SHANK'S
MARE

SHANK'S MARE

A Compendium of Remarkable Walks

EDITED BY

RON STRICKLAND

PARAGON HOUSE

New York

First edition, 1988

Published in the United States by

Paragon House Publishers
90 Fifth Avenue
New York, NY 10011

Due to limitations of space, acknowledgments begin on a separate page following the Contents pages.

Library of Congress Cataloging-in-Publication Data

Strickland, Ron.
  Shank's mare: a compendium of remarkable walks / by Ron Strickland.—1st ed.
    p. cm.
  ISBN 1-55778-074-9. ISBN 1-55778-097-8 (pbk.)
  1. Walking in literature. 2. Travel in literature.
3. Literature, Modern—20th century. I. Title.
PN6071.W3S76 1988
808.8'0355—dc19   87-30888

Manufactured in the United States of America

Contents

Acknowledgments

Grateful acknowledgment is made to the following for permission to use material:

Holland Press for "My African Journey" by Winston Churchill. Reprinted by permission of Holland Press, London.

Viking Penguin Inc. for "Mahatma Gandhi's March Across India" by Ved Mehta. From *Mahatma Gandhi and His Apostles* by Ved Mehta. Copyright © 1976 by Ved Mehta. All rights reserved. Reprinted by permission of Viking Penguin Inc.

James Morris for his "Coronation Everest."

Little, Brown and Company for "First on the Moon" by Neil Armstrong. From *First on the Moon* by Neil Armstrong, Michael Collins and Edwin E. Aldrin, Jr. Copyright © 1970 by Little, Brown and Company. Reprinted by permission.

Curtis Brown Ltd. for "A Short Walk in the Hindu Kush" by Eric Newby. Reprinted by permission of Curtis Brown Ltd.

Eland Books for "Kenya Diary" by Richard Meinertzhagen. Reprinted by permission of the publisher.

Simon and Schuster, Inc. for "A Day at Kora" by George Adamson. From *My Pride and Joy.* Copyright © 1986 by George Adamson. Reprinted by permission of the publisher.

Simon and Schuster, Inc. for "North of South" by Shiva Naipaul. From *North of South: an African Journey* by Shiva Naipaul. Copyright © 1978, 1979 by Shiva Naipaul. Reprinted by permission of Simon and Schuster, Inc.

Random House, Inc. for "African Calliope" by Edward Hoagland. From *African Calliope* by Edward Hoagland. Copyright © 1978 by Edward Hoagland. Reprinted by permission of Random House, Inc.

Houghton Mifflin Company for "Gorillas in the Mist" by Dian Fossey. From *Gorillas in the Mist* by Dian Fossey. Copyright © 1983 by Dian Fossey. Reprinted by permission of Houghton Mifflin Company.

Constable Publishers for "Journey to the Jade Sea" by John Hillaby. From *Journey to the Jade Sea* by John Hillaby. Reprinted by permission of the publisher.

Simon and Schuster, Inc. for "In Southern Light" by Alex Shoumantoff. From *In Southern Light: Trekking Through Zaire and the Amazon.* Copyright © 1986 by Alex Shoumantoff. Reprinted by permission of Simon and Schuster, Inc.

Syracuse University Press for "Shahhat: An Egyptian" by Richard Critchfield. Reprinted by permission of Syracuse University Press.

Harcourt Brace Jovanovich for "Wind, Sand and Stars" by Antoine de Saint-Exupéry. From *Wind, Sand and Stars*, copyright © 1939 by Antoine de Saint-Exupéry;

renewed 1967 by Lewis Galantiere. Reprinted by permission of Harcourt Brace Jovanovich, Inc.

Harper & Row for "The Gulag Archipelago" by Aleksandr I. Solzhenitsyn. From *The Gulag Archipelago* by Aleksandr I. Solzhenitsyn. Copyright © 1974 by Aleksandr I. Solzhenitsyn. English language translation copyright © 1975 by Harper and Row Publishers, Inc. Reprinted by permission of the publisher.

Beacon Press for "Mans' Search for Meaning" by Viktor E. Frankl. From *Man's Search for Meaning* by Viktor E. Frankl. Copyright © 1959, 1962, 1984 by Viktor E. Frankl. Reprinted by permission of Beacon Press.

David R. Godine Publishers, Inc. for "War in Val D'Orcia" by Iris Origo. From *War in Val D'Orcia: an Italian War Diary 1943–44* by Iris Origo. Used by permission of David R. Godine Publishers, Inc.

Penguin Books, Ltd. for "The Roads to Sata" by Alan Booth. From *The Roads to Sata*, copyright © 1985 by Alan Booth. Reprinted by permission of Penguin Books, Ltd.

William Morrow and Co., Inc., for "Japanese Pilgrimage" by Oliver Statler. From *Japanese Pilgrimage* by Oliver Statler. Copyright © 1983 by Oliver Statler. By permission of William Morrow and Co.

Curtis Brown, Ltd. for "Letter to Henry Miller on Walks with George Katsimbalis" by Lawrence Durrell. From *Lawrence Durrell & Henry Miller*, edited by George Wickes. Copyright © 1964. Reprinted by permission of Curtis Brown Ltd., New York.

Little, Brown and Company for "On the Shores of the Mediterranean" by Eric Newby. From *On the Shores of the Mediterranean* by Eric Newby. Copyright © 1984 by Eric Newby. By permission of Little, Brown and Company.

Monthly Review Press for "Long March Veterans" by Agnes Smedley. From *The Great Road: the Life and Times of Chuh Teh* by Agnes Smedley. Copyright © 1956, 1972, by Agnes Smedley. Reprinted by permission of Monthly Review Foundation.

New American Library for "The Armies of the Night" by Norman Mailer. From *The Armies of the Night: History as a Novel/The Novel as History* by Norman Mailer. Copyright © 1968 by Norman Mailer. Reprinted by arrangement with New American Library, New York, New York.

Macmillan Publishing Company for "The Royal Road to Romance" by Richard Halliburton. Reprinted with permission of Macmillan Publishing Company from *The Royal Road to Romance* by Richard Halliburton. Copyright © 1925 by Macmillan Publishing Company. Copyright renewed 1953.

Hamish Hamilton Ltd. for "Kailas" by Peter Somerville-Large. From *To the Navel of the World* by Peter Somerville-Large. Reprinted by permission of the publisher.

The Estate of Ion L. Idriess for "My Mate Dick" by Ion L. Idriess.

Simon and Schuster, Inc. for "In Patagonia" by Bruce Chatwin. From *In Patagonia* by Bruce Chatwin. Copyright © 1980 by Bruce Chatwin. Reprinted by permission of Simon and Schuster, Inc.

Jeremy P. Tarcher, Inc. for "Brazilian Adventure" by Peter Fleming. From *Brazilian Adventure* by Peter Fleming. Copyright © 1983. Reprinted by permission of Jeremy P. Tarcher, Inc.

Sterling Lord Literistic, Inc. for "Ninety-two Days: A Tropical Journey" by Evelyn

Waugh. From *Ninety-two Days* by Evelyn Waugh. Copyright © 1934, 1986 by Evelyn Waugh. Reprinted by Permission of Sterling Lord Literistic, Inc.

Viking Penguin Inc. for "The Cloud Forest" by Peter Matthiessen. From *The Cloud Forest: A Chronicle of the South American Wilderness* by Peter Matthiessen. Reprinted by permission of the publisher.

Ecco Press for "Smara: The Forbidden City" by Michel Vieuchange. Reprinted by permission of the publisher.

Viking Penguin Inc. for "Who Goes Out in the Midday Sun?" by Benedict Allen. From *Who Goes Out in the Midday Sun?* by Benedict Allen. Copyright © 1985, 1986. Reprinted by permission of Viking Penguin Inc.

Alfred A. Knopf, Inc. for "Walk to Huayapa" by D.H. Lawrence. From *Mornings in Mexico* by D.H. Lawrence. Copyright © 1927 by D.H. Lawrence and renewed 1955 by Frieda Lawrence Ravagli. Reprinted by permission of Alfred A. Knopf, Inc.

Macmillan Publishing Company for "Journey to Kars" by Philip Glazebrook. Excerpted from *A Journey to Kars*. Copyright © 1984 Philip Glazebrook. Reprinted with permission of Atheneum Publishers, an imprint of Macmillan Publishing Company.

Houghton Mifflin Company for "Walking Through Israel" by Daniel Gavron. From *Walking Through Israel* by Daniel Gavron. Copyright © 1980 by Daniel Gavron. Reprinted by permission of Houghton Mifflin Company.

Curtis Brown Group Ltd. for "A Friend Revisited" by C.S. Lewis. From *C.S. Lewis: Images of His World*. Reproduced by permission of Curtis Brown Ltd., London, on behalf of the Estate of C.S. Lewis.

Viking Penguin Inc. for "On Foot to Constantinople: From the Hook of Holland to the Middle Danube" by Patrick Leigh Fermor. From *Between the Woods and the Water: On Foot to Constantinople from the Hook of Holland: The Middle Danube to the Iron Gates* by Patrick Leigh Fermor. Copyright © 1986. Reprinted by permission of Viking Penguin, Inc.

Victor Gollancz Ltd. for "Hamish's Groats End Walk" by Hamish Brown. Reprinted by permission of the publisher.

Gwen Moffat for her "Space Below My Feet."

Farrar, Straus and Giroux, Inc. for "A Walk Along the Boyne" by Anthony Bailey. Excerpt from *Spring Jaunts* by Anthony Bailey. Copyright © 1986 by Anthony Bailey. Also appeared originally in *The New Yorker* and *Acts of Union*, published by Random House. Reprinted by permission of Farrar, Straus and Giroux, Inc.

Macmillan Publishing Company for "Frank O'Connor, Poet" by James Matthews. From *Voices: A Life of Frank O'Connor* by James Matthews. Copyright © 1983 by James Matthews. Reprinted with the permission of Atheneum Publishers, an imprint of Macmillan Publishing Company.

Estate of Vladimir Nabokov for "Butterfly Walks" by Vladimir Nabokov. From *Speak, Memory*, copyright © 1947, 1951, 1960, 1966 by Vladimir Nabokov. By arrangement with the Estate of Vladimir Nabokov.

Harcourt Brace Jovanovich for, Inc. "The Star Thrower" by Loren Eiseley. From *That Unexpected Universe* by Loren Eiseley. Copyright © 1969 by Loren Eiseley. Reprinted by permission of Harcourt Brace Jovanovich, Inc.

Random House, Inc. for "Sigmund Freud's Alpine Walks" by Ronald W. Clark.

From *Freud: the Man and the Cause* by Ronald W. Clark. Copyright © 1980 by E.M. Partners, AG. Reprinted by permission of Random House, Inc.

Stein and Day Publishers for "A Parade in Zurich" by Herbert Kubly. From the book *Native's Return* by Herbert Kubly. Copyright © 1981 by Herbert Kubly. Reprinted with permission of Stein and Day Publishers.

Macmillan Publishing Company for "A Moveable Feast" by Ernest Hemingway. Excerpted from *A Moveable Feast*, by Ernest Hemingway. Copyright © 1964 Mary Hemingway. Reprinted with the permission of Charles Scribner's Sons, an imprint of Macmillan Publishing Company.

Harcourt Brace Jovanovich, Inc. for "Paris Diary" by Anaïs Nin. Excerpt from *The Diary of Anaïs Nin 1931–1934*, copyright © 1966 by Anaïs Nin. Reprinted by permission of Harcourt Brace Jovanovich, Inc.

Dodd, Mead and Company for "A Traveller in Italy" by H.V. Morton. From *A Traveller in Italy* by H.V. Morton. Reprinted by permission of Dodd, Mead and Company.

Oxford Illustrated Press for "Mean Feat" by John Waite. From *Mean Feat* by John Waite. Reprinted by permission of the publisher.

Hodder & Stoughton Ltd. for "Dreams of Distant Treks" by Eric Shipton. From *That Untravelled World* by Eric Shipton. Reprinted by permission of Hodder & Stoughton Ltd.

The New York Times for "The Alps, On Foot" by Adam Nicolson. Copyright © 1986 by The New York Times Company. Reprinted by permission. Permission for this piece has also been granted by its author.

Charles Konopa for his "The Reason Why."

Harper & Row for "A Walk to Fred's Grave" by E.B. White. From *Bedfellows* by E.B. White. Copyright © 1956 by E.B. White. Reprinted by permission of Harper & Row Publishers, Inc.

Joe Malone for his "Roaming the Streets of Henry Miller, Then and Now." Copyright © 1981 by Joe Malone. Originally published in the Brooklyn College Alumni Literary Review.

Harcourt Brace Jovanovich, Inc. for "A Walker in the City" by Alfred Kazin. Excerpt from *A Walker in the City*, copyright © 1951, 1979 by Alfred Kazin. Reprinted by permission of Harcourt Brace Jovanovich, Inc.

University of Pittsburgh Press for "The People of Penn's Woods West" by Lee Gutkind. Reprinted from *The People of Penn's Woods West*, copyright © 1984 by Lee Gutkind. Reprinted by permission of the University of Pittsburgh Press.

Henry Holt and Company, Inc. for "Northern Farm" by Henry Beston. From *Northern Farm: A Chronicle of Maine* by Henry Beston. Copyright © 1948 by Henry Beston. Copyright © 1976 by Elizabeth Coatsworth Beston. Reprinted by permission of Henry Holt and Company, Inc.

Michael Frome for his "Strangers in High Places."

Lawton Chiles for his unpublished diary, "Diary of the 'Walking Senator.' "

Caitlin Gareth for her "Walking My Dog in Montrose Park."

Walking Magazine for "Organized Labor" by Nell Platt. Copyright © 1988, Raben Publishing Co., 711 Boylston St., Boston, MA 02116.

St. Martin's Press, Inc. for "Backpacking with Jack Kerouac" by Gary Snyder. From *Jack's Book: An Oral Biography of Jack Kerouac* by Barry Gifford and Lawrence

Lee. Copyright © 1978. Reprinted by permission of St. Martin's Press, Inc., New York.

Curtis Brown, Ltd. for "A Zen Hike with Bill Graham" by Herbert Gold. From *A Walk on the West Side: California on the Brink* by Herbert Gold. Copyright © 1981 by Herbert Gold. Reprinted by permission of Curtis Brown, Ltd.

Alfred A. Knopf, Inc. for "The Man Who Walked Through Time" by Colin Fletcher. From *The Man Who Walked Through Time* by Colin Fletcher. Copyright © 1967 by Colin Fletcher. Reprinted by permission of Alfred A. Knopf, Inc.

Don Congdon Associates, Inc. for "Desert Solitaire" by Edward Abbey. From *Desert Solitaire* by Edward Abbey. Copyright © 1968 by Edward Abbey. Reprinted by permission of Don Congdon Associates, Inc.

Backpacker Magazine for "In Love with Tundra" by Patricia Armstrong.

Vanguard Press for "The Pacific Coast Ranges" by Lois Crisler. Reprinted from a chapter by Lois Crisler in *The Pacific Coast Ranges*, edited by Roderick Peattie, by permission of the publisher, Vanguard Press, Inc. Copyright © 1946 by Vanguard Press, Inc. Renewed © 1973 by Vanguard Press, Inc.

Houghton Mifflin Company for "The Conquest of Mount McKinley" by Belmore Browne. From *The Conquest of Mount McKinley* by Belmore Browne. Copyright © 1956 by Houghton Mifflin Company. Reprinted by permission of Houghton Mifflin Company.

University of California Press for "Alaska Wilderness" by Robert Marshall. From *Alaska Wilderness: Exploring Central Brooks* by Robert Marshall. Copyright © 1956 The Regents of the University of California.

Introduction

"Shank's mare" is an old Scottish term referring to the way a horseless person gets about on his own shanks or legs. Walking is also called "shank's pony." Whatever the name, consider this a personal invitation to join me on a vicarious trek.

This *Shank's Mare* sampler is your introduction to some of my favorite twentieth-century walkers. Here you will stroll with them in literary Paris, tropical jungles, lunar space, world war, African veldt, Antarctic cold, and Cape Cod sand. With this book as your letter of introduction you will time travel across the most diverse century in history.

Walking always has the potential to make a good story. It has the advantage of a definite beginning and end. Life afoot is rich with possibility. Adventure calls.

Each walker brings back what he or she can. England's John Hillaby, hiking through suburban sprawl, would probably emerge with an insightful essay about middle class culture and the reactions of dogs and automobile addicts to a man on foot. New England's Dudley Cammett Lunt, walking for miles at a popular beach resort, would certainly report back miracles of Nature unseen by thousands of less observant souls.

Shank's Mare is fun. Come participate in Eric Newby's encounter with a famed English explorer. "Thesiger's caravan was abreast of us now, and his horses lurching to a standstill on the execrable track." There, with his "two villainous-looking tribesmen," was Thesiger himself, "a great, long-striding crag of a man, with an outcrop for a nose and as hard as nails, in an old tweed jacket of the sort worn by Eton boys, a pair of thin grey cotton trousers, rope-soled Persian slippers and a woollen cap comforter."

Come meet Winston Churchill on safari in East Africa.

Walker, come along with us.

Ah, here is naked-but-for-his-boots Colin Fletcher, striding across the Tonto Platform deep in the Grand Canyon. Whoa! I see Michael Harman walking from San Francisco to Manhattan. And there's my hero Henry Beston putting his Maine farm to bed as the earth livens to the sound of spring's melting snow and ice.

In *Shank's Mare* everyone speaks through a common language of walking.

Since we are to be companions of the road, let me tell you about myself and about how *Shank's Mare* came to be. As a teenager and as an under-graduate I was an incurable rambler, at first on day trips in the fields and woods of Rhode Island and Delaware, and then on overnight hikes away from Georgetown University. Early on I fell in love with the romance of trails. Whenever I crossed one of the long distance footpaths I felt a tug. The very names "Appalachian Trail" or "Pacific Crest Trail" were enough to set my heart astir.

By the time I was in my mid-twenties I was hooked.

Ostensibly I rambled in order to see what was over the next hill or to revel in the familiarity of favorite spots. In retrospect I now know that my compass was preset for another declination, for curiosity about people and Nature. Although walking as a health measure has recently overtaken jogging in popularity, fitness and longevity were not my goals out on the trails and byways.

Instead I loved nature and adventure and the freedom that wilderness backpacking brought. As I wrote in *Pacific Northwest Trail Guide* (1984), "Walking is beautifully simple. Long-distance walking has the purity and economy of well-lived days. Trekking is both aesthetically pleasing and phys-ically demanding. For many of us, walking is a must, a passion."

That type of enthusiasm about walking is much closer to nineteenth-century Romanticism than to today's fitness boom.

In 1968 my hometown friend, Paris Walters of Newark, Delaware persuaded me to fly west to hike in grander surroundings. He had already hiked all of the 900-mile Pacific Crest Trail in Washington and Oregon. After a week-long trial hike on the Long Trail in Vermont, I flew to Seattle and launched myself on a three-week jaunt through the North Cascades. It was good beyond my wildest dreams.

Two years later, restless in graduate school, I escaped again to Wash-ington state and began a series of summer explorations for a future east–west national scenic trail. Eventually these Pacific Northwest Trail adven-tures were told in *Going The Distance* (1988). That book was slow aborning, however, and in 1978 matters had taken a surprising turn when I became an oral history interviewer.

After moving to Seattle in 1977 to be nearer to the PNT, I began to record its old-timers' tales. As I later wrote in *River Pigs And Cayuses*, I spent "dizzying blurs of months haunting woodlots, back porches, corrals, fishing schooners, ranch kitchens, Scout camps, log cabins, saltwater beaches, overgrown Indian trails, game refuges, forgotten mines, and wil-derness mountains."

Soon I was as fascinated with oral history as I had been earlier with contour maps and distant horizons.

River Pigs And Cayuses appeared in 1984.

In 1986 I published *Vermonters: Oral Histories from Down Country to the Northeast Kingdom.* Soon I was spending month after month searching for interesting *Texans* and *Californians.* Hundreds of individuals came before my microphone and camera. Before I knew it I was creating a series of oral history portraits of every region of the United States. As publisher deadlines drew near, I realized that I had no more time for long distance walking. What to do?

Fortunately the solution was near at hand in the library where I was researching California and Texas. There I could read about walking even if I could no longer do much of it myself.

I approached vicarious adventure with the same excitement that I had felt in the early days of exploring the Pacific Northwest Trail. There was plenty of material to read because during the 1970s America and Europe had experienced a surge of new interest in walking. Guidebooks and how-to-walk books proliferated. A technological revolution transformed the old world of Trapper Nelsons and Army ponchos. Miracle fabrics lightened our loads. With these changes came new journals, trail clubs, fad hikers, and, in the United States, the National Trails System. Walking's old trickle of books and articles became a flood.

Great! That should make putting together an anthology easy, right?

Wrong. The new literature of walking was often disappointing. Somebody would tell about his or her distances, dilemmas, and days in a hiking club or magazine article that might provide a fair outline of what could be expected on trail X but that did very little to make me care about the person taking the hike. I wanted to find the same degree of interest in the walkers that I had discovered in my oral history interviews.

Thus I have often looked to writers for whom the walking was incidental to other purposes. I have wanted to fill every page of this book with walkers so in love with their subjects—whether Vladimir Nabokov with butterflies or Patricia Armstrong with tundra flowers—that they make me want to rush to join them. Most of all I appreciate a highly personal point of view. Though both Colin Fletcher and Edward Abbey write about Southwest deserts, no one would ever confuse the two. Such walkers are eccentrics in the most positive sense of the word. I appreciate the desert rituals of Colin Fletcher in preparing his tea and pampering his feet. Colin Fletcher does not equal the single mindedness of, say, Richard Burton walking undetected to Mecca in 1853, but he is probably as hooked on walking as any contemporary Californian can be.

Good walking and good reading go together. There is no better vicarious pleasure than tramping obscure byways with someone whose writing is elegant and who appreciates the poetry of names. With such a person we are ready for anything. Perhaps a chance encounter with an old Kentuckian like the one whom trans-America walker Michael Harman met in Missouri in 1904:

While walking the track, several miles east of Little Blue, Mo., I met an old, old man, with a long white beard, hobbling along with the aid of a walking stick, and carrying a bundle.

"Where are you going, young man?" he inquired.

"I'm on a walk from San Francisco to New York City," I answered.

"Walking from San Francisco to New York," he repeated slowly, "I wouldn't do that for all the money in the world."

"Oh, it's not so hard after one becomes accustomed to it," was my reply.

"Yes, it's true. I guess h—— would be all right after one became accustomed to it," he answered, "but come and spend the night with me in my shack up in the woods, and I want you distinctly to understand, young man, that I'm the only man in Jackson County who would extend you hospitality. They are a bad lot these Missourians, a very bad lot; and I have been here long enough to find them out, over forty years."

Invited to Albertus Babe Kelly's shack, Harman felt obliged to share a white lightning toast:

Here is to dear old Kentucky,
The land of the rich blue-grass;
And to Missouri eternal damnation,
Which is only fit for an ass.

Sometimes the theme of the journey is a metaphor for the ups and downs of life. John Hillaby in *A Walk Through Europe* says at one point, "I sat there, writing up notes about the night of the storm and the old lady and, above all, about how fortune changed, almost from hour to hour."

Fortune, fate—a distance walker is confronted almost daily by odd turns of events and strange coincidences. Sometimes in the wilderness I have wanted to see a certain person and have chanced upon him farther down the trail. At other times I have felt the cleansing humility that comes from long immersion in the wilderness.

Ultimately the nature writers are my favorite walkers. They see the sights I want to see and they feel the things I feel. I think often of Henry Beston (*The Outermost House*) and of his starry excursions beside the black Atlantic.

One July night, as I returned at three o'clock from an expedition north, the whole night, in one strange, burning instant, turned into a phantom day. I stopped and, questioning, stared about. An enormous meteor, the largest I have ever seen, was consuming itself in an effulgence of light west of the zenith. Beach and dune and ocean appeared out of nothing, shadowless and motionless, a landscape whose every tremor and vibration were stilled, a landscape in a dream.

The physical sensations of walking are part of that same Nature. In my own *Going The Distance* I tell of the euphoria that the homely act of putting one foot in front of the other produced in me while hiking the Pacific Northwest Trail.

> The surge of well-being within me became a rhythm of feet, legs, chest, and arms. This trail was often in trees so there were no distractions from the physical sensations which propelled me up the mountain. . . . I pushed into my pack straps and leaned forward into the slope. I felt very good. I was moving fast under a form-fitting, weightless pack. The trail dropped away beneath my tan and blue striped feet.

As the months passed I concluded that there was no way to place a value on that inner joy.

Just as there is no way to force it into being. It comes with the welcome surprise of a cairn in a mountain fog and brings the confidence that you are on the right path. Such feelings combine the ecstasy of childhood with the joy of the mountains and the contentment of maturity.

Shank's Mare began as relief for my own enforced sedentariness. If I could not be out walking myself, I could spend some time each day reading about other people's walks.

Excellent anthologies of largely nineteenth-century material had already appeared but I soon realized that I wanted walkers from the twentieth century, the same period that I was probing in my oral history research. Furthermore I wanted to find a collection of writers whose walking experiences hinted at the incredible variety of life in this century.

Our century has seen more extremes of invention, suffering, and hope than any other. In my oral history work I have interviewed both a woman who migrated to Texas in a covered wagon and a man who flew from Texas to the moon. But however fascinating such technological change is, it is not my primary interest. I prefer to learn what people *feel* about their experiences.

And *you* can help me. I am seeking additional walking adventures that broaden our understanding of people, places, and events. Please help me to find adventure, comradeship, and insight in distant and near decades and countries. Who are your favorite twentieth-century walkers? Please send your suggestions for additional selections for a year 2000 edition of this anthology to me % Paragon House.

Shank's Mare is like the gorp mixture that hikers love to eat. There is a little of everything here. Urban strolls. Country rambles. Wilderness bushwhacks. Spiritual quests. Survival epics. Nature paeans. Walks on major trails and on obscure byways. *Shank's Mare* is a trek through the nearness and the strangeness of our own century.

Come you strollers and boulevardiers. You flaneurs, distance demons, and armchair wanderers. Wonderful things are on the horizon. There is Hamish Brown waking as the Scottish morning glows through the walls of his tent. "Sunrise comes out of the pit, as we do and is a fearsome, tingling marvel, before which we bow in awe."

And look! There is the redoubtable H. V. Morton strolling through a Mantuan night under a full moon that is transforming the city into "the backcloth of an opera."

Amid the unspeakable horror of a Nazi death camp slave laborer Viktor Frankl marches to work while dreaming of his beloved.

Gandhi walks to the sea to make salt in defiance of the British Raj.

As walkers we all have our own pace, whether we are distance seekers or deep thinkers. *Shank's Mare*'s moods are as varied as its speakers:

Antoine de Saint-Exupéry (wandering, lost in the Libyan desert): "These are the cares of men alive in every fibre, and I cannot help thinking them more important than the fretful choosing of a nightclub in which to spend the evening."

Ion Idriess (searching for pay dirt in Australia): " . . . just after dawn, with pick and dish on shoulder, joyously we strode out for the hills, looking for gold."

Iris Origo (after escaping World War II shelling on foot in northern Italy): "When I look back upon these years of tension and expectation, of destruction and sorrow, it is individual acts of kindness, courage, or faith that illuminate them; it is in them that I trust."

These selections were written by scientists, novelists, essayists, explorers, refugees, prisoners, poets, soldiers, environmentalists, diarists, astronauts, psychiatrists, senators. These selections vary greatly in their emphases on adventure, reflection, and reporting. However, my favorites are usually those in which the character of the teller is most clearly revealed. As an oral history interviewer, these are people I would like to have met. Rosa Parks of civil rights fame, for instance. She had a lot of unwanted walking to do, to and from work, when she was boycotting Montgomery, Alabama's segregated buses in 1955. Daily she found inner strength to make that walk. "My feet are tired," she said, "but my soul is at rest."

After beginning with a few classic at the Indian Ocean, Mount Everest, and the moon, we proceed to Africa. Next come some chronological selections from the late 1930s, World War II, and the reconstruction era. The Long March blends into the march on the Pentagon. Richard Halliburton takes us on *The Royal Road to Romance*. Our new friends tell of Australia, South America, the Middle East, Britain, Ireland, Europe, and America. The flame of life leaps from author to author.

Voluntary walking is not a rejection of technology as much as it is a reaffirmation of the pleasure of having two legs. I, for instance, am planning a hike right now. And I am as excited about it as when, at the age of fifteen, I bought my first boots. There is the excitement of getting my gear together, of buying the food, of studying the maps and planning the route.

Watch out! By the time you finish this book you will be as restless as I am today. And foot powders can't cure *this* itch.

A century ago someone feeling this way would "light out for the territory" or stampede off on the latest gold rush.

If you are as hopelessly romantic as I am, just the sight of your old boots, compass, or pack is enough to boost your pulse rate. But for all of us wanderers, backpackers, and armchair Marco Polos there is no use in just pacing the floor.

So lace up your boots, roll up your sleeves, and set out with me, shank's mare, in search of friends who are waiting just down the trail.

Let's go walking!

SHANK'S
MARE

Winston Churchill

My African Journey

In 1908 Britain's twentieth century champion of empire journeyed across Kenya and Uganda hunting and sightseeing. The classic era of on-foot exploration and safaris was fast coming to an end.

* * *

Early in the morning of November 23rd our party set off upon this journey. Travelling by marches from camp to camp plays a regular part in the life of the average Central African officer. He goes "on Safari" as the Boer "on trek." It is a recognized state of being, which often lasts for weeks, and sometimes for months. He learns to think of ten days "Safari" as we at home think of going to Scotland, and twenty days' "Safari" as if it were less than the journey to Paris. "Safari" is itself a Swahili word of Arabic origin, meaning an expedition and all that pertains to it. It comprises yourself and everybody and everything you take with you—food, tents, rifles, clothing, cooks, servants, escort, porters—but especially porters. Out of the range of steam the porter is the primary factor. This ragged figure, tottering along under his load, is the unit of locomotion and the limit of possibility. Without porters you cannot move. With them you move ten or twelve miles a day, if all is well. How much can he carry? How far can he carry it? These are the questions which govern alike your calculations and your fate.

Every morning the porters are divided into batches of about twenty, each under its headman. The loads, which are supposed to average about sixty-five pounds, are also roughly parcelled out. As each batch starts off, the next rushes up to the succeeding heap of loads, and there is a quarter of an hour of screaming and pushing—the strongest men making a beeline for the lightest-looking loads, and being beaten off by the grim but voluble headman, the weakest weeping feebly beside a mountainous pile, till a distribution has been achieved with rough justice, and the troop in its turn marches off with indescribable ululations testifying and ministering to the spirit in which they mean to accomplish the day's journey.

While these problems were being imperfectly solved, I walked down with the Governor and one of the Engineer officers to the Ripon Falls, which are but half a mile from the Commissioner's house, and the sound of whose waters filled the air. Although the cataract is on a moderate scale, both in height and volume, its aspect—and still more its situation—is impressive. The exit or overflow of the Great Lake is closed by a natural rampart or ridge of black rock, broken or worn away in two main gaps to release the waters. Through these the Nile leaps at once into majestic being, and enters upon its course as a perfect river three hundred yards wide. Standing upon the reverse side of the wall of rock, one's eye may be almost on a plane with the shining levels of the Lake. At your very feet, literally a yard away, a vast green slope of water races downward. Below are foaming rapids, fringed by splendid trees, and pools from which great fish leap continually in the sunlight. We must have spent three hours watching the waters and revolving plans to harness and bridle them. So much power running to waste, such a coign of vantage unoccupied, such a lever to control the natural forces of Africa ungripped, cannot but vex and stimulate the imagination. And what fun to make the immemorial Nile begin its journey by diving through a turbine! But to our tale.

The porters had by now got far on their road, and we must pad after them through the full blaze of noon. The Governor of Uganda and his officers have to return to Entebbe by the steamer, so it is here I bid them good-bye and good luck, and with a final look at Ripon Falls, gleaming and resounding below, I climb the slopes of the river bank and walk off into the forest. The native path struck north-east from the Nile, and led into a hilly and densely wooded region. The elephant grass on each side of the track rose fifteen feet high. In the valleys great trees grew and arched above our heads, laced and twined together with curtains of flowering creepers. Here and there a glade opened to the right or left, and patches of vivid sunlight splashed into the gloom. Around the crossings of little streams butterflies danced in brilliant ballets. Many kinds of birds flew about the trees. The jungle was haunted by game—utterly lost in its dense entanglements. And I think it a sensation all by itself to walk on your own feet, and staff in hand, along these mysterious paths, amid such beautiful, yet sinister, surroundings, and realize that one is really in the centre of Africa, and a long way from Piccadilly or Pall Mall.

Our first march was about fourteen miles, and as we had not started till the hot hours of the day were upon us, it was enough and to spare so far as I was concerned. Uphill and downhill wandered our path, now plunged in the twilight of a forest valley, now winding up the side of a scorched hill, and I had for some time been hoping to see the camp round every corner, when at last we reached it. It consisted of two rows of green tents and a large "banda," or rest house, as big as a large barn in England, standing in a nice trim clearing. These "bandas" are a great feature of African travel; and the dutiful chief through whose territory we are passing had taken pains to make them on the most elaborate scale. He was not long in making his appearance with presents of various kinds. A lanky, black-faced sheep, with a fat tail as big as a pumpkin, was dragged forward, bleating, by two retainers. Others brought live hens and earthenware jars of milk and baskets of little round eggs. The chief was a tall, intelligent-looking man, with the winning smile and attractive manners characteristic of the country, and made his salutations with a fine air of dignity and friendship.

The house he had prepared for us was built of bamboo framework, supported upon a central row of Y-shaped tree stems, with a high–pitched roof heavily thatched with elephant grass, and walls of wattled reeds. The floors of African "bandas" when newly made are beautifully smooth and clean, and strewn with fresh green rushes; the interior is often cunningly divided into various apartments, and the main building is connected with kitchens and offices of the same unsubstantial texture by veranda-shaded passages. In fact, they prove a high degree of social knowledge and taste in the natives, who make them with almost incredible rapidity from the vegetation of the surrounding jungle; and the sensation of entering one of these lofty, dim, cool, and spacious interiors, and sinking into the soft rush bed of the floor, with something to drink which is, at any rate, not tepid, well repays the glaring severities of a march under an equatorial sun. The "banda," however, is a luxury of which the traveller should beware, for if it has stood for more than a week it becomes the home of innumerable insects, many of approved malevolence and venom, and spirillum fever is almost invariably caught from sleeping in old shelters or on disused camping grounds.

Life "on Safari" is rewarded by a sense of completeness and self-satisfied detachment. You have got to "do" so many miles a day, and when you have "done" them your day's work is over. 'Tis a simple programme, which leaves nothing more to be demanded or desired. Very early in the morning, often an hour before daybreak, the bugles of the King's African Rifles sounded reveille. Everyone dresses hurriedly by candlelight, eats a dim breakfast while dawn approaches; tents collapse, and porters struggle off with their burdens. Then the march begins . . .

There is no surer way of keeping fit in Uganda than to walk twelve or fifteen miles a day.

Ved Mehta

Mahatma Gandhi's March Across India

Strange as it may seem now, the twentieth century has been the century of empire. Never before in history were so many lands and peoples under the domination of so few.

The British Empire was the greatest empire of all. Not only was it true that the sun never set on its red splash across the world map but also that, when it disintegrated, the end came amazingly fast.

A little man on foot was one of the principal dismantlers of empire. Mahatma ("Great Spirit") Gandhi was sixty when he led a march across India to the sea to protest the British salt laws. Within a short time the once all-powerful British Raj was history. Ved Mehta's book Mahatma Gandhi and His Apostles describes this unravelling.

Ved Mehta quotes an Englishman who knew the century's greatest proponent of nonviolence. Gandhi, said Woodrow Wyatt, habitually walked about wearing only a sort of loincloth of homespun white cotton. "He wanted to wear or use only what was within the means of any peasant, however poor. He mostly went barefoot or wore wooden clogs. When he went on long walks, he wore a pair of leather sandals, and sometimes also a white cheesecloth shawl around his shoulders and a white kerchief on his head, tied under his chin."

Each day, after his early morning prayers and correspondence Gandhi took a walk through the flat country surrounding his central India ashram. Woodrow Wyatt described it this way:

At six-thirty, he always fastened his pocket watch to the waist of his dhoti with a safety pin, slipped his feet into his leather sandals, took up a tall bamboo staff, and set out for his morning walk, along the dirt road toward Wardha. Most of the time, the sun was already quite hot, the air was dry, and the earth smelled of stale manure. Many of us rushed after him, clamoring for his attention. A number were less nimble footed than he and almost had to run to keep up with him—he took such long, quick strides. The children of the ashram danced around him, pestering him *with their questions. They had little opportunity to spend time with him otherwise, so they made the most of his walks. I remember that one of them said, "Bapu, in the Bhagavad Gita the hero Arjuna asks short questions and Lord Krishna gives long answers. But when we ask you questions, you always give us short answers." Bapu laughed, and said, "Lord Krishna had only one Arjuna to contend with. I have dozens of you."*

Along the way, Bapu greeted pilgrims who had come great distances for their darshane, and peasants who had left off their work in the fields to watch him go by. Sometimes, when he got a little tired, he gave his staff to the first person who reached for it, and put his hands on the shoulders of the sisters walking beside him. These "walking sticks," as he affectionately called them, were usually Sister Abha and Sister Sushila. Sister Sushila was about ten years older than Sister Abha and was as domineeering and pushy as Sister Abha was quiet and retiring. Bapu invariably asked them, "Did you have a good bowel movement this morning, sisters?" Constipation was the commonest complaint in the ashram, and no one thought anything of talking about it. Bapu taught us to be open about everything—with him and with each other. His standard prescription for constipation was more vegetables, and, if that didn't work, an enema, which he taught us to administer to each other without any embarrassment.

We often met Ba [Gandhi's wife] on our way back. She didn't go on Bapu's long walks. Instead, she bathed, read a little of the Ramayana, and then took a stroll through the ashram with some of the other older women. She was about the same age as Bapu, and, like him, she was toothless. Her face was quite sunken, but she always looked contented. By the time Bapu returned to his hut, it was about seven-thirty. Sister Abha took off Bapu's sandals, which were covered with dust and caked with mud, cleaned them with a rag, and put them out in the sun to air.

*   *   *

On January 1, 1930, Congress defiantly unfurled a flag for independent India and so opened its campaign for all-out independence.

Everyone in the Congress now looked to Gandhi to find an issue around which the whole country could be rallied nonviolently, and within two months he did find one. His "inner voice" told him to lead a civil-disobedience campaign against the salt-tax laws, on the model of his 1913 satyagraha campaign in South Africa. First, he wrote to Lord Irwin, the Viceroy:

The iniquities [of the tax laws in general and the salt laws in particular] . . . are maintained in order to carry on a foreign administration, demonstrably the most expensive in the world. Take your own salary. . . . You are getting over 700 rupees per day against India's average income of less than two annas per day. . . . Thus you are getting much over five thousand times India's average income. . . . On bended knee, I ask you to ponder over this phenomenon. I have taken a personal illustration to drive home a painful truth. I have too great a regard for you as a man to wish to hurt your feelings. . . .

But a system that provides for such an arrangement deserves to be summarily scrapped; . . . nothing but unadulterated non-violence can check the organized violence of the British government. . . .

But if you cannot see your way to deal with these evils and my letter makes no appeal to your heart, on the eleventh day of this month, I shall proceed with such co-workers of the ashram as I can take, to disregard the provisions of the salt laws.

The Viceroy, rather than enter into a discussion with Gandhi or arrest him, contented himself with having his secretary write a formal acknowledgment of Gandhi's letter.

Under the salt laws, the government enjoyed a monopoly on salt mining, levied a sales tax on salt, and forbade Indians to make their own salt or to use contraband salt. A large number of Indians lived on plains not far from the sea and could easily have made their own salt by drying out seawater in the sun. For the Indians, salt was as essential as air and water: most of them labored long hours in the fields in blistering heat and ate only lentils, bread, and salt. Gandhi came to look upon the salt tax as a tax on Indian sweat and blood.

On March 12, 1930, Gandhi—accompanied by scores of ashram residents; workers in what he had named his Constructive Programme, a movement for social reform; and press correspondents—set out for Dandi, a coastal town two hundred miles south of the ashram, where he planned to publicly flout the salt laws, vowing that he would not return to the Sabarmati Ashram until they had been repealed. Every day, he marched about twelve miles, then stopped for the night in a village, where he held a prayer meeting and gave a talk about the salt laws and the Constructive Programme, on occasion mentioning the second Bardoli campaign as an inspiring example of both the potency of nonviolence and his countrymen's capacity for it. Every evening, too, he found time to do an hour's spinning and to keep his diary and correspondence up to date. Some villagers joined the march; others sprinkled water along Gandhi's path to settle the dust, and strewed leaves and flower petals before him.

Gandhi's journey to Dandi was compared by his disciples and followers to Jesus's journey to Jerusalem; many Hindus who could read bought copies of the Bible and read it. Gandhi himself apparently thought that he might have to die in Dandi, as Jesus died in Jerusalem. He and his followers arrived there on April 5th and spent the night praying on the beach. In the morning, he walked into the sea to bathe and purify himself. Then he and his followers went through the process of making salt from seawater and so became criminals in the eyes of the law. He and his followers camped near Dandi for the next month, making and selling small quantities of salt, and waiting to see what the government would do. At first, the government did nothing, in the expectation that Gandhi's bizarre campaign would spend itself. But the story of the salt march and Gandhi's illicit activities was reported around the world, and in India more and more people began going on symbolic salt marches of their own. Up and down the coasts, on the beaches, and on the banks of brackish streams—wherever there was salt to be found—people became satyagrahis and broke the law. Scarcely any violence was reported. The satyagrahis waded into the sea, collected salt water in pans, watched it evaporate in the sun, and shared the precious salt left behind. The authorities, completely underestimating the symbolic power of Gandhi's action, ridiculed the idea that the British raj could be dissolved in pans of seawater. Not much salt was actually produced, but stories of selling and used contraband salt were widely told to dramatize the evils of the British system. Civil disobedience spread to other forms of protest and soon far surpassed the noncooperation campaign of 1920 and 1921. In fact, the 1930 effort became the largest protest movement that Gandhi ever led.

The government had continued to follow a policy of restraint in the hope of diffusing the force of the movement, but at last it decided to act, and on May 5th, in the middle of the night, the police appeared at Gandhi's camp and arrested him. His arrest was followed by government action against practically anyone who was involved in an important way in the civil-disobedience campaign. Webb Miller, a United Press correspondent, described what happened on May 21st to a march designed to raid the government's Dharasana Salt Works, a hundred and fifty miles north of Bombay:

> Suddenly at a word of command, scores of native policemen rushed upon the advancing marchers and rained blows on their heads with their steel-shod lathis. Not one of the marchers even raised an arm to fend off the blows. They went down like ten-pins. From where I stood I heard the sickening whack of the clubs on unprotected skulls. The waiting crowd of marchers groaned and sucked in their breath in sympathetic pain at every blow. . . . They marched steadily, with heads up, without the encouragement of music or cheering or any possibility that they might escape serious injury or death. The police rushed out

and methodically and mechanically beat down the second column.
There was no fight, no struggle; the marchers simply walked forward
till struck down.

By midsummer, according to one estimate, as many as a hundred
thousand satyagrahis, including most of the major and minor Congress leaders, were in jail.

Civil disobedience nevertheless continued in India, and it was against
that background that, in November, the Round Table Conference was con-
vened in London. Britain was represented by delegates from the Labour,
Conservative, and Liberal Parties, and, except for the Congress, practically
all important sections of Indian opinion were represented, in the persons of
some of the most important potentates of the Indian princely states and
preeminent leaders of the All-India Muslim League—a minority religious
party that from its founding, in 1906, had dedicated itself to greater representation of Muslims in the government. The conference lasted over two
months and ended with unanimous agreement on a new system of federal
government for India, which would grant Indians some measure of respon-
sible self-government both in the provinces and at the center. The princes
agreed to the federation partly because they were afraid of the effects of the
civil-disobedience movement in their states; the Muslim Leaguers agreed
to it partly because they looked upon the Indian princes—whether Hindu
or Muslim—as allies against rule by the Congress, which amounted to populist Hindu domination; and the British agreed to it partly because they saw
in the federation a way of safeguarding minority interests while allowing
greater Indian participation in the government. The agreement had the effect
of making many Hindus, including members of the Congress, abandon their
civil disobedience, and at the same time raised the expectations of Muslim
Leaguers about their role in any future Indian government. When the conference adjourned, Prime Minister MacDonald expressed the hope that the
Congress would participate in a second Round Table Conference. In January,
1931, Gandhi and many other Congress leaders were therefore released
from jail, and Gandhi was invited to New Delhi for preliminary discussions
with the Viceroy.

In New Delhi, Gandhi often went five miles on foot from a friend's
house, where he was staying, to the Viceroy's palace for the discussions. In
England, Winston Churchill, among other upholders of the Empire, declared himself humiliated and revolted by the "spectacle of this one-time
Inner Temple lawyer, now seditious fakir, striding half-naked up the steps
on the Viceroy's palace, there to negotiate and to parley on equal terms with
the representative of the King-Emperor."

James Morris

Coronation Everest

Queen Elizabeth II's coronation on June 2, 1953 was enlivened by the last minute announcement that a British expedition had put two men on the summit of the world's highest mountain. As befit the occasion London's stately newspaper The Times *broke the news via a secret dispatch from a correspondent who had traveled with the climbers. James Morris (later Jan Morris) outfoxed his Fleet Street competitors with a clever system of codes and runners and muddled through with a superbly British combination of pluck and humor. This is from his book,* Coronation Everest.

*   *   *

Half past two on the afternoon of May 30 I scribbled it all down in a tattered old notebook, drinking in the flavor of the occasion, basking in the aura of incredulous delight that now flooded through our little camp. The talk was endless and vivacious, and would no doubt continue throughout that long summer afternoon and into the night; but there were only three full days to the Coronation, and as I scribbled I realized that I must start down the mountain again that very afternoon, to get a message off to Namche the next morning. This time there would be no night's rest at Camp III. I must go straight down the icefall to Base camp that evening. My body, still aching from the upward climb in the morning, did not like the sound of this at all; but at the back of my slightly befuddled brain a small voice told me that there could be no argument. Wilfred Noyce had always planned to make this last dash down the mountainside for me; but now I was here myself, and need not bother him.

"I'll come with you, James!" said Michael Westmacott instantly, when I told them my plans; and remembering the newly oozing ice bog of the route, I accepted his offer gratefully. We loaded our rucksacks, fastened our crampons, shook hands all round, and set off down the slope. "Good luck!" a voice called from the dome tent; I turned to wave my thanks, and stood for a moment (till the rope tugged me on) looking at the blank face of Lhotse, just falling into shadow, and the little clump of happy tents that was Camp IV. Christmas angels were in the Cwm that day.

So we strode off together down the valley. In a downhill climb the most experienced man should travel last; but I was so obviously in a condition of impending disintegration, and the way was so sticky and unpleasant from the thaw, that Westmacott went first, and I followed. At the head of the Cwm, though we did not know it, Wilfrid Noyce, Charles Wylie, and some Sherpas were making their way down to Camp IV from the Lhotse Face, where they had been packing up the tents to bring them lower. As they crossed a small ridge they caught sight of our two small figures, far below, all alone in the Cwm and traveling hard towards Camp III. Perhaps there were ghosts about, Noyce thought as he watched our dour silent progress; the angel theory did not occur to him.

For me it was a wet and floundering march. So soft, receptive and greedy was the snow that at almost every step I sank deeply into it, often up to my thighs, and had then to extricate myself with infinite trouble, with that confounded rope (connecting me with Westmacott) rapidly getting tauter as I struggled, until suddenly there would be a great sharp pull upon it, and Mike would turn around to see what was happening, and find me sprawling and flapping in the snow, like some tiresome sea creature on the sand. I remember vividly the labour and the discomfort of it all, with the wet seeping into my boots, and the shaft of my ice axe sinking into the snow, my head heavy and my brain muzzy but excited. As we travelled down the Cwm, so the sun went down, and the valley was plunged into shadow, chilling and unfriendly.

Here and there were our footsteps of the morning's journey, barely recognizable now, but squashy and distorted, as if Snowmen had passed that way. Long and deep were the crevasses that evening, and as we crossed them their cool interiors seemed almost inviting in their placidity. The shadows chased us down the snow, elongated like a dream figure, with my old hat swollen on my head and my ice axe, like a friar's stave, swinging my hand. Before long we were peering ahead through the dark, still struggling and slipping, but still moving steadily down the mountain.

Camp III again, in the half-light. We stopped for lemonade and sweets, and I looked about me with a sudden pang of regret at the melting plateau, the sagging tents, and the tottering wireless aerial, the odd boxes and packing cases. I would never set foot on this place again; this was my good-bye to the mountain. So befuddled was I by the altitude and the exertion, so feverish of emotion, that a hot tear came to my eye as I sat there shivering in the cold, my boots soggy and my head throbbing, looking about me at the loathsome decaying wilderness of ice that surrounded us.

Down we plunged into the icefall, and I realized again what an odious place it had become. The bigness and messiness and cruelty of it all weighed heavily upon me, a most depressing sensation. Any grandeur the icefall possessed had gone, and squalidness had overcome it. Now more than ever it was a moving thing; seracs were disintegrating, plateaus splitting, ice towers visibly melting; and there were creaking, groaning and cracking noises.

> The ice was here, the ice was there,
> The ice was all around;
> It cracked and growled, and roared and howled,
> Like noises in a swound!

Through this pile of white muck we sped, and as we travelled I wondered (in a hazy sort of way) what we would find at the bottom. How many Izards or Jacksons had encamped at Base Camp in my absence, setting up their transmitters, poised to fall upon the descending Sherpas? Was there any conceivable way in which the news of the ascent could have reached the glacier already? Nobody had preceded us down the mountain, but what about telepathy, mystic links, smoke signals, choughs, spiders, swounds? What if I arrived at camp to find that my news was already on its way to London and some eager Fleet Street office? I shuddered at the thought, and taking a moment off to hitch up my rucksack, nearly fell headlong into a crevasse.

"Stay where you are," said Westmacott a little sharply. "And belay me if you can!"

One of his pole bridges, across a yawning chasm, had been loosened by the thaw, and looked horribly unsafe. I thrust my ice axe into the snow and put the rope around it while Westmacott gently edged himself across. I could just see him there in the gloom, precariously balanced. One pole was lashed to another, and he had to move them around, or tie them again, or turn them over, or hitch them up, or do something or other to ensure that we were not precipitated into the depths, as Peacock once remarked, in the smallest possible fraction of the infinite divisibility of time. This, after a few anxious and shivery moments, he did; and I followed him cautiously across the void.

Who would have thought, when Hunt accepted me over that admirable lunch at the Garrick Club, that my assignment would end like this, scrambling dizzily and feverishly down the icefall of Everest in the growing darkness? Who could have supposed that I would ever find myself in quite so historically romantic a situation, dashing down the flanks of the greatest of mountains to deliver a message for the Coronation of Queen Elizabeth II? It was all perfectly—*oops, steady, nasty slippery bit!*—all perfectly ridiculous. It must all be some midnight dream, by brandy out of Gruyère; or a wild boyhood speculation, projected by some intricate mechanism of the time-space theory. Slithering down the mountain with the news from Everest! What poppycock!

"Do try and wake up," said Westmacott. "It would be a help if you'd belay me sometimes!"

I murmured my apologies, blushing in the dark. Indeed by now, as we passed the tents of Camp II, I was a pitiful passenger. All the pieces of equipment fastened to my person seemed to be coming undone. The ice axe constantly slipped from my fingers and had to be picked up. The rope threatened to unloose itself. The laces of my boots trailed. The fastening of one of my crampons had broken, so that the thing was half on, half off my foot, and kept tripping me up. I had torn my windproof jacket on an ice spur, and a big flap of its red material kept blowing about me in the wind. My rucksack, heavy with kit, had slipped on its harness, so that it now bumped uncomfortably about in the small of my back . . .

Still we went on, my footsteps growing slower and wearier and more fumbling, and even Westmacott rather tired by now. Presently we made out the black murk that was the valley of the Khumbu; and shortly afterwards we lost our way. Everything had changed so in the thaw. Nothing was familiar. The little red route flags were useless. There was no sign of a track. We stood baffled for a few moments, faced with an empty, desert-like snow plateau, almost at the foot of the icefall. Then: "Come on," said Westmacott boldly, "we'll try this way! We'll glissade down this slope here!"

He launched himself upon the slope, skidding down with a slithery crunching noise. I followed him at once, and, unable to avoid a hard ice block at the bottom, stubbed my toe so violently that my big toenail came off. The agony of it! It was like something in an old Hollywood comedy, with indignity piled upon indignity, and the poor comic hero all but obliterated by misfortune!

But I had little time to brood upon it, for Westmacott was away again already, and the rope was pulling at me. As we neared the bottom of the icefall, the nature of the ground became even more distasteful. The little glacier rivulets which had run through this section had become swift-flowing torrents. Sometimes we balanced our shaky way along the edge of them; sometimes we jumped across; sometimes, willy-nilly, we waded through the chill water, which eddied into our boots and made them squish as we walked.

At last, at the beginning of the glacier moraine, I thought I would go no farther. It was pitch black by now, and Westmacott was no more than a suggestion in front of me. I sat down on a boulder, panting and distraught, and disregarded the sudden sharp pull of the rope (like totally ignoring a bite on a deep-sea fishing line).

"What's the matter?"

"I think I'm going to stop here for a bit," (as casually as I could manage it) "and get my breath back. I'll just sit here quietly for a minute or two. You go on, Mike, don't bother about me."

There was a slight pause at the other end of the rope.

"Don't be so ridiculous," said Westmacott: and so definitive was this pronouncement that I heaved myself to my feet again and followed him down the glacier. Indeed, we were almost there. The ground was familiar again, and above us loomed the neighborly silhouette of Pumori. The icefall was a jumbled dream behind us. I felt in the pocket of my windproof to make sure my notes were there, with the little typed code I was going to use. All was safe.

Presently there was a bobbing light in front of us; and out of the gloom appeared an elderly Sherpa with a lantern, grinning at us through the darkness. He helped us off with our crampons and took the ice axe from my hand, which was unaccountably shaking with the exertion.

"Anybody arrived at Base Camp?" I asked him quickly, thinking of those transmitters. "Is Mr. Jackson here again, or Mr. Tiwari?"

"Nobody, sahib," he replied. "There's nobody here but us Sherpas. How are things on the mountain, sahib? Is all well up there?"

All well, I told him, shaking his good old hand. All very well.

So we plunged into our tents. There were some letters, and some newspapers, and a hot meal soon appeared. Mike came to join me in eating it, and we squeezed into my tent comfortably, and ate and read there in the warm. I was exhausted, for the climb from III to IV and thence down to base was no easy day's excursion for a beginner; and it seemed to me that the icefall, in its present debased and degenerate condition, had been nothing short of nightmarish.

"Was it really as bad as all that?" I asked. "Or was it just me?"

"It was bad!" Westmacott replied shortly, peering at me benevolently over his spectacles, like a scholarly physician prescribing some good old-fashioned potion.

We lay and lazed there for some time, and chatted about it, and remembered now and then that Everest had been climbed, and wondered how the news would be received in London. I made a few tentative conjectures about honours lists. "Sir Edmund Hillary" certainly sounded odd. What about Tenzing? "Sir Tenzing and Lady Norkay?" "Lord Norkay of Chomolungma?" But no, he was Indian, or Nepalese (nobody quite knew which) and could qualify for no such resplendent titles: he would be honoured royally anyway. We heaved a few sleepy sighs of satisfaction, and presently Westmacott eased himself gradually out of the tent. I thanked him for all his kindness on the icefall, and we said good night.

Before I could go to sleep, though, I had a job to do. Leaning over in my sleeping bag with infinite discomfort, for my legs were as stiff as ramrods and patches of sunburn on various parts of my body made movement very painful, I extracted my typewriter from a pile of clothing and propped it on my knees to write a message. This was that brief dispatch of victory I had dreamed about through the months. Oh Mr. Tiwari at Namche and Mr. Summerhayes at Katmandu! Oh you watchful radio men in Whitehall! Oh telephone operators, typists and subeditors, readers, listeners, statesmen, generals, Presidents, Kings, Queens and Archbishops! I have a message for you!

Now then, let me see. Pull out the crumpled paper code; turn up the flickering hurricane lamp, it's getting dark in here; paper in the typewriter, don't bother with a carbon; prop up your legs with an old kit bag stuffed with sweaters and socks; choose your words with a dirty broken-nailed finger; and here it goes!

Snow conditions bad stop advanced base abandoned yesterday stop awaiting improvement

Which being interpreted would mean:

Summit of Everest reached on May 29 by Hillary and Tenzing.

I checked it for accuracy. Everything was right. I checked it again. Everything was still right. I took it out of the typewriter and began to fold it up to place it in its envelopes: but as I did so, I thought the words over, and recalled the wonder and delight of the occasion, and remembered that dear old Sherpa who had greeted us with his lantern, an hour or two before, when we had fallen out of the icefall.

All well! I added to the bottom of my message.

[Beyond Namche Bazar, two days later. Morris's runners have been carrying his message to an expectant world.]

As we descended a strange and uncomfortable lassitude overcame me, the effect perhaps of de-acclimatization. I had been weak on the glacier high above; now I was not only weak, but intolerably lazy. I could hardly bring myself to move my limbs, or urge my lungs to operate; and often, as we made our way along the stream, I would take off my pack and sit down upon a rock, burying my head in my arms, trying to recover my resolution. It was too ridiculous. The path was easy, the country delightful; the monsoon was about to burst, and there was a smell of fresh moisture in the air; but there, it had been a long three months on Everest, and a long, long march from Lake Camp, and my body and spirit were rebelling.

It was evening now. The air was cool and scented. Pine trees were all about us again, and lush foliage, and the roar of the swollen river rang in our ears. On the west bank of the Dudh Khosi, about six miles south of Namche Bazar, there was a Sherpa hamlet called Benkar. There, as the dusk settled about us, we halted for the night. In a small square clearing among the houses Sonam set up my tent, and I erected the aerial of my radio receiver. The Sherpas, in their usual way, marched boldly into the houses round about and established themselves among the straw, fires, and potatoes of the upstairs rooms. Soon there was a smell of roasting and the fragrance of tea. As I sat outside my tent meditating, with only a few urchins standing impassively in front of me, Sonam emerged with a huge plate of scrawny chicken, a mug of *chang*, tea, chocolate, and *chuppatis*.

How far had my news gone, I wondered as I ate? Was it already winging its way to England from Katmandu; or was it still plodding over the Himalayan foothills in the hands of those determined runners? Would tomorrow, June 2, be both Coronation and Everest Day? Or would the ascent fall upon London later, like a last splendid chime of the Abbey bells? There was no way of knowing; I was alone in a void; the chicken was tough; the urchins unnerving; I went to bed.

But the morning broke fair. Lazily, as the sunshine crept up my sleeping bag, I reached a hand out of my mummied wrappings towards the knob of the wireless. A moment of fumbling; a few crackles and hisses; and then the voice of an Englishman.

Everest had been climbed, he said. Queen Elizabeth had been given the news on the eve of her Coronation. The crowds waiting in the wet London streets had cheered and danced to hear of it. After thirty years of endeavor, spanning a generation, the top of the earth had been reached and one of the greatest of all adventures accomplished. This news of Coronation Everest (said that good man in London) had been first announced in a copyright dispatch in the *Times*.

I jumped out of my bed, spilling the bedclothes about me, tearing open the tent flap, leaping into the open in my filthy shirt, my broken boots, my torn trousers; my face was thickly bearded, my skin cracked with sun and cold, my voice hoarse. But I shouted to my Sherpas, whose bleary eyes were appearing from the neighboring windows:

"Chomolungma finished! Everest done with! All okay!"

"Okay, sahib!" the Sherpas shouted back. "Breakfast now?"

Neil Armstrong

First on the Moon

"That's one small step for a man, one giant leap for mankind." So saying, spacecraft commander Neil Armstrong became the first person to walk on the moon. His two-hour excursion in 1969 with Edwin Aldrin, Jr. was seen by many of his fellow earthlings via simultaneous television. But no one really knew in advance what the lunar walking conditions would be like until that historic first step.

As it happened, Armstrong's boots barely sank into the mysterious soil. "Maybe an eighth of an inch, but I can see the footprints of my boots and the treads in the fine sandy particles."

He could move around easily! "There seems to be no difficulty . . . It's even perhaps easier than the simulation at one-sixth G . . . It's actually no trouble to walk around."

The following excerpts from First On The Moon *include both Armstrong's later recollections and his actual radio transmissions from Tranquility base, where the two pioneers deployed experiments and collected rock samples.*

* * *

Of all the spectacular views we had, the most impressive to me was on the way to the moon, when we flew through its shadow. We were still thousands of miles away, but close enough so that the moon almost filled our circular window. It was eclipsing the sun, from our position, and the corona of the sun was visible around the limb of the moon as a gigantic lens-shaped or saucer-shaped light, stretching out to several lunar diameters. It was magnificent, but the moon was even more so. We were in its shadow, so there was no part of it illuminated by the sun. It was illuminated only by earthshine. It made the moon appear blue-gray, and the entire scene looked decidedly three-dimensional.

I was really aware, visually aware, that the moon was in fact a sphere, not a disc. It seemed almost as if it were showing us its roundness, its similarity in shape to our earth, in a sort of welcome. I was sure that it would be a hospitable host. It had been awaiting its first visitors for a long time.

* * *

We are landed in a relatively smooth crater field of elongated second-ary—circular secondary craters, most of which have raised rims, irrespective of their size . . . The ground mass throughout the area is a very fine sand to a silt. I'd say the thing that would be most like it on earth is powdered graphite. Immersed in this ground mass are a wide variety of rock shapes, sizes, textures, rounded and angular . . . The boulders range generally up to two feet with a few larger than that. Now some of the boulders are lying on top of the surface, some are partially exposed, and some are just barely exposed.

Aldrin: "It's a very simple matter to hop down from one step to the next." *Armstrong:* "Yes, I found it to be very comfortable, and walking is also very comfortable. You've got three more steps and then a long one." *Aldrin:* "Okay, I'm going to leave that one foot up there and both hands down to about the fourth rung up." *Armstrong:* "There you go." *Aldrin:* "Okay. Now I think I'll do the same." *Armstrong:* "A little more. About another inch. There you got it. That's a good step, about a three-footer." *Aldrin:* "Beautiful view." Ten-fifteen in the evening, Houston time . . . [They were now both on the moon, and for a few seconds they were awed in spite of themselves.]

"Isn't that something?" Armstrong asked. "Magnificent sight out here."

"Magnificent desolation," Aldrin said.

[*Aldrin.*] Neil and I are both fairly reticent people, and we don't go in for free exchanges of sentiment. Even during our long training we didn't have many free exchanges. But there was that moment on the moon, a brief moment, in which we sort of looked at each other and slapped each other on the shoulder—that was about the space available—and said, "We made it. Good show." Or something like that . . .

Aldrin: "Reaching down fairly easy. Can't get my suit dirty at this stage." *Aldrin:* "The mass of the backpack does have some effect on inertia." *Armstrong:* "You're standing on a rock, a big rock there now." *Aldrin:* "This pad sure didn't sink much." *Armstrong:* "No, it didn't . . . I wonder if that right under the engine is where the probe might have hit . . . Yes, I think that's a good representation of our sideward velocity at touchdown there." *Aldrin:* "Can't say too much for the—for the visibility here in the LM shadow without the visor up . . . [static] . . ."

Houston (McCandless): Try again, please, Buzz—you're cutting out.

Aldrin: "I say, the rocks are rather slippery . . . very powdery surface when the sun hits. The powder fills up all the very little fine porouses. My boot tends to slide over it rather easily . . . about to lose my balance in one direction and recovery is quite natural and very easy . . . and moving arms around—Jack [Schmitt, astronaut-scientist], doesn't lift your feet off the surface . . . We're not quite that lightfooted . . . Got to be careful that you are leaning in the direction you want to go, otherwise you . . . [static] . . . In other words, you have to cross your foot over to stay underneath where your center of mass is. Say, Neil, didn't I say we might see some purple rocks?" *Armstrong:* "Find the purple rocks?" *Aldrin:* "Yes, they are small, sparkly . . . [static] . . . I would make a first guess, some sort of biotite. We'll leave that to the lunar analysts, but . . . [static] . . ."

Armstrong: " . . . the little hill just beyond the shadow of the LM is a pair of elongated craters about—that will be the pair together—is forty feet long and twenty feet across, and they're probably six feet deep. We'll probably get some more work in there later. [One hour and 7 minutes expended . . . Aldrin was now erecting the solar wind experiment, that aluminum foil window shade . . .]

Aldrin: Incidentally, you can use the shadow that the staff makes to line this up perpendicular to the sun . . . Some of these small depressions, of the boot toes, when moved slowly, produce clods of about three inches. It could suggest exactly what the Surveyor pictures showed when the scoop pushed away a little bit. You get a force transmitted through the upper surface of the soil and about five or six inches of . . . [static] . . . breaks loose and moves as if it were caked on the surface though in fact it really isn't.

Armstrong: I noticed in the soft spots where we had footprints nearly an inch deep that the soil is very cohesive, and it will retain a slope of probably seventy degrees . . . [static] . . . footprints.

Aldrin: "The blue color of my boot had completely disappeared now into this—still don't know exactly what color to describe this other than grayish-cocoa color. It appears to be covering most of the lighter part of the boot . . . very fine particles . . . " [One hour and a half expended on the support systems, the backpacks . . .]

Aldrin: "As I look around the area, the contrast in general is . . . [static] . . . looking down sun, zero phase, it's a very light-colored gray, light gray color. I see a halo around my own shadow, around the shadow of my helmet. Then as I look off cross-sun, the contrast becomes strongest . . . [static] . . . in that the surrounding color is still fairly light as you look down into the sun. . . ." *Aldrin:* "considerably darker in texture . . . " [Armstrong on the television screen carrying the lunar scoop . . .] *Aldrin:* "Right in this area, there are two craters. The one that's right in front of me now—as I look off in about the eleven o'clock position from the spacecraft. About thirty to thirty-five feet across. There are several rocks and boulders about six to eight inches across . . . many sizes . . . [static] . . . "

The moon was a very natural and very pleasant environment in which to work. It had many of the advantages of zero-gravity, but it was in a sense less *lonesome* than zero G, where you always have to pay attention to securing attachment points to give you some means of leverage. In one-sixth gravity, on the moon, you had a distinct feeling of being *somewhere*, and you had a constant, though at many times ill-defined, sense of direction and force.

One interesting thing was that the horizontal reference on the moon is not at all well defined. That is, it's difficult to know when you are leaning forward or backward and to what degree. This fact, coupled, with the rather limited field of vision from our helmets, made local features of the moon appear to change slope, depending on which way you were looking and how you were standing. The weight of the backpack tends to pull you backward, and you must consciously lean forward just a little to compensate. I believe someone has described the posture as "tired ape"—almost erect but slumped forward a little. It was difficult sometimes to know when you were standing erect. It felt as if you could lean farther in any direction, without losing your balance, than on earth. By far the easiest and most natural way to move on the surface of the moon is to put one foot in front of the other. The kangaroo hop did work, but it led to some instability; there was not so much control when you were moving around.

As we deployed our experiments on the surface we had to jettison things like lanyards, retaining fasteners, etc., and some of these we tossed away. The objects would go away with a slow, lazy motion. If anyone tried to throw a baseball back and forth in that atmosphere he would have difficulty, at first, acclimatizing himself to that slow, lazy trajectory; but I believe he could adapt to it quite readily.

Eric Newby

A Short Walk in the Hindu Kush

In the mid-1950s mountaineering novice and London couturier Eric Newby made a quixotic trek across the mountain wastes of the Nuristan region of Afghanistan with another Englishman and a few feckless retainers. As Evelyn Waugh said in the preface of this "very English" book, "Mr. Newby is the latest, but, I pray, not the last of a whimsical tradition. And in his writing he has all the marks of his not entirely absurd antecedents. The understatement, the self-ridicule, the delight in the foreignness of foreigners, the complete denial of any attempt to enlist the sympathies of his readers in the hardships he has capriciously invited; finally in his formal self-effacement in the presence of the specialist (with the essential reserve of unexpressed self-respect) which concludes almost too abruptly this beguiling narrative . . ."

* * *

We crossed the river by a bridge, went up through the village of Shahnaiz, and downhill towards the lower Panjshir.

"Look," said Hugh, "it must be Thesiger."

Coming towards us out of the great gorge where the river thundered was a small caravan like our own. He named an English explorer, a remarkable throwback to the Victorian era, a fluent speaker of Arabic, a very brave man, who has twice crossed the Empty Quarter and, apart from a few weeks every year, has passed his entire life among primitive peoples.

We had been on the march for a month. We were all rather jaded; the horses were galled because the drivers were careless of them, and their ribs stood out because they had been in places only fit for mules and forded innumerable torrents filled with slippery rocks as big as footballs; the drivers had run out of tobacco and were pining for their wives; there was no more sugar to put in the tea, no more jam, no more cigarettes and I was reading *The Hound of the Baskervilles* for the third time; all of us suffered from a persistent dysentery. The ecstatic sensations we had experienced at a higher altitude were beginning to wear off. It was not a particularly gay party.

Thesiger's caravan was abreast of us now, and his horses lurching to a standstill on the execrable track. They were deep-loaded with great wooden presses marked "British Museum," and black tin trunks (like the ones my solicitors have, marked "Not Russel-Jones" or "All Bishop of Chichester").

The party consisted of two villainous-looking tribesmen dressed like royal mourners in long overcoats reaching to the ankles; a shivering Tajik cook, to whom some strange mutation had given bright red hair, unsuitably dressed for Central Asia in crippling pointed brown shoes and natty socks supported by suspenders, but no trousers; the interpreter, a gloomy-looking middle-class Afghan in a coma of fatigue, wearing dark glasses, a double-breasted lounge suit, and an American hat with stitching all over it; and Thesiger himself, a great, long-striding crag of a man, with an outcrop for a nose and bushy eyebrows, forty-five years old and as hard as nails, in an old tweed jacket of the sort worn by Eton boys, a pair of thin grey cotton trousers, rope-soled Persian slippers and a woollen cap comforter.

"Turn around," he said, "you'll stay the night with us. We're going to kill some chickens."

We tried to explain that we had to get to Kabul, that we wanted our mail, but our men, who professed to understand no English but were reluctant to pass through the gorges at night, had already turned the horses and were making for the collection of miserable hovels that was the nearest village.

Soon we were sitting on a carpet under some mulberry trees, surrounded by the entire population, with all Thesiger's belongings piled up behind us.

"Can't speak a word of the language," he said cheerfully, "know a lot of the Koran by heart but not a word of Persian. Still, it's not really necessary. Here, you," he shouted at the cook, who had only entered his service the day before and had never seen another Englishman. "Make some green tea and a lot of chicken and rice—three chickens."

"No good bothering the interpreter," he went on. "The poor fellow's got a sty, that's why we only did seventeen miles today. It's no good doing too much at first, especially as he's not feeling well."

The chickens were produced. They were very old; in the half-light they looked like pterodactyls.

"Are they expensive?"

"The power of Britain never grows less," said the headman, lying superbly. "That means they are very expensive," said the interpreter, rousing himself.

Soon the cook was back, semaphoring desperately.

"Speak up, can't understand a thing. You want sugar? Why don't you say so? He produced a large bunch of keys, like a housekeeper in some stately home. All that evening he was opening and shutting boxes so that I had tantalizing glimpses of the contents of an explorer's luggage—a telescope, a string vest. *The Charterhouse of Parma, Du Côté de Chez Swann,* some fishhooks and the 1/1,000,000 map of Afghanistan—not like mine, a sodden pulp, but neatly dissected, mounted between marbled boards.

"That cook's going to die," said Thesiger; "hasn't got a coat and look at his feet. We're nine thousand feet if we're an inch here. How high's the Chamar Pass?" We told him sixteen thousand feet. "Get yourself a coat and boots, do you hear?" he shouted in the direction of the campfire.

After two hours the chickens arrived; they were like elastic, only the rice and gravy were delicious. Famished, we wrestled with the bones in the darkness.

"England's going to pot," said Thesiger, as Hugh and I lay smoking the interpreter's king-size cigarettes, the first for a fortnight. "Look at this shirt, I've only had it three years, now it's splitting. Same with tailors; Gull and Croke made me a pair of whipcord trousers to go to the Atlas Mountains. Sixteen guineas—wore a hole in them in a fortnight. Bought half a dozen shotguns to give to my headman, well-known make, twenty guineas apiece, absolute rubbish."

He began to tell me about his Arabs.

"I give them powders for worms and that sort of thing." I asked him about surgery. "I take off fingers and there's a lot of surgery to be done; they're frightened of their own doctors because they're not clean."

"Do you do it? Cutting off fingers?"

"Hundreds of them," he said dreamily, for it was very late. "Lord, yes. Why, the other day I took out an eye. I enjoyed that."

"Let's turn in," he said.

The ground was like iron with sharp rocks sticking up out of it. We started to blow up our air beds. "God, you must be a couple of pansies," said Thesiger.

Richard Meinertzhagen

Kenya Diary

By the beginning of the twenty-first century East Africa's wildlife heritage will probably be lost forever. Not long ago, however, the mountains, plains, and lakes teemed with game and the ecosystems functioned in all their grandeur. Richard Meinertzhagen's Kenya Diary *(1902–1906) takes us back to a time in Kenya before all the lions had become zoo animals and before all the tribes had become pacified.*

In 1902, Richard Meinertzhagern (1878–1967) was a young army officer, newly stationed with the King's African Rifles in the East African Protectorate (Kenya). He was sent on safari to take command of the army detachment at Fort Hall. He and his caravan of porters walked to this station near Mount Kenya, marvelling at the wildlife along the way. "Made a long march today of about 23 miles over rough country" is his typically terse comment during the four-day walk to the outpost that consisted of two grass huts enclosed by a stone wall and a ditch.

At Fort Hall, in "undulating country covered with low brush," the new arrival met the English District Officer, a civilian named Tate, and the English police officer named Hemsted.

To our refined sensibilities at the end of the twentieth century Richard Meinertzhagen at the beginning of the century was a blood-thirsty fellow, blasting away at the ubiquitous wildlife and the miscreant natives with equal gusto. But he was also amazingly prescient about the end of Empire. He once told the High Commissioner that the Africans' "interests must prevail over the interests of strangers" and that the country would ultimately belong to them, not Europeans.

* * *

I was out at dawn after the wounded impala and on the way killed another waterbuck. No sooner had I got on to last night's blood spoor of the impala than I saw 8 lion trotting across a piece of open grass towards a large reed bed. They were some 300 yards distant. I only had time to spot one maned lion among them when they got into the reeds. At the spot where they entered the reeds I saw several heads looking at me, so I walked slowly in their direction and at 150 yards took a shot at one of their heads but missed. There were several snarls and roars, but they all disappeared. I was now at a loss to know what to do. The reed bed was some 5 acres in extent and dense. It was bounded on one side by the Tana River and on the other by about 300 yards of short grass. I only had two nervous niggers with me, so I sent one up to Fort Hall for Hemsted, while I and the other watched the reed bed to see that the lion did not break out. At 2:39 P.M. Hemsted arrived and we proceeded to walk through the reeds. Of course we never saw one, but we frequently heard them as they dashed through the reeds. One of our niggers saw one close to him and fled. So at dark we had to abandon the attempt.

[I did not realise at the time how foolhardy we were. To try to walk up 8 lion in dense reeds is asking for trouble; we should have left them alone and waited outside at dusk, when no doubt we should have got a shot as they started off on their evening hunt.]

When I saw the lion first in the open, they appeared more like fat, sleek sheep and not a bit like the King of Beasts. But the sight of 8 lion all in a bunch made my mouth water a bit. I noticed that lion spoor is much smaller than that of the tiger.

I left the waterbuck's carcass out tonight and shall visit it tomorrow at dawn in the hope of finding some lion eating it.

JUNE 24, 1902. MERAGUA RIVER

I was out before dawn to watch the waterbuck carcass but saw nothing; the lion must have polished him off in the middle of the night, for the carcass was picked dry and numerous fresh lion tracks were in the neighbourhood. I saw some impala about 400 yards away and was just going to stalk them when a couple of rhinoceros trotted out of the bush within 30 yards of me, heading for the reed bed. I quickly slipped a solid bullet into my Mannlicher and fired at the largest beast at 75 yards. Both animals turned and ran back across me towards some scrub. The smaller of the two held its tail erect while the larger one did not, so I presumed my bullet had had effect. I followed them and found them standing together among some thorn scrub in which they were almost invisible. Creeping to within 40 yards I put a second bullet into the beast's shoulder, at which she headed again for the reed patch. I knew she was badly hit by the way she ran, so I gave her another two shots, both of which hit her in the ribs. I rushed after them, and just before entering the reeds the large beast turned and faced me in the open. I sat down and fired at her chest, whereat she turned towards the reeds, and walked slowly into them, so that I lost sight of her. As I did not fancy walking up wounded rhinoceroses with a Mannlicher, I sent to camp for my 8 bore cannon. When this arrived I followed the spoor cautiously into the reeds and soon caught sight of the smaller beast standing watching me. As this beast was only three-quarters grown I did not wish to kill him, so tried to frighten him away. I threw stones and cartridges and shouted but he merely snorted at me, though he stood but 20 yards from me. Eventually I fired off the 8 bore, at which he crashed into the reeds and I saw him no more. The larger beast, an old female, was lying dead a few yards further on. I photographed her and then commenced to cut her up. Her dorsal skin was nearly two inches thick. I was sorry to find her in an advanced state of pregnancy, for I cut from her a perfect young rhino, just ready to be born. It had hair round the eyes and on the face, back and rump. In adult rhino there is only hair on the eyelashes, tail and ears. I skinned the young one complete and shall have it set up.

The horns of the cow are poor and much worn, which denotes an old beast. We had some difficulty in removing them, but by working under them with a knife for nearly two hours we eventually removed them from the skull. The horns of a rhino are not attached to the skull but grow on the skin, being really congealed hair. The whole camp having come to the scene, and a hunting party of Wakikuyu having also turned up, all the meat was taken away. The beast was so heavy that it took 10 of us to turn her over.

In the afternoon I killed a buck oribi at 40 yards with my Mannlicher.

[I described these oribi as a new race in the *Proceedings of the Zoological Society* some years later, naming them *kenyae*. They are closely allied to Haggard's oribi.]

JUNE 25, 1902. FORT HALL

Tomorrow being Coronation Day, Tate asked me to shoot some haartebeeste for meat for the natives at the festivities at Fort Hall. He sent down 20 porters to carry meat and I shot 2 haartebeeste for them.

I walked back to Fort Hall in the evening, having shot 3 waterbuck, 2 impala, 3 haartebeeste, a rhino, a red lynx and an oribi, and having seen 8 lion. I killed everything with my Mannlicher, with which I am well pleased. I used nothing but hollow-pointed bullets, except for the solids I used on the rhino.

Tate has returned from his tour, and he, Hemsted and I all feed together. I like both Tate and Hemsted.

My pay in India was exactly £108 a year, and now I find myself with £400 a year under cheaper conditions, for outside luxuries such as cartridges, alcohol, etc., living is absurdly cheap. Eggs three a penny, sheep 3 rupees, a chicken half a rupee, and we grow our own vegetables. My daily expenditure on food is only about the equivalent of 2s. a day. So, with the small allowance Father gives me, I am rapidly becoming a capitalist.

[On joining the K.A.R. my capital value was £0. On leaving the K.A.R. after nearly 5 years I found myself possessed of over £3000.]

JUNE 26, 1902. FORT HALL

Today being the Coronation Day of King Edward, we decided to have a general holiday and a military review, and give the local savages a treat. All the local chiefs were invited to come in, and the haartebeeste meat, supplemented by an ox and a goat, was distributed among them. We had a little ceremonial drill in the *boma*, which consisted of a sort of amateur trooping of the colour. I marched my detachment of 22 men about the station, firing an occasional *feu de joie* will ball ammunition, and frequently presenting arms to a Union Jack on a pole. I could not help smiling at the rather Gilbertian touch to the whole proceedings, but our hearts were in the right place.

Tate gave the savages a speech in Swahili, but he might as well have spoken in English for aught the Wakikuyu understood. The natives, of course, thought we had all gone mad and understood nothing of the proceedings. Hemsted, in as ragged clothes as his 30 police, stood to attention for 35 minutes, not daring to give a word of command, which he knew no man of his would either understand or obey.

In the afternoon the natives gave us a treat. A large party of young men and girls danced together for many a hot hour. To my mind the dance was most suggestive and immoral, but that did not make it any the less interesting. I imagine the origin of all dancing is to incite or play on the sexual senses. In the dances I witnessed this afternoon the last phase is the bolting of the lady into the bush, hotly pursued by the young man. As both are almost nude, and as the girl is invariably caught and tripped up, the climax of a Kikuyu dance can best be imagined. It certainly could not be introduced into Belgravia, though modern dancing in England is sometimes little better than these savage displays in tropical Africa.

The men dancers had their heads smeared with red earth saturated with sheep's fat, and were bedecked with beads and copper wire, which gave them the look of veritable little demons. The grimaces they make as they dance made me roar with laughter, and the efforts of the men to finish up the final dance with the girl they fancy were too ludicrous. They, of course, take the whole proceeding most seriously. Most dancing is done with the heads and shoulders, the legs having but one step, which is continually repeated. The women wriggle at the hips.

We also tried some sports, which were not a success, as the winner always had to fight the rest afterwards. I noted that the winner of a race 2¼ miles long did the course in exactly 14 minutes. There was also a tug-of-war between my men and the police, which my men won. That again led to a free fight later on.

I found out a curious custom among the Wakikuyu. There is a bird here which lives in the forest called a plantain-eater. It is about the size of a cuckoo, has a crest, and is dull green in colour with brilliant crimson on the webs of the primary feathers. It is apparently a custom among the Wakikuyu that once a year every unmarried girl who has reached the age of puberty—that is to say, over about 11 or 12 years—must wear one of these crimson wing feathers in her head ornaments, and that while she so wears it she is not allowed to say No to any man, but can dispense with it as soon as the man has satisfied himself. She need only wear the feather on one day in the year, and on that day must travel at least once to the nearest village by daylight. Of course in most instances the appointed day for wearing the feather is arranged with the girl's favourite young man. The custom is aimed at making it uncomfortable for young girls who refuse to marry.

I discovered this custom by accident. I passed a girl on the road wearing such a feather. She smiled at me in a rather awkward manner, and was at once seized round the waist by a young man who was walking near me and carried off into the bush, where after a brief struggle all was silent. As I was unable to understand such impetuous behavior on the part of the Kikuyu and the lack of resistance on the part of the girl, I enquired of the Government interpreter, who told me the above detail. He added that any girl misusing a scarlet feather, or using it more than once a year, was subjected to a severe beating by the whole of her village as a loose character.

JULY 6, 1902. THIKA RIVER

At 9:30 yesterday morning a native youth came into the *boma* (Fort Hall) with the story that the mail party had been cut up and destroyed by Wakikuyu on the Thika River while on its way into Nairobi. We at first thought it was a lie or another outrage by a well-known man-eating lion on the Thika River. But at noon our worst fears were realised, when a message from Hemsted, who is working on the road about 15 miles from here, brought definite information that the mail had been cut up on the Thika and 29 miles from here. Three porters and a policeman had been murdered, and some others travelling with the mail had been wounded.

[See also September 7, 1902; the culprits turned out to be the Kihimbuini people, a section of the Merouka Kikuyu. They got well punished.]

On hearing this I collected 20 of my men and started off at once for the scene of the outrage, with food for 5 days. When we reached Punda Milia camp, some 15 miles on the road, it began to get dark and 5 of my 8 porters ran away, so I commandeered another 5 from the road working party. As some of my men and porters could not keep up with the 5 miles an hour at which I was travelling, I went ahead with but 4 of my men. Hemsted had meanwhile also proceeded to the scene, but as he had but 2 rather unreliable policemen with him I was anxious to reach him as soon as possible. We had a long and weary march, with occasional showers. We reached the Thika River at 2:40 A.M., where I was relieved to find Hemsted safe. I think he was mighty glad to see me. The last few miles of my night march were far from pleasant, for we were passing through a district doubly dangerous. There was the risk of having my small party rushed by the Wakikuyu, or attacked by the famous man-eating lion of these parts. The night was pitch dark, and when about a mile from the Thika we heard a lion roaring not far from us; soon afterwards a lion kept parallel with us and only a few yards away, as was clear from the low grunts which were continually made. This induced us to fix our bayonets and proceed with great caution.

Hemsted had arrived here yesterday evening and found a dreadful scene. The 3 dead porters had not been buried and were smelling. The wounded, comprising 9 men and 2 women, were lying about groaning, and were a mass of flies and maggots. Several unwounded survivors had not attempted to get them water or to assist in any way. One of the survivors gave me the following account.

The party had built for themselves a small thorn *zariba* in which they were all asleep, when about 10 P.M. a large party of Wakikuyu rushed them, spearing and shooting arrows in all directions. The one policeman fired a shot, at which all the Wakikuyu fled. The mail bag was untouched, so also was a piece of rhino skin and some trophies which I was sending into Nairobi. I fancy the whole business was done by the Merouka tribe, who live in the neighbourhood, and was prompted by the sheer love of killing. They are notorious for their lust for blood. In their hurry to decamp they have left several spears, bows and arrows in the grass, some of which I have collected.

Some of the wounded are in a bad condition. I have sent Hemsted back to Fort Hall for medical stores, and have sent a runner to Nairobi for a doctor, but I fear both will be some time in reaching me. Two of the most seriously wounded are women. One has a spear thrust under the right arm, and as it comes out under her left arm, I wonder she is alive. The spear had not been extracted, Hemsted not having been able to face it. After a severe tug I managed to pull it out and stuffed the hole with permanganate. The other woman has a bad wound in the stomach and from the wound protruded some part of her inside which might have been anything. It was a mass of maggots, so I cut it off with a pair of scissors and sewed up the hole, having stuffed it with permanganate. Both are in bad pain and I doubt if they can live. A Masai with a spear wound in his lungs may die at any moment. Dressing the wounds of these poor wounded is quite the worst job I have ever undertaken, for my only medical stores are permanganate, cotton-wool and lanoline. I have also administered large doses of tea and whisky, and I can do no more. The flies are a great nuisance, so I have rigged up some shelters for the wounded and have detailed natives to continually fan them with brushwood fans.

But my main work today has been the construction of a stiff thorn *zariba* which cannot be rushed by natives. The rest of my men having arrived here this afternoon, I forwarded the mail bags to Nairobi. The garrison of my post is now 15 rifles and myself.

Just before dark I took a stroll round camp to see if there were any signs of lion. I shot a waterbuck within 150 yards of camp and got all the meat into the *zariba* before nightfall. I have set all hands on to make soup for the wounded.

Immediately after dark we heard natives calling on the other side of the river, doubtless a scouting party of the Wakikuyu, to see what was happening. A few fire signals were made, so we all stood to arms for an hour. But as a precaution I have 4 double sentries round the camp this evening.

JULY 7, 1902. THIKA RIVER

In spite of all my precautions, last night proved that my defences were inadequate against lion. About 10 P.M. a small party with stores and an escort of 15 police arrived from Fort Hall. We let them into the *zariba*, and I again dressed the wounds with the carbolic which had been sent out, and gave the two women a good injection of morphia. I then lay down on my bed. The night was stuffy and I was sleeping out. Suddenly a piercing cry rang out from a man who was sitting round a camp fire with his comrades. I jumped up with my revolver, thinking the natives had got in, and just had time to see by the failing light of the camp fires the image of a lion jumping over my *zariba* with a man in his mouth. We fired in his direction in the hope of making him drop his victim, but we failed. It appears that the lion leaped into the *zariba* and seized a porter by the buttocks, but, on this man yelling, let go his hold and seized the next man by the throat, probably killing him instantly, and decamped over the thorn *zariba*. I rushed out of the *zariba* into the dark with a lamp and my rifle, but we could neither hear nor see anything, so returned.

I then attended to the porter's buttocks. The lion had gripped him firmly and had punctured his skin with the four canine teeth. I washed these wounds out with strong carbolic and dressed them. No sooner had I completed this than two lion began to roar and grunt quite close to the *zariba*. Whenever they roared we fired a few cartridges in their direction, and this went on for two hours before they finally made off. But as I was still nervous about a second attack by perhaps more than one lion I sat up all night to encourage the sentries, whose nerves were on the verge of collapse.

As soon as it was light enough to see this morning I tracked the man-eating lion. The trail was not difficult to follow, owing to the broken bead necklaces, small pieces of cloth, a certain amount of blood and the claw marks of the galloping lion as he tore across the soft mud near camp. Though his victim had been silent it was clear that a struggle had taken place, for there were marks on the ground where the man had dug his fingers in to try to stop himself. He had also pulled out a handful from the lion's mane. The fact that he had been seized by the neck would account for his inability to shout. Some 300 yards from camp we came to the site of the last struggle. The grass was drenched with blood, and covered with small pieces of bone and human skin and the man's skull. It was obvious that more than one lion had partaken of this ghastly feast. The ground was now rocky and tracking became impossible, so we abandoned the idea of going further. Doubtless the party of lion are at this moment not far distant and probably lying up in the thick fringe of bush along the Thika River. I have several men out watching for any signs of them.

[On December 26, 1903 I killed both the man-eating lion and the lioness.]

The porter suffering from the lion's teeth is doing well, but the carbolic I stuffed into his wounds this morning hurts more than the wounds themselves. The other wounded are in a bad condition. The Masai has developed pneumonia and is unconscious. He will die before tomorrow. The woman with the stomach wound is much worse and is exuding a sort of green fluid from the wound. She is suffering terrible pain, so I have given her a real good dose of morphia. My carbolic is almost exhausted and I am using my shirts and pyjamas as bandages.

I had patrols out all day. One of them sighted a party of armed savages, and, acting under my orders, opened fire, killing one of their number, whose arms they brought back to camp. So that's good. I have turned all available hands on to increase the thorn zariba, and we are now impregnable against natives. A lion might jump over it, but he could never get back with a man in his mouth, for it is now 7 feet high and 4 feet thick.

I retrieved the rest of the waterbuck which I shot yesterday, and also killed a buck Thomson's gazelle, and the camp is now busy making soup. There seems to be plenty of game about here, for this evening I saw lots of zebra, waterbuck, impala, gazelle, ostrich, wildebeeste, haartebeeste and steinbock.

George Adamson

A Day at Kora

George Adamson was a jack-of-all-trades and game warden in Kenya before embarking on an unusual retirement with his wife, Joy, of releasing tame lions into the wilds. Their adventures resulted in several books including the bestseller Born Free *(1960). The worldwide popularity of that book (and of "Born Free," the movie) was probably due to its romantic theme and setting but George Adamson's life as described in* My Pride and Joy *(1987) is not the African idyll of our imaginations. "Destroying the wilderness," he wrote, "and robbing its prospects of peace and of game, man leaves only the promise of danger. He has killed ten of my lions and murdered my wife."*

George Adamson was born in India in 1906 and moved to East Africa at an early age. His remote camp at Kora is the scene of his ongoing attempt to repatriate urban or orphaned lions to the wilds. Each day he walks his camp lions several miles to the Tana River. Almost every day visitors hope to participate in this most extraordinary of walks.

Those who live close to and identify with wild animals often have a radically different sense of their nature and worth. The great Henry Beston called our fellow creatures "other nations." George Adamson summed it up this way, "Believing, as I now do, that the larger social animals are closer to man than is usually admitted, I believe also that they have moral rights which are similar to man's. The corollary of this is that people are much closer to animals, in their genetic impulses and social behaviour, than they care to admit. I sometimes examine my own nature in this light."

This selection is from My Pride and Joy.

* * *

Day starts when the fan-tailed ravens, regular as clockwork, call us with their raucous croaking at dawn. For the next twenty minutes the rumpus rises to a crescendo as they flap around Hamisi, trying to steal his eggs. He usually fobs them off with a biscuit.

As my campbed is next to the two lion enclosures, at the end of the camp, I sometimes wake up to find a pair of cubs lying only a few inches away from my nose, on the other side of the wire. By sleeping next to me they learn that human beings do not necessarily represent a threat. I had to keep two young lions, Suleiman and Sheba, who had been sent to us by a ranching friend called Ken Clarke, penned up for several weeks before they calmed down; Suleiman had been grazed by the bullet which killed his mother. They were over a year old, and their mother had been shot for persistent cattle-raiding; I took them as I could not bear the thought of them going to a zoo. Once the young lions are settled, I wander in as soon as I am up, with a bucket of water or tit-bit of meat. If they rub their heads against my knee the first battle to win their trust has been won.

After a quick cup of tea I get ready to walk the lions down to the river. Hamisi breaks off washing the pans and gives my tracker a cold thermos and packet of biscuits. Tony arranges for our driver to hitch the trailer to the Landrover and fetch water. Terence briefs his road gang for the day. There is a fearful cackle as the guinea fowl and hornbills clear off with the last of the millet or Terence's Weetabix. Most of the lions spend the night outside camp and it is intriguing to see how newcomers react to their first taste of freedom. Usually they have got the measure of the pride after watching them carefully through the wire: once outside they approach their elders with diffident greetings, like dogs.

So far none of them has bolted. Nevertheless this initial introduction to the rest of the pride is an acid test of their nerve. The younger the cubs the sooner they are likely to be accepted. Normally they approach the dominant male and work their way down through the hierarchy. The warmer the feelings between two lions, the more affectionately they rub cheeks and run them sinuously down each other's flanks. This tactile sense is obviously of great importance. Suleiman and Sheba were treated much more suspiciously than most other newcomers, partly because they were at least a year old and partly because the pride was already over a dozen strong and beginning to break up. Nevertheless they were tolerated on occasional walks.

As soon as the pride moves off all its senses are alert to the engrossing world of the bush. Lions have superb vision for spotting movement and instinctively shift to the highest ground for the best look-out: that is why mine have always lorded it from the tops of my Landrovers. Being nocturnal their night vision is excellent too.

When I came to Kora I grew more aware of how important scent is to lions. In this dense bush, where visibility is often down to fifty yards or less, I have seen them set off after a giraffe which has been browsing five or six hundred yards away. They also have a different and no doubt instinctive understanding of scent. When they come across a big ball of elephant dung, or one of those middens made by the families of little dik dik antelopes, they love to roll in it. I suppose it is to disguise their scent, which to the human nose is rather like honeyed tobacco, for they never roll in the droppings of lions, hyenas or jackals.

Lions have very keen ears. I have known them to pick up a sound eight miles away, which was well beyond the power of human hearing. Their voice plays an important part in their social life and they seem to appreciate that a rock or a cliff can boost their full-scale territorial roaring. They have a whole repertoire of lesser noises—puffs and whuffs, miaows and purrs, moans, yowls, grunts and growls.

Although their basic diet depends on the local game they certainly have a discriminating palate. They relish zebra meat as much as they scorn baboon, unless they are starving. Like dogs they occasionally feel the urge to eat grass. Once I put out poisoned meat to get rid of some hyenas, but found to my dismay it had been taken by lions. I followed their tracks and came to a place where a lion had been sick. In the vomit were some chewed berries of *Cordia gharaf*. They have a bitter taste and I am sure they were eaten as an emetic.

While roaring is the most obvious method of proclaiming territory the pride is constantly employing another on our walks—marking. Young lions piddle, females squat, and adult males deliver backward, well-aimed squirts, scented from an anal gland. By this means the native lions and mine are constantly exchanging challenge, information and insult.

The principal aim of our walks is to provide fun and game, but sometimes we run into trouble. If they try to take on the rare buffalo we meet, the younger lions are in for a shock, but it is essential for them to be completely at home in the bush and to get the measure of the different game. I cannot teach them to hunt, any more than their mothers or their elders can. Lions are born with the instinctive ability to stalk and to kill— I have seen it proved over and over again—but only experience will perfect these skill and experience is what I can offer.

While we are walking I talk to the lions. They must know my voice so well that they automatically pick up its intonations of encouragement, approval, reassurance, caution, command and rebuke. It would be lunacy, not to say disastrous, to try to dominate them as some people train dogs.

They know very well when you are angry, will often respond to a shouted "No!", and will respect you if you stand your ground and move towards them—whereas retreating is dangerous. What matters is that they recognise a voice and authority. Even so you can never rely on them entirely. When it rains, and the temperature drops, they can become uncomfortably boisterous. I do not carry a rifle or revolver whenever I leave camp just for protection against irascible rhinos.

By the time we get down to the river I am ready for a cool glass of gin from the thermos and, as the sun will be getting warm, the lions are quite happy to flop down on the sand or mess about in the shallows. Lions are among the laziest animals on earth and like to spend most of the day dozing, although if very hungry they will spring up at the chance of a kill whatever the heat.

It is extremely beautiful down by the Tana. The stretch we make for is more than a hundred yards wide if you take in the stream, the pools, the shallows, the rocks and the sand. There is shade from the palms and acacias, which are much taller here than those in the bush round the camp. Terence has identified all the plants and the shrubs—the deadly datura or moonflower with its lovely white trumpets, the sweet scented henna and the red-berried salvadora, so attractive to birds.

The game fades away at the approach of the lions but the baboons chatter and bark on the opposite bank, while the hippos wallow and snort out in the silted red water. Close in it is hard to tell if a dark ridged shape, gliding along with the current, is a log or a crocodile. The birds seem to have no fear of the lions and if I sit quietly a succession of waders will drop down to the river—silent white egrets and honking purple-black hadada ibis, mottled Egyptian geese and the formidable carnivorous sentries, goliath herons, tall yellow-billed storks and the large marabous, with their wicked beaks pressed against the scrotum-pink sacs on their chests.

Peaceful as it is, warmed by the sun and cooled by the contents of my thermos, I am always a little uneasy when I am here with the lions. After it has rained they make a frightful fuss when they have to walk through a puddle, but if something excites their interest on the other side of the river they plunge straight into the stream and swim directly across, despite the strength of the current. My worry is that crocodiles have drowned at least one of my lions and may easily account for others.

I usually walk the younger lions back to camp for lunch; in the first few weeks they are inclined to come to a call, like a dog. I leave the older ones by the river, or on Kora Rock, which we pass on the way. They are probably still there when I go down in the evening—or will come to me quickly if I call them with a megaphone.

I have had some tricky moments up on the rocks. Early one morning, in 1977, I let Suleiman and Sheba out of their enclosure to spend the day in the bush, while I drove to the hill to look for a lioness with cubs. I climbed to the foot of some cliffs where I thought her lair might be, but could see no sign of them.

As I started down Suleiman and Sheba appeared. They were in a playful mood and while I fended off Sheba, who butted me from the front, Suleiman jumped on my back, grabbing me by the neck and bringing me down on the steep hillside. I tried to beat him off, whacking him over my shoulder with a stick. This made him angry and he started to growl, sinking his teeth in the back of my neck. It was no longer play.

Luckily I was wearing my revolver because my search for the lioness and cubs might well have brought me face to face with a cobra or leopard while I was poking about in the rocks. I drew the gun now with the notion of firing a shot over Suleiman's head to scare him off. When I pulled the trigger there was just a dull click. It happened a second time and with a fearful chill I realised I had probably forgotten to load it. My hand was no longer steady as I broke the gun open to work out my chances. At least there was a round in each of the chambers and as Suleiman still had his teeth in my neck—I could feel the blood trickling down my shoulders and the sweat coming out on my forehead—I decided to try again. This time I managed to get two shots off into the air. They had not the slightest effect.

Suleiman bit harder. In sheer desperation I pointed the revolver backwards over my shoulder, and fired straight at him. Immediately he let go and, looking startled, went and sat twenty feet off with Sheba, who had leapt back at the sound of the first two shots. I could see blood on his muzzle and more on his neck.

I was bleeding profusely myself and wondered what the hell to do next. Tony Fitzjohn was away in Nairobi. Terence was off on safari and our radio was out of action. I therefore concentrated on getting down to the car and back into camp, where at least I had disinfectant and dressings. By the time I got the Landrover into camp I was feeling exceedingly groggy.

To my surprise it was Terence who opened the gates at the sound of my engine. He had got in only a few minutes before me. He helped me clean up the bites, and then he set off on an eighty-mile journey to the nearest medical post, which was in permanent touch with Nairobi. I did not get much sleep during the night and felt very worried about Suleiman, as I had no idea how badly I had wounded him. I rather feared the worst as Sheba had appeared in the evening without him. Next morning, much to my relief, Suleiman turned up. The pistol bullet had run across the top of his shoulders and lodged under the skin. He looked little the worse for it and was as friendly as ever. My own damage might have been worse too. The Flying Doctor took me to hospital in Nairobi and as the wound did not go septic I was out in a week.

Few of our morning walks end as eventfully as this one and the camp we return to at midday has calmed down after the bustle at breakfast. By now the temperature is 100 degrees. The lions lie flat out under the trees. All the other animals too, the reptiles, the birds and even the insects are silent and still, each in its own patch of shade. Our lunch is like a movie in slow motion with the sound turned down. It is an effort to eat, to drink, to puff my pipe. Terence and I nod in our chairs. Dry leaves crack under the scorching heat of the sun like tiny pistol shots.

I know that if I surrender to sleep, just as I get on to my bed, I shall hear the persistent and approaching drone of a small plane heading for camp. I recently counted from my visitors book that two hundred and ninety-seven people made their way to Kora last year. As always, while friends bring their news and their views, strangers ask questions. I do my best to give answers.

"Yes, after their first week or two the lions are entirely free to come and go as they please—unless they are damaged or ill, in which case I bring them into camp to look after them."

"I'm sorry, I can only take people out on foot if I know that the lions are well away from camp."

"Sadly it is true. One of the lions did kill a man here; but that's a long time ago now."

"Well, the danger is really more to Tony and me than anyone else, as we spend so much of the day with the lions."

"No. In a funny way the danger is part of the attraction—as it presumably is for racing drivers or people who sail round the world single-handed."

"As a matter of fact nobody pays us. We have to raise money to keep ourselves going as best we can."

"Why do I do it?" That is the most difficult question of all. "Well, I suppose it is to give the lions the chance of a decent life. A lion is not a lion if it is only free to eat, to sleep and to copulate. It deserves to be free to hunt and to choose its own prey; to look for and find its own mate; to fight for and hold its own territory; and to die where it was born—in the wild. It should have the same rights as we have."

Shiva Naipaul

North of South

Social observation is one of the great pleasures of urban strolls. Few writers have refined this art more than Shiva Naipaul. Born in Trinidad of Indian ancestry and educated in England, he brought his outsider's eye to 1970s Africa. In North Of South *(1978) he reports on a walk along Kenyatta Avenue in Nairobi, Kenya where he has just had an unpleasant altercation with a shoeshine boy.*

* * *

Andrew, I would guess, was in his early twenties. We had met in the street when I stopped him to ask the way. He wore a striped suit, platformed shoes and carried a leather briefcase. Rather than explain, he offered to escort me personally, brushing aside my objections. "I'll take you," he said firmly.

Having delivered me safely, he announced his intention to wait for me.

"That isn't necessary," I said, wary now of his generosity.

"I'll wait."

"But I don't know how long I'll be."

"That's all right. I have nothing else to do." He was quietly adamant.

He was as good as his word. An hour later I found him where I had left him. He fell in step a pace or two behind me, as self-effacing as a shadow, and followed me back to the hotel. He touched my arm as I entered the lounge. No doubt he was expecting to be paid for his services. After my misadventure with the shoeshine boy, I dreaded the prospect of another scene. Hesitantly, not knowing whether it was too much or too little or—come to that—whether he would be offended by my presumption, I offered him ten shillings. He took the note, folded it neatly and put it in his breast pocket. But he still showed not the slightest inclination to depart.

"You want *more* money?"

"I don't want more money," he said. "I want to give you this." He held out a stylishly printed calling card. "Andrew Njenga. Office Furniture Salesman." An address and telephone number were supplied.

I returned the card. "I don't need any office furniture. Sorry."

"You keep it," he said. "It's for you. If you give me your card, we could write to each other."

"I don't have a card."

This appeared to astonish him. However, ready for any emergency, he produced an address book and a pencil. "You can write your address in here," he said.

"But why do you want us to write to each other?"

"I would like you as a pen pal," he said. "I like writing to pen pals."

I was touched, rebuking myself for my churlishness. I wrote my address in his book. Anxious now to make up for my gracelessness, I offered to buy him a drink. He accepted the invitation with alacrity.

We descended soft-carpeted stairs to the dimly lit bar, virtually deserted at that relatively early hour of the afternoon. Soon, though, it would be overrun by tourists, office workers and harlots. Canned music drifted dismally through the air-conditioned gloom. Andrew ordered a beer.

"Why don't you have a calling card?" he asked.

"I never thought of it."

"You should. All my friends have them." He took a card from his wallet and stared pensively at it. I felt he was looking at an alter ego; that the printed card helped to make him real to himself, to lend credence to his city existence.

He asked me if I was married. I said I was.

"How many cows did you have to give?"

"Cows?"

"How many did you have to give to your wife's family?"

"I didn't have to give any."

"None at all?"

"None at all."

Andrew loosened his tie knot. He looked somber. "You are a lucky man. I had to give my wife's family four cows. And what's more, one of them was pregnant." He sipped his beer.

"My real ambition," he said suddenly, "is to be a lawyer or an engineer. But for that I need a scholarship."

"Won't the government give you one?"

"I have tried. I don't have the correct qualifications." He stirred the frothy crest of his beer with a finger. "My only hope is that one day I might be lucky enough to meet some rich person who will help me. I know somebody who got a scholarship like that."

"Who gave it to him?"

"A German lady. I hear the Germans are nice people. I keep hoping I would meet someone like that. Someone who will take me away with them and give me good studies."

"Maybe you will."

"Maybe." He gazed despondently around the room. Not a rich German lady in sight. He stared at me. "You must be a wealthy man."

"Me! What ever gave you that idea? I'm not rich at all. I'm very, very poor."

"They say all you Asians have a lot of money."

"I'm an exceptional Asian. I have no money at all."

"You can't be that poor if you are able to travel all the way to Kenya. You must have a lot of *savings* in the bank." His bright, clear eyes shone with worldly wisdom. "How else could you afford to come all this way?"

"Somebody paid for me to come."

"You mean somebody gave you a scholarship?"

"Well . . ."

"You are a lucky man," he said. "I wish I could be as lucky as you."

He finished his beer; I bought him another one. The first whore of the evening had arrived. She was garbed in an ankle-length, contour-hugging dress. A white knitted shawl was draped about her bare, bony shoulders. She carried a tiny silver lamé purse suspended from a cord which was looped around her wrist. A necklace glittered on her bosom. Her severely straightened hair shone like lacquered wire in the dim electric glow. She glanced without interest at us before perching on a bar stool. The slit up the side of the dress bared an expanse of black flesh. She conversed lightly and familiarly with the barman.

"That one," Andrew said, "I know her well. She only goes with the *mzungus.*" He gazed sadly at her. "She is very beautiful. The *mzungus* always get the best."

I did not know how to console him.

He finished his beer. "Come," he said, abruptly cheerful. "I'll take you for a walk. I'll show you some of the sights of Nairobi."

Kenyatta Avenue was crowded with office workers on their way home. The late-afternoon light, luminously yellow, was hazed with the fertile red dust of Kikuyuland. Spaced like sentries at regular intervals along the pavement, the shoeshine boys, surrounded by an array of tins and bottles and brushes, kept their eyes fixed on the shoes of the pedestrians. My rheumy-eyed Kikuyu was, fortunately, stationed on the far bank of the avenue. On the numerous newsstands, row upon row of the latest pornographic magazines from the West were on display. What did someone like Andrew make of these provocative displays? Did he regard it as one more token of the new-forged "equality" between black and white? More than time seems to have flown since the days when "respect" was regarded by the European settlers as a near-mystical tribute to be paid by black to white, a surer safeguard of their survival than superior firepower. Respect, Elspeth Huxley has candidly observed, was, for the European, "an invisible coat of mail . . .

the least rent or puncture might . . . split the whole garment asunder and expose its wearer in all his human vulnerability."

Exposure has come in a more literal way than she could ever have imagined. That very week, at the Sombrero Night Club, Beauty Lee, "the International Striptease Artiste" (European, but of no precise provenance) was supposed to be performing on stage three times nightly. The Monro Massage Salon was enticing customers with its African, Asian and European masseuses. Naturally, not everyone approves. The long-settled British, those to whom the Norfolk Hotel is a last embattled outpost of settler civilization, remain aloof and tight-lipped. The blame is generally—and quite rightly— placed on those Europeans without adequate colonial experience—the Swedes, the Danes, the Germans, even the Swiss. One Swiss lady had caused a minor ripple of scandal when she disappeared into the bush with her African lover.

The beggars on Kenyatta Avenue, like the shoeshine boys and the stands selling pornographic magazines, had their own clearly demarcated territories. Most were maimed. Lepers with truncated arms and legs were a common sight; but even more numerous than the lepers were the victims of severe bone malformation, the result of calcium deficiency. This affliction ravages the human frame, reducing it to a tangled wreckage of atrophied limbs. Occasionally, the beggars are rounded up and sent off somewhere, hidden from sensitive tourist eyes. When I was in Mombasa just before the height of the tourist season, they lined the length of Kilindini Road like gargoyles. Some weeks later a friend of mine visited Mombasa. He was surprised when I brought the subject up: he had not seen a single beggar and had come away with the impression that Kenya was a happy, prosperous country composed largely of polite, well-trained waiters. But the roundups have only a temporary success. Like the shantytowns which are periodically razed, like the prostitutes who, now and again, are subjected to culling campaigns (these last can never be entirely eliminated for two reasons— their numbers are far too great, and they are an inseparable adjunct of the tourist trade: the Germans are particularly addicted to what is called the "sex-safari"), they always spring up again.

Andrew stopped and stared into the window of a shoe shop. He said he needed new shoes. "Those are nice," he said, pointing at a multicolored, platformed pair.

I pretended not to hear. We walked on, turning left up a side street lined, I noted anxiously, with clothes shops. I tried to divert his attention. "What would you do if you became a lawyer—or an engineer—and made a lot of money?"

"I'd buy a big farm and grow tea on it." He looked at me wisely. "You get a very good price for tea these days." He paused by a shop window. "Those are nice jeans."

"And what else would you do if you were rich?" We walked on.

"I would buy a Mercedez-Benz." He laughed. "Then I'd get all the beautiful women. The Wabenzi always have beautiful women." ("Wabenzi" is the pleasantly jocular term used to describe the nouveau-riche black middle class—they who have eaten well of the fruit of Uhuru. They signal their status by the acquisition, at the first opportunity, of a Mercedes-Benz. Hence, the Wabenzi—the Benz tribe.) Andrew stopped again. "That is a pretty shirt. A special offer . . ."

"What about your wife? Wouldn't she get jealous if she knew you were driving other women about in your Mercedes?"

"My wife will be looking after the *shamba* [homestead]. Anyway, I will give her lots of money." He stopped again. "That is a nice belt . . ."

"I read in the newspapers that the government was going to pass a law that would throw people guilty of adultery into jail." We walked on.

"It won't work."

"Why not?"

"If they did, they would have to throw nearly every Member of Parliament into jail. Maybe even . . ." He teetered on the verge of sacrilege. "It won't work," he said.

Before us loomed the many-storeyed tower of the Kenyatta Conference Centre, symbol of Nairobi's grandeur and aggressive contemporaneity. A few people strolled on the flagged terrace in front of it. Beds of flowers glowed in the deepening twilight. The terrace was dominated by a statue of Kenyatta raised aloft on a pedestal. He was attired in full academic regalia, his hand clasped on his robed lap. He brooded massively, portentously, over the monumental scene. However, the fountain at the base of the pedestal was not in operation, and the basin was empty.

By the time we regained the avenue, darkness had fallen. Baton-wielding watchmen warmed their hands over braziers in the doorways of shuttered shops. Neon lights flashed their inane Morse. The hour was early, but the avenue was already deserted. A curio seller was shutting up his stall; the shoeshine boys had packed up and gone home; the beggars had retreated before the chill of the Highlands night. Little groups of whores congregated disconsolately under the street lamps. They hung out their tongues at us, swayed their hips. "Want fuck? I give you nice fuck, darling."

Andrew paused by one of the pornographic displays. He picked up a magazine.

"You will buy this for me?"

I was too tired to argue. I bought it for him. He slipped it into his briefcase.

Andrew accompanied me back to the hotel. "Tomorrow," he said, "I go home to my *shamba* near Kisumu. Every weekend I go there." He laughed. "I am a different man when I work on my *shamba*. When I take off all these clothes, you would find it hard to recognize me. You will write to me?"

"I will write to you if you write to me."

We shook hands. He wandered off, swinging his briefcase, dreaming, perhaps, of the rich German lady who might stop him on the street any day to ask the way; of the "scholarship" she might offer him; of the Mercedes-Benz that might one day be his and the beautiful women it would bring. What a ragbag of fantasies must whirl in that head! Within twenty-four hours, the office furniture salesman with his elegantly printed calling cards would, as he himself had said, become unrecognizable. He was an unstable compound of urban and peasant man.

"The settler's town," Franz Fanon wrote, "is a strongly built town, all made of stone and steel. It is a brightly lit town . . . a well-fed town, an easy going town . . . a town of white people, of foreigners . . . The look that the native turns on the settler's town is a look of lust, a look of envy; it expresses his dreams of possession: to sit at the settler's table, to sleep in the settler's bed, with his wife if possible . . . there is no native who does not dream at least once a day of setting himself up in the settler's place."

Nairobi, with its broad avenues, its multistoreyed hotels, its travel agencies, its boutiques, its nightclubs, its striptease "artistes" and massage parlors, its two casinos, is not even a settler's town—not any more. It is a tourist town; and the tourist town is, by its very nature, a fantastical place, a kind of papier-mâché confection. Its quintessential expression is the international hotel. In the eyes of native and tourist alike, international hotels are dream palaces. But the tourist has this advantage: he *knows* it is a dream; he knows that at the end of two or three weeks he will fly away and return to an everyday world. The native cannot make the distinction. The abnormal becomes the stamping ground of his visions of "progress" and "development" because it is only the abnormal he sees. He is vulnerable. He is defenseless. Culturally, he is in much the same position as those aboriginal peoples who were wiped out by imported Old World diseases. Black and white meet and mingle at the point of fantasy, aggravating an already deformed vision. Fantasy is piled on fantasy. For as long as he can afford it, Andrew will sit in darkened, air-conditioned bars and dream of miraculous rescue.

Edward Hoagland

African Calliope

The "Third World" is a peculiarly twentieth century expression mean-ing the developing, politicallty-unaligned countries of Asia, Africa, and Latin America. Despite better communications, mass tourism, and the Peace Corps, the daily realities of Third World life are still much less understood by most Westerners than the arcana of moon shots and space walks.

One man who has accepted the contemporary writer's challenge to portray overseas peoples to his countrymen is Edward Hoagland. In his walks with a Sudanese hunter near the Ugandan border, as described in this selection from African Calliope: A Journey to the Sudan *(1979) he learned as much about the value of his own boots as he did about the esthetic value of the birds and beasts of the forest.*

* * *

Ordinarily the policeman was not allowed to have any bullets, but he had been issued a few after the emergency, with which to repel a conjectural invasion from the Uganda border by Sadiq al-Mahdi. He would be the first legal officer of the Sudan whom an invader encountered. Usually he had only the rifle—a British .303, from the King's African Rifles, pre-World War II—and no ammunition, because in a manner of speaking, it was the village's gun, and the people were former Anya Nya. One day, before the emergency, he had been kind enough to loan it to Ilariyo when Ilariyo took me on a meat hunt for buffalo. They both decided I'd be safer if Ilariyo hunted with the rifle instead of with his bow, and Ilariyo did have bullets. Before he'd been disarmed at the end of The Troubles, he'd hidden some, and so at a couple of junctures when the policeman had needed a means of defense in facing a husband wielding a spear against an adulterer flailing an ax, he had come to Ilariyo, who had dug up one or two bullets for him, cleaning them off with kerosene.

Unfortunately, on our way to kill the buffalo, Ilariyo shot at a red bushbuck, browsing deerlike along the Kinyeti below us. Although he wounded it, it got away and the explosion scared the buffalo herd, as an arrow would not have done. He ran ahead of me just quickly enough to glimpse them as they fled.

Several buffalo had tapeworms; big white cast-off segments gleamed in their stools. And there was a corncob on the path, where a hunter before us had sat and eaten lunch. We looked at a eucalyptus tree whose bark the buffalo and bushbuck had knawed. An elephant had rubbed moss off another tree eight feet up. We saw a number of places where one or another elephant had forced a solitary path uphill through the undergrowth. On high ground, a half-mile from the buffalo lick we had visited, some of the buffalo had a pawing and rolling spot.

On other walks, the bracken fern and burdock and raspberries made me feel as if I were strolling at home, though the bamboo and Abysinnian banana plants did not. Fifty feet high, in the forks of large trees that were flossy with moss, delicate species of tree ferns grew, and green and brown vines and gray, beardlike lichens hung down. These were gigantic trees, with whole separate levels of epiphytic life sprouting from them. Every so often, up in the crown, a family of blue monkeys ripped through the leaves, leaping, catching and propelling themselves again with feet and hands—a wizened, bald baby clinging to its mother's chest—to get out of Ilariyo's bow's range. Close up, the adults are comely creatures, equipped with white gorgets, full cheeks, grayish backs, and rufous rumps, carrying their tails in a high loop. But Ilariyo fitted an arrow to his bowstring the instant they revealed themselves, so any monkey that had lingered to show its plumage would have fetched up in the pot.

They whistled and chattered once they were at a safe distance, whereas the colobus monkeys had a cry like a frog's croak, amplified. Colobuses are heavier, like decorative, long-tailed, light-boned, arboreal baboons. They have white cheeks, foreheads and beards, and white, long-haired flank ruffs, and bushy white ends to their tails, set off by a contrasting body that is black otherwise. Their long hair apparently acts as a parachute as they sail between the trees, but when they sit on a limb, their splendid tails seem to hang down poignantly, if you are with somebody hunting them.

Bushbuck give a sharp bark of alarm, deeper in pitch than that of American deer—like a German shepherd's, but abbreviated. The ones I handled were dead, with the snared neck bent horribly backwards against the ribs, as the log drag had held it while the legs tugged the body forward. Goat-sized, with goat-shaped horns with three spiral ridges and a white flag of a tail, white spots on the haunches and vertical stripes on the body, they seemed to sigh when Ilariyo released the swollen neck from its circle of wire and the air trapped inside the dead lungs was exhaled at last. The "necktie," as he called it—World War II telegraph wire—had rubbed off a circle of hair, where ants fed on the reddened skin. If the animal had lain for awhile, there was gas in the belly, too, which Ilariyo forced out by carefully treading on it, first placing the carcass in the river shallows. When I accompanied him, slowing him down, he was likely to leave it there for the time being, weighted with rocks in the cold water, where the meat would keep longer and bush pigs wouldn't smell it. A horde of them might have devoured his catch. Instead, a leopard—a night traveler, like the pigs—found one of the bushbuck we had left, yanked it out of the stream and ate from a hind leg and from some of the organs.

Ilariyo lopped a twig with his *panga* (machete) to remind himself where he had set a snare, leaving it to me to sit and listen to the birds, while he hurried to thickets further on. He had long feet, all tendons; long shins or shanks, whitened from the wear and tear where the brush just off the path was scarcely penetrable. He'd had three years' schooling altogether, in Arabic, but without that, could convey affectingly by signals the sufferings of an elephant that poachers had killed, whose skull we found. He pointed to the blaze marks on two trees where it had hit its tusks, venting its pain and rage, though at the same time he smiled slightly, because, after all, he might have been one of the poachers himself.

He had a flicking motion with which he dismissed his disappointment when game got away, and handed me his bow to lean on in crossing the footlogs that led away from this bog, which by general agreement among the village hunters had been assigned to him. He said that a leopard skin could bring about $110, nine months' wages, on the black market, and pointed to where a bushbuck had nibbled a charred stick in the ashes of a campfire; and at more elephant tusk and shoulder smudges on some of the trees—no anguish in them—as we went on. Without speaking or glancing around to see whether I was watching properly, he flapped his arms in just the subtle manner of any number of different birds, to warn me which kind was starting to fly up ahead of us.

There was a greater variety and mix of timbre to the bird calls than I was used to, in America. The wading birds, the birds in the brush, and then a whole forest ensemble struck up behind us as we climbed on a slant and descended the intervening ridges on our way home. Usually I'd stop along and swim in the Kinyeti when we crossed it again before we reached Gilo. I'd see five kinds of butterfly, brilliant blue and iridescent green, drinking at a hole in the sand, and a huge, green-abdomened grasshopper whose wings opened out even more beautifully than the butterflies—red, purple, black, and green.

Cold water, warm sun, no biting flies. Squirrel, mouse, and monkey tracks. To hunker naked on a riverbank in the heart of Africa was quite dramatic, if you thought about it—drama, like sex, being primarily in the mind. Because I had worked in a circus many years before, I wasn't afraid of the idea that elephants and leopards might be roaming about within a mile or two, and swam in a deep trout hole with as much pleasure as in a mountain stream in Vermont. Afterwards, I sat for an hour, not thinking or stirring, resting on a log and listening to the water, digging my toes in the sand. Above me in the canopy of trees were birds purposeful in their calling, and birds oblivious-sounding as a pondful of peepers. Jay-like or crow-like calls, and long pretty narratives. A bird with a two-note, bell-toned, knocking rhythm; another with a song like a nasal, high-range oboe. Some displayed their songs as their sweetest and proudest possession; others hacked with them as a weapon. One communicated like a lovely flageolet, endlessly charming; another used wheezy, repetitive, upward whistles. There were birds that sang in a rattling chatter, a minatory, suspicious chipping; and one-note birds; and birds that commanded a grand, waving banner of ten or twelve or fifteen notes. Also, what I took to be cicadas singing.

Once in a while another hunter, silently returning to Gilo, would pass me. As he crossed the little river on a footlog, he averted his eyes politely from my body, but found it more difficult to avoid staring at my boots and other clothing piled together on the farther bank. The one object I think I might have been killed for was those boots. If he was not as naked as I was, he was wearing some absurd and ragged scrap of suburbiana—a plaid sport jacket, a paisley vest—donated by a church group in America. Though I had had to punch new holes in my belt, as the heat and diet of this drastic continent had slimmed me down quickly toward that frantically ectomorphic archetype which most expatriates in Africa attain soon enough—*the pink spider*, as Juba's black sophisticates used to say, looking at one of us appraisingly—I was never as skinny as one of those hunters.

Dian Fossey

Gorillas in the Mist

Dian Fossey spent almost twenty years studying mountain gorillas at her Karisoke Research Centre in Rwanda's Virunga Mountains. Her long war against poachers resulted in her own murder in 1986. She is buried in the cemetery where she had often interred the remains of slaughtered gorillas.

The following passage from Gorillas in the Mist *(1983) describes the way she began her research at Karisoke.*

* * *

The path that we followed between the herbaceous slopes on our right and the saddle terrain slightly below on our left was more defined than it had been in the village because it was kept open by elephant and buffalo as well as by an overflow from numerous streams draining off the mountain.

The first hour and a half of the climb was the steepest part and, as the altitude increased, breathing—for me at least—became somewhat of a raspy affair. I was delighted when the porters wanted to stop for a rest and a smoke. The spot they chose was a small meadow clearing where elephant and buffalo droppings had accumulated around a stream running through the middle of the clearing. The air was pure elixir and the running water refreshingly sweet and cold. The heavy fog and drizzle were just beginning to give way to the promise of welcomed sun. For the first time I could fully appreciate the extent of the herbaceous foliage that abounded on Visoke's steeper slopes to the north side of our trail. The terrain seemed to be very promising gorilla country. I grew tremendously eager to discover what lay ahead west of us, deeper within the heartland of the Virungas.

Considerably apprehensive, the porters were now quieter than they had been far below in their village. Nevertheless, they were willing to go on even though it seemed that only a few had ever been this far into the mountains before. We continued climbing at an easier gradient for more than an hour before coming to the beginning of a long meadow corridor densely carpeted with a variety of grasses, clovers, and wildflowers. Distributed throughout the meadows, like so many powerful sentries, stood magnificent *Hagenia* trees, bearded by long lacy strands of lichen flowing from their orchid-laden limbs. The entire scene was backlit by sunlight, giving all a spectacular dimension no camera could record or eye believe. I have yet to see a more impressive spot in all the Virungas or a more ideal location for gorilla research.

Exactly at 4:30 P.M. on September 24, 1967, I established the Karisoke Research Centre—"Kari" for the first four letters of Mt. Karisimbi that overlooked my camp from the south; "soke" for the last four letters of Mt. Visoke, whose slopes rose north some 12,172 feet immediately behind the 10,000-foot campsite.

With the site chosen, the next logical step was the selection of a Rwandese camp staff from the lineup of porters. A number of men were eager for permanent work, and in no time at all I had the beginnings of the Karisoke staff helping to set up tents, boil water, collect firewood, and unpack essential supplies and equipment. My tent was set up alongside a swiftly flowing creek. About one hundred yards farther back in the meadow nestled closely to Mt. Visoke's slopes, another tent was set up for the newly chosen African staff recruited from the porter line.

Since that day I have never had the slightest difficulty in recalling the elation felt upon being able to renew my research with the mountain gorilla. Little did I know then that by setting up two small tents in the wilderness of the Virungas I had launched the beginnings of what was to become an internationally renowned research station eventually to be utilized by students and scientists from many countries. As a pioneer I sometimes did endure loneliness, but I have reaped a tremendous satisfaction that followers will never be able to know.

A distinct language barrier existed between the Rwandese and myself during the early days following Karisoke's establishment. Alyette DeMunck, who had an excellent command of languages, had to leave following a mere few days at camp. I spoke only Swahili and the Rwandese only Kinyarwanda. Thus, much of our communication was carried out via hand gestures, head nods, or facial expressions. Africans have a great facility for learning languages quickly because they do not tend to rely on the crutch of books. It was therefore easier for me to teach the men Swahili than for them to try to teach me Kinyarwanda.

Most of the Rwandese porters I hired that day have remained with me as loyal and dedicated assistants. Some of the men enjoyed being in the forest, so I trained them, just as Sanwekwe had trained me, in tracking skills. . . .

A good six months were to pass before the men felt confident enough to go out in the forest and track by themselves. Even then they clearly preferred not going more than an hour from camp and were reluctant to follow trails older than two or three days because of the distances involved.

With old trails two trackers, rather than one, went out together. Much of the terrain was still unfamiliar to them and they retained a natural apprehension of possible encounters with wildlife or poachers.

Teaching Rwandese how to track was far easier than instructing the students who eventually came to Karisoke. The locals' senses, especially their eyesight, were more acute. When training anyone, I always led the way for a couple of days, explaining the factors that determined the route taken. Sometimes I purposely strayed from an actual gorilla trail (occasionally unintentionally) to see how long it would take those behind me to realize the error. Another beneficial teaching ruse was furtively to press a series of my own knuckleprints along a section of damp earth going in the opposite direction to the knuckleprints of the gorillas being followed. How Sanwekwe would have loved this bit of chicanery! Those being trained would excitedly discover my knuckleprints and confidently follow them only to find no gorilla spoor ahead. This method proved to be the best way to teach people not to blunder when on difficult trails—trails on grassy meadows or rocky slopes in particular, where even one bootprint can destroy a vital tracking clue.

Following a gorilla track in thick herbaceous foliage is in fact child's play. Most vegetation bends in the direction of a group's travel, knuckleprints may be found impressed upon intermittent dirt patches or trails, and chains of gorilla dung deposits provide other clues as to the direction of the animals' passage. The individuals of a calmly moving group do not travel one after another. There may be nearly as many trails as group members, so I attempt always to follow the most central trail. Numerous cul-de-sacs occur wherever individuals depart from the main route to go off and feed by themselves. I learned eventually that the false leads could be identified by the presence of two layers of foliage. The top one is bent in the direction of the group's travel and the lower is bent in the opposite direction where an individual has gone off on its own before returning to the group.

In extremely dense, tall foliage, much circuitous tracking time could be saved by looking ahead of a group's trail for signs of disturbance of vegetation or of branches in distant trees where gorillas have climbed to feed. This technique was especially helpful in the saddle areas, where gorilla spoor could be nearly eradicated by passage of elephant or large herds of buffalo. The ground signs that might survive between the miniature craters left by the elephants' feet are the gorillas' typical trilocular dung deposits or their feeding remnants, such as the unmistakable peelings of thistle and celery stalks. Often, gorilla trail merges briefly with or zigzags in and out of buffalo trail. Whenever this happens and visual cues are obscured by vegetation I feel with my fingers for the deep imprints left by the cloven hooves of the buffalo to realize that I am on the wrong path. Because gorillas always seek fresh untrampled vegetation for feeding purposes, they seldom travel along buffalo trails for any distance.

Unfortunately, the reverse is not true. Characteristically bovine in nature, buffalo are very trail-oriented, particularly in thick vegetation. Upon encountering gorilla trails, they often follow them like so many cows heading for the barn. On several occasions, without intention I found myself following gorillas who were in turn being followed by buffalo. Twice the gorillas, either in vexation or perhaps with a sense of joie de vivre, turned and charged directly toward the buffalo, which speedily turned tail and retreated unknowingly toward me. In retrospect, the subsequent confrontations had all the comical ingredients of a Laurel and Hardy movie. I had the option of climbing any available tree or diving head-first into vegetation—too often nettles—that fringed the trail of the oncoming herd. I was always more than willing to let buffalo have the right-of-way. This is one of the first rules any person must learn when working in the domain of wild animals and is one that some learn the hard way.

Tracking is an enjoyable challenge, though there were times when trackers became convinced that their four-legged quarry had sprouted wings, so faint were the clues. This was especially true when trying to follow the trail of a lone silverback gorilla rather than a group, trails more than a week old, trails crossing relatively barren regions such as meadows or lava rock-slides, and trails traversed by ungulates sharing the gorillas' terrain.

One morning along the trail of a lone silverback I was belly-crawling under a long dank tunnel roofed by a fallen *Hagenia* tree and sided by dense vines. With relief I saw a sunlit opening about fifteen feet ahead and wormed toward it enthusiastically while dragging my knapsack behind me. Upon reaching it I grabbed on to what appeared to be the base of a sapling in order to pull myself out of the gloomy tunnel confines. The intended support not only hauled me out of the tunnel but dragged me through several feet of nettles before I had the sense to let go of the left leg of a very surprised buffalo. The odoriferous deposits of his justifiable fright took several days to wash out of my hair and clothing.

John Hillaby

Journey to the Jade Sea

Journey To The Jade Sea (1964) is my favorite of John Hillaby's long distance walking books. In 1962 this walking Englishman made an 1100-mile foot safari (with camels) through the deserts south and east of Lake Rudolf in Kenya's Northern Frontier District. He later reported that before setting out he had received excellent advice from "that prince of modern travelers, Wilfred Thesiger," including, "to carry a lot of medicine instead of useless trinkets and knicknacks, and to wear tennis shoes rather than bush boots."

* * *

During the talk round the fireside that night I heard the word *upepo* mentioned again and again. It meant wind, the great wind that roared west from beyond Kulal and thrashed the shores of the lake. As there was a light wind blowing at the time, I began to wonder what the morning would bring and whether we should be able to reach water by dusk, that is if we delayed our departure until midday as I had planned. But like most of my apprehensions, they disappeared overnight. The morning was hot, bright and scarcely breezy. At high noon, when we strode out of the shadow of the palms, the heights of Pel danced in the heat.

We walked for about four miles before I began to understand the curious topography of the gap. The symmetry was such that the mountain flanks on either side disappeared into the distance like railway lines or the perspective of a Dali landscape. The topmost tip of Kulal was just visible ahead, but with every step we took it seemed to rise a little from the floor of the lava below the crest of the escarpment.

The heat became intense. Apart from observing with monotonous regularity that there were "forks in the sun" the men said very little. Goiti urged the camels forward with a throaty "hodai!" repeated at intervals. I never discovered what *hodai* meant, if indeed, it meant anything. And Goiti soon tired of saying it.

During the afternoon I discovered that Lelean could determine the sex of distant travelers by the way they sparkled in the sun. Samburu women positively glitter with reflected points of light. They wear polished necklaces and amulets on their arms and the majority of them are tightly encased in brass bangles from their knees to their ankles. It was somewhat more difficult to spot a man from a twinkle of light reflected from a spearhead but I checked the determination with field glasses and Lelean was rarely wrong, even when the traveler was a dot on the horizon or partly hidden away in the bush. At one point our game was enlivened with a touch of drama when it looked as if we had located a poacher.

The flash came from the tip of a spear about a mile away. Lelean said "a man" and then became tense at what he saw through the glasses. The man seemed to be crouching and instead of carrying his spear over his shoulder like any respectable Samburu, the weapon was "at the ready", point foremost in the manner of a lance.

Lelean loped after him; I followed, panting in the heat. It was not an ideal afternoon for a cross-country run. When we got close the spear carrier turned out to be a very old man who could neither move quickly nor stand upright. His spear was rusty and blunt. It had not been used for years and, far from poaching, he explained in a quavering voice that he had lost one of his cows. He was looking for it. Had we seen it? I shook my head; Lelean said something uncomplimentary in Samburu and we hurried back to the camels with considerably less enthusiasm for our little game.

Shortly before sundown we marched over a ridge and looked down on to a lunar landscape of lava; it stretched out into infinity. Although the hot wind blew against us, gently, everything was deathly still; I had the impression that we alone were alive in a dead world. There was not even a drop of water in the Anderi *lugga*. This was not a serious matter; we carried an emergency supply of four gallons; there were said to be one or two permanent waterholes immediately ahead of us, and at worst we could march through the night to the lake which was marked on the map as "brackish but drinkable." What annoyed me was that although I had carefully consulted the map and sought local advice about the watering point, I had been completely misled by the men who wanted to stay in South Horr as long as they could. As there would be light for about another hour we decided to march on until we found a sheltered camping site.

It was hot, uphill work and the track had almost disappeared. The route was marked only by lumps of brown and black lava which were smaller in size than the big, jagged lumps on either side of us. Seen from a distance, the lava walls to the west and the north were apparently smooth and flat-topped, like railway embankments, but at close quarters they were seen to be composed of lumps of tightly packed slag and pumice stone, hot to the touch and riddled with holes like a Gruyère cheese.

Lake Rudolf, or the Jade Sea as some explorers have called it, was discovered on March 6, 1888 by the Austrian Count Teleki von Szek. He

was an interesting man who had made an ambitious foot safari across almost
the whole of East Africa accompanied by three Swahilis, six guides, eight
Somalis, fifteen *askaris*, over 200 porters and his faithful, plodding, dull-
witted biographer, Lt. Ludwig von Höhnel. What little we know of the
count himself comes through the laborious and sycophantic prose of the
lieutenant, poured out in two large volumes. When he was within a mile or
two of where we were looking for a camping site, von Höhnel wrote:

> The mountain district between us and the lake was, in fact, a
> veritable hell, consisting of a series of parallel heights, running from
> north to south which we had to cut across in a north-westerly fashion.
> The slopes of these mountains were steep precipices, most of them
> quite insurmountable, and those that were not were strewn with
> blackish-brown blocks of rock or of loose scoriae. The narrow valleys
> were encumbered with stones or debris, or with deep loose sand in
> which our feet sank, making progress difficult. And when the sun rose
> higher, its rays were reflected from the smooth brownish-black surface
> of the rock, causing an almost intolerable glare, whilst a burning wind
> from the south whirled the sand in our faces, and almost blew the loads
> off the heads of the men.

Far from blowing the loads off our camels, the wind for the most part
was no more than a warm, sustained breeze. It neither rose nor fell for
periods of about half an hour and then, quite unexpectedly, came a sound
like a long, drawn-out moan from the direction of Julal. After a few seconds,
the increase in velocity was reflected in a scurry of dust devils, almost at
our feet. My floppy bush hat blew off once or twice and I had to pull it
down over the side of my face. At the onset of the gusts the camels veered
a little and had to be dragged back on to what passed for the track. Their
gait became slower as they breasted the wind; they had to be hauled rather
than led across the shattered rock. In this fashion we found shelter in a small
depression in the lava which I shall always remember with distaste.

I used half my water allocation that night on a brew of tea; there was
not enough for a wash and I was not prepared to rinse my hands and face
in camel urine as the boys did. Supper was a meagre affair of a little roasted
bird on a plate of cold baked beans. I shot the bird, a dikkop or thick-knees,
as it flapped off a slab of rock, crying mournfully. I don't know what it lived
on. Nothing grew in the little valley except a few twisted thorn trees.

As I sat on my canvas chair, sipping tea, everything seemed to resolve
itself into the absence of water. I had made a bad mistake in not setting out
with more than an emergency supply. It would not have happened if I had
paid more attention to the map and less to gossip. The water in the Anderi
was up in the hills and not at the point where we crossed the *lugga*. It would

have been better had we camped in the stream bed and sent out a party to look for a well.

Mezek came up to ask whether he should erect the tent; the alternative was that I should sleep in the open. I agreed that the tent might be blown away but remembering the hyena that bit off the end of my gym shoe, I told him to put the mosquito net over my bed. Mezek pouted and reminded me of the *upepo*. Thinking this an excuse to avoid work, I told him to get on with the job without furthur argument. I regretted this later in the evening when a gust picked the net up like a handkerchief and threw it into one of the twisted trees. It took us about half an hour to unhook it, badly torn, from the claw-like thorns.

Despite the wind there was a vast assemblage of stars and once, when I awoke, I tried to work out the time from the position of the pointers in the constellations of the Great Bear. Due, I suppose, to our position within two degrees of the equator, the Bear was lying with its feet in the air and its tail almost brushing the horizon.

I remembered that in Arabia they speak of the northeast wind as the Na'ashi and say that it blows from the very centre of the constellation. "Can'st thou guide the Bear with her train?" asked the Lord of Job when he spoke from a whirlwind. As I gazed at the pointers I wondered whether the pattern of stars was a finger beckoning us on or a fist with the thumb pointing ominously down.

The wind began to rise at dawn until at times it had some of the skull-wrinkling intensity of a scream. The hot blast of air might have come from a furnace. When the thorn trees shrilled and sand began to pile up against my pillow I had no desire to do anything except stay precisely where I was, curled up under a dirty brown sheet on the ground. It seemed as if the expedition had come to a dead stop before we had even reached the lake. [Lake Rudolf.] In fact, if the men had not been so cheerful about the wind I might have ordered a smart countermarch back to the South Horr valley. Yet, Mezek seemed to think it funny when a gush of precious tea was carried away like a spume before it reached the cup; Lelean conceded that the *upepo* was very bad but he thought it would soon die down and Karo laughed uproariously when my sheet blew away. He bounded after it, whooping and cheering. This did me a lot of good. Our affairs, as I saw it, might have been much worse. I got up, ate a mouthful of moistened porridge oats and dates, and went off on my own to see what the landscape looked like from the top of a nearby hill.

It looked bad. No tracks were visible in any direction. The foot of Mount Kulal and the Longippi Hills were hidden in orange-coloured streamers of wind-driven sand. The foreground was entirely covered by lava boulders and clusters of polished rock which had either collapsed like bombed houses or seemed to be on the point of collapsing. I walked back to the camp, leaning against the wind. My impression was that it was less violent than it had been at dawn. When we began to lumber foward at nine o'clock I got some comfort from the fact that if we could put up with the hard going until the midday halt it was unlikely we should find conditions much worse anywhere else.

At this point in the journey I want to say plainly that I felt both apprehensive and jubilant—apprehensive for obvious reasons; jubilant because I felt physically competent to walk as far as the camels would take us. My feet were tougher than they had ever been before. This was largely due to Thesiger's advice about wearing canvas shoes; it was the best I could have had. The men wore their variation of Somali sandals made out of pieces of discarded tyres. Among the lava the straps broke and they pulled out the tacks with their teeth, hammering the strips together with a stone. The canvas shoes were more adaptable. When the going was easy I pulled out the laces and slouched along, sometimes taking the shoes off altogether for short periods, walking barefoot in the dust, a delightful sensation. But during the rock-hopping stages I put them on again and laced them up for ankle support.

After about an hour I realized we had gained more height than I had imagined during the latter part of the previous stage. Mountains which had appeared insignificant suddenly rose to an impressive height, yet because of some optical illusion I was never sure whether I was looking at a pile a rocks in the immediate foreground or a range on the horizon.

Lelean was concerned about the haze ahead of us. He said it was a very bad sandstorm and indicated that we should avoid it if we could. To this I readily agreed even if it meant spending a night with no more than a gallon of water among us. Although it streamed along some two or three miles to our left, the corridor of blown sand looked dense and suffocating. Dust devils scurried towards us and I was relieved when the haze veered away.

Lelean led the column but after shouting questions at him above the noise of the wind I could not be sure whether we had reached the famous Sirima track which led direct to the lake. It looked as if he intended to seek shelter behind the Longippi Hills. To avoid the sandstorm we took a northerly course. Despite my good intentions about using the map and compass I had made a singularly bad attempt at taking a cross bearing on two distant peaks. Far from being the mountain I thought it was, one turned out to be a little pimple of rock on a distant mound of lava and the other slowly disappeared like the Cheshire Cat until only the fragments remained suspended in the sky. It looked as if it had exploded; it was, in fact, a mirage.

Hopping along, dodging the boulders and trying to keep my mind off a cool, clear lake of drinkable water, I thought of Teleki and von Höhnel who had marched this way without the certain knowledge that there was a lake ahead of them. In their diary they wrote:

"No living creature shared the solitude with us, and as far as our glass could reach there was nothing to be seen but desert, desert everywhere. To all this was added the scorching heat and the ceaseless buffeting of the sand-laden wind against which we were powerless to protect ourselves."

Alex Shoumantoff

In Southern Light

In the late twentieth century the public rightfully confuses the differ-
ence between travel and tourism. "Travel" to the hard-core traveler
is etymologically close to the Middle English word travailen, *meaning*
to labor or to toil. Travel necessarily includes a large element of work
and self-discovery. "Tourism" on the other hand should signify a type
of mobile entertainment.

Worldwide, as the amount of tourism continues its dramatic in-
crease, the number of true travelers cannot keep pace. Democratically,
of course, everyone should be allowed the snobbish luxury of thinking
that his or her trip is the greatest thing since Burton or Livingston set
off on foot across the dark continent.

Oh, but how I love a true traveler. Especially a foot traveler. Alex
Shoumantoff is such a person.

This New Yorker *staff writer makes the sort of journeys that are*
travel at its best. He works at getting into fascinating cross-cultural
situations and then bringing back insights about ordinary people in
distant (usually subtropical) parts of the world.

The following account from In Southern Light: Trekking through
Zaire and the Amazon *(1986) describes part of his 100-mile trek through*
remote Zairian jungles in search of pygmies. The Efe (or BaMbuti)
people are known as part of the largest group of hunter/gatherers in
the world and a solo walk with them through their equatorial forests
would still be true "travel" for us as much as it was for Stanley in the
nineteenth century.

Beginning at the Ituri forest town of Opoku, Alex Shoumantoff
hired two Zairois guides and walked into the jungle.

One remarkable aspect of this hike was that despite all of the
turmoil of the preceding century many of the people he met had seen
so few white people that they were terrified of him. For all they knew,
he might have been some Arab slaver out of the not-so-distant past.

They need not have worried. This latest muzungu *[white man]*
had not come to eat or enslave them. He had simply come to understand

them. The twelve-day hike—on which he lost fifteen pounds—was true travel, a sensitive appreciation of another culture.

Alex Shoumantoff worked at his walk into pygmy life. He is a traveller!

* * *

In the morning Bob took me to Opoku and introduced me to two of the younger, more progressive men there, who weren't so afraid of *muzungus*. Their names were Baudouin and Gamaembi. Baudouin spoke a little French—the official language of Zaire, which few BaLese and no Efe speak or understand—and Gamaembi knew it quite well, so we could communicate. They also spoke their own language, KiLese, as well as Swahili, the lingua franca of the region, neither of which I knew. Like many male Zairois born in 1955, Baudouin had been named for the King of the Belgians, who had toured the Congo that year. He had another, "authentic" name, Apabu, probably given by his father, but Baudouin was one of many who had not got the word about Mobutu's 1972 *authenticité* decree. He was about five feet tall, with a large head, a high shiny forehead, and lighter skin than most of the villagers. He thought he had pygmy blood, although his father was a Lende, from near Uganda, and his mother a Lese. He had grown up with her in her village—his father had abandoned them when he was little—and his strongest connection to Opoku was a leprotic aunt, whose claw hand I shook, reaching into an enclosure where she and two other women were gaily shelling peanuts. People liked to employ him, but they did not feel obligated to him, because he was an immigrant and not in their *fungu*, or clan—the patrilineal kinship group to which every Lese's allegiance is unquestioning. In many ways, he was more like a pygmy than like a villager. His best friend, Manuele, was an Efe. So was his wife. It was a mark of his low status that he didn't have a BaLese wife. His personality—the air of mischief, the spoiling for fun, the way he dissolved into laughter at the slightest provocation—was Efe, and, like the Efe, he loved marijuana.

Gamaembi (ex-Dieudonné—the European name, it seemed, of every third man in Zaire) was twenty-two, four inches taller than Baudouin, darker-skinned, and well built, with broad shoulders, strong arms and legs, a slim waist, and not an ounce of fat. "Gamaembi" means "the man without a chief." He was the last son of the late *capita*, or headman, of Opoku. One of his brothers was almost sixty, one of his sisters was married to a son of the chief of the *collectivité*, and some of the *capitas* of the villages in the forest were his relatives. Besides being well connected, he had walked to Epini a few years earlier and knew the way, so I couldn't have had a better guide. He was about to plant a peanut *shamba*, but when I offered to pay him five zaires a day, he decided to come. Five zaires was then officially worth about a dollar-fifty. At the "parallel" (black market) rate—the one that mattered—five zaires was worth only fifty cents, but that was still good money to Gamaembi: double what the Greek coffee planters in Digbo, twenty miles up the road, were paying. He and his half brother Kuri were raising money to open a store in Opoku. (The nearest store was in Digbo.) I made the same offer to Baudouin, and he accepted. The three of us shook hands and agreed to set out in the morning.

Later in the day Baudouin appeared in camp and asked if I could advance him some of his pay so he could buy some *bangi* for the trip. Richard advised me to hold the *bangi* for Baudouin, or he would smoke it all at once. I gave him ten zaires and in the evening he turned over six little balls of the herb, wrapped in *mangungu* leaf.

That night, I made a final inventory of my gear. For clothing, I had shorts (long pants are cumbersome in the jungle), jogging shoes, heavy knee socks, a couple of T-shirts, a blue cap, a poncho that doubled as a ground cloth, a sweatshirt to put on at night, flannel pajamas, and bedroom slippers. I had a bottle of alcohol to rub down my arms and legs with; cuts and insect bites infect easily in the humid tropics, and alcohol not only disinfects them but reduces the urge to scratch. My medicine chest—an empty coffee can— contained Merthiolate; a course of the broad-spectrum antibiotic ampicillin; paregoric and Lomotil for diarrhea; chloroquine and primaquine for malaria; effervescent Vitamin C tablets; and gamma globulin, which offers transient protection against hepatitis A (but does nothing for hepatitis B, which I eventually came down with), and a syringe to inject it with. I had already given myself a shot that was good for thirty days. Elizabeth supplied me with a handful of aspirin for "public relations," and some little white pills to be taken twice a week against African river blindness, which is transmitted by black flies. Richard lent me a lightweight sleeping bag, and Nadine told me three good sentences to know in Swahili: *Kwenda nzuri* (Go well); *Bakie nzuri* (Stay well); *Lala nzuri* (Sleep well). I had field guides to the birds, butterflies, and large mammals of Africa, and a stack of empty notebooks. All this fit into a long brown canvas dufflebag, whose strap I put over my forehead as a tumpline, letting the bag hang behind. Once your neck muscles have got used to it, this system—which most of the people in South America, Africa, and Asia use to carry heavy loads—works better in the forest than a backpack, because your shoulders aren't pinned down and it is easier to raise your arms to negotiate vines and branches.

The guitar was in a black vinyl case, and in my side bag were a Nik-kormat camera with a macro lens for close shots of butterflies and flowers; a small Sony tape recorder; a small pair of six-power Nikon binoculars; my passport, traveler's checks, return air ticket, and the brick of zaires. I also had a large, lethal-looking folding knife, such as the carpenters in my home-town wear in cases on their belts. I figured I owed it to my family to have it along. The provisions and trade items—the hand mirrors, salt, a dozen bars of soap, and a carton of Tumbaco—were in a burlap sack, as were two cans of sardines and enough rice, beans, peanuts, and plantains to last the three of us two days. After that we would be dependent on hunting and gathering and on trading with the people in the forest. For cooking, I had a small aluminum pot with a lid and a detachable handle; for illumination a flashlight, a dozen candles, and several hundred matches. I had also brought a dozen plastic Ziploc bags. They didn't weigh much and always came in handy for sequestering things.

At three o'clock the next morning—it was a Thursday—I tapped at the small wicker door of one of the huts in Opoku and whispered "Baudouin." He came out rubbing the sleep from his eyes, and we set off walking through the misty *shambas* behind the village. It was oddly quiet, the lull before dawn. Not a frog, insect, hyrax, colobus, or bird to be heard.

At daybreak, amid a growing bee hum, with more and more birds coming in, giving their position, from every direction, we reached Ondi-komvu, a suburb of Opoku, consisting of three huts, one of which was inhabited by Gamaembi and his wife, Anna. He came out looking dapper in red shorts and a red T-shirt, with a red vinyl side bag that contained a toothbrush, a comb, and a change of clothes. He contributed some palm oil and some peanut butter that his wife had ground the night before. Baudouin put the oil, which was in a plastic bottle, and the peanut butter, which was wrapped in leaves, into the burlap sack. He wore a white shirt and a pair of long brown pants, which he stooped to roll up over his strong thighs when, soon after leaving Ondikomvu, we entered the forest.

"Do you have forest like this in America?" Gamaembi asked. He was in the lead, carrying my duffelbag and holding a small bow and about a dozen arrows. Baudouin was next, carrying the burlap sack by a tumpline he had made from the inner bark of a tree. I followed close behind, with my side bag and Gamaembi's and the guitar.

"No, not exactly," I said. "It isn't as thick with shrubs and vines. There aren't so many kinds of trees, and it isn't so green."

Gamaembi's response was to turn over a leaf with a silver underside. "This is another leaf," he said.

Baudouin and Gamaembi walked with slightly bowed legs, gripping the ground with spread toes. I said I envied them that contact. "Of course, we would like to have shoes if we could afford them," Gamaembi told me, "but in the forest we prefer bare feet." As we passed through a slanting shaft of light, I was for some reason reminded of an incident in my early childhood. I could almost bring the specific place and time into focus, but at the last moment they faded into only a sensation.

After a while, we came to a smoky clearing with half a dozen domes of *mangungu* thatch in it. They were the smallest dwellings I had ever seen, like tropical igloos or the nests of some gregarious ground creature. I could not quite have stretched out in one. Two Efe women, squatting before a little fire that smoldered at the meeting point of three logs, got up and, without daring to look at me, bravely took my extended hand. A man and another woman came out of one of the huts. The man was very muscular, like a wrestler, and his arms and legs looked slightly long in relation to his torso. He stood about four feet nine and, except for a rag tucked through a vine belt, he was naked. The women, who were a few inches shorter, wore similar loincloths. They had black circles of plant juice painted on their arms and legs and black lines on their faces, much as some Amazon Indian women have, and their teeth were chipped to points. Two of them were old—over thirty—with wrinkled breasts sagging over their bellies. The average life span of an Efe, with infant mortality taken into account, is forty, although some live to be eighty. I passed the man and each of the women cigarettes, which they took, still not looking at me. I took out my guitar and played them a high-stepping rag called "The St. Louis Tickle." Their reaction was guarded, but they understood that it was music. The man went to his hut and, returning with a little five-string harp, plucked a single open minor chord over and over for about a minute. I recorded it. Then I recorded the woman, who, after much giggling and several false starts, broke into a haunting three-part yodel to a cross rhythm that one of them kept by slapping her thigh. "It is a song of joy," Gamaembi explained when they had stopped, "about their child being old enough to be sent to his hut for the first time after disobeying his mother." They listened intently as I played it back to them, and when it was over they looked at each other with sly, knowing smiles, burst into laughter, and slapped each other's open palms, like basketball players who have just scored. I had always thought that "giving skin" was something American blacks had invented—part of a routine that the members of a particular oppressed minority had made up to support each other. It is equally intriguing that the BaLese use the word "bad" in the approving way, and "brother" in the loosely fraternal way that some American blacks do.

We crossed a little river called the Afalabombi. Baudouin's tumpline had frayed and was coming apart, and while he was off peeling a new one Gamaembi picked a nearby *mangungu* leaf, folded it into a cone, dipped it in the river, and passed it to me. Baudouin returned with a long strip of bark and wrapped it around the neck of the burlap sack, leaving a loop that he slipped over his head, and we started out again.

After several hours, we reached the top of a viewless hill. "This is where we stop and rest whenever we are here," Gamaembi informed me. He spread out a few handy *mangungu* leaves for me to sit on, while Baudouin tore a square from an old, khaki-colored *mangungu* leaf, sprinkled Tumbaco and *bangi* on it, and rolled himself a joint. The leaf had the body of a thin sheet of paper etched with tough little fibres. *Mangungu* seemed to have a thousand and one uses.

We were sitting in a grove of hundred-and-fifty-foot strangler figs. The species, *Ficus thonningii*, is partial to high, well-drained sites. Each tree had started as a seed dropped by a bird in the crotch of a different species of tree which had originally occupied the site. Like wax melting down the side of a candle, the roots had descended from the seeds, mingled and merged, and eventually smothered the host tree out of existence. At the same time, usually about thirty feet from the ground, a trunk had ascended from the seed and shot up for a hundred feet or so before finally branching into a crown. Gamaembi cut into a huge buttress of anastomosed fig root with the edge of an iron arrowhead, and a sticky white latex bubbled out. "Along the rivers, we line traps with the milk of this tree and bait them with seeds," he said. "Birds walk in and get stuck." He said the tree was called *popo* and was one of those whose inner bark the Efe and some of the older BaLese pounded into loincloths.

We sat eating peanut butter with our fingers. I noticed that Gamaembi had both metal-tipped arrows and arrows with plain, sharpened shafts which had been dipped in the sap of a vine of the biologically active genus *Strophanthus*—a sap that paralyzes monkeys and makes them release the branches they are holding. I asked if he was a good shot, and he said, without a trace of ego, "We are all good shots." I never got to see him in action, although we ran into quite a lot of game. He carried the bow in case of attack from animals or spirits, not for hunting.

When we started walking again, Baudouin pointed out on the edge of the path a bent-over branch with a noose on the end of it for snaring little forest antelopes. Most of them are duikers, six species of which inhabit the Ituri Forest. The smallest and most abundant, the blue duiker, is not much bigger than a dachshund. There are also Bates's pygmy antelope and the water chevrotain, a diminutive relative of deer which has some affinities with pigs. Of these, the wildlife ecologist John Hart, who has spent five years in the forest, has told me, only the pygmy antelope, which frequents the edges of *shambas*, subsists on leaves. The rest browse on fallen fruit, seeds, flowers, and mushrooms. There are very few deep-forest leaf-eaters in the Ituri. All the monkeys (except the colobuses), and even the forest elephants, are frugivorous. The reason for this may be that here the cost to a tree of losing its leaves is tremendous. Most of the trees are not deciduous, and because they do not flush a new set of leaves each year their foliage is heavily protected—in most cases by toxic or indigestible secondary compounds, but sometimes by thorns or prickly hairs or by sophisticated symbiotic relationships with stinging insects. A few species have evolved extra-floral nectaries, which attract fire ants; no one would want to brush against these leaves, let alone try to eat them. Life for a tree in such a forest is not easy. Many trees spend years, or even their whole lives, no more than a yard tall, waiting for a gap to open in the canopy, and at this stage they are most vulnerable. When an opening does present itself, they shoot up with amazing speed.

Gamaembi picked some white-gilled mushrooms with light-gray caps and foot-long taproots. He said they were called *imamburama* and were good to eat. That evening, we ate them sautéed in *mafuta* with rice and sardines, and they were good. We would sleep on *mangungu* pallets in a lean-to on the Afande River which two men from Opoku had recently built as a fishing and trapping camp. After supper, I tried one of Baudouin's joints. The *bangi* was very smooth and relaxing, but it wasn't conducive to clear thought, and when I got up to poke the fire back to life I discovered that it made tedious demands on motor coordination. Gamaembi didn't touch the stuff. "For me, life is already wonderful," he explained.

He and Baudouin were fascinated by the color plates in Jean Dorst and Pierre Dandelot's *Field Guide to the Larger Mammals of Africa*, which we pored over with a flashlight. I wrote down in phonetic spelling the Swahili and KiLese names of the animals they recognized. I asked about leopards. Gamaembi said that a day in from the road they were quite common— especially along rivers. "We can hear him sing, cry, *être dans la folie pour rien*, purr happily after killing an antelope," he said. He told me that you could hit a giant forest hog with a hundred arrows before it died, but that with a spear it only took once or twice. I asked about butterflies. The BaLese have many names for bees, but for butterflies they use only the general Swahili word, *kipepéo*. "Butterflies are bad for us, because we have no use for them," Gamaembi said.

"To me, the butterfly is the insect that climbs trees and eats the leaves," Baudouin remarked.

"Butterflies are metamorphoses," Gamaembi said. "We eat the caterpillars but not the butterflies."

"I love the forest, monsieur," Gamaembi said a little later, as we lay in the darkness. "To know its situation, to find all the marvellous little things and the mountains in it."

Late in the night, it started to pour, but the roof was good and we stayed dry. In the morning, the river was muddy and swollen, way up over the rocks and prostrate trees I had walked out on the evening before. "Friday the twenty-seventh. The quality of our drinking water has taken a turn for the worse," I entered in a journal I was keeping. "We can look forward to a day of gray dampness." The river was now as wide as the trees along its bank were tall. If one of the trees had fallen over, it would have been just long enough to cross on. I noticed several pendulous socks hanging in a tree on the other side. They were the nests of malimbe weavers and looked much like the nests of the yellow-rumped cacique of the Amazon.

The malimbes were already off somewhere, perhaps flocking with greenbuls, bulbuls, and flycatchers. Africa has at least ninety kinds of weaver.

We were ready to go at 6:30 A.M., but as I was zipping up the duffelbag the side caught on my pajamas and, trying to free it, I forced it off one of its tracks. "What are we going to do now?" I asked Gamaembi. He started to work—removing the staple at the base of the tracks, rethreading the slide, putting back the staple—and in five minutes it was fixed. I was impressed, having operated hundreds of zippers but never having come to terms with one. I tended to take the mechanisms in my life for granted—even had a slight aversion to them—but Gamaembi approached them with deep respect and curiosity. If in the United States the zipper in my pants had broken, I reflected, I would probably have thrown them away and bought a new pair. But this was not a throw-it-away society. There were no spare parts, no convenient repair shops. If something broke, you had no choice but to try to fix it.

We crossed the Afande half a mile downstream, inching along a partly submerged log. Almost at the end, I lost my balance and fell into furious brown water; I expected to be swept away, but it was only knee-deep. The three of us laughed, realizing we could have just waded across. Soon afterward, we crossed another river—the Afalu—and then we reached the first village in the forest: Zalondi.

Gamaembi had been explaining as we walked that in 1942 the men of his tribe had been forced by the Belgians to come out of the forest and build the road that went past Opoku. The road was needed to bring up war matériel to the Sudan, and after it was built the men were sent out to collect wild rubber, which was also needed. It was a period of great hardship for the BaLese. The men were separated from their wives and their *shambas*. There was little to eat. If they did not bring in their quota of rubber, they were beaten. After the war, the BaLese men were forced to live near the road— where they could be kept track of—to keep the road in repair, and to grow cash crops like peanuts, rice, and cotton. Their women joined them, and the villages in the forest were abandoned. Maintenance of the road stopped abruptly with independence. Some of the BaLese immediately went back to their *matongo*, their *ancienne place* in the forest, and started new villages, but most of them remained on the road. It was disappearing, becoming not much more than a path. Because of the widespread gonorrhea and other diseases, the population along the road was in decline. More BaLese were giving up on the promises of the road and were returning to their *matongos*. In the past few years, a dozen new villages had started in the forest. The *collectivité*, like much of the country, was in a state of active regression.

Zalondi was a recent recolonization of one of the ancestral village sites. It consisted of three huts in a clearing surrounded by immense banana trees. The *capita*, a young man who was a friend of Gamaembi's, welcomed us warmly. In broken French, he told me that he had come to Zalondi a year ago, "for a rest." He went on to say, "There is too much *dérangement*, too many thieves. I was getting tired of the police taking my chickens, and officials of the *collectivité* dropping in and expecting to be fed." Thirty Efe had a camp nearby, and a group of women and children from it were sitting in a doorway of one of the huts, all heaped together, nursing babies, combing each other's hair, enjoying each other's warmth. A sweet lanolin smell emanated from them. The oldest woman, a withered grandmother, puffed marijuana in a wooden pipe whose stem was the hollowed three-foot midrib of a banana leaf. The Efe like to smoke a lot of *bangi* before they go hunting, Bob told me—especially when they are going for elephant—or before they climb a honey tree, but sometimes they smoke so much it leaves them dazed and their projects are abandoned.

We traded a bar of soap for a hand of pudgy bananas that were only a few inches long, and traded some of Baudouin's *bangi* for a comb of thick, dark honey. The bananas were wonderfully sweet, and the honey was so strong I felt a surge of energy from it almost immediately. Bob had told me that during July and August, the wettest months, the Efe roam the forest and eat nothing else. The start of the honey season is signalled by a long, woeful, high-pitched cry that is heard in the distance. The Efe say the sound is made by a newt who is about to lay her eggs and die, and that that is why her cry is woeful; but it is actually made by a crake. No later than five-thirty in the morning, before the bees have left their hives, the Efe men fan out in groups of five or six, approaching trees and tilting their heads. When one of them hears a tree humming with the promise of honey, he blows a flute made from a sapling, as a joyous announcement to the others, and breaks branches around the bee tree to mark the site. After a man has found three or four such trees, he goes back with his companions (not necessarily right away but within several weeks) to get the honey, a procedure that may require daring feats of engineering, since the hive is often a hundred feet up and a bridge from a smaller tree—sometimes several bridges—must be built. On the spot, the men weave from *mangungu* two baskets—one for the honey, the other to fill with burning wet leaves—and the man who found the bees' hole climbs to it, and smokes the hive; after waiting for the bees to go into a torpor, he widens the hole with an axe and chops out the honey. When he returns to the ground, more often than not he will eat several pounds of honey and get on a sugar high—becoming excited to the point of screaming about the next tree he is going to raid. (The Efe seem immune to the nausea and chills of hyperglycemia.) A good hive can yield from twenty to twenty-five pounds of honey, and what the finder does not eat he brings to his wife and relatives. At the start of the honey season, the BaLese villages give the Efe big *chungus*—aluminum pots capable of holding forty pounds of honey—which the Efe bring back full and trade for cloth. One

year, there may be a bumper crop of honey, the next almost none, where-
upon the Efe become uncharacteristically sad for that season.

The village clearing was swarming with bees (one stung me on the
neck when I brushed it accidentally with my hands) and with skippers that
had dull brown wings and stout green bodies—a species known as the striped
policeman. Several chickens and emaciated dogs were snapping up the butterflies. The dogs were small, with curly tails, and were mostly hound. The
breed is called the African barkless dog, because they don't vocalize as much
as other dogs; they are thought to be like the first dogs that lived with man.
Dogs are very important for driving game. Before a drive starts, Bob had
told me, the Efe tie wooden clappers around the necks of the dogs, about
half of which belong to the BaLese villagers. One man, the beater, sings
and shouts continually to keep the dogs moving. Four hundred yards from
where the drive begins, the other men wait in a semicircle, very still, for
panicky duikers to streak within bowshot. The hunters do not shoot at anything over thirty feet away; it is too chancy through the trees. Once an animal
is hit, the dogs keep it on the move until it drops or passes by another
hunter, who is waiting motionless to finish it off with another arrow.

I took out my camera and aimed it at three teen-age Efe girls, and
they ran in mock terror behind a hut, where I could hear them giggling. I
tried to photograph another Efe woman and her children, but she shooed
them from the man-eating *muzungu*, so I gave up on taking pictures and
turned on my Sony. When the girls behind the hut heard the three women
I had recorded the day before, they returned and, not to be outdone,
launched into a three-part yodel, breaking their voices on throaty *aOO's*
that came with the haphazard timing of frogs in chorus or katydids in late
August. The girls were as shy as birds, and their music was cosmic; their
yodels seemed to resonate indefinitely. The way each took a different note
is called hocket singing, but their collective sound, unlike contemporary
Western music, came out in a pentatonic scale; it was based almost entirely
on the dominant, with the occasional addition of sevenths, and was nearly
always in a descending pattern. Every few seconds, another rhythm, another
melody blended in. The Belgian ethnomusicologist Benoit Quersin has described the pygmies' music as *"polyphonie en cascade."* There is nothing
quite like it elsewhere in Africa or in any other place.

The *capita* of Zalondi told Gamaembi of a village that had been started
since his last visit. It was up the Mubilinga River, and we could go to it
instead of to three villages that Gamaembi was already familiar with. I said
it sounded like a good idea. When we were back in the forest, I asked to
go first, so I could learn to find the way. The path was well worn and about
a foot wide—twice as wide as an Amazonian footpath, because the Indians
put one foot directly in front of the other as they lope along. Sometimes it
had lots of little offshoots. It wasn't easy to tell the ones that were shortcuts

from the animal trails that petered into nothing. The elephant trails, which crossed the path from time to time and sometimes followed it for a stretch, were deep and especially confusing. Sometimes the path would split in two, which meant that up ahead a tree had fallen across the original route. You took the newer-looking detour. Snapped saplings always meant something— usually that someone had rights to a nearby honey tree. Once, we came across a message carved on a tree in Swahili. It said, according to Gamaembi:

> I came by here in December, when you had gone in search of honey. Bring me some quickly.
>
> Sekuri

In time, I learned to let my feet make the decisions, and they were usually right.

Richard Critchfield

Shahhat: An Egyptian

It is difficult to believe that until 1935, the majority of Americans were country folk. Urbanization has proceeded so fast in the United States that by the year 2000 only about one percent of Americans will still be farming.

    Yet, amazingly, most of the world's people still live in traditional villages. When that villager compares the backbreaking toil and uncertain rewards of rural work with the glittering prospects of the city, the latter becomes a magnet for more millions. The hegira accelerates. Like our grandparents used to say, "You can't keep em down on the farm anymore."

    Richard Critchfield has spent a lifetime living with villagers around the world. In Shahhat: An Egyptian *(1978) he tells of one upper Nile peasant whose feelings of numbness and confusion are little different from those of John Steinbeck's 1930s Okies.*

*   *   *

Shahhat hurriedly climbed the narrow trail which traversed the rocky cliff face, not stopping until he reached the highest ridge away from the valley toward the empty desert. His muscles ached, sweat ran into his eyes, he breathed heavily, filling his lungs with fresh cool air. All about him was sky, an intense blue above the dusty haze of desert and valley. He wrapped his arms tightly around his chest as if against some inward chill, holding his body tensely, like a beggar hounded from the streets, broken and powerless, or a kicked animal which expects to be kicked again. He sat for a long time this way without moving. He looked like someone lost in space, frozen forever in a pose of despair.

    Time passed. The sun began its descent. Soon it sank into a dusty purple mist on the desert's edge. The air grew cold as if to remind him of the narrow limits of man's freedom. Shahhat stirred, knowing he would soon have to return to the valley just to keep warm.

    Over and over he asked himself, "What am I going to do?" Like anyone numb and paralyzed with depression, he was unable to think beyond the question to any future. He had spoken of going away, to Suez or other Arab lands, but in his *fellah's* heart he felt to leave his village was to die. He stared into the desert where nothing but sand dunes stretched to the horizon, and he longed to lose himself forever in such calm emptiness. The rocky cliffs would keep the world away and protect him in boundless space. "The Bedouin lives the best," he thought. "He can take his freedom. When a man lives in a village and becomes a villager, there is always trouble. Two or three Bedouins alone in the desert would take care of each other and love each other much."

Vaguely he imagined himself, a man, a tiny speck, disappearing into this vast uninhabited solitude. Sand and rock might be his only companions, but he would not fear the emptiness nor the echo that would reverberate with his every footfall. He longed to escape into this free life he had never lived. Perhaps he dimly recalled things heard about Arabia long ago. Or he had inherited this vision of a life of freedom along with his flesh and blood from his Bedouin ancestors. He kept his eyes fixed on the desert a long while.

It was getting colder. He climbed up to a rocky outcropping and looked down the sheer drop of the cliffs to the slopes and valley below. In the fading light the houses and trees, the flat green plain with its broad, winding river, the ruined temples, the canals and roads, were so diminished, and the people, as they moved about, such tiny specks, they seemed illimitably distant and remote. He could see, strung out a mile from south to north on the slopes just below, the twisting road to the Valley of the Queens, the two crumbling stone giants of the Colossi of Memnon, the Rammuseum to the left, the canyon into the cliffside temple of Hatchepsut, and winding above it, the trail up the ridge and down again to the Valley of the Kings. All these Shahhat had known since childhood. The stone reliefs and hiero-glyphics might tell of wars and massacres, but the blood and misery was long past; now they were just pictures on a wall, and the ruins had the same soothing calm of the desert.

It was almost dark, but to the north, around a bend in the river, he could see the white sails of three *fellucas*. To Shahhat, the Nile was *el Bahr*. The sea. The giver of life. This was the month, August, when the river always rose to flood its banks. Now, just since his fifteenth year, the High Dam at Aswan had held back these waters. The Nile would never flood again. Shah-hat wondered what his life would have been like if the river had not been tamed. Poorer, but lived in the old natural rhythms and certainties. For the dam had brought the incessant field work, even in hottest summer. It had brought the diesel pumps, the fights to load sugar cane, the feuds and frustrations. It had created the inspectors, the Lameis, the Faruks, the Hagg Abd el Mantalebs. It had fed his mother's extravagance and fierce expec-tations. To Shahhat, order and reason were limited and no scientific or technical progress could enlarge them; rather they made life more difficult. For did not hidden demons, blind fate, the solicitations of Satan, the hot fury of one's own blood, await every man in ambush at the crossroads? Why, then change?

He heard distant sounds of life and listened, straining his ears. He could make out the doleful braying of a donkey. A vendor's familiar wailing cry, "Onions sweet as honey!" A bagpipe playing a wedding tune and the faint wail of mourning women. Someone had married, and someone had died. He thought of his mother the night before, gossiping about the comedy of village life. And of Batah, lying in the road. At once the sense of numb despair returned.

The moon started to rise. It was almost full as tomorrow would be the last day of the Feast of Abu Hagag. The valley grew dark, and around the huddled masses of houses and trees began to flow a sea of thin, moonlit mist, and, what remained long in Shahhat's memory, wisps of vapor, white as ghosts, floated slowly across the open expanse of fields. Near the moon, yellow and enormous as it rose over the curve of the ridge, swarmed transparent patches of cloud. The whole Nile Valley, it seemed, was made of black shadows and wandering wisps of light. At first he saw no sign of life. Then small twinkling yellow glows appeared here and there, village oil lamps, however feebly, reaching even these heights.

And Shahat felt as if Allah himself were close, looking down, just as he was, from the sky. The star-filled desert sky was so deep and incomprehensible that he imagined it was from here that the angels watched and saw all that was going on below. In the valley Satan and his genii might make men evil and violent. But here at least, high on the desert ridge, all was peaceful, and Allah ruled unchallenged. As he looked down into the shadowed valley, Shahhat remembered Suniya's words that the sunrise was like the land expressing thanks. He had teased her for being *pharaoni*, worshipping the sun. But now he thought perhaps the earth was waiting to emerge into goodness, just as the sun would rise in a few more hours over the Arabian Desert from the night.

Life might seem unrelenting and absurd. But things were what they were, predestined, and part of Allah's plan. That was what human life meant. "Everything is from Allah," he said aloud. "I cannot decide anything. Everything we are is from him."

The path down the cliff face was steep but Shahhat did not think abut his strength nor where he put his feet. Sometimes the moon shone in front of him, sometimes behind. As he neared the lower slopes the jackals out on the desert began their hideous, derisive cries. To Shahhat they were like Satan's demons, taunting him with doubts, "See what will happen, Shahhat, what will happen to you?"

Antoine de Saint-Exupéry

Wind, Sand and Stars

The mid-1930s was aviation's pioneering era of distance, endurance, and speed records, and of the technological advance that led to the fighting machines of World War II. On December 29, 1935, veteran French airman Antoine de Saint-Exupéry set off with his mechanic Prévot on an ambitious flight from Paris to Saigon. Lost in the black night of the Libyan desert, their Simoon *crashed at 170 miles per hour onto a rocky, sandy plateau. The men were miraculously uninjured. By luck they began to walk northeast after three days of indecision. They were eventually saved but not until experiencing nights spent buried in sand as protection from the cold winds. And not until they had gone through blinding days of torture by thirst and sun.*

Almost a decade, later during the summer of 1944, the author of Wind, Sand and Stars (1939) *and of* The Little Prince *disappeared over the Mediterranean while on a military reconnaisance flight.*

* * *

Flying is a man's job and its worries are a man's worries. A pilot's business is with the wind, with the stars, with night, with sand, with the sea. He strives to outwit the forces of nature. He stares in expectancy for the coming of dawn the way a gardener awaits the coming of spring. He looks forward to port as to a promised land, and truth for him is what lives in the stars.

I have nothing to complain of. For three days I have tramped the desert, have known the pangs of thirst, have followed false scents in the sand, have pinned my faith on the dew. I have struggled to rejoin my kind, whose very existence on earth I had forgotten. These are the cares of men alive in every fibre, and I cannot help thinking them more important than the fretful choosing of a nightclub in which to spend the evening. Compare the one life with the other, and all things considered this is luxury! I have no regrets. I have gambled and lost. It was all in the day's work. At least I have had the unforgettable taste of the sea on my lips.

I am not talking about living dangerously. Such words are meaningless to me. The toreador does not stir me to enthusiasm. It is not danger I love. I know what I love. It is life.

The sky seemed to me faintly bright. I drew up one arm through the sand. There was a bit of the torn parachute within reach, and I ran my hand over it. It was bone dry. Let's see. Dew falls at dawn. Here was dawn risen and no moisture on the cloth. My mind was befuddled and I heard myself say: "There is a dry heart here, a dry heart that cannot know the relief of tears."

I scrambled to my feet. "We're off, Prévot," I said. "Our throats are still open. Get along, man!"

The wind that shrivels up a man in nineteen hours was now blowing out of the west. My gullet was not yet shut, but it was hard and painful and I could feel that there was a rasp in it. Soon that cough would begin that I had been told about and was now expecting. My tongue was becoming a nuisance. But most serious of all, I was beginning to see shining spots before my eyes. When those spots changed into flames, I should simply lie down.

The first morning hours were cool and we took advantage of them to get on at a good pace. We knew that once the sun was high there would be no more walking for us. We no longer had the right to sweat. Certainly not to stop and catch our breath. This coolness was merely the coolness of low humidity. The prevailing wind was coming from the desert, and under its soft and treacherous caress the blood was being dried out of us.

Our first day's nourishment had been a few grapes. In the next three days each of us ate half an orange and a bit of cake. If we had anything left now, we couldn't have eaten it because we had no saliva with which to masticate it. But I had stopped being hungry. Thirsty I was, yes, and it seemed to me that I was suffering less from thirst itself than from the effects of thirst. Gullet hard. Tongue like plaster of Paris. A rasping in the throat. A horrible taste in the mouth.

All these sensations were new to me, and though I believed water could rid me of them, nothing in my memory associated them with water. Thirst had become more and more a disease and less and less a craving. I began to realize that the thought of water and fruit was now less agonizing than it had been. I was forgetting the radiance of the orange, just as I was forgetting the eyes under the hat brim. Perhaps I was forgetting everything.

We had sat down after all, but it could not be for long. Nevertheless, it was impossible to go five hundred yards without our legs giving way. To stretch out on the sand would be marvelous—but it could not be.

The landscape had begun to change. Rocky places grew rarer and the sand was now firm beneath our feet. A mile ahead stood dunes and on those dunes we could see a scrubby vegetation. At least this sand was preferable to the steely surface over which we had been trudging. This was the golden desert. This might have been the Sahara. It was in a sense my country.

Two hundred yards had now become our limit, but we had determined to carry on until we reached the vegetation. Better than that we could not hope to do. A week later, when we went back over our traces in a car to have a look at the *Simoon*, I measured this last lap and found that it was just short of fifty miles. All told we had done one hundred and twenty-four miles.

The previous day I had tramped without hope. Today the word "hope" had grown meaningless. Today we were tramping simply because we were tramping. Probably oxen work for the same reason. Yesterday I had dreamed of a paradise of orange trees. Today I would not give a button for paradise; I did not believe oranges existed. When I thought about myself I found in me nothing but a heart squeezed dry. I was tottering but emotionless. I felt no distress whatever, and in a way I regretted it: misery would have seemed to me as sweet as water. I might then have felt sorry for myself and commiserated with myself as with a friend. But I had not a friend left on earth.

Later, when we were rescued, seeing our burnt-out eyes men thought we must have called aloud and wept and suffered. But cries of despair, misery, sobbing grief are a kind of wealth, and we possessed no wealth. When a young girl is disappointed in love she weeps and knows sorrow. Sorrow is one of the vibrations that prove the fact of living. I felt no sorrow. I was the desert. I could no longer summon those moving visions towards which I should have loved to stretch forth arms. The sun had dried up the springs of tears in me.

And yet, what was that? A ripple of hope went through me like a faint breeze over a lake. What was this sign that had awakened my instinct before knocking on the door of my consciousness? Nothing had changed, and yet everything was changed. This sheet of sand, these low hummocks and sparse tufts of verdure that had been a landscape, were now become a stage setting. Thus far the stage was empty, but the scene was set. I looked at Prévot. The same astonishing thing had happened to him as to me, but he was as far from guessing its significance as I was.

I swear to you that something is about to happen. I swear that life has sprung in this desert. I swear that this emptiness, this stillness, has suddenly become more stirring than a tumult on a public square.

"Prévot! Footprints! We are saved!"

We had wandered from the trail of the human species; we had cast ourselves forth from the tribe; we had found ourselves alone on earth and forgotten by the universal migration; and here, imprinted in the sand, were the divine and naked feet of man!

"Look, Prévot, here two men stood together and then separated."

"Here a camel knelt."

"Here . . ."

But it was not true that we were already saved. It was not enough to squat down and wait. Before long we should be past saving. Once the cough has begun, the progress made by thirst is swift.

Still, I believed in that caravan swaying somewhere in the desert, heavy with its cargo of treasure.

We went on. Suddenly I heard a cock crow. I remembered what Guillaumet had told me: "Towards the end I heard cocks crowing in the Andes. And I heard the railway train." The instant the cock crowed I thought of Guillaumet and I said to myself: "First it was my eyes that played tricks on me. I suppose this is another of the effects of thirst. Probably my ears have merely held out longer than my eyes." But Prévot grabbed my arm:

"Did you hear that?"

"What?"

"The cock."

"Why . . . why, yes, I did."

To myself I said: "Fool! Get it through your head! This means life!"

I had one last hallucination—three dogs chasing one another. Prévot looked, but could not see them. However, both of us waved our arms at a Bedouin. Both of us shouted with all the breath in our bodies, and laughed for happiness.

But our voices could not carry thirty yards. The Bedouin on his slow-moving camel had come into view behind a dune and now he was moving slowly out of sight. The man was proably the only Arab in this desert, sent by a demon to materialize and vanish before the eyes of us who could not run.

We saw in profile on the dune another Arab. We shouted but our shouts were whispers. We waved our arms and it seemed to us that they must fill the sky with monstrous signals. Still the Bedouin stared with averted face away from us.

At last, slowly, slowly, he began a right angle turn in our direction. At the very second when his eyes met ours, thirst would vanish and by this man would death and the mirages be wiped out. Let this man but make a quarter-turn left and the world is changed. Let him but bring his torso round, but sweep the scene with a glance, and like a god he can create life.

The miracle had come to pass. He was walking towards us over the sand like a god over the waves.

The Arab looked at us without a word. He placed his hands upon our shoulders and we obeyed him: we stretched out upon the sand. Race, language, religion were forgotten. There was only this humble nomad with the hands of an archangel on our shoulders.

Face to the sand, we waited. And when the water came, we drank like calves with our faces in the basin, and with a greediness which alarmed the

Bedouin so that from time to time he pulled us back. But as soon as his hand fell away from us we plunged our faces anew into the water.

Water, thou hast no taste, no color, no odor; canst not be defined, art relished while ever mysterious. Not necessary to life, but rather life itself, thou fillest us with a gratification that exceeds the delight of the senses. By thy might, there return into us treasures that we had abandoned. By thy grace, there are released in us all the dried-up runnels of our heart. Of the riches that exist in the world, thou are the rarest and also the most delicate— thou so pure within the bowels of the earth! A man may die of thirst lying beside a magnesium spring. He may die within reach of a salt lake. He may die though he hold in his hand a jug of dew, if it be inhabited by evil salts. For thou, water, art a proud divinity, allowing no alteration, no foreignness in thy being. And the joy that thou spreadest is an infinitely simple joy.

You, Bedouin of Libya who saved our lives, though you will dwell for ever in my memory yet I shall never be able to recapture your features. You are Humanity and your face comes into my mind simply as man incarnate. You, our beloved fellowman, did not know who we might be, and yet you recognized us without fail. And I, in my turn, shall recognize you in the faces of all mankind. You came towards me in an aureole of charity and magnanimity bearing the gift of water. All my friends and all my enemies marched towards me in your person. It did not seem to me that you were rescuing me: rather did it seem that you were forgiving me. And I felt I had no enemy left in all the world.

This is the end of my story. Lifted on to a camel, we went on for three hours. Then, broken with weariness, we asked to be set down at a camp while the cameleers went on ahead for help. Towards six in the evening a car manned by armed Bedouins came to fetch us. A half-hour later we were set down at the house of a Swiss engineer named Raccaud who was operating a soda factory beside saline deposits in the desert. He was unforgettably kind to us. By midnight we were in Cairo.

I awoke between white sheets. Through the curtains came the rays of a sun that was no longer an enemy. I spread butter and honey on my bread. I smiled. I recaptured the savor of my childhood and all its marvels. And I read and reread the telegram from those dearest to me in all the world whose three words had shattered me:

"So terribly happy!"

Aleksandr I. Solzhenitsyn

The Gulag Archipelago

The name Siberia has enjoyed the same currency in the twentieth century that it did in the nineteenth—as a dreaded destination for Russia's prisoners. Whether those prisoners were Tsarist or Soviet made little difference to the individual slave laborer.

In Solzhenitsyn's The Gulag Archipelago *(1973) we feel what it is like to walk from the nightmare of a railway flatcar journey to a new prison camp site. As we walk, the dead cold of Siberian winter closes in around us.*

*　*　*

No, damn that red cattle car train too, even though it did carry the prisoners straight to their destination without changing trains. Anyone who has ever been in one will never forget it. Just as well get to camp sooner! Just as well arrive sooner.

A human being is all hope and impatience. As if the Security officer in camp will be anymore humane or the stoolies any less unscrupulous. It's just the other way around. As if they won't force us to the ground with those same threats and those same police dogs when we arrive: "Sit down!" As if there will be less snow on the ground in camp than what has sifted through into the cattle cars. As if it means that we've already gotten to where we're going when they begin to unload us and won't be carried farther in open flatcars on a narrow-gauge track. (And how can they carry us in open flatcars? How can we be kept under guard? That's a problem for the convoy. And here is how they do it: They order us to lie down all huddled together and they cover us with one big tarpaulin, like the sailors in the motion picture *Potemkin* before they're to be executed. And say thank you for the tarpaulin too. In the North, in October, Olenyev and his comrades had the luck to have to sit in open flatcars all day long. They had already embarked, but no locomotive had come. First it rained. Then it froze. And the zeks' rags froze on them.) The tiny train will jerk and toss as it moves, and the sides of the flatcar will begin to crack and break, and the bouncing will hurl someone off the car and under the wheels. And here is a riddle: If one is traveling sixty miles from Dudinka through Arctic frost in open flatcars on the narrow-gauge track, then where are the thieves going to be? Answer: In the middle of each flatcar, so the livestock around them will keep them warm and keep them from falling under the train themselves. Right answer! Question: What will the zeks see at the end of this narrow-gauge track (1939)? Will there be any buildings there? No, not a one. Any dugouts? Yes, but already occupied, not for them. And does that mean that the first thing they do will be to dig themselves dugouts? No, because how can they dig in the Arctic winter? Instead, they will be sent out to mine metal. And where will they live? What—live? Oh, yes, live . . . They will live in tents.

But will there always be a narrow-gauge track? No, of course not. The train arrived: Yertsovo Station, February 1938. The railroad cars were opened up at night. Bonfires were lit alongside the train and disembarkation took place by their light; then a count-off, forming up, and a count-off again. The temperature was 32 degrees beglow zero Centigrade. The prisoners' transport train had come from the Donbas, and all the prisoners had been arrested back in the summer and were wearing low shoes, oxfords, even sandals. They tried to warm themselves at the fires, but the guards chased them away: that's not what the fires were there for; they were there to give light. Fingers grew numb almost instantly. The snow filled the thin shoes and didn't even melt. There was no mercy and the order was given: "Fall in! Form up! One step to the right or left and we'll fire without warning. Forward march!" The dogs on their chains howled at their favorite command, at the excitement of the moment. The convoy guards marched ahead in their sheepskin coats—and the doomed prisoners in their summer clothes marched through deep snow on a totally untraveled road somewhere into the dark taiga, nary a light ahead. The northern lights gleamed—for them it was their first and probably their last view of them. The fir trees crackled in the frost. The ill-shod prisoners paced and trod down the snow, their feet and legs growing numb from the cold.

Or, as another example, here is a January 1945 arrival at Pechora. ("Our armies have captured Warsaw! Our armies have cut off East Prussia!") An empty snowy field. The prisoners were tossed out of cars, made to sit down in the snow by sixes, painstakingly counted off, miscounted, and counted again. They were ordered to stand up and then were harried through a snowy virgin waste for four miles. This prisoner transport was also from the south—from Moldavia. And everyone was wearing leather shoes. The police dogs were right on their heels, and the dogs pushed the zeks in the last row with their paws on their backs, breathing on the backs of their heads. (Two priests were in that row—old gray-haired Father Fyodor Florya and young Father Viktor Shipovalnikov, who was helping to hold him up.) What a use for police dogs? No, what self-restraint it showed on the dogs' part! After all, they wanted to bite so badly!

Finally they arrived. There was a camp reception bath; they had to undress in one cabin, run across the yard naked, and wash in another. But all this was bearable now: the worst was over. They had *arrived*. Twilight fell. And all of a sudden it was learned there was no room for them; the camp wasn't ready to receive the prisoner transport. And after the bath, the prisoners were again formed up, counted, surrounded by dogs, and were marched *back* to their prisoner-transport train all those four miles, but this time in the dark. And the car doors had been left open all those hours, and had lost even their earlier, pitiful measure of warmth, and then all the coal had been burned up by the end of the journey and there was nowhere to get any more now. And in these circumstances, they froze all night and in the morning were given dried carp (and anyone who wanted to drink could chew snow), and then marched back along the same road again.

And this, after all, was an episode with a *happy* ending. In this case, the camp at least *existed*. If it couldn't accept them today, it would tomorrow. But it was not at all unusual for the red trains to arrive nowhere, and the end of the journey often marked the opening day of a *new* camp. They might simply stop somewhere in the taiga under the northern lights and nail to a fir tree a sign reading: "FIRST OLP."* And there they would chew on dried fish for a week and try to mix their flour with snow.

But if a camp had been set up there even two weeks earlier, that already spelled comfort; hot food would have been cooked; and even if there were no bowls, the first and second courses would nonetheless be mixed together in washbasins for six prisoners to eat from at the same time; and this group of six would form a circle (there was no tables or chairs yet), and two of them would hold onto the handles of the washbasin with their left hands and would eat with their right hands, taking turns. Am I repeating myself? No, this was Perebory in 1937, as reported by Loshchilin. It is not I who am repeating myself, but Gulag.

Next they would assign the newcomers brigade leaders from among the camp veterans, who would quickly *teach them to live*, to make do, to submit to discipline, and to cheat. And from their very first morning, they would march off to work because the chimes of the clock of the great Epoch were striking and could not wait. The Soviet Union is not, after all, some Tsarist hard-labor Akatui for you, where prisoners got three days' rest after they arrived.

* OLP = *Otdelny Lagerny Punkt* = Separate Camp Site.

Viktor E. Frankl

Man's Search for Meaning

Dr. Viktor E. Frankl, M.D., Ph.D. spent three years at forced labor in Nazi death camps. His experiences there later became the basis for his creation of logotherapy, the "third school" of Viennese psychiatry. On one walk he learned the truth of Nietzsche's statement that, "He who has a why to live can bear with almost any how."

* * *

In spite of all the enforced physical and mental primitiveness of the life in a concentration camp, it was possible for spiritual life to deepen. Sensitive people who were used to a rich intellectual life may have suffered much pain (they were often of a delicate constitution), but the damage to their inner selves was less. They were able to retreat from their terrible surroundings to a life of inner riches and spiritual freedom. Only in this way can one explain the apparent paradox that some prisoners of a less hardy makeup often seemed to survive camp life better than did those of a robust nature. In order to make myself clear, I am forced to fall back on personal experience. Let me tell what happened on those early mornings when we had to march to our work site.

There were shouted commands: "Detachment, forward march! Left-2-3-4! Left-2-3-4! Left-2-3-4! Left-2-3-4! First man about, left and left and left and left! Caps off!" These words sound in my ears even now. At the order "Caps off!" we passed the gate of the camp, and searchlights were trained upon us. Whoever did not march smartly got a kick. And worse off was the man who, because of the cold, had pulled his cap back over his ears before permission was given.

We stumbled on in the darkness, over big stones and through large puddles, along the one road leading from the camp. The accompanying guards kept shouting at us and driving us with the butts of their rifles. Anyone with very sore feet supported himself on his neighbor's arm. Hardly a word was spoken; the icy wind did not encourage talk. Hiding his mouth behind his upturned collar, the man marching next to me whispered suddenly: "If our wives could see us now! I do hope they are better off in their camps and don't know what is happening to us."

79

That brought thoughts of my own wife to mind. And as we stumbled on for miles, slipping on icy spots, supporting each other time and again, dragging one another up and onward, nothing was said, but we both knew: each of us was thinking of his wife. Occasionally I looked at the sky, where the stars were fading and the pink light of the morning was beginning to spread behind a dark bank of clouds. But my mind clung to my wife's image, imagining it with an uncanny acuteness. I heard her answering me, saw her smile, her frank and encouraging look. Real or not, her look was then more luminous than the sun which was beginning to rise.

A thought transfixed me: for the first time in my life I saw the truth as it is set into song by so many poets, proclaimed as the final wisdom by so many thinkers. The truth—that love is the ultimate and the highest goal to which man can aspire. Then I grasped the meaning of the greatest secret that human poetry and human thought and belief have to impart: *The salvation of man is through love and in love.* I understood how a man who has nothing left in this world still may know bliss, be it only for a brief moment, in the contemplation of his beloved. In a position of utter desolation, when man cannot express himself in positive action, when his only achievement may consist in enduring his sufferings in the right way—an honorable way— in such a position man can, through loving contemplation of the image he carries of his beloved, achieve fulfillment. For the first time in my life I was able to understand the meaning of the words, "The angels are lost in perpetual contemplation of an infinite glory."

In front of me a man stumbled and those following him fell on top of him. The guard rushed over and used his whip on them all. Thus my thoughts were interrupted for a few minutes. But soon my soul found its way back from the prisoner's existence to another world, and I resumed talk with my loved one: I asked her questions, and she answered; she questioned me in turn, and I answered.

"Stop!" We had arrived at our work site. Everybody rushed into the dark hut in the hope of getting a fairly decent tool. Each prisoner got a spade or a pickaxe.

"Can't you hurry up, you pigs?" Soon we had resumed the previous day's positions in the ditch. The frozen ground cracked under the point of the pickaxes, and sparks flew. The men were silent, their brains numb.

My mind still clung to the image of my wife. A thought crossed my mind: I didn't even know if she were still alive. I knew only one thing— which I have learned well by now: Love goes very far beyond the physical person of the beloved. It finds its deepest meaning in his spiritual being, his inner self. Whether or not he is actually present, whether or not he is still alive at all, ceases somehow to be of importance.

I did not know whether my wife was alive, and I had no means of finding out (during all my prison life there was no outgoing or incoming mail); but at that moment it ceased to matter. There was no need for me to know; nothing could touch the strength of my love, my thoughts, and the image of my beloved. Had I known then that my wife was dead, I think that I would still have given myself, undisturbed by that knowledge, to the contemplation of her image, and that my mental conversation with her would have been just as vivid and just as satisfying. "Set me like a seal upon thy heart, love is as strong as death."

Any attempt at fighting the camp's psychopathological influence on the prisoner by psychotherapeutic or psychohygienic methods had to aim at giving him inner strength by pointing out to him a future goal to which he could look forward. Instinctively some of the prisoners attempted to find one on their own. It is a peculiarity of man that he can only live by looking to the future—*sub specie aeternitatis*. And this is his salvation in the most difficult moments of his existence, although he sometimes has to force his mind to the task.

I remember a personal experience. Almost in tears from pain (I had terrible sores on my feet from wearing torn shoes), I limped a few kilometers with our long column of men from the camp to our work site. Very cold, bitter winds struck us. I kept thinking of the endless little problems of our miserable life. What would there be to eat tonight? If a piece of sausage came as extra ration, should I exchange it for a piece of bread? Should I trade my last cigarette, which was left from a bonus I received a fortnight ago, for a bowl of soup? How could I get a piece of wire to replace the fragment which served as one of my shoelaces? Would I get to our work site in time to join my usual working party or would I have to join another, which might have a brutal foreman? What could I do to get on good terms with the Capo, who could help me to obtain work in camp instead of undertaking this horribly long daily march?

I became disgusted with the state of affairs which compelled me, daily and hourly, to think of only such trivial things. I forced my thoughts to turn to another subject. Suddenly I saw myself standing on the platform of a well-lit, warm and pleasant lecture room. In front of me sat an attentive audience on comfortable upholstered seats. I was giving a lecture on the psychology of the concentration camp! All that oppressed me at that moment became objective, seen and described from the remote viewpoint of science. By this method I succeeded somehow in rising above the situation, above the sufferings of the moment, and I observed them as if they were already of the past. Both I and my troubles became the object of an interesting psycho-scientific study undertaken by myself. What does Spinoza say in his *Ethics?*— "*Affectus, qui passio est, desinit esse passio simulatque eius claram et distinctam formamus ideam.*" Emotion, which is suffering, ceases to be suffering as soon as we form a clear and precise picture of it.

Iris Origo

War in Val D'Orcia

*In this "isms"-polluted century it has not been unusual at any one time
for millions of people to be victims of this or that ideology. Italy in
1943–44 was a perfect example. Civil war, massive invasion, and brutal
reprisals were daily realities.*

*War in Val D'Orcia (1947) is Iris Origo's diary describing her
struggle to keep her large Tuscan hill farm operating as a refuge for
her family and peasants, for escaped Allied POWs, for resistance fighters, and for dozens of war orphans.*

*Finally the fighting between the retreating German army and the
invading Allies forced Iris Origo and her orphans to abandon the farm
for a dangerous walk to safety.*

*Immediately after the war was over Iris Origo wrote, "When I
look back upon these years of tension and expectation, of destruction
and sorrow, it is individual acts of kindness, courage or faith that
illuminate them; it is in them that I trust."*

*"These—the shared, simple acts of everyday life—are the realities
on which international understanding can be built. In these, and in
the realization that has come to many thousands, that people of other
nations are, after all just like themselves, we may, perhaps, place our
hopes."*

* * *

JUNE 22ND

The day begins badly. During the first lull in the firing a tragic procession
begins to struggle down to our cellar: those of our farmers who, until then,
have preferred to take shelter in the woods. All night they have been under
fire, and their drawn, terrified faces bear witness to what they have been
through. They thankfully take refuge in the cellar and the vat room—old
men, women, and children—about sixty more people to shelter and feed.
An old grandmother from a neighboring farm is among them; half paralysed,

with a weak heart, she has been dragged along by her son and daughter, and now collapses, utterly exhausted. The babies whimper from cold and hunger. The older children go and whisper to ours, frightening them with the tales that I have tried to spare them until now. We go up to the kitchen (since fortunately the lull still continues) and produce hot barley-coffee and bread and milk, the keeper having succeeded in finding and milking the cows. The farmers' account of their nights in the woods is not such as to encourage us to try to get through to the Allied lines with the children, a plan which again, this morning, we had considered. Sporadic firing goes on all through the morning.

This glimpse of a tiny segment of the front increases my conviction of the wastefulness of this kind of warfare, the disproportion between the human suffering involved and the military results achieved. In the last five days I have seen Radicofani and Contignana destroyed, the countryside and farms studded with shell holes, girls raped, and human beings and cattle killed. Otherwise the events of the last week have had little enough effect upon either side: it is the civilians who have suffered.

LATER

The above reflections were written during a lull in the shelling, in the kitchen, while boiling some milk for the children. But, in the midst of them, a louder burst of shellfire than any we had experienced brought me down to the cellar, where we turned on the gramophone and started songs with the children and waited. "Now," we felt, "it really is beginning." It had already been evident for some hours that shells of larger caliber were now being used, and both Antonio and I (though fortunately no one else) realized that the cellar was by no means proof against them. After a while, in another slight lull, the door opened, and a German sergeant came in: space would at once be required, he said, in the cellar (already filled to overflowing) for some German troops. A few minutes later an officer appeared: "You must get out," he said, "and get the children away. You can't keep them here. And we need the cellar." (That same morning we had again asked this officer what we should do with the children, and he had said emphatically, "Stay on!") "If you get out at once," he added, "you may be able to get out of range during this lull." There followed a few minutes of considerable confusion. Antonio and I were beseiged by a crowd of terrified people, asking what and where they should go, what they should take with them, what they should leave behind, and so on. We could only answer: "At once. To Montepulciano or Chianciano, wherever you have friends. Take only what you can carry with you—the clothes on your back, and some food."

The babies were howling, and, with Donata in my arms, I couldn't help Schwester much, but we managed to pack a basket with the babies' food, and the pram with some of their clothes and nappies. I took a tiny case, which we had in the cellar, containing a change of underclothes for Antonio and me, a pair of shoes, some soap and eau de cologne and face powder, my clock and Giorgio's photographs; and that is all that we now possess. Each of the children carried his own coat and jersey. The grown-ups each carried a baby, or a sack of bread. And so, in a long, straggling line, with the children clutching at our skirts, half walking, half running, we started off down the Chianciano road.

I did not think, then, that we should get all the children through safely. We had been warned to stick to the middle of the road, to avoid mines, and to keep spread out, so as not to attract the attention of Allied planes. German soldiers, working at mine-laying, looked up in astonishment as we passed. "Du lieber Gott! What are those children doing here?" Some corpses lay, uncovered, by the roadside. A German Red Cross lorry came tearing up the hill, nearly running over us. And all the time the shells were falling, some nearer, some farther off, and the planes flew overhead. The children were very good, the older ones carrying whatever they could, the smaller ones stumbling along as fast as their small legs could carry them. Donata shouted with glee on Antonio's shoulder. No one cried except the tiny babies, but now and again there was a wail: "I can't go so fast!" and someone would pick up that child for a few hundred yards. The sun was blazing overhead, the hill very steep, and none of us had had any food since early breakfast. But every stumbling, weary step was taking us farther away from the cellar, and from what was still to come.

When we got to the top of the hill before Cianciano we divided into two parties. Those who had friends in Chiaciano went on there, the rest of us, sixty in all (of whom four were babies in arms, and twenty-eight others children) started across country towards Montepulciano. The road itself was, we knew, under continual shellfire, but we hoped to be able to cut across to the Villa Bianca crossroads. The first part went well, and when at last we had a ridge between us and La Foce, we called a first halt. The children fell exhausted and thankful on the ground, only to rise again hastily, having sat down on an anthill. They made, indeed, much more fuss about the ants than about the shells.

The shelling seemed farther off, the mined path was behind us, and a peasant brought us glasses of water. Until then, there had been no moment in which to stop and think, but now we began to realize, with dismay, all that we had left behind. The people in the vat room—had they been warned? No one knew, and we looked at each other in horror. Then at last Assunta remembered: "Yes, she had seen the fattore go in to warn them." But what they could do next it was difficult to imagine, for the old grandmother who was with them was unable to walk, and there were also several children. Probably they would merely hide in terror in a ditch. One could only pray that none of them would be killed.

And then there was Giorgio's body. We had hoped to bury him the night before, so that at least we could show his grave to his family when we are able to trace them, but the firing on the road to the cemetery prevented us from getting there. so we had had to leave him in that little room, unburied.

And then the dogs—they, too, had been forgotten. We fed them up to yesterday, but in the hurry of leaving we did not remember to go up to the kennels (five hundred yards away, and under shell fire) to fetch them. And poor Gambolino, the poodle, is terribly gun-shy. Even if he is not killed he will go almost mad with fear. It does not bear thinking of.

After a brief rest (too brief, but as long as we dared) we went on again— Antonio and the keeper, Porciani, taking the longer and more dangerous road, on which the pram could be pushed, and the rest of us scrambling along a rough track up and down steep gulleys. The children were getting very tired, but struggled manfully on, and we lifted them over the steepest places. Twice planes came hovering us, and we all crouched down in a ditch. Then when we came out into the open cornland, beyond Pianoia, came the worst part of the journey. The shelling had begun again, and on the Montepulciano road, a few hundred yards below us, shells were bursting with a terrific din. The children were afraid to go on, but on we must. Some more planes came over, and we lay down for cover in the tall corn. I remember thinking at that moment, with Benedetta lying beside me and two other children clutching at my skirts: "This can't be real—this isn't really happening."

At last we reached a farm on the road, occupied by a German Red Cross unit, and there again we got some water and a short rest. But the officer came out and, hearing that it was a *Kinderheim*, gave us disconcerting advice: take refuge at once in the Capuchin convent on the hill, he said, and don't push on to Montepulciano. "What is happening at La Foce today, will happen here tomorrow." For a minute we hesitated, but the convent, we knew, had no food and no sort of shelter, so we decided to risk it and push on. From this point onward, the Germans said, the road was safe, and so we took it, a long, straggling, footsore procession. Half an hour after we had passed, that very stretch of road was shelled.

After four hours we got to San Biagio, at the foot of the Montepulciano hill, and there sat down in a ditch for a breather before the last pull. We were very tired now, and a dreadful thought came over us: "What if the Braccis should have left?" "What if we find no shelter here?" But as we sat there, a little group of Montepulciano citizens appeared, then yet another: they had seen us from the ramparts, and were coming down to meet us with open arms. Never was there a more touching welcome. Many of them were partisans; others were refugees themselves from the south whom we had helped; yet others old friends among the Montepulciano workmen. They shouldered the children and our packages, and in a triumphant procession, cheered by so much kindness, we climbed up the village street, Antonio at the head, with Donata on his shoulder. Bracci and his wife Margherita came out to meet us, the children were at once settled on cushions on the terrace, and the Montepulcianesi vied with each other in offering accommodation. Antonio and I acted as billeting officers. Three went to one house, four to another, and the Braccis nobly took in not only our whole family, but all the refugee children as well. The Braccis' mattresses and blankets, which had been walled up, were pulled out again and laid on the ground, the children (after a meal of bread and cheese) put to bed, and at last we were able to wash and rest. Only one child was the worse for the terrible experience: Rino, who had a touch of the sun and suddenly fainted. Benedetta (sharing a bed with me) woke up, when I came to bed, to say: "We've left the bangs behind at last, haven't we?" and then fell into a twelve hours' sleep.

We have left behind everything that we possess, but never in my life have I felt so rich and so thankful as looking down on all the children as they lay asleep. Whatever may happen tomorrow, tonight they are safe and sound!

Alan Booth

The Roads to Sata

In The Roads To Sata (1985) Alan Booth concludes, after a two-thousand mile walk from the northern tip of Hokkaido to the southern tip of Kyushu, that he cannot really understand Japan. An Englishman who had lived in Japan for a quarter of his life, he took four months off to scrutinize the country to "come to grips with the business of living here, and get a clearer picture, for better or worse." At the end of it all he felt that he had "learned a bit about Japan and a lot about myself."

I only wish that Alan Booth's daily distances had been recorded in ri, the traditional Japanese measurement, officially pegged at 3.927 kilometers.

> *One ri—as I came to know in practice—was the distance that a man with a burden would aim to cover in an hour on mountain roads. The kilometer was invented for the convenience of machinery. The ri was an entirely human measure, which is why it had no chance of surviving. We tell the time in digits and bleeps, and distance is not distance if you can't divide it by ten.*

Hanawa is a town in the north of Honshu Island.

* * *

The road began to curve, though the land was flat and the mountains of Hachimantai reared up like a stage set. In the brief intervals between the torrents of rain, the layers of cloud that hovered round the mountains would rise and fall as though on pulleys. First the clouds would hide the peaks so that the mountains looked flat-topped like tables, then they would sink to hide the slopes and the peaks would jut up above the clouds like a landscape in a charcoal painting. When the rain ceased, the light had the chilling quality of old silver, but when the rain came on again it smothered everything—the peaks, the clouds, the distant farms. I sheltered for an hour in someone's back shed and scooted on again to find a grocer's shop where I sat, sodden, eating apples while the thunder drove the grocer's children frantic.

In a lull I reached the town of Hanawa. It was a little after midday. I ate lunch in a restaurant where the walls were covered with posters announcing a festival, and the restaurant owner stamped about, cursing the rain and worrying that the festival would be canceled.

"You mean it's today?"

"Today and tomorrow."

"Here?"

"Over towards the station." The owner squinted at me from behind the counter. "You mean to say that's not what you've come for?"

"I'd no idea."

The owner scoffed. "There's no other damn reason to come here. You might at least stay for that."

I needed no persuading. The weather was foul to walk in and the prospect of a festival—however threatened—was the perfect excuse for a dry afternoon. I took a room in a ryokan near the station, hung my dripping clothes over an oil stove, and spent a couple of hours sprawled on tatami mats, sipping green tea and listening to the thunder ripple across the valley.

By early evening the rain had stopped and I strolled out of the ryokan to find the road in front of the station transformed into an open-air bazaar. It was lined with dozens of pink-draped stalls, all hung with red-and-white paper lanterns, selling fireworks, goldfish, stag beetles, terrapins, candyfloss, robot masks, octopus, and ginger. There were rifle ranges and hoopla stands, and in a shelter between the pumps of a petrol station sat six or seven policemen with megaphones, sipping tea and trying not to look enthused. Beyond the stalls, on the main street of the town, was a collection of large wooden platforms on wheels, and on each of the platforms stood a huge *taiko* drum. Hordes of young children in bright summer yukatas were clambering over the platforms and beating the drums with curved wooden sticks. Out of the shops and houses flocked the fathers—firemen, bank clerks, postmen, farmers—dressed either in yukatas or in white shorts and the belted blue tunics called *happi*. There was mayhem as the fathers tried to wrest the drumsticks from their wriggling sons, and the noise of the drums and the screams and the laughter had reached a climax when the downpour began again.

It fell without thunder but it fell as solidly as it had fallen for most of the day, and the cries of the children when their mothers scuttled forward to drag them off the streets mingled with the curses of their fathers as they swarmed onto the platforms and struggled to haul tarpaulins over the drums. The tarpaulins were sodden and heavy with a day's rain and the drums were twice the height of a man.

I fled into the first dry space I could see—a canvas tent that turned out to be the festival organizers' headquarters. The organizers sat behind a row of trestle tables, scowling at the rain, complaining to their wives, and drinking large quantities of beer. We gaped at each other for a few seconds, till I was invited to sit down at one of the tables and submit to beer and questions.

"What do you think of festivals?"

"I like them when it doesn't rain."

For a long moment my presence was ignored.

"That is to say, I like them anyway. Especially festivals in small towns."

An organizer topped up my glass.

"I like festivals where tourists are not important, festivals where they'd just as soon tourists didn't come. The festivals I've seen in large cities like Kyoto and Kanazawa seemed mainly for the benefit of the tourist trade, whereas a festival in a small town like this one is an event for working people and their families. That," I continued, growing radical, "is what a festival ought to be, not an annual bonus for some travel agent."

This heady speech earned me a plate of salami and a bottle of beer I was allowed to pour myself.

"And what do you think of Akita *bijin?*"

Akita is famous for its beautiful women (*bijun*), a fact that I had noted long ago and tended to dismiss as a partisan myth until, wandering about the streets of Hanawa in the rain, I found that my mouth kept dropping open and that I was devoting about a quarter of one eye to the taiko drums.

"My daughter is a *bijin*," an elderly festival organizer chuckled. "She's twenty-four."

"How very nice . . ."

"It's a pity she's married. You could have married her."

His wife, I supposed, was the woman choking in the corner. His daughter stayed wisely out of sight. And before I could ask about nieces and distant cousins, the rain stopped as suddenly as it had started, and the organizers packed me off to the station square where "the real festival," they said, was about to commence.

In the station square stood eighteen of the wooden platforms in a semicircle facing the gathering crowd. Nine of the platforms supported taiko drums, and on the other nine stood rectangular paper lanterns, all taller by half than the massive taiko, and lit from inside by candles so that the red-and-gold hand-painted pictures on them glowed and flickered with life. Some were of heroes from the Kabuki theater with masses of black hair, white-and-blue faces, and bright scarlet eyes. Others were of feudal warriors, grimacing under fierce horned helmets. On some, the warriors were locked in combat, a tangle of long white-bladed swords and black, glinting halberds. On others, a single warrior rode in arrogant splendor, his horse's jaws a mass of foam, his armor bristling with arrows.

The nine drums thundered in unison, pounded by the fathers now, not the sons. Each drum required two men to beat it, and they hammered out a single rhythm that had already reached a powerful crescendo and was still mounting as the noise and excitement of the crowd mounted with it. Sweat poured off the faces of the drummers and the trails of it glistened in the light of the candles. So violently did they hurl themselves at the drums, and so powerfully did each stroke take its toll on the whole body, that a man could not play for more than three or four minutes before stumbling away, as another took his place, and collapsing on a bench to tip cold sakè down his throat and bury his face in a towel.

The taiko is an instrument that demands more than technique. It is an obstinate instrument. It will resist and resist the drift of the music until the sheer energy of the man who plays it at last excites the god in the drum, and the rhythms then flow naturally from him till his arms grow weak with exhaustion. The wise player circumvents the drum's resistance by taking so much sakè into his body that the god in the drum has no alternative but to assume command at the outset.

I have to suppose that the god in the drum can also read minds, for as I moved in and out of the crowd, past the lanterns and the benches and the crates of bottles, a young man wearing a white plastic raincoat came up and thrust a paper cup of sakè into my hand and asked me if I would like to play. I said that I would, but that I would require more sakè. More sakè came. The crowd around us began to bubble. Three drummers offered me the use of their sticks, and after I had drained a third paper cup I took my place by the side of a drum and waited for the right-hand drummer to tire. Then, when my turn came, I stepped up to the drum, saluted it with the sticks, and whacked it.

The crowd went silly. "Look at this! Look at this! A gaijin! A gaijin playing the taiko!" Flash guns went off, crates were upended, parents pushed their children forward and craned their necks and stamped and clapped, and I felt the sakè curl in my stomach and grinned at the drummer on the left of the drum, a middle-aged man who said "Yah!" and grinned back, and the god in the drum was kind to us both.

I have no idea how long I played. Twice the left-hand drummer changed and twice the drumsticks slipped out of my hands. When I came away I was drenched in sweat, and I sat on a bench with a towel round my head, guzzling sakè and laughing like an idiot.

They had seen me from the ryokan windows, and when I got back, they danced about the entrance hall while I beat the floor with a pair of slippers. Then they ushered me into the front parlor where a college professor in a suit and spectacles presented me with his namecard and commenced to give us all a lecture.

"You see, the festival is a Tanabata festival and so it has its origins in eighth-century China where it commemorated the annual union of the two stars Altair and Vega. Up to the nineteenth century . . ."

Someone had poured me a cup of sakè.

"Up to the nineteenth century the festival was celebrated on the seventh night of the seventh month, but when Japan adopted the Gregorian calendar Tanabata was incorporated into the general celebrations of August. The Nebuta lanterns of Aomori . . ."

"Excuse me, professor . . . ," I said, grinning inanely while the parlor audience held its breath, ". . . but have you ever played the sakè after three cups of drum?"

The professor expressed his puzzlement.

"I mean to say," I said, attempting a northern dialect to hisses of delight, "have you ever played the taiko after drinking three cups of sakè?"

The professor admitted that he never had.

"The professor knows an awful lot about festivals," said the mistress of the ryokan, beside herself with joy.

In the streets the fathers were lighting fireworks for their sons. I felt happy for the firework sellers, who were the only stallkeepers that had not been doing a brisk trade. In the bath, when I let my ears sink under the water, the water throbbed to the rhythm of the drums, and when I got out of the bath and stood drying on the mat, my hands were still tapping out the rhythm on the windowsill. It was a long time before I could get to sleep, but I didn't mind. That night I knew an awful lot about festivals.

Oliver Statler

Japanese Pilgrimage

Religious pilgrimages have ever been associated with walking, whether the hajji's encirclement of the Kaaba in Mecca or the English pilgrim's walk to the shrine of St. Thomas à Becket at Canterbury. Japan has an extraordinary route that roughly traces the mountainous circumference of Shikoku Island, Japan's fourth largest. Almost a thousand miles long, this pilgrimage honors Kobo Daishi, the founder and saint of a major sect of Japanese Buddhism named Shingon. The Daishi lived from 774 to 835 and was acknowledged in China as the master of Esoteric Buddhism, which he imported to and adapted in Japan. His teachings emphasized the welcome idea that enlightenment is possible in this life.

The Shikoku pilgrimage commemorates the Daishi's travels about his home island; its route visits mountains, passes, farmlands, and coastlines. Eighty-four legend-rich temples enrich the journey of the henro (pilgrim).

Beginning in 1968 an American named Oliver Statler made the Shikoku tour several times. In his delightful book Japanese Pilgrimage *(1983), he suggests that the core experience of Buddhism is not a liturgy or belief system but the Path, surely an excellent metaphor for what we do as distance walkers.*

> There are pilgrimages all over the world. In most, one travels to a place or places hallowed by events that took place there. One goes; one reaches one's goal; one returns. There are pilgrimages in India that follow a spiral route, moving around a mountain in a narrowing circle, gradually approaching the summit, the goal. But this Shikoku pilgrimage is the only pilgrimage I know of that is essentially a circle. It has no beginning and no end. Like the quest for enlightenment, it is unending.

* * *

The evening that we spent at Ashizuri and Temple Thirty-eight brought to a close an especially fine day: sunny, warm, and very clear. After supper we walked again to the cliff to face the sea that holy men sailed into, seeking Kannon's Fudaraku. The only clouds were the vapor trails of training jets, marking the darkening sky with long calligraphic strokes. The moon was a slender crescent that would hold water. We remarked on the long spell of beautiful weather we had enjoyed.

Perhaps we should learn not to do that. During the night I became aware of a growling wind. When we rise the weather has changed around: it is gray, chilly, and blowing a gale.

But the road is pleasant, narrow and little used, bordered on our right by woods and our left by the rocky coast, pounded today by a somber sea.

The rain holds off until late morning, a few splatters and then a downpour. If we were bright we would stop for the day. Instead we walk on along something more river than road until two compassionate foresters stop and give us a lift to the next town, where some concerned and friendly folk find a place for us at an inn that has gone out of business but is willing to take us in. When we go to bed the storm is still at it. Sheets of rain and blasts of wind slam the old house: it trembles and groans.

But in the morning the sun is out. We skirt a coast guarded by bastions of black rock. The ocean heaves and smashes at them, still seething from yesterday's storm. A few fishermen in rowboats looking small and vulnerable ride the swells, rising and falling, appearing and disappearing. On a beach a woman digging for clams is eyed by a hawk that soars above her. Landward are black crows and black butterflies and mountains of black rock touched with spring's green.

But the wind—it fights us every step of the way. Gripping my sedge hat I watch a bird fly into it and lose headway. At my feet a woolly caterpillar is picked up and blown from the macadam. Conversation is impossible; words are torn from our lips and scattered.

At the head of each narrow bay we thread the lanes of a fishing village. At the last one that shows on our maps we stop for lunch. It is too small to have a restaurant but we find a food shop tended by a smiling woman from her bright kitchen overlooking it. We buy half a dozen eggs and cheerfully she boils them for us. We buy a package of bread; she loans us her toaster and insists on giving us butter. We buy a can of peaches and eat them from her dishes.

Soon we leave the coast and climb into the hills. Deep in the forest we find the bangai we have been looking for. In Shinnen's time Moon-Mountain Temple, it is today Moon-Mountain Shrine. Here is an institution that weathered the separation of Shinto and Buddhism without catching its breath. The priest of those days simply changed from Buddhist to Shinto robes and continued to perform the same services he always had. He preserved his institution, kept it open.

Perhaps he was able to do this because he was a long distance from the castle town and fief headquarters, perhaps because this place always had a strong Shinto flavor, perhaps because he was the kind of man he was. Other Buddhist priests tried it; some went insane, some committed suicide.

But here is Moon-Mountain Shrine, maintained by his descendant, an elderly man retired from teaching. He tells us that the central altar enshrines the same object it did in Buddhist days, a sacred stone with the shape and the glow of the moon half at the wane; he implies that the people pray more often at a small chapel dedicated to the Daishi. He seems pleased to see us: one henro came last year; we are the first this year (only April 29 and traffic has already doubled).

The next day we reach Temple Thirty-nine, the last in Tosa. Quiet, rural, it possesses a national treasure, a bell cast in 911 at a temple called Miroku. The priest says there has never been a Miroku Temple on Shikoku, and he supposes it was cast in Nara or Kyoto. Legend says it was brought here from the palace of the Dragon King of the Sea by a great red turtle that rose, bell on back, from a pool formed by a spring the Daishi had brought forth. For a moment I wonder whether this tale might signify that the bell was recovered from the wreck of a boat that sank offshore. But I put this thought out of my mind: here in the compound for all to see is the pool, and the turtle is memorialized in red concrete.

The priest escorts us a few hundred yards to the innermost altar. We pass a lone farmer scything a field of wheat and come to a flooded field with a crop we have seen in both Awa and Tosa but could not identify: clumps of slender green grasses like long pine needles. The priest tells us that they are the reeds that are woven to make the covers of tatami mats. Now they are about as high as the wheat the farmer is harvesting but they will grow almost as tall as a man. The seedlings are transplanted in the coldest season and the reeds are harvested in the hottest. They used to be grown almost exclusively in Okayama Prefecture but they do not tolerate contamination: pollution on the other side of the Inland Sea has brought this crop to Shikoku.

Hanging inside the little chapel are large red banners, many of them, each bearing the name, age, and address of someone whose prayers to the Yakushi of this temple have been attended by recovery from illness. Outside are dozens—no, hundreds—of little flags, red and white, planted in the ground, signifying the same blessing. "There are innumerable stories of cures," the priest murmurs, "from tuberculosis, blindness, paralysis—but the stories are no different. I suppose, from those of any other temple."

He reflects. "To intellectuals, religion seems strange. But the point of the religious life is mental and spiritual training, and that cannot be achieved by oneself. We need help from some source like Buddha or Kobo Daishi or Yakushi." He considers us. "The point of the pilgrimage is to improve oneself by enduring and overcoming difficulties."

Now we leave Tosa. In the old days there was just one authorized exit, a mountain pass called Pine Tree Ascent right on the border between Tosa and Iyo. There is always something significant about crossing a pass. A scholar has noted that the Japanese word for "mountainpass" originates from a verb meaning "to offer," "because travelers always had to offer something to the god of the pass as a prayer for safe journey (a custom also seen in Korea, Mongolia, and Tibet). . . . There are many instances where large mounds have accumulated from the offerings of small stones."

At Pine Tree Ascent was a barrier gate. There was a flood of Tosa edicts, one every three or four years for more than two centuries, stipulating that it was the only point where travelers might cross the long border with Iyo. Of course henro who had entered Tosa by evading the barrier gate at the other side of the province had no choice but to try to evade Pine Tree Ascent—and, if caught, suffer being flogged or branded or both before being forcibly ejected.

Tosa guards also became unpleasant if outgoing henro had overstayed their authorized thirty days, while they doggedly examined incoming henro—those performing the pilgrimage in reverse order—to screen out spies, rogues, vagabonds, jugglers, minstrels, and monkey trainers.

Many henro of those times, on leaving this province where they felt so abused, would squat with their backs to it and augment the memorial to "the Devil's Land," a quite different offering from the usual one at a pass. Writing in 1927, Alfred Bohner reported that the Dung Monument no longer existed but that vegetation grew very rank where it had.

On a contrasting note, praise was lavished on the prospect from the summit: "The entire bay of Sukumo stretched before me: its countless islands, its bizarre tongues of land, its winding arms of the sea." And, "Kyushu was within reach of my staff while the towering mountains of Iyo lay at my feet." That 1819 henro from Tosa here surrendered his exit permit and received a new pass permitting him to reenter at the other side of the province. Then, overcome by the view and sentiment at leaving his home country, he composed a haiku before continuing.

For years I did not attempt Pine Tree Ascent, having been assured by presumably knowledgeable folk on both sides of the pass that the path no longer existed, that it had disintegrated and disappeared completely when a new road was built around the mountain instead of over it. But I have learned to distrust such advice and I was haunted by the feeling that I should try to find the old path. Last year, walking with friends in the heat of summer when the dirt and roar of traffic on the highway seemed almost intolerable, I suggested that I was willing to risk losing some hours in the search if they were. We struck off into the countryside toward the hills.

Trying from our maps to figure the best approach, we began to climb along a little wooded road. Around a curve we found an old man, comfortably stripped down to some baggy cotton trousers, with a cart that had started life as a baby buggy. In it were a couple of mats to sit on and something to eat and drink. I am sure he was up there for peace and quiet away from his family. He told us we were on the wrong road; we should start from the village where he lived and he led us back.

In the village he turned us over to a farmer who said that yes indeed, the path still existed, and pointed to the ridgeline high above. "That's the border between Tosa and Iyo," he said. "On this side the path is good, but on the Iyo side it's not well maintained," and he started us out.

It *was* a good path, only a bit overgrown. The weeds had been cut back not much earlier but thistles had already sprung up and were nettlesome. As we gained altitude we began to get those belauded views, the coastline, islands, the strait between Shikoku and Kyushu. We had not gone far when a boy appeared at our heels, a smiling kid who fairly sprinted up the path wearing rubber sandals. Clearly the mountain was familar to him. When we began to find divergent paths and were unsure, we moved him up front. Someone murmured, not facetiously, that Kobo Daishi had appeared to guide us.

We had trouble only with the last hundred yards or so, where timber had recently been harvested and the path destroyed in the process, as usually happens; it takes a while for feet that know the mountain to mark the path again. We struggled up, mostly on all fours, but the ridgeline was so close there was no sense of being lost.

Once we gained the ridge all was easy again; through a break in the forest another sweeping view and then the pass. Two memorial stones, quite new, mark the site, but of the buildings that used to stand here—the barrier was a bit lower but up here were two teahouses (where everyone stopped to rest and where henro overtaken by darkness could spend the night) and a chapel enshrining a statue of the Daishi—nothing remains save a bit of stone wall.

I already knew the story of that Daishi. When the new road was built travelers over the pass became so few that the teahouses were abandoned, and about fifty years ago the people of a village on the Iyo side decided to bring the chapel down where they could care for it. A bit later a meeting hall was built nearby and the horses tethered there made the surroundings much too dirty for the Daishi. Finally the old men's club of the town at the foot of the mountain offered a suitable location and the villagers accepted gratefully. One of the members of the club has shown me to the little chapel that stands on the grounds of the chamber of commerce building, the town's social center. Inside was a crutch, offered by someone who no longer needed it; this Daishi, he told me, is renowned for its power to help cripples. And there was the image: a seated figure about two feet high, carved in sections— primitive art with simple strength.

Once we achieved the pass we sat to rest like thousands of henro before us, and pulled from our packs some of the snacks we always carried. The boy, having delivered us, vanished just when we wanted to share our food with him, but almost immediately the farmer who had set us on the path appeared. "I saw that you were having difficulty," he said, "so I hurried up to help." He sat with us in the little clearing, chatting and eating, until we started down into Iyo. He had been wrong about only one thing: on the Tosa side it was certainly a good path, except for that last short stretch, but on the Iyo side it was even better—clean, often shaded, and with lovely views of the mountains and valleys. Unfortunately it ended where a great gash had been cut in the slope to build a new highway, and we had to inch our way down to the road.

And so Morikawa and I, now that we know the path exists, cross the border from Tosa to Iyo over Pine Tree Ascent as henro should. In the town we find a comfortable inn and then we go to pray before the Daishi. Presently we are relaxing in a hot bath. As we are finishing our dinner and it is growing dark, two new guests, young men, limp past the open doors of our room. They are so evidently footsore that Morikawa grins in sympathy. "Henro," he says.

After they have bathed and dined we call on them. The older, whom I guess to be in his thirties, does the talking. He tells us that he works in an office in Osaka. Year before last he began his pilgrimage and he has continued it every time he could get a few days' holiday. Sometimes the younger chap has accompanied him, sometimes not. They have walked the pilgrimage not in sequence but choosing a section according to the time available. (Japanese employees are granted a week or two of annual holiday but few consider it within the work ethic to take it.)

We are now in the midst of what is called Golden Week: seven days that include three holidays—April 29, the Emperor's birthday; May 3, Constitution Day, celebrating the new constitution; and May 5, the ancient festival of Boys' Day (now given the unisex name Children's Day). By using the weekend and taking one day off from work, these two have given themselves five days. They traveled all last night to make an early start this morning. They have today walked more than forty miles, and worshiped at Temple Forty along the way. We admit that to us such a walk seems almost impossible, and the spokesman grimaces and says they don't waste time; they maintain a fast pace and they even walk while they eat.

By walking a hundred and fifty miles more and worshiping at the three temples along the way, the older will close the last gap: he will complete his pilgrimage on this holiday and he will have walked every foot of the way. We admire him for that and tell him so. He says that he enjoys walking and he needs exercise and release from the tensions of the office. They both envy our being able to do the pilgrimage all at once and in so leisurely a manner; they make us feel privileged.

As we are saying good night he asks whether we have heard that a man at the unlucky age of forty-two should make the pilgrimage. He does not look that old . . . is he thinking of his next pilgrimage?

Lawrence Durrell

Letter to Henry Miller on Walks with George Katsimbalis

In The Colossus of Maroussi, *the American novelist Henry Miller tells of meeting Greek storyteller George Katsimbalis in pre-war Greece and of trying to sell him on Sherwood Anderson, "the one American writer of our time who has walked the streets of our American cities as a genuine poet." Since the Greek hadn't heard of Anderson, Miller spoke passionately "about writers who walk the streets in America and are not recognized until they are ready for the grave."*

The friendship that developed between the American and the Greek led in 1941 to Miller's The Colussus of Maroussi, *in which Katsimbalis has "the general physique of a bull, the tenaciousness of a vulture, the agility of a leopard, the tenderness of a lamb, and the coyness of a dove."*

After the war a mutual friend, British novelist Lawrence Durrell, returned to Athens and sent news to Miller of his walks with the war-weary but undefeated Katsimbalis. "I walked beside the Colossus in a daze," wrote Durrell, "listening to his great voice filling in the span of years that had separated us with stories of all they had passed through."

* * *

MOI, BMA, Rhodes, MEF

[February 1946]

Henry my dear:

I have just spent a week in Athens and am still bewildered by the warmth of my reception there, both from those I knew, and from all those unlikely people whose existence I had forgotten: the Institute porter, a girl student, the kiosk man from whom I bought the paper and a pack of cigarettes every day, Andrew in whose little bar we drank so often. For the first day I was in a whirlwind of embraces and tears and kisses. And most wonderful of all, most mysterious, was that Athens was under deep snow: purple and bistre shadows under the Acropolis, steamy breath of oxen and men. I walked beside the Colossus in a daze listening to his great voice filling in the span of years that had separated us with stories of all they had passed through. Neither Katsimbalis nor Seferis have changed—though the world has changed a good deal round them. Athens is unbelievably sad, crowded, ill-housed, with money practically worthless and prices soaring: and yet in some singular way what they have gone through has made them gentle and friendly and sympathetic to each other as they have never been before. Even in George, behind the tremendous effervescence, you feel a repose and resignation—as of someone who has faced death in his imagination for a long time, so that it has detached him from ordinary life—which is only after all the joy of expectation. Yet the stories are more wonderful than ever. When I next write I will tell you the story of Palamas' funeral—at which George suddenly shouted insults at the German embassy representative who was laying a wreath on the tomb, and began to sing the national anthem, then forbidden under pain of death. "Like a man in a nightmare . . . yes . . . ten thousand people . . . no one would sing . . . my voice broke on the top notes . . . eyes bulged . . . finished the first verse alone amidst a terrified silence of the crowd . . . I was trembling all over . . . Aspasia trying to shut me up . . . Seferis' sister pulling my arm . . . felt as if I had gone mad, quite mad . . . Terrific hush in the crowd and everywhere people whispering, 'By God, it's Katsimbalis . . . it's Katsimbalis . . .' I started the second verse alone . . . not a voice raised to help me . . . German looking round angrily . . . felt like a drowning man in the middle of that huge crowd . . . Then over opposite me saw a fat Corfiot friend of mine . . . fat man but a big rich voice . . . He joined in and we finished the second verse together . . . Then suddenly as if you had thrown a switch the roar of the crowd took it up and we sang it with tears running down our faces . . ." Of course after this demonstration George was in danger of being shot and was terrified for some time. His description of hiding here and there is very funny. And of course there are other wonderful stories. But I feel that in some peculiar way Athens is very sad and exhausted at the moment. Write to George Katsimbalis, care of the British Council, Kiphissia Road, Athens, and to Seferis, Political Adviser to the Regent, The Regency, Kiphissia Road, Athens. Send them books, any and every kind. And if you have a few pounds from time to time send it to George to use at his own discretion to help Greek poets: many of them are starving, Sekilianos among them. I saw the little captain Antoniou too—he has been through it, though he is as silent and smiling as ever. I'm afraid you will have to give Athens a year or two to settle down politically etc. before you can think of going there. But keep in touch and don't be worried if they don't write; they are working sixteen hours a day and meet only rarely. But the intellectual hunger is terrific . . .

Love to you three,
Larry

Eric Newby

On the Shores of the Mediterranean

Among all the scams and dodges of impoverished post-war Naples, none would be more bizarre to serious walkers today than the scarpe scompagnate *and no service more welcome than that of the* solchanello. *This account is from Newby's 1984 book,* On the Shores of the Mediterranean.

* * *

Until recently there were *solchanelli*, mobile shoe repairers. A *solchanello* carried the tools of his trade in a basket with a board on top which he used as a seat on which he could squat down anywhere and begin work. Uttering a strange cry, *"Chià-è! Chià-è!,"* to attract attention, he would sometimes latch onto some unfortunate person with a hole in one of his shoes or a sole coming off and follow him, sometimes for miles, all the while reminding the victim of the defect in an insistent monotone until whoever it was, unable to stand it any more, sank down in despair on the nearest doorstep and allowed the *solchanello* to carry out the repair.

In Naples the loss of one of a pair of shoes does not necessarily mean that the other will not have a long and useful life ahead of it, even if it is not sold to some unfortunate person with only one leg. It is still possible to find what are known as *scarpe scompagnate*, unaccompanied shoes, in the great market for new and second-hand shoes, which, weather permitting, takes place every Monday and Friday in Corso Malta, an interminable, dead-straight street that runs northwards from the Carcere Guidizario on Via Nuove Poggioreale to Doganella, at the foot of the hill where the cemeteries begin.

Few people, even Napoletani, buy one shoe. Some, however, can be persuaded to buy two shoes which do not match. Luccano de Crescenza recorded a conversation in dialect between a potential buyer of two odd shoes and a vendor of *scarpe scompagnate* which went more or less as follows:

"But these shoes are different, one from the other!"

"No signuri, so tale e quale—they are exactly alike!"

"Well, they look different to me."

"And what does it matter if they look different? That's only when you're standing still. Once you start walking they will look exactly the same—*tale e quale*. Let me tell you about shoes. What do they do, shoes? They walk. And when they walk one goes in front and the other goes behind, like this. In this way no one can know that they are not *tale e quale*."

"But that means I can never stop walking."

"How does it mean you can't ever stop walking? All you have to do when you stop is to rest one shoe on top of the other."

Agnes Smedley
Long March Veterans

The Chinese Communist Long March of 1934–36 is one of the greatest mass hikes in recorded history. Of the 86,000 people who began the escape from Nationalist encirclement in southern China, only 4,000 managed to walk the full 6,000 miles through western China and around north to Beijing. Mao Zedong's forces had to cross twenty-four rivers and eighteen mountain ranges while fighting for their lives. Survivors whom Agnes Smedley recorded in The Great Road *(1956) told of waist deep mud on the Great Snow Mountain and of Fan warriors who rolled boulders off mountainsides onto the Communist Chinese marchers.*

*   *   *

A political worker with whom I talked said he thought the worst mountain to cross was Kuchow, which was not so high as others but was completely covered with forests so dense that they shut out all light. The troops climbed this mountain in a pouring rain, wading in mud up to their hips and pulling themselves out by the branches of trees.

"After that," the man continued, "the Chiachinshan range was the worst—most of our comrades thought it was the worst of all. When we came to it we had already crossed many mountains and many of our men were exhausted. Before crossing, General Chu Teh made an inspection of every unit, looking at our shoes, lifting packs to test the weight, inquiring about everyone's health, and instructing medical units to march in the rear to care for exhausted or older people who fell behind. He encouraged us to put forth every effort.

"Chiachinshan is blanketed in eternal snow. There are great glaciers in its chasms and everything is white and silent. We were heavily burdened because each man had to carry enough food and fuel to last ten days. Our food was anything we could buy—chiefly corn, though we had a little buckwheat and some peppers. We carried our food in long cloth pouches over our shoulders. General Chu carried his food like everyone else. He had a horse but he gave it to sick or wounded men to ride.

"We would not have suffered so much, or had such heavy losses in life, if we had been able to buy rice. The change from rice to a corn diet gave our men diarrhea and other stomach disorders. The corn passed straight through them—they couldn't digest it at all. Another torment was lice. Wherever we slept in the huts of the people, the lice seemed to come up out of the earthen floor to settle on us. Everybody had lice, everybody hunted lice."

Of all the men who talked of crossing Chiachinshan, however, Tung Piwu seemed the most graphic. A learned man of fifty, Mr. Tung was one of the earliest Communists. In describing the crossing of Chiachinshan, he said:

"We started out at early dawn. There was no path at all, but peasants said that tribesmen came over the mountains on raids, and we could cross if they could. So we started straight up the mountain, heading for a pass near the summit. Heavy fogs swirled about us, there was a high wind, and halfway up it began to rain. As we climbed higher and higher we were caught in a terrible hailstorm and the air became so thin that we could hardly breathe at all. Speech was completely impossible and the cold so dreadful that our breath froze and our hands and lips turned blue. Men and animals staggered and fell into chasms and disappeared forever. Those who sat down to rest or to relieve themselves froze to death on the spot. Exhausted political workers encouraged men by sign and touch to continue moving, indicating that the pass was just ahead.

"By nightfall we had crossed, at an altitude of 16,000 feet, and that night we bivouacked in a valley where there was no sign of human life. While most of us were stretched out exhausted, General Chu came around to make his usual inspection. He was very weary, for he had walked with the troops. Yet nothing ever prevented him from making his rounds. He gave me half of a little dried beef which he had in his pocket. He encouraged everyone and said we had crossed the worst peak and it was only a few more days to Moukung.

"To avoid enemy bombers, we arose at midnight and began climbing the next peak. It rained, then snowed, and the fierce wind whipped our bodies, and more men died of cold and exhaustion.

"The last peak in the range, which we estimated to be eighty li (twenty-seven miles) from base to summit, was terrible. Hundreds of our men died there. They would sit down to rest or relieve themselves, and never get up. All along the route we kept reaching down to pull men to their feet only to find that they were already dead.

"When we finally reached a valley and found a cluster of tribal houses, we gathered around and rejoiced at the mere sight of human habitation. The tribespeople had fled because we were Chinese, and centuries of cruel oppression had engendered in them fear and hatred of every Chinese. We had a number of Lolo tribesmen with us, but they also could not understand the tribal language in these areas.

"I lost track of time, but I think it was middle or late June when we finally reached a broad valley dotted with many tribal villages of huts or black yourts made of yak wool. Here were great fields of barley, two breeds of wheat, millet and peas, and herds of pigs, yak, sheep, and goats. We established such friendly relations as we could with the tribespeople and bought food from them. We paid for our food with national currency.

"By that time we had so many sick and exhausted men that our main forces decided to rest for a week while Peng Teh-huai led eleven regiments ahead to establish contact with our Fourth Front Red Army in the Moukung, Lianghokow, Lifan, and Maosien districts. The Fourth Front Red Army had occupied these areas for a number of months, but there were still many mountains and rivers to cross before we reached it. The mountains were not so terrible as those behind us, but the whole territory ahead was peopled with fierce Fan tribes who fought every step of our advance."

One of the political workers who went with Peng's vanguards told this story:

"For four days we fought Fan tribesmen in the Black Water River region and finally reached a shabby little village called Weiku. The people had evacuated and destroyed the rope suspension bridge over the river. They took up positions on high, precipitous cliffs directly behind Weiku and rolled huge boulders down the mountainside against us. Peng had to send troops to drive them away.

"Everywhere from the cliffs and mountains we heard the tribal horns calling men to battle: WUNG-G-G-G! WUNG-G-G-G! WUNG-G-G-G-G-G-G!

"Our troops had begun building a pontoon bridge when we saw a column of armed men coming down from the hills on the far shore, running and shouting, but the roar of the river was so great that we could not hear them. One of them wrapped a message around a stone and hurled it across to us. It read:

'We're Fourth Front Red Army troops. Forty li up the river at Inien is a rope suspension bridge where you can cross.'

"On the way to Inien we passed through empty tribal villages where the Fan tribesmen again hurled boulders down from overhanging cliffs. The river at Inien was wider than at Weiku and the rope suspension bridge had been destroyed. Again we saw marching men, and when they reached the bank a Fan guide who was with them threw a message across the river to us. It was from Hsu Hsiang-chien.

"We all marched back to Weiku where our engineers constructed a pontoon bridge and we crossed the Black Water River and united with our comrades. We embraced, we sang and wept."

Norman Mailer

The Armies of the Night

In October 1967 the first of the anti-Vietnam War mass marches con-
verged on the Pentagon across the Potomac River from Washington,
D.C. Among the hippies, students, and other youth were celebrities
such as critic Dwight Macdonald, poet Robert Lowell, and novelist
Norman Mailer, who "were requested to get up in the front row, where
the notables were to lead the March, a row obviously to be consecrated
for the mass media."

In this first century of "media events," the March on the Pentagon
was a classic drama played out for the press. "Newsreel, still, and
television cameras were clicking and rounding and snapping and zoom-
ing before the first rank was even formed."

* * *

It had been a particularly onerous wait for the Critic, the Poet, and
the Novelist. They had talked to people, met people, chatted with other
notables like Sidney Lens and Monsignor Rice of Pittsburgh (to whom Lowell
had confessed with an enigmatic smile that he was now a "lapsed Catholic,"
a remark which brought no rush of sympathy from the priest, more a thought-
ful non-approving grunt) they had lolled about in the sun, watched the Black
contingent drift off in an Oriental scramble of secret signals, had passed
around chocolate bars in lieu of lunch, Mailer refusing a bite (he had the
uncharacteristic conviction he must not eat or drink until the March was
over, or he would spoil the now undeniable clarity and sweet anticipation
of his nerves) and had finally contented each other with wry twists of the
eyebrow at the interminable tedium of the speeches. No use to tell oneself
that the people who spoke had worked hard to prepare this March, and so
were entitled to their reward. Bugger all reward. Half the troops would
desert if the speeches went on. (And in fact half the troops did—no telling
how many more would have set out if the invitation to move to the Pentagon
had followed the noontime exhilaration of the music.) Mailer, of course, had
been preparing an extempore speech for the odd chance they might call on
him; he would have liked to address fifty or one hundred thousand people:

the beginning of a twenty year war is here today in our March, he might have said, rising to the occasion—but the call never came, which did little to improve his patience.

Well, finally they were now set to go. The March was to begin on a road which separated the upper and lower levels of steps at Lincoln Memorial, and debauched in about two hundred feet onto the Arlington Memorial Bridge, a span some half-mile long which was to lead to a traffic circle on the Virginia side—how better to know one has crossed the border from one state to another than by encountering a traffic circle? Then they would strike out to the Pentagon. Mailer, of course, knew little of this yet—he was certainly too nearsighted to see that far ahead, and much too vain to wear his eyeglasses before hundreds of Leicas and Nikons and Exactas in the hands of professional photographers. No, rather he stood in the makings of the front line of notables (which was having as much trouble being formed as the makings in a cigarette put together by an amateur cowboy.) Notables kept being crowded into the second rank by notables less notable than themselves, so they made great efforts to get back to the front rank which promptly buckled. Then upstarts and arrivistes tried to infiltrate the flanks of this front line which naturally created a tangle. At least sixty people were trying to get into a front line which was not wide enough for forty. It was not unlike the squeeze at a football game—whoever cheers most and sits down last has no seat. Next the order was passed—still impossible to move out—to link arms. Mailer's arm was promptly taken by Sid Lens, an old radical leader from the Fellowship of Reconciliation, who had the red meaty face and cunning look of a man who has been in many a trade union harangue, war, stampede, and squeeze-out over the years, and has lasted, sir, has lasted like one of those tough-skinned balloons with a lead bottom which always spring up when you strike them. If a Committee from the Feature Formers Guild of Heaven had been given instructions to design a face which was halfway in appearance between Sidney Lens and Robert Lowell, they might have come up with Norman Mailer; stationed between Lens and Lowell he felt the separate halves of his nature well-represented; which gave little pleasure, for no American citizen likes to link arms at once with the two ends of his practical working-day good American schizophrenia. So Mailer managed in the general wrestling, buckling, and staggering of the line to work around to the other side of Lowell, and leave to Lens the cartel of being stationed between Lowell and Macdonald—which is probably what Lens had wanted from the beginning, and was why, old pirate of union negotiations, he had chosen to begin in the first place with Mailer. (Modern politics may be built on the art of attaining specific ends by requesting others.)

At any rate, despite all strainings and waverings, the ranks began to form behind the first rank, and a hollow square of young Mobilization monitors formed up ahead of the leading rank of notables in order to sweep like a plug or a piston along the bridge, thus keeping infiltrators from passing the flanks and destroying the front of the March, but the notables in consequence were shifted down from the forwardmost line to what was now no more than the third line, to Mailer's disappointment, for he had been pleased to be in the front rank, in fact had fought doggedly to keep position there, anticipating at the end of the March a confrontation face to face with the eyes of soldiers guarding an entrance to the Pentagon, and thought if his head was to be busted this day, let it be before the eyes of America's TV viewers tonight.

Besides, back in the third row, the danger from behind was no longer to be disregarded. After fifteen minutes of pushing, eddying, compressing, and decompressing from ranks, the March at last started up in a circus-full of performers, an ABC or CBS open convertible with a built-on camera platform was riding in privileged position five yards in front of them with TV executives, cameramen, and technicians hanging on, leaning out, off on their own crisis run as they crawled along in front. Two monitors kept working like cheerleaders through portable loudspeakers to dress the front rank, which kept billowing and shearing under the pulses of inertia and momentum from the ranks behind, and a troop of helicopters, maybe as many as eight or ten, went into action overhead, while ten to twenty cameramen, movie and still, walking backward, wheeling, swinging from flank to flank, danced in the hollow square.

Picture then this mass, bored for hours by speeches, not elated at the beginning of the March, now made irritable by delay, now compressed, all old latent pips of claustrophobia popping out of the crush, and picture them as they stepped out toward the bridge, monitors in the lead, hollow square behind, next the line of notables with tens, then hundreds of lines squeezing up behind, helicopters overhead, police gunning motorcycles, cameras spinning their gears like the winging of horseflies, TV car bursting seams with hysterically overworked technicians, sun beating overhead—this huge avalanche of people rumbled forward thirty feet and came to a stop in disorder, the lines behind breaking and warping and melding into themselves to make a crowd not a parade, and some jam-up at the front, just what no one knew, now they were moving again. Forty more feet. They stopped. At this rate it would take six hours to reach the Pentagon. And a murmur came up from behind of huge discontent, hot huge yet, huge in the potential of its discontent. "Let's get going," people in the front lines were calling out.

The monitors reformed the hollow square, maneuvering interlopers to the side with a maximum of politeness for the circumstances. Now again, the procession inched forward. The problem was at last apparent—it was to keep everybody from engorging the entrance to the bridge before the first ranks of the March were actually upon it.

During this delay, the notables came to be familiar with one monitor, a young pale Negro with a small portable battery-pack loudspeaker who kept addressing the line with sharp little commands, "Move up here, please; move back there now, will you now! Come on! Let's get it going. Follow me, keep my pace. No, stop! Stop right there!" The notables were getting raw recruit training: Dr. Spock and Janey Spock, Lens, Lowell, Mailer, Macdonald, Dellinger, Jerry Rubin—if the Negroes had left the March en masse, the exception here left behind was obviously embodying any desire for total representation of his people. A pale dirty cream in color, nobody could ever say he had lost his black—Mailer wasn't there to speak for the other notables, but *he* hadn't been ordered about so continuously since his first day in the Army. In fact, it was like old times on the Left when you took any Negro into the club that you could get. The white monitors for the Mobilization looked in the main to be college students, not unathletic, chosen where possible for their ability to handle the March with a minimum of force. (Such at least was their function for the March—later some were to be active at the Pentagon, some to be arrested.) But the pale Negro was no heroic paradigm of a noble African; rather he had a screeching birdlike voice which cut to the marrow of all good nerve, and the sort of conniving pimp's face which Midwestern bellboys used to develop by taking an extra dollar from the hotel whore. "Dress up that front line, there, dress it up, what's the matter with all of you? Come on, cooperate with me. Help me keep this thing moving right," he drilled through the loudspeaker like an angry hospital nurse dealing with some well-whipped orphans. But, in fact, they were not moving at this moment, just milling and filing. He had gone too far.

"Look here," said Lowell to the monitor in a no-nonsense voice, "we're perfectly willing to cooperate with you, but there's no need to yell and get officious. Be sensible."

This emptied the pale Negro's balloon. He was sensible for the rest of the March. Mailer was now admiring again the banker manqué in Lowell— no mean banker had been lost to Boston when Lowell put his hand to the pen.

Once again they began to move, once again the camera whirred, the television convertible crawled ahead, the helicopters hung above, motors chopping, motorcycles gargled in low gear, the hollow square stepped out on the bridge, and the line of notables, and the first ranks behind. For a hundred yards they moved in a slow uneven step, arms locked, advancing for ten paces, halting for five seconds, moving again, the shock and release of the stop, then the start, traveling in waves down the thick close-packed ranks—from above, from the helicopters, it must have looked like the pulsations in the progression of a caterpillar.

Then came a long halt. It went on for ten minutes. They were now a third of the way across the bridge with hundreds of ranks massed solidly behind them all the way back to the entrance of the bridge. There, a fearful congestion like a crowd trying to push out of a stadium exit and not succeeding, rather pressing in on people ahead, produced an urgency at the rear which began to make itself felt up front; underneath the tension of secretly wondering what they would do when they reached the Pentagon was now added the frustration of being unable to move! Full of excitement, not without fear, the crowd jammed upon the bridge were in danger of turning unruly. "Why don't we move? Why don't we just move ahead?" said a boy behind Mailer. He literally pushed against the line of notables, thus jamming into a professor named Donald Kalish, one of the leaders of the Mobilization. "I came here to get to the Pentagon," said the boy, "not to wait in line like this."

Something was wrong, Mailer decided. It would make sense to send provocateurs to start violence within the ranks on the bridge—the entire March could be lost, or spoiled, before it reached the Pentagon. "Let's get going," shouted the boy, "let's go. I don't want to be held up . . . I want to get to those soldiers at the Pentagon."

Yes, his voice had no real ring, Mailer decided, his dialogue was wrong. And to the mix of adrenaline in circulation, came another, one he did not like to feel arriving, for it left him tense if he could not use it: he was getting ready for a fight. He would of course not throw the first punch, not ever! that would be just what he would need for his reputation. To throw the punch which started the rumble which wrecked the March on the Pentagon! And every camera in town to pick up the action. No, Mailer was merely getting prepared for the kid to swing, and so covertly studying him. The kid was probably no fighter—his nose was too long and pointed for that; he had never caught anything on the nose, that was obvious, but still he had some kind of snap in him, he was confident of possessing something. Possibly he had a good left hook, probably good enough to drop a man if he caught him by surprise; then he would drive a kick into the ear—that might be his style. Mailer was full of adrenaline now—how fortunate his hangover was modest, or his brain would be left smoking like an electric hot plate.

"They're not going to hold me here," said the kid, looking ugly, again shoving into Kalish.

"Now, son, take it easy," said Kalish.

"What are they all, yellow?" screamed the kid. "Let's get going. That's what we're here for."

"Hey, let's not lose our cool," said Mailer in his imitation of Marlon Brando's voice in *The Wild One*. It was a fair imitation and often came to his larynx on the rip tide of adrenaline. But that was not the key to lock this kid up today.

"I want to move," said the boy.

"Why don't you join the monitors," said Kalish. It was a simple suggestion. The boy could hardly refuse. He left his spot and sauntered up ahead; soon he was in the line of sweepers. But the nascent general in Mailer was much annoyed, as if somehow he had been derelict in not holding the agent provocateur where he belonged, back at his own rank.

"It was the only thing to do," said Kalish. "The monitors will be able to handle him better than we can." Mailer felt a too generous portion of middle age in the communality Kalish had just granted him.

Richard Halliburton

The Royal Road to Romance

Escaping from the "dullness" and "futility" of Princeton undergraduate life, Richard Halliburton set out penniless around the world in the early 1920s, hungering for romantic vistas, peoples, and places. His insouciant accounts of youthful adventure have fascinated generations of dreamers. In The Royal Road To Romance *(1925), one of his treks was a 500-mile roundtrip to Ladakh, a province of Kashmir on the Tibetan side of the Himalayas.*

* * *

All the cooks in the city [Srinagar, Kashmir] seemed to know about our decision to visit Ladakh as soon as we did, judging by the dozen that had lined up outside the office to mob us as we came out. We chose the one who spoke the best English and who said he could make corn muffins. His name was Mohammed, which we soon abbreviated to "Mo," later expanded to "Moses," and finally, thinking that this might have some weight in converting him from the crescent to the cross, to "Holy Moses." Under his experienced guidance we secured a goodly supply of jam, spices and olive oil, forgetting the meal for the muffins. For ourselves we purchased a blanket, an extra bottle of ink, and a new toothbrush apiece. Thus armed against any event, we were all ready to undertake the five-hundred-mile tramp trip over the Himalayas and be gone six weeks.

By the light of the moon we loaded Holy Moses and our few supplies into a small barge in which we were to reach Ganderbal, the first stage of our journey, by water. Then we set sail.

The memory of other poetic nights has come and gone, but the memory of this will never go. As David and I, weary from the day's work, lay on the floor of the barge, two tireless rowers propelled us under the seven bridges of the Jhelum, past the fantastic, moonlit houses, more jumbled and grotesque than ever in the dimness. A wedding-party, singing to the music of native instruments, sailed by in a huge gondola, pushed forward by twenty gondoliers whose twenty heart-shaped blades flashed with every stroke. Their craft was ablaze with paper lanterns, and decorated with garlands of jasmine and chains of dahlias which drooped into the water and trailed behind on the wake of glittering ripples. In a hubbub of song and revelry they swept past and sped beyond, sending back in ever fainter tones the strains of music and laughter, till distance deadened every sound and left the lake to stillness—and to us. Then quietly through the night we floated on across the cool calm surface of the Dahl, where the wind and the lotus-leaves brushed so gently as we passed that we were lulled to sleep.

At the head of the Scind Valley up which we moved toward the crest of the first range to be surmounted, we entered the Zogi Pass, which while it is only eleven thousand five hundred feet, is one of the most notorious defiles in India. The tropical rains from the peninsula turn to snow upon its heights, and a trail of animal carcasses and human graves bears witness to its bloodthirsty disposition. In fact the very day we made our crossing the corpse of an unfortunate coolie, lost the winter before, was just emerging from a snowdrift. This in itself would have dampened the gay spirits David and I had enjoyed for weeks, but to make life a completely dreary affair, the enveloping clouds, for sixteen miles over the pass, poured sleet upon us. Nor did that night spent at eleven thousand feet bring relief. Rain fell in torrents upon the cooking-fire; the wind penetrated to the very marrow; and only a large bottle of brandy bequeathed by Mr. C—saved us from total extinction.

Next morning the arctic storm rumbled away into the mountains, and a true June day dawned in its place. How contrasted was the nature of things on this side of the range! The ascending slopes had been all forest and flowers, the descending were only barrenness and desolation, as it continued to be all the way to Leh, with only a patch of oasis here and there to prevent the country from being a veritable desert. Our pass soon narrowed into a canyon with sheer rock sides and a seething, thrashing torrent roaring at the bottom. Day after day we followed the mule-trail along the face of such a gorge, stopping noon and night at the tiny villages that came from ten to twenty miles apart at places where the walls opened wide enough to permit them.

On the tenth day the summit of our trail to Leh was reached—fourteen thousand feet! From this commanding point we saw the Himalayas spreading for a hundred miles in all directions. Fourteen thousand, the top of things in most mountains, is in this region often only the plateau from which the peaks begin to rise. All about us snowy pinnacles reached to twenty-five thousand feet, and one, endless miles to the north, was Godwin-Austen, twenty-eight thousand two hundred and sixty, topped in the entire world by Everest only. There was not a tree or a blade of grass to be seen in this vast sweep, since it seldom rains. In their places were colors of an astonishing prodigality—vertical veins of brilliant orange and red and purple, streaking upward until they met the inevitable robe of clouds and diadem of snow.

Snuggled against this third and highest range, we came upon our first

Tibetan village, Lamayuru; and at the sight of this amazing community, felt we beheld another world. The contrast of sterile granite that we had seen for days with the sudden fresh verdure of irrigated rice paddies gave us a distinct shock. Stuck on a cliff straight above the canyon floor appeared the huts and caves of the citizens, while on the very brink of the highest rock perched a good example of the "gompa" or lama monastery, where dwells the only spiritual or civil authority the country knows.

No sooner had we halted at a cleared space that lay in the shadow of the overhanging village than the greater part of the male population came down from the cliff-tops to surround us—all real Ladakis, with Chinese faces and long loose clothes of gray wool. Each of the men was resplendent in jewelry, with silver ear-hoops dangling to his shoulders and colored necklaces reaching to his waist. Even the poorest muleteer possessed a bracelet or two. The average citizen of Lamayuru, however, was such a symphony of dirt and gray that not even these jewels could give him much of a swagger appearance.

They had seen few white men, and none at all who traveled as we did, with only one servant and no mounts. An exclamation of surprise went up when they saw us unpack the ponies, extract the cooking utensils and assist in the preparation of a meal, which, when served in our own quaint way, attracted the circle of staring citizens to very close range where they sat spellbound by our strange manipulation of scrambled eggs. Next morning we awoke to find every window and roof sprinkled with curious villagers, who from their superimposed seats could look down upon the making of our toilet. Never before or since have I dressed so publicly. As they seemed fascinated by the spectacle, David and I obliged them by an extravagant employment of toothbrush, soap and comb.

The monastery roof was packed with dozens of red-gowned monks, perched three or four hundred feet above, who scampered out of sight when they saw us begin to climb to their stronghold. We stumbled through black tunnels, up ladders and precipitous steps, through a mystic maze of passages, emerging, under the guidance of a priest, into the innermost shrine. Here the images of Buddha, in gold, wood and bronze, sat leering fatly down at the burning incense and at the rows of dull brass bowls, filled with oil and grain, placed before them as offerings. The light was just strong enough to give the gaudily-colored and elaborately-carved room a fantastic, mysterious atmosphere that fascinated yet repelled us. Horrible demons grinned from the walls, and equally terrifying masks hung from the ceiling beams. The lama form of Buddhism has been described as a religion of juggling, idolatry and mechanics, and this shrine exemplified very well these elements. Prayer flags and wheels decorated every building, and our ecclesiastic guide, spinning each of the latter as he passed, allowed us to give them a slap to our own credit. While we were not having a particularly hard time of it, a word to the fates from Buddha would not do any harm.

We were led into a great hall, whence came the babble of many voices, and found there, seated on long rows of benches, the entire population of the monastery—over two hundred—chanting passages from their sacred books. The "books" consisted of great stacks of printed cardboards, one by two feet, each one of which was placed beneath the stack as it was read through. Such a bedlam of voices one never heard, though it all stopped instantly the moment we walked in. The students, ranging from half-grown boys to old graybeards, stared at us as we stared back at them, and I do not know which side was the more awestruck.

We were escorted to the monastery trail on the back side of the cliff, and managed to toboggan down it to the floor of the canyon, where the path to Leh, met once more, continued to lead us through more painted gorges, more terrific heat, over higher passes and across more arid deserts.

We were now in the heart of Ladakh, and indeed it was like nothing else on earth. The entire country seemed to be falling to pieces. The mountains, higher than ever, were cracked into fragments and in the form of shale were slipping into the Indus River which raged beside us like a Niagara. Pinnacled on the cliffs about were the skeletons of ancient citadels and crag-topping castles, indicating that four centuries ago, before the feudal lords had been displaced by Lhasa, Ladakh was a far more populous and powerful state. These once haughty fortresses are in utter ruin today and do their share in giving the whole landscape the illusion of falling to pieces.

The rarity of the atmosphere is to blame for another of Ladakh's mad characteristics—its phenomenal climate. The film of moistureless air is so thin that it has neither resistance to the tropical desert sun nor the ability to retain heat after the sun is gone. In consequence this region suffers from abnormally cold weather along with abnormally hot. In summer, the season of our expedition, the thermometer climbs to one hundred twenty degrees in the sun and then drops at night to forty. The shadow of a cloud brought a chill, where the moment before we had been miserable from the scorching heat. In winter, though there is almost no snow, zero is not uncommon after sundown of the very day when it had been eighty-five. Consequently David and I spent a good part of our time putting on and taking off and putting on and taking off clothes in an effort to meet the demands of this temperamental climate.

One afternoon, sixteen days after our departure from Srinagar, we turned an unexpected corner and bumped abruptly into Leh—or at least it seemed so. But it was an illusion, since the vast and dominating castle of the rajah, enthroned on the ridge above the city, was ten miles distant. Not until we had trudged four hours more through ankle-deep sand did we reach the entrance gate, assist our pack ponies over the two-foot threshold, and find ourselves the cynosure of all eyes in one of the world's most curious capitals.

Mary Crawford

Trekking with Harry

*In some circumstances walking has the element of leadership about it.
After all, isn't marching (which is a form of organized walking) often
touted in officer training schools as leadership education?*

*Professor Mary Crawford of Pennsylvania learned about the
pluses and minuses of traditional male leadership in the mountains of
Nepal. She is a professor of psychology who once wrote about trekking,
"As we trekked farther up the lonely trail I began to experience a
profound sense of peace and serenity. Far from the responsibilities of
job and family, my only task to keep walking, my mind floated free."*

"Trekking with Harry" originally appeared in Mountain Gazette,
November 1977.

* * *

The Sherpas who live here can lift their eyes every day to the great
Himalayan peaks—Kwangde (20,320 feet), Thamserku (21,730 feet), Kang-
tega (22,340 feet), Ama Dablam (22,494 feet), Nuptse (25,850 feet), Lhotse
(27,890 feet) and Everest itself—Chomolungma. Their Buddhist faith assures
them they'll be reincarnated in an endless cycle, perhaps to live at the foot
of these mountains again. To my best knowledge, I'll only live once. That's
really why I'm here. My once, I'm determined, will include a pilgrimage
to Chomolungma.

The trail is a well-established one. We fly into Lukla, 175 miles from
Kathmandu, and start walking northeast past the main Sherpa trading center
of Namche Bazaar, on to the monastery at Thangboche (13,000 feet), then
to Pheriche in its cold, narrow valley and finally to the Everest base camp
(18,000 feet). Hundreds of trekkers follow this route every year. Not a few
of them regret it. And every year some die because they ignore the signs
of altitude sickness.

The Polish doctor-mountaineer working for the Himalayan Rescue Association at Pheriche tells me, "The French are the worst. They have a
certain arrogance about the mountains. Maybe they've done some technical
climbing in the Alps. So they think trekking should be easy." He shows me

a hand-lettered chart on his wall comparing our altitude at Pheriche (14,000 feet) with the summit of Mont Blanc (15,780 feet) and explaining that this altitude provides only half the oxygen available at sea level. "Remember," warns the Himalayan Rescue Association trekker's booklet, "the Himalayas begin where other mountain ranges leave off."

Still, it's a trail that almost anyone can walk. My companions and I are proof enough of that.

My first reaction on meeting them in Kathmandu is dismay. There's an eighteen-year-old boy on his first trip away from home, and already so zonked on the local *ganja* that his ability to communicate ends with a sweet, spacey smile. I label him Baby Tommy in my mind. Who will get to be mommy and daddy? There are three women. Only one, Joanne, is an experienced climber and hiker. Another is already reduced to weeping by the travails of the Delhi airport. Our leader is a woman, too; Sarah is an independent trekker on her sixth trip to base camp. Then there are the three married couples, fiftyish but fit. The husbands are little boys playing explorer: the wives—makeup, diamond jewelry, grandchildren stories—seem not quite sure what they're doing here. It doesn't take an expert on human behavior to perceive that we are a wildly heterogeneous group. At home, we'd never have chosen one anothers' company. Now we have to live in isolation together for two-and-a-half weeks on the trail.

The airstrip at Lukla is at 10,300 feet. We spend a day or two acclimatizing by walking to nearby villages and back. Ahead of us is Kwangde, a portent of peaks to come.

Right away we give one another plenty of hassles. People complain about the food, accuse one another of hogging the best mattresses and tents, argue about who's to blame for everything from lost luggage to diarrhea. Tommy notes that people keep treating him like a baby. I gently suggest to the others that if we stop playing parents, perhaps Tommy will stop playing child.

Harry the Big Businessman disagrees. "That kid needs his ass kicked and if nobody else will do it, I will!" Okay. So Harry and I are not exactly kindred spirits. He's *allowed* his wife to come along on the condition that she always walk behind him and hike no farther or higher than he does. It's hard for me to empathize with a person who needs to outshine his wife. It's no easier for Harry to empathize with me. More than once he soliloquizes, "It's a man's world in these mountains." It seems that he barely restrains himself from adding, "So what the hell are you doing here?"

Once on the trail, we spread out, and tensions begin to dissipate. We're walking eight to eleven miles a day, moving easily along well-trodden trails. With Sherpas and yaks to carry our gear, we experience the luxury of walking unburdened. Dwarf blue gentian and edelweiss bloom everywhere. The vegetation is a strange mixture of alpine and tropical: spindly pines and barberry along with twenty-foot rhododendron and pale wispy moss draping juniper bushes.

We decide to trek west to Thami, a village near the Tibetan border: The side trip will help us acclimatize and give us a chance to see a village where few trekkers go. The local people carry on clandestine trading with Tibet by crossing the nearby Tesi Lapcha pass, an ancient Nepali-Tibetan trading route. We set off from our camp above Namche after Sarah describes our destination, the only village in the valley. It's a beautiful morning's walk, and I begin to feel the expanding serenity that only the mountains can bring about. On my left roars the icy, opaque Bhote Kosi. By now I'm getting used to the 13,000-foot altitude, and I feel strong and happy. I keep my distance from the others: no hassles today.

The mist is closing in by the time I reach Thami, at about four in the afternoon. Our campsite by the river is damp and chilly. Joanne is already there, and the Sherpas are busy setting up tents and starting the cooking fire. One by one the others join us. After a while, somebody says, "Where's Tommy?" People look at each other blankly. He's gone.

Six o'clock comes, cold and dark, and still no Tommy. Somebody remembers that he'd bought crampons and a small Sherpa sitting mat that morning in Namche. Good God, is he trying to climb a mountain? Our sirdar, Nima Chottar, returns from the monastery above the valley and reports that Tommy passed there two hours earlier, heading up onto the ridge. There are no trails and no shelter past the monastery.

Dinner is a dismal time. We alternate between outrage at Tommy's stupidity, guilt at not having given him the supervision he so clearly needed and fear for his safety. Harry's wife, Peg, offers a prayer: "May God in his infinite wisdom see fit to compensate for Tommy's lack of wisdom."

As for me, I'm really angry. What if that stupid kid's broken a leg and we have to carry him back to Kathmandu? I want to go to Everest! Then I imagine him lying in a ravine, cold and frightened, and I feel rotten for worrying about my vacation.

It's getting colder, and the wind's come up. Most of the Sherpas—Pasang, Nima Chottar and Pemba Dorje—have gone up the mountain past the monastery to search for Tommy. We sit, worrying, around the fire. People ruminate endlessly. How could he have missed the village? How did he get so far ahead of everybody else? Why didn't he ask for shelter at the monastery? What does he think he's doing up on the goddamn mountain at night? He has no jacket or hat, no sleeping bag, no food. The tale of the crampons and Sherpa mat is retold. A villager brings a confused report that Tommy was seen at dusk by a yak-herder high on the mountain—sitting on a rock, writing something on a piece of paper.

Fatigue and worry are overtaking us. Is he writing a farewell note before he starts climbing? Does he mean to kill himself? No. He's a baby, but he's not crazy or suicidal. I reassure Harry that smoking a little dope does not automatically qualify a person as a hopeless psychotic. Tommy's just lost, the victim of his lack of experience and judgement.

I hope.

The Sherpas return at 5 A.M., exhausted, and another contingent heads up the hill. After breakfast, Sarah marshals us all for a hike. There's nothing we can do for Tommy, so we keep busy.

We return to camp at three in the afternoon to find a dazed and miserable Tommy laid out in the dining tent. His lips are cracked, his face chapped raw, his hands trembling. He'd stumbled into a creek in the dark, and spent the night crouched, wet and freezing, beneath a tiny rock overhang at 14,000 feet. But aside from fatigue and fright, he's okay. Incredibly, he's angry with us. "It's all Sarah's fault," he insists. "I was only looking for the village."

Harry towers over him. "Boy," he says, "You're in big trouble."

In fact, Tommy *is* in big trouble, and not just because he's annoyed Harry. He was found by a contingent of Nepali police patrolling the forbidden Tibetan boundary. Tommy had wandered a bit too close to the border. The penalty: five months in jail, bring your own food.

These same police are now relaxing in the sweet afternoon sunshine of our camp. They are willing to be reasonable about this jail business, it seems, but such reasonableness is contingent on a proper respect for their power. The Sherpas, well versed in the rules of this game, have already sent to the village for a kettle or two of *chang*, the national rice beer, and are whipping up a mid-afternoon snack for our guests. Our dried eggs, yak butter and cheese become splendid omelettes, and are served with appropriate deference. Our cigarettes are passed.

Afternoon slips into evening as the *chang*-drinking, eating and merriment go on. We firmly repress our jumbled emotions of anger and relief at Tommy as we play at entertaining our friends the police. The evening is a masterpiece of fake hilarity. The campfire is piled higher. Women arrive from the village and begin dancing and singing. We respond with songs of our own.

> "Daisy, Daisy, give me your answer, do-o-o
> I'm half cra-a-azy, all for the love of you. . . ."

I'm half crazy, all right. I can't believe this is happening. After traveling halfway around the world to see the mountains of Nepal, I'm sitting here instead trying to placate a group of policemen. I help myself to another cup of *chang*.

In the morning the police are gone. Tommy is still with us, and everybody has a headache.

We walk upward. From Kumjung we ponder Ama Dablam, a dream-symbol of a mountain, perfect in its solitary symmetry. The monsoon this year has been a bad one, and in spots the trail and bridges are washed out. The temporary bridges are skimpy arrangements of loose logs and vines; they sway and creak with every step. I walk along easily enough, but when it comes time to scramble up a steep riverbank, my heart pounds and I lean against a spindly tree, gasping for breath.

Now we are drawing closer to Ama Dablam. We climb a ridge above Pheriche and look across the valley to its face. We are standing at 15,000 feet, and the mountain is just beginning. Past the end of the long valley, the great peaks of the Himalayas rise in a massive arc around us—Lhotse. Lhotse Shar, Cho Polu, Makalu.

Past Pheriche the trail heads upward again. It is colder now, and the ground ever more rocky and barren. Nothing grows here but sparse, low grass and lichen. We camp at the tiny settlement of Lobuche (16,000 feet) —hardly more than a stone hut or two. Directly east is Nuptse, very close. The afternoon sun is caught in its snows, pink and golden. Nuptse seems to float in the dazzle.

Harry is critical of our food. He proposes that we buy a chicken or two from the villagers and have a big barbecue; he volunteers to be in charge of everything. Sarah explains that the villages here are very small and very poor. It would take a village's whole chicken population to feed us, *if* they could be bought, and then there'd be no more eggs for the villagers. Besides, firewood is scarce and should be used only when necessary. She explains that it's important to minimize the impact of our presence on the Sherpa way of life.

Harry is not persuaded. He talks meat half the day and makes plans for a big barbecue on the way down.

Walking laboriously upward, I have plenty of time to think about Harry. Back home, he's clearly done all right for himself—a big house in Houston, a ski condominium at Vail, a twin-engine Beechcraft, the whole lot. He's used to being in charge; that's his whole life. Basically, Harry believes that people are naturally lazy and don't want to think for themselves; They *need* to be closely watched and told what to do. This is why it's so natural for him to play parent to Tommy and to try to take over Sarah's job. I don't *like* the fact that he's this way, but I can sympathize. Here we are in the mountains, where our only tasks are to keep walking and to get along with each other. Harry's a man without a job.

After eleven days on the trail, we're approaching our highest camp, Gorak Shep—a Tolkienesque name for a cold and lonely spot. We walk directly beneath the face of Nuptse, along the terminal moraine of the Khumbu Glacier, and reach our campsite at midday. We decide to climb Kala Patar, a rocky hill (18,500 feet) at the foot of Pumori (23,442 feet) for a sweeping view of the glacier, the Everest base camp and beyond into Tibet. Most of the way, the path slopes easily upward, though the altitude makes me focus on every step and every breath. The last few hundred feet are a scramble over loose rock. Then, panting and triumphant, I'm at the top. I look across to Everest—Chomolungma, goddess mother of the earth. In the dazzling clear air I can see the north peak (inside Tibet), the base camp area and Khumbu icefall, the west shoulder and the summit, nearly bare of snow. To the east is the mighty flank of Nuptse; avalanches rumble down its side. Further eastward, across the jumbled wasteland of the glacier, is Ama Dablam. In every direction there is only ice and snow and rock, without the slightest hint of human existence.

The four women who have climbed all the way—Peg, Joanne, Sarah and I—ask Harry to take our picture together. We raise our fists high in cheerful salute to one another.

"Put your arms down," Harry mutters. "I don't like that women's lib stuff."

Six days later, we trek wearily into Lukla. The weather has turned unseasonably wet, and the last day's walk down from Namche has been a misery of cold rain beating through our clothes and turning the trail to mud and slime. But Lukla is a misery of another sort: in the gray gloom we see dozens of tents. Every available inch of land has a trekker camped on it. In the past nine days, only four flights have been able to get in from Kathmandu. Meanwhile, nearly 200 trekkers and their Sherpas have come down from the mountains. Food is short. Sanitation is terrible. Lukla is the only route out of the wilderness except for the grueling ten-day walk to Kathmandu. And the rain clouds hang in the pass.

What the hell can we do? The dozen or so trek leaders try to reassure their groups. But Royal Nepali Air Corporation (RNAC) schedules only four flights a day to Lukla, even when the weather is perfect. This means that fifty-six people at the most will get out the day the clouds lift. Worse, if a scheduled flight is cancelled, its ticket-holders go to the bottom of the list—those who've been here longest could be among the last to leave. I have a little fantasy—the sun shines, a plane comes in, a smiling group of fourteen trekkers ambles down from Nanche waving their official tickets. The 300 longtime Lukla campers part to let them through, then smile and wave goodbye as the plane lifts into the air. . . .

Sure. What's more likely is a bloody fistfight. And what about the sick ones?

Nobody knows what to do. Part of the problem is that the trekkers are in small groups, all strangers to the others. German, Austrian, Japanese, American, British and French stick with their own, in separate camps. Each leader is looking out for his or her own group members and maneuvering to get them on the first planes. Not that it matters—nobody's going anywhere anyway. Every morning the crowd milling at the top of the runway is bigger and more disgruntled. People tell anyone who'll listen why they should be the first to go—ran out of money, gotta get to my job, booked a tour of India, got bronchitis, got a bad knee—the chorus of complaints rises to meet the thick white clouds above us.

Throughout all this, Harry has tried hard to be patient. But the confusion and lack of direction are too much for him. Suddenly, he takes over. Within minutes, all the group leaders are organized under his direction: On his orders, they're assembling all the trekkers for a grand noontime demonstration at the RNAC radio shack. The plan is to scare the hell out of the radio people (who have been utterly indifferent to our plight) and force them to send messages to our embassies and RNAC headquarters.

Ten minutes before noon, I step out of the lodge to join a huge crowd of men and women flowing toward the radio shack. Some are carrying ice axes, ski poles, or stout wooden sticks. Others pick up hefty rocks from the abundant supply on the airstrip. We surround the shack—a determined-looking bunch, I think. Joanne and I stand on a rock at the head of the group and help lead the shouting.

Harry relays our demands: top priority to our evacuation, extra planes to be stationed ready outside Kathmandu so that we can move fast when the weather changes, helicopter evacuation for the sick, messages to our embassies and our families detailing our critical situation. The RNAC people are clearly impressed—in fact, they appear to be terrified.

Harry is almost visibly expanding with power and authority as he addresses the crowd. There is no question—German and Japanese and British alike acknowledge him as leader.

We schedule a 4 P.M. repeat demonstration, just to keep the situation fresh in the radio operator's mind. The second gathering is even more impressive: more ice axes, a few rocks tossed harmlessly against the radio shack, more chants and shouting. It's like being back in the sixties, standing around and yelling, "We want out!" And it seems to be working. The Nepalis are a gentle and pacifist people. Our unseemly aggressive display has convinced the radio operator that mayhem is nigh. Hopefully, he's conveying this firm belief to the people with the airplanes.

Meanwhile, Harry has disappeared into the lodge with his band of group leaders. Many hours later, they emerge. Harry has drawn up a master list that specifies the exact order in which every one of the more than 300 trekkers will get on the plane. The basic plan is: sick people first, with illness certified by doctors drawn from among the trekkers. Then trekkers go in the order in which they arrived at Lukla, regardless of official tickets or RNAC rules. The leaders of the most recently arrived groups have been persuaded to ask their members to voluntarily surrender their tickets, thus possibly delaying their own escape by days or weeks in favor of those who've

been stranded longest. So skilled is Harry's assumption of power that everyone agrees without protest. It is clear to everyone that his plan is the fairest
possible solution.

Harry has quietly placed himself at the bottom of the list.

When the planes finally come, it's a circus. The sky fills with the drone
of engines; chickens and goats and children scurry from the rocky airstrip;
a cheer goes up. Three hundred people crowd the edges of the field; the
air is alive with their excitement. Harry is in the center of it all, issuing
"official" boarding passes from his list.

The first plane discharges a contingent of police—proof enough, as
they stand uneasily between us and the aircraft, that our message has been
understood in Kathmandu.

I'm on the sixth plane, along with Joanne and Tommy. The scene has
grown zanier and more euphoric all morning. The entire Royal Nepali air
fleet seems to be at Lukla. At one point there are three twin Otters and two
five-person Pilatus Porters crammed on the tiny airstrip. The RNAC officials
have early on capitulated completely to Harry. Police and pilots and trekkers
alike address him respectfully as "Captain Sahib" and await his nod to board
or take off. And Harry is loving it, in his element at last.

People are laughing, singing, waving goodby to their friends. I climb
on the little plane and hold my breath as it lurches down the rocky strip,
engines screaming, and lifts suddenly into the sky. I look down at the deep,
lonely valleys and then across at the wondrous desolation of the great white
peaks. There are tears in my eyes. I notice that Joanne's eyes are shiny,
too. The strain of it all has caught up with us.

Chances are I will never come back here. But I blow my nose and tell
myself I don't need to. I've seen the mountains and I've learned a few things
on the long walk. One pilgrimage to Chomolungma is enough.

Peter Somerville-Large

Kailas

At the age of sixty Peter Somerville-Large made the Tibetan pilgrimage to the holy mountain of Kailas. The veteran walker was not a religious pilgrim but a curious Irishman. He was not a penitent, though his sixteen-day truck ride to reach the Kailas trail must have been torture. His visit occurred at a time not long after Tibet had been reopened to Westerners and after the Kailas pilgrimage had reemerged from the darkness of China's Cultural Revolution.

Even at the end of the enlightened twentieth century the ancient link between religious faith and walking continues in some isolated corners of the world. I like this tie-in to the past. Through our own feet we can rediscover what mystics and wanderers have felt before us. Wars of religion have smeared our century with blood; perhaps killing in the name of god will never end. But who would have expected that believers would still be making centuries-old treks to sacred mountains? How long, I wonder, will Kailas remain the province of pilgrims rather than of tourists? As Peter Somerville-Large put it, "In the Skanda Purana is written: 'There are no mountains like the Himalaya, for in them are Kailas and Manasarowar.' "

The following excerpt is from To The Navel Of The World *(1987).*

* * *

When we looked at the circle of orange-coloured hills grouped around the snow-covered lignam, Kailas seemed an intimidating distance away. First there was a river to be crossed, then a baked clay corridor, then the mountain. One of the geologists casually mentioned the existence of a pilgrim resthouse.

"I do not know where," he said, shrugging his shoulders, but adding that the driver might know. He meant the driver of the lorry, and he had to wait for an hour for him to catch up. He confirmed the news, before we drove on a few miles to a dusty track. We were deposited, together with our baggage, beside sloping ground covered with small prickly bushes. A couple of miles away, the line of red foothills met the ground, half-concealing the dome of Kailas which glinted in the sun above them.

The holy mountain of Kailas is unique in its phallic symmetry. Its shape, which has been compared to temples in South India, is one of those rarities in nature, a perfectly regular form, four sides of a crude style facing the four corners of the compass as sharply defined as if they had been chiselled by an axe. Traditionally they are said to be composed of crystal and different jewels, but in fact the mountain is geologically significant as the world's highest deposit of tertiary conglomerate. In other words, it is a giant mound of cemented gravel.

Remotely placed near the world's largest snow barrier among the head-streams of four mighty and holy rivers, the Ganges, the Indus, the Brahmaputra and the Sutlej, the two sacred destinations of pilgrims, the mountain of Kailas and the oval lake of Manasarowar beside it, present in geographical fact the images of natural harmony that are essential to Tibetan and Hindu philosophy. The union of balancing and opposing forces, earth and water, male and female, are here for the pilgrim to see. The image of the mountain, reflected in architecture all over South Asia as far away as Indonesia, evokes the idea of the world Pillar, and suggests the symbol of the Mandala. Kailas was holy for the old followers of shamism with their wild gods; it is holy for Buddhists and it is holy for Hindus. Shiva, the creator and destroyer, is a god of mountains, and Kailas which he shares with his *shakti*, the goddess Devi, who represents the female aspects of Shiva's qualities, is his special abode and Paradise. The Tibetan counterparts of Shiva and Devi, the four-faced demon Demchog and his consort, Dorje Phangmo, also have their home among the snows of this eastern Olympus where beliefs of Hindu and Buddhist alike are fused in perpetual holiness.

The sacred mountain spire loomed in the distance behind a row of splintered orange hills which seemed sharp as sharks' teeth. The sun was blindingly hot. Caroline took up one pack and I carried the others, dropping them along the way in clusters. We moved very slowly along the track.

After a few hundred yards Caroline said, "I think I'll go on. You bring up everything."

I watched her bound away towards a little building surrounded by an encampment of huts, behind which the dome of Kailas showed over its guard of foothills. I followed on slowly with a back-stitch gait, carrying some baggage forward, going back for the rest and taking that beyond the load in front. After about an hour I reached a rough road where groups of women carrying enormous loads were striding along, and a lorry went by crammed with nomads who looked like Red Indians. These were pilgrims. Then a pretty girl caught sight of me and came rushing down to pick up some of the bags and toss them easily up on her back. Further on I could see Caroline standing outside the gate of a walled enclosure that surrounded a low building. She was talking to two men.

When I at last came to the gate I was met by a Tibetan and another Oriental, a plump middle-aged man in a bright blue jacket and yellow cap.

The Tibetan was Dorje, who ran this guesthouse for pilgrims. The other:

"I am Dr. Kazuhiko Tamanura, Professor of Tourism from Doshisha University, Kyoto, Japan." Kazi, as we came to know him, smiled and shook hands, dismissing the girl who had carried my bags with a few sweets.

Dorje helped us bring the bags inside and assigned us a room. He was in charge of this very ancient pilgrimage centre, originally built by a king of Bhutan for the benefit of pilgrims from outside Tibet. Controlled by the Bhutanese for centuries, Tarchan was independent of the Gartok Viceroys, and remote and far away, ignored any directives from Lhasa. The lamas who ran it were called Dashok, and they seem to have had a certain style. When Colonel Sherring visited Tarchan in 1905 everyone in the place was drunk; twenty years later, when Colonel Ruttledge journeyed here across the Western Himalayas, the Dashok still appeared to be drunk.

Before 1981 the pilgrimage had been suspended for a twenty-year period, during which any manifestation of Buddhist ceremony was forbidden. Now religion was acceptable once more, and back in China fifty million Christians were allowed to go to church again. Here in western Tibet, after the eclipse of the Cultural Revolution, the resthouse had been rebuilt specifically to accommodate Indian and Nepalese pilgrims. A trickle had already journeyed here across the Himalayas during the three years since the parikarama and festival of Kailas had been resumed, but until this year no foreigners from the West had been here for at least thirty-five years. This year a number of outsiders had made the journey to Tarchan:

One American, who hired two jeeps and drove here from Lhasa. He got official permission by paying thousands of dollars to China Travel. Remembered because he only drank beer.

One Austrian who also paid thousand of dollars to China Travel.

Dr. Kazuhiko from Kyoto, Japan.

Two impoverished Irish travellers.

The room we were assigned was simple—no washbasin, no beds, just sacks filled with dried pellets of sheep dung. But it was our first room since leaving Snowlands in Lhasa that didn't smell of urine, and on the whole it was clean. Caroline had a fit of housekeeping. The mud floor was washed and brushed out, the sacks of sheep shit were arranged to make mattresses for our sleeping bags, a clothes line was erected. At her end of the room she made a primitive table out of a plank and a couple of rocks on which she laid out her face creams and washing things, her Walkman, books, camera films and tapes in neat piles.

"I can't stand dirt."

At my end things were less tidy.

"How can you live like that? You really are at home in a country where people never change their clothes."

In the evening the Japanese professor entertained us. First he gave us a glass of Japanese whisky, and then out of a large cardboard box he took packets of dried seaweed, prawn chips, dried vegetables and strips of processed beef which he heated on a gas burner.

"Perhaps you like green tea?" he asked as various Tibetans crowded round the door to have a look. Kazi was a member of the Chinese–Japanese Friendship Mountaineering Expedition which at this very moment was engaged in climbing Memonani, a peak in the Gurla Mandhata mountain range which we could see from the guesthouse. Twenty-five Japanese and Chinese were out on the slopes of what would be for a very short time the second highest virgin peak in the world. The Japanese had worked for almost twenty years to get here; negotiation was sweetened by staggering sums of money, paid for, so Kazi assured us, by the richest man in Japan.

"You see, we must each pay twenty thousand dollars for the permission. We also give four new Japanese Landcruisers as a big bribe. The Chinese are clever people and climbing mountains is political. If we reach the summit—and there are many problems, plenty of dangerous blue ice on the way—everyone will be pleased. Already a celebration dinner is planned in Beijing. Very good for Japanese–Chinese trade." The food we were eating, so similar to what was on offer in the Khumbu area, was part of the expedition's general supplies. Around his room were stacked pieces of equipment donated by Japanese industries, offering a dazzling display of Nippon technology, expensive cameras, sound equipment, jostling with gadgets I didn't recognize. This was stuff that had been left behind; there were plenty more aids to modern mountaineering up on Memonani.

Before we retired Kazi lent us an extra gas stove and that night we enjoyed a cup of tea.

Caroline said: "Don't use two bags. If you remember to use them carefully, one bag is ample for two cups. We aren't millionaires." The sheep dung pellets felt like plastic chips.

It was strange to get up without the feeling of "Oh God, can we find a lorry today?" At Tarchan there was no prospect of officials strolling around in green jackets asking awkward questions.

There was peace. Being so close to Kailas—called Tise by Tibetans—was a source of wonder. When you looked out you could see the fretted line of snowpeaks. Sir Thomas Holditch observed how "the chief obstacles to Tibetan exploration have been the mountain barriers which surround the plateau, massed together like a series of gigantic walls. They rise in a region of unbroken silence like gigantic frosted fortresses until their white towers are lost in the sky." Behind the peaks on the far horizon were Kashmir and Ladakh, Nepal and the Indian plains.

Directly in front of Tarchan the prow of Memonani shone white in the sun, and below the Gurla mountains among which Memonani starred were the lakes of Manasarowar and Rakas Tal, associated in holy unity with Kailas. Manasarowar, in particular, is sacred, and the pilgrim who reaches its shores acquired immeasurable merit. For the Hindu it is as good a place to die as anywhere along the Ganges.

For the first time since entering Tibet our lives took in a settled pattern. In the morning I would get up and collect the glacial water from the stream that ran down through the pilgrim encampment from the nearby mountain. Upstream, above the encampment, naturally; there followed a long process of filtering and boiling. The boiling was presumably cosmetic, since boiling point was low, and tea was never quite hot enough. Caroline had fixed up the ground sheet from our tent to be hung over the window by night, but, when we took it down by day, onlookers would instantly gather to look through and watch us wash clothes, cook, read and quarrel. Caroline wandered around in her chuba like a convalescent in a cottage hospital.

Behind the pilgrims' resthouse were the remains of the old gompa surrounded by tents with the cone of Kailas shining behind its back. One morning I investigated the old building which for centuries must have been the only solid habitation for scores of miles that had a roof and walls. Until the resthouse was built in 1982, this important centre for pilgrims had been allowed to decay. I walked through the small bare rooms where the lamas had lived and prayed and got drunk, where shepherds now camped down with their meagre possessions . . . a few battered tin pots, or a tea churn with a long elegant brassbound stem. A sheep peered at me from a doorway and an old woman wrapped in a bright Aztec patterned shawl was cooking over a fire. She smiled and said something, but I couldn't stay; the smell of burning dung and damp earth and years of unwashed communal life was overpowering. I felt as if my head was on fire and each short breath made me gasp. In the next dark room a rickety ladder led upwards, and in seconds I was out on the roof, breathing the rarified cold air, looking down on the shimmering golden plain with its two lakes and the background of the Gurla mountains. Behind them I could see more lines of mountains, the Himalayan barrier which was like so many breaking waves.

The lamas had gone. Would the Chinese let any trickle back for the sake of the pilgrim trade? People give you different figures. One estimate has about 120,000 monks in Tibet in 1959 and 2,711 monasteries, many of which were destroyed during the upheaval because they were centres of rebellion. After the fighting many were razed for buiding material before the further destruction of the Cultural Revolution. At present, nine monasteries with lamas remain in the whole of Tibet.

Perhaps things would change with the new tolerance. Here was Tarchan rebuilt and functioning as a hostel. This was its third year. Most of the rooms would remain empty until the end of June or the beginning of July when small contingents of Indians and Nepalese would come this way after the passes were free of snow. Tibetan pilgrims did not aspire to stay indoors, but camped all around outside. At this time during the first weeks of June Tarchan accommodated, beside ourselves, Kazi, Dorje, Dorje's aunt and another old lady with cracked blue-tinted glasses and a face as wrinkled as W. H. Auden's, who almost qualified for Holditch's severe estimate of Tibetan looks: "The life they lead on these sublime heights has wrinkled them exceedingly, the old people being especially hideous." Witchlike, she was followed everywhere by a small brown cat.

Dorje, a small, sinewy man with a cast eye, could just remember the old unchanged Tibet, warts and all, before the Chinese swept in. He fled into exile in India, where he learnt English, returning to his own country in 1970 to look after his sick father. During the Cultural Revolution his ability to speak English was regarded with the greatest suspicion.

"They said I was a spy." He did not enlarge on his personal experience of persecution during the years when thousands were killed in a period of unprecedented violence, and much of the social and cultural fabric of Tibetan life was destroyed. The memory is recent, but like so many other Buddhists Dorje displayed a lack of bitterness almost incomprehensible to Westerners; the passive acceptance of suffering is an intrinsic part of the Buddhist path to perfection.

"It is not that we do not care. But our beliefs make us realise how little time we spend in this world."

"And those who died?"

"They have their reward."

By day most activity was centred around the small yard crammed with pilgrims' belongings—piles of bags and bound pieces of sheepskin, firewood, posteen coats and supplies of herbs gathered daily for medicinal purposes and left to dry in the sun. Just north of Kailas are important salt deposits, and the whole area used to have a thriving wool trade. We had assumed that sheep caravans travelling between Tibet and India and Nepal had ceased, but we were to find that we were mistaken.

All around us were nomads with their animals. In the early morning I watched them milking their sheep before letting them go free on the mountains, absorbed by the daily spectacle of hundreds of bleating ewes and the gaudy clothes of those who tended them. Getting the ewes into parallel lines for milking, facing each other, heads interlocking, took time and expertise. A description of 1906 shows that the method has not changed. "These latter are tied neck to neck in a long line, so closely together that movement is impossible, alternate animals looking in different directions, and the women go up and down the line with great rapidity." Later, when the sun got up people and animals vanished into the hills. A man or woman with a staggering amount of sheep would fade away, expressing a potent force of freedom. The Chinese have had little luck with cooperatives in Tibet.

Often Kazi would invite us for a meal. Why wasn't he on the mountain

with the rest of the Chinese–Japanese Friendship Expedition? He was engaged on important research on pilgrims. While his colleagues were busy
on their virgin peak, he was a star turn down at Tarchan, as he made a
detailed study of the pilgrims and their motives for coming to Kailas. He
walked around armed with notebooks, sketchbooks, index cards, typed ques-
tionnaires and flipover counter-check lists, tape recorder and Polaroid
camera.

The Polaroid was part of his irresistible interviewing technique. After
he had questioned his pilgrim, he immediately photographed him, giving
him a free coloured print, while keeping a second picture to be filed with
his notes. Sometimes he handed out cigarettes, a pen or pencil. Most people
had never seen photographs of themselves before. All day long the little
courtyard was filled with eager interviewees, monks and shepherds, nomads
and merchants from Lhasa, mountain men with their families, who had come
from all over the country to the spiritual heart of the Himalayas and the
centre of the universe. The pilgrimage to Kailas was the fulfilment of a lifetime's ambition, which the coming of Communism had not diminished, and
Dr. Kazi was one of their rewards.

Dorje was essential to Kazi as interpreter. Squatting together, they
would begin their day's work. The Japanese had a shy diffident manner,
which put the pilgrims at their ease as Dorje translated. You could see them
beginning to enjoy the questions.

"Please ask him the colour of his tent—is it white or brown?"

"White."

"How many sheep does he own?"

"Sixty."

"Has he heard of Japan?"

"No."

"Why does he come here?"

"For the future life."

"How many days did he travel from his home?"

"Twenty."

Kazi noted everything down, earnings, the food the pilgrims ate,
whether they could read or write, probable age. Occasionally he made a
mistake.

"You must not ask if he is married," Dorje said. "That is unlucky."

When everything was written down the Polaroid was produced, the
moment everyone was waiting for. Often it was the signal for the pilgrim to
go off and change into his best clothes. Here were four young nomads with
their wives, swashbuckling figures in embroidered hats and cloaks, two
brandishing ornate daggers which intensified the impression of cavaliers. In
the old days almost every man carried a sword or a gun. The wives in long
black dresses, their hair braided to the height of mantillas, stuck out their

tongues and giggled. A tall youth displayed his new cloak edged with fox fur, an old man in a shaggy chuba appeared dazed as he held the little piece of card and watched his figure slowly emerge. And so they came day after day, all morning and during the hot windy afternoon.

Then Kazi decided to do the parikarama around Kailas in the steps of his compatriot, Ekai Kawaguchi, who circled Kailas in 1900.

There are three paths of pilgrimage around the mountain. Most pilgrims take the widest and lowest. One tour is adequate, but many do three or thirteen a particularly holy number. Those who complete twenty-one parikaramas are considered worthy to attempt the middle circuit high across the four faces of the mountain. There is a higher route still, only attainable by those who have achieved an advanced state of Buddhahood, culminating in the hundred and eighth circuit, which is said to ensure Nirvana.

One circuit would do for Kazi. We watched him depart with his two porters and return two days later exhausted, to receive our congratulations before collapsing in his room.

"It was so difficult. I am not used to such things, and you can have no idea how dreadful was the track."

We planned to follow his example. Originally we toyed with the idea of going around on a yak like Sven Hedin or Ekai Kawaguchi, even though this meant less merit. I would have thought it would have added an added measure of penance. There were no riding yaks available. Dorje's was far away grazing on a mountain. "Everyone knows my yak."

He found a young brother and sister who were willing to carry our bags. Pusu Seren Urju and Pusu Chorten were a handsome pair with apple-red cheeks indicating high quantities of red corpuscles in their blood, who found working for foreigners hilarious. Their laughter was uproarious as we showed them our rucksacks, bags, tents, provisions, all to be taken along. First the girl was loaded, and then the boy, everything tied on and balanced by straps across the forehead.

As we left the courtyard Kazi was back at work, three pigtailed nomads standing in front of him waiting for the magic moment when the camera appeared. Outside the guesthouse another lorry crowded with pilgrims roared up after a journey from somewhere far away which must have involved a penitential degree of discomfort. They climbed down laughing and smiling; the sight of Kailas over their heads in the sun was the glorious indication of journey's end. They had little in the way of baggage or food. There were men and women, old men and old women, and babies wrapped in sheepskin. In June it could still snow, and every night water froze solid; summer was short like life itself.

We followed our porters, strapped and bent down with our bundles, as they led us round the edge of the hills. The girl, wearing a fringed scarf that covered her head, a furry jacket and long dress, carried my rucksack, the heavy green army bag and her own rug. Her brother's load was much lighter.

Pale yellow flowers bloomed among the rocks, and, as the sun came up behind our backs and warmed us, the light picked out details like a probing torch. A mani wall of stones, elaborately carved with sacred texts and figures of Buddha, had stood there over the centuries as a reminder of our transitory existence. A hare twitched his ears as he saw us pass, and others bounded across the grass, tame as dogs. Reverence for life, the philosophy that Albert Schweitzer shared with Buddhists, ensured that this morning the tame hares around Kailas had their place in the Buddhist cosmology. (Not everyone feels this way. Hares are incorporated in the Sino–Tibetan cuisine, and numerous English travellers have shot and eaten them.)

The waterless air conveyed the sun's rays in relays as it hit the plain, changing it from green to golden brown, coral pink and gold. The colours evoked Blake and his natural world to which hares belong. We walked in a silence which in Tibet has a quality of its own. "A four dimensional space silence," Fosco Maraini called it. "There is the yellow ochre silence of the rocks, the blue-green silence of the ice-peaks; the silence of the valleys over which hawks wheel in the sun; and there is the silence that purifies everything, dries the butter, pulverises the bones and leaves in the mind an inexpressible dreamy sweetness, as if one had attained some ancient fatherland lost since the beginning of history."

We came up to a young man prostrating himself along the route. It would take him about twelve days to complete the circuit, following the prescribed rules for covering the ground. There is the way to stand and lift your arms, the way you pause and pray and measure your length. The distance around Kailas is about fifty kilometres, much of it over snow and rocks and stones. He wore the uniform of prostrating pilgrims, the protective sheepskin apron and wooden blocks strapped to his hands. Beyond him we caught up with two more men making the same progress, and we would pass many more.

All morning we followed the traditional route towards Kailas, a dusty trail marked out with little piles of stones and chortons stuck with blue, white, red and yellow flags. Pilgrims were walking and praying around each one. At midday we turned our backs on the plain at a place where another chorton covered in tattered flags marked the first important point of the circuit. It stood at the foot of the circle of high buff-coloured hills that had seemed red or orange when seen from a distance guarding Kailas; now the holy mountain towered in front of us.

At 22,000 feet Kailas is a modest peak compared to many Himalayan giants, but its shape is striking and unmistakable. It has been compard to a chorton, the handle of a millstone, a great lignam. "The eastern face is crystal, the south is sapphire, the west is ruby and the north is gold," one legend said; another claimed it was clothed with fragrant flowers and shrubs. Sven Hedin was more prosaic; he considered Kailas "a tetrahedron set in a prism." At some periods during the summer the ridges on the south face, catching unmelted snow, are seen to record the holy mark of the swastika.

Rather than trying to capture the ecstasies of pilgrims, it is safer to record the impressions of strangers. "It is incomparably the most famous mountain in the world," Sven Hedin wrote, "Mount Everest and Mont Blanc cannot vie with it." An earlier lone traveller, Henry Strachey, catching sight of Kailas's snows in the summer of 1864, considered it the most beautiful mountain he had ever seen, "a king of mountains, full of majesty."

A hot wind stirred up the dust as we walked towards a gorge that opened out from the rust-coloured rocks with Kailas above our heads. Two horsemen were riding towards us, the hard wooden saddles of their ponies placed on embroidered saddle cloths; their plaited manes and tails were tied with pink bows. The riders, wearing fur coats, fur hats and high decorated fur boots, spurred their mounts beside a stream known as God's River, trotting on what appeared to be bright green grass. But when we came closer and the ponies were urged past us, the green dissolved and, like other spectacles in the thin air, turned out to be hallucinatory; all I could see were specks of burnt foliage among the rocks.

A little further on we came to a huge wooden pole covered with coloured yak skins whose streamers tumbling from its head gave it the look of a giant maypole. In a land without trees, the sight of such a giant which must have been carried up painstakingly from the forests of the Himalayas was a startling herald to the entrance of the gorge. Inside, the path followed a dark, cold valley; above our heads one side was crossed with moving shadows, while the other sparkled in light where the world of snow and ice began above the crests of stone. Occasionally there was the thunder of an avalanche, the crack of falling rocks, a distant puff of snow and a long silence. Beside us the murmur of the little river continued undisturbed, a burble like monks praying in the dark.

We joined a group of pilgrims camping under a mani wall glistening with butter spread over the years. Two men and their wives, one with a parcelled baby, welcomed us and offered us tea. They had lit a small fire using the same sort of pellets of sheep shit on which we had been trying to sleep for a week. The smallest and most ordinary things would keep them alive on the parikarama, ground-up barley meal taken from a leather bag, rancid butter swirling in the bowls of luke-warm brick tea which they shared with us.

After we had swallowed tea and tsampa in the cold, the family went ahead, while we continued more slowly among the stream of pilgrims who walked and prayed, spun prayer wheels, or carried poles or staves, usually with prayer flags tied to the tips to help them over the rocks. There were also a number of Nepalese pilgrims carrying umbrellas. Now we reached another chorton where pilgrims stopped and prayed, circling it in the prescribed clockwise direction. Here was the family who had given us tea going round briskly, baby bundled on his mother's back, reciting their mantras and religious texts while we gasped for breath. This chorton had an imprint of Buddha's foot, the next one along decked with flags contained the bones of a holy man, and now we were passing a cave revered as a place of particular sanctity because it was once the abode of an ascetic. It may well have been one of those where in the old days lamas were walled up for a grim bout of meditation.

We continued to follow the track beside God's River, our porters trotting many yards in front, occasionally stopping so that we could catch up. Along the way groups of pilgrims travelled with us, many passing us, others stopping to pray or picnic, the occasional dogged prostrator inching his way up the dark valley. Above us was still the steep line of corrugated brown peaks that guarded Kailas, and from time to time the holy mountain would emerge from a cauldron of clouds with snow running down its shoulder like a Christmas pudding. Once Caroline stopped and took out her paintbox to sketch the dome in the freezing air before it vanished again in swirling mist. The effect on passing pilgrims of seeing a recognizable image of their holy mountain was electrifying. They stopped, stared and muttered; one elderly nomad, his face scorched by sun and wind, snatched up the still-wet watercolour and reverently touched his forehead with it.

At noon we camped beside the frozen river bed. Kazi's stove didn't work.

Any benign and profound thoughts about holy places and the nature of pilgrimage and faith evaporated in a high altitude fit of rage. All over the Himalayas I had been demonstrating either the failure of Western technology in the face of challenge, or the paucity of my travel budget. But I had thought the Japanese might have come up with something more efficient. We watched water remain sullen, leaving rice half-raw, while the busy little flame of our porters' turd fire a few yards away mocked us as it cooked their tsampa.

No need to linger. Beyond the river the track twisted in a gentle bow and the valley widened as we started to climb towards the Dolma Pass. Among the weeping spires of ice and frozen waterfall, we came across a large herd of yaks, big Tibetan yaks with fringes over their eyes and rivers of hair falling down to tiny protruding legs. Some were golden, others spotted or dabbled with white, but most of them were black as ebony. What did they live on? Moss, perhaps, lichen? There was nothing visible for them to graze on in this wilderness, certainly nothing in the way of grass. "Pousse-Cailloux" of the Army Transport Corps watched yaks grazing in empty country on their way to Lhasa. "Smooth your hand along the table. Bare. Just like that." He had great admiration for "an uncouth beast of burden which in some primeval fashion, seemed to be able to pick up a living off the bitter barrens across which we were slowly advancing. Watch it for an hour when turned loose to 'graze.' At the end of the time you would swear a solemn oath that its diet was stones and shingle. As a matter of fact, it seems to be able to dig up with its great fore-feet a subsoil saxifrage moss of sorts, a thing which must be almost chemically concentrated nourishment to support such a vast and hairy bulk."

How spoilt Sod and Mucker had been compared to their cousins snatching meagre grazing beneath Kailas. Big as these yak were, wild yak would be bigger. My ambition to see a wild yak was not fulfilled—unless, I torture myself, somewhere on our journey a herd or an individual might have passed in view of one of the lorries in which we rode. There must be some left. Western Tibet used to be famous for its herds of wild yak, drong in Tibetan. They are massive animals, standing six feet high in the withers with a reputation of being as ferocious as lions. Given the temperament of domesticated yak, that must be true. Drong have been hunted to the edge of extinction, since, unlike their domesticated cousins, they failed to qualify among Tibetans for the license to live. No doubt the Chinese have taken pot shots at wild yaks; there is no estimate of surviving numbers. Heinrich Harrer saw herds during his escape; earlier, Colonel Bailey described a huge herd he saw grazing near his camp in the region of Geer. "I saw what I think was one of the finest and most impressive sights in my life. As soon as they smelt a man, the whole herd lifted their heads, waved their big bushy tails over their backs, and as though drilled, galloped off."

We were climbing at over 18,000 feet, moving very slowly alongside all the pilgrims, every now and then passing someone flat on his stomach. At one of our numerous pauses for breath Caroline encountered an old lady resting, wrinkled like a relief map of the Himalayas.

"She's exactly your age," Caroline said.

I recalled Po Chu-i's thoughts on being sixty. In Arthur Waley's translation:

Between thirty and forty one is distracted by the Five Lusts;
Between seventy and eighty one is prey to a hundred diseases . . .
I am still short of illness and decay and far from decrepit age.
Strength of limb I still possess to seek the rivers and hills.

Among the men Sven Hedin brought with him on his trans-Himalayan expedition was an old man of sixty-two who was so keen to travel "that he had the forethought to pack up a shroud that he might be buried decently if he died on the way." It was comforting to remember he had survived.

By dusk we had been walking for almost twelve hours; the gleaming sides of Kailas were directly above us and it was very cold. In the old days there used to be four monasteries along the route, "like jewels in a bracelet," to shelter travellers—three were near the summit of the pass. But up here nothing remained to welcome pilgrims, and we were lucky to erect our tent inside the shelter of what seemed to be a run-down yersa situated beside an abyss. A camp site for ascetics—no prospect of keeping warm as icy winds rattled the tent's sides. Outside were the porters; from time to time we heard a song or the hum of a mantra.

"For God's sake, shouldn't we ask them to come in?"

"How do you think they can possibly squeeze in beside us?"

It was true that the tent was crowded out and with the best will in the world there was no room for two other bodies. We were not breaking any rules. A traveller who came here in 1848 explained the procedure:

"We carried two small tents eight or ten feet in length, one for our own use, the other for the Bhotias; and if it is asked how our sixteen men shall get into one such tent, it must be explained that there is an aristocracy in the heart of the snowy mountains—and that the underlings were expected to lie wholly in the open air day and night, which they did without any apparent inconvenience." A hundred years on, Professor Tucci mentioned how Tibetans slept out in the open wrapped in their robes and woollen blankets.

But 19,000 feet up at the summit of the Dolma Pass? Brother and sister were softly praying outside. Their prayers may have kept them warmer than I was in my sleeping bag. "Perfectly adequate for sub-zero conditions."

At dawn Kazi's stove failed us again before we resumed climbing. Our porters appeared none the worse for wear. Nor did the pilgrims who climbed with us, without visible sign of camping gear.

The sun ascended slowly as we walked in Indian file, our porters moving steadily in front of us, towards another snow field, behind a group of pilgrims which included our hosts of the day before. The baby's fur-wrapped head stuck out of a sack, alert black eyes looked back at us from a small crimson face. The crowd of pilgrims was becoming denser, and more and more were prostrated on the wrinkled icy surface of the pass.

Caroline wore chuba and face mask, although why she needed a face mask at 18,589 feet was a mystery. It was midday and we had reached the very top of the pass, where a large pillar of black stone decorated with flags cut the skyline. The Dolma Rock marked the culmination of the pilgrimage. The shining polished appearance of the bottom part of the monolith came from butter smeared on the sides as far as human arms could reach. Numerous small objects were embedded in the grease. In the old days a pilgrim would smear a bit of butter on the stone, pluck out a lock of his hair and slap it into the butter. According to Sven Hedin, the stone resembled "a huge wig-block, from which black locks of hair flutter in the wind. . . . Teeth are even stuck in the chinks of the Dolma Rock, forming whole rosaries of teeth."

Today's offerings were a lot less grisly, just coins and bank notes, a few sweets and nuts, a piece of chewing gum and a photograph of the Dalai Lama. Would I revive an old custom by leaving my own teeth there?

We were in a state of immense exhaustion, as mountain sickness increasingly claimed us with shortness of breath and a headache that made me feel that my skull was much too small to contain my brain. For a long time we sat gasping, watching the column of pilgrims pass, praying and touching the great rock. Behind us, far below, other figures were waiting patiently in an endless line like the famous photograph of the Klondyke.

Somewhere hidden in the snowfield was the holy lake of Gaurikund which remained frozen all the year. Later in the summer when the snow retreated and it was uncovered for a few weeks, the faithful would break the ice and place a little water on their heads. Now they could only wait their turn to greet the holy pillar with reverence. We watched a group of shaggy men carrying spears as they prayed and touched the great lignam. Then a family group, then more nomads and their women—all those we had seen arriving at Tarchan on foot and in lorries from vast distances to conclude their pilgrimage with a journey of immense hardship. The sight of so many trudging through the snow, waiting to make their devotions at the shining black, butter-smeared, flag-hung rock standing in snow and ice was sublime. When Sven Hedin saw a similar line of pilgrims eighty years ago he observed how "they feel no weariness, for they know that every step improves their prospects of the world beyond the river of death."

We were the intruders, myself and Caroline with her camera and sketch book. No doubt the next thing would be a film crew. I wondered how much longer Kailas would remain isolated from outsiders and nonbelievers. Would foreigners travel this way in the numbers that wandered under Everest, to mingle with the great queue of the devout below us?

Time had fled and we had recovered enough to begin the descent from the pass through another steep slippery valley of snow and ice. A line of pilgrims was holding hands to try and stop slipping since there were no aids to safety, no guides or ropes or handholds. I watched men and women of all ages, arm in arm, slithering down the bone-breaking ice. My contemporary was there, being helped down by her daughter, a handsome young woman wearing long earrings of coral and seed pearls. Slowly, slowly we made progress down the slippery trail, and then Kailas was behind us with all its ice and mystery. We came to a different world, a windy valley free of snow through which a stream bubbled over rocks. With muted green, brown and grey colours predominating, it resembled a glen in Donegal except that yaks were grazing with the sheep, and there was not a blade of grass to be seen. The bright greens that shone with a quality of stained glass could only be mistaken for grass at a distance—when you looked closely you found lichens and moss growing all over the rock.

We stopped to eat and once again the gas burner lost out against dung fires as women in their long dresses went searching for fuel. Yak turds were king-sized, sheep pellets smaller and harder work to gather. Dung-collecting is part of the daily round, and at any nomad encampment you can watch people moving about slowly looking for argols (a much prettier word than turds). The yak provides not only meat, milk, butter, cheese and wool, but also fuel. In a country without trees, the large yak dropping is important for making a fire, and the very survival of many nomads would be in doubt without the yak standing by. Père Huc, the Lazarist missionary father who travelled in Tibet in the early nineteenth century, described how "when one is lucky enough to find half concealed among the grasses an argol recommended for its size and dryness, there comes over the heart a tranquil joy, one of those sudden emotions which create a transient happiness." Today at the foothills of Kailas they were much in demand, but there seemed to be enough for all; soon blue pillars of smoke rose all round us for the last meal of the pilgrimage.

The final stage back to the resthouse took a further three hours. Snow was falling, and some shepherds, immobile as snowmen, stood and watched us pass in the blizzard. We went down round the last bluff and hill towards the familiar plain.

At the point where the valley opened up to the plain we found a small derelict gompa whose sole inhabitant was a very old lama with whom we drank tea. This was the only holy building left on the parikarama; the monasteries of Juntilphu and Nandi Phu with its offerings of matchlocks, swords and shields and a pair of elephant tusks, and Diripu, which were all situated near the summit of the pass, have been destroyed. Juntilphu and Nandi Phu had been maintained by the same Bhutanese authority that controlled Tarchan. Although this one remaining temple was a bleak little place without thangkas, shrines or gilded Buddhas, it appeared to have a future—workmen were repairing it after the long night of the Cultural Revolution.

We reached Tarchan in the evening when the rays of the setting sun were touching the distant mountains; snow peak after peak was caught in the light before vanishing suddenly in darkness. We passed a herd of sheep marching across the hills throwing up dust, each animal carrying two small woollen bags strapped to its back. Then Tarchan came in sight.

The parikarama of about twenty-eight miles had taken us two days.

"I was worried about you," Dorje said. "Such an old man walking the round."

Ion L. Idriess

My Mate Dick

Gold! Throughout the century the lure of buried wealth has continued to lure men to the wilderness. Gold in Alaska and the North Cascades. Copper in South America. Uranium in Utah. Gems in Africa. Wherever men prospected that big jackpot always glistened just over the next hill.

When Ion Idriess and his young partner Dick explored Australia's Cape York Peninsula before World War I it was still such a wild region that gold was likely to be beneath their feet anywhere they walked. This piece is from the book My Mate Dick *(1962).*

* * *

Next morning just after dawn, with pick and dish on shoulder, joyously we strode out for the hills, looking for gold.

A beautiful sunrise—on such a day we simply *had* to be lucky. As we set out from camp to cross the grassy valley a parrot with piercing shriek sped overhead in a flash of gold, of purple and green. In long swooping dives he sped right across the valley, a rippling sheen of opal in the sunlight.

"He's leading us straight to our spot of gold!" laughed Dick.

My mate was just a tiny bit inclined to see good omens. His eyes were bright as he gazed at the dark range looming ahead of us. It was ever thus. Each day we'd set out full of hope and corned-beef and damper—when we had it.

"Let's try new country," suggested Dick eagerly. "After all, we've barely started on our tucker yet."

"Right-on!" I agreed.

We were only play-acting, of course, with the suggestion of trying "new country," for gold had already been found along the Starcke. Every prospector dreams of finding new country, but he must have at least six months' supply of tucker and the horses to carry it. For all that, there still was ample new country hereabout, we could see it stretching away far north up the Peninsula. While to the west—well, of course, we could not see behind this mass of ranges, the foothills of which Dick was about to climb.

As he veered away from the low country and the dozen blue-black dumps that indicated the workings he put on the pace and I knew we were in for a long and rough day.

And we were. Climbing forest spurs, down into precipitous ravines, up again into patches of gloomy scrub, until we were well away from the Starcke workings. Then digging out and washing dish after dish of wash-dirt, hard as we could go, then on again, seeking this one faint elusive chance, a patch of fresh ground. There were thousands of square miles of fresh ground, of course, but what we were so hopefully seeking was but a few yards of untouched country carrying alluvial gold. Thus with eyes to reef and dyke along the hillsides, eyes directed below to wash-dirt of creek, gully, and ravine, we trudged across a wild bushland joyous with bird-life, scented by flowering timbers of open forest and the dense tangle of jungle-scrub that line many of these mountain streams. And in mid-afternoon we paused on top of a razor-back spur, staring away down at one of these, gazing down on a black roof of interlocking tree-tops bound through and through by giant looping cables and riotous vine and creeper. I glanced expressively at the sun; we were miles away from camp, and it would be a long, rough walk back, with no such help as tracks in this country, of course.

Dick merely shrugged and cautiously began to slide down the spur, for the ravine banks were steep as the roof of a house, even steeper in places. He slipped, flung out arms to save himself, and the shovel and prospecting dish went flying. The dish, already spinning, hit the slope and shot away into space, hit the slope again and sailed out, a glinting, spinning disc in the sunlight, to vanish in a sway of vines deep into those tree-tops below. The long-handled shovel with gathering speed followed it down the incline, the heavy blade swaying as it slithered, for all the world like a hammer-headed snake in desperate flight.

Dick, who had landed thump on his tail, sat up to swear energetically as we watched the dish vanish within that still swaying foliage. And my mate Dick, for all his boyishness, could really swear when thoroughly put out, which his tail seemed to be, for he was tenderly patting it. Of course, now we must find that dish; we could not replace it this side of Cooktown. A prospector without a dish feels as lonely as a dog without fleas.

"Why not leave the dashed thing until morning?" I suggested mildly. "We've a long way back to camp."

"Not on your flaming life, Cyclone!" snapped Dick as he scrambled up and gingerly stepped out, or rather down again. "I'm going to find that dish and try that creek if I have to camp there all night!"

Dick could look very determined. I followed cautiously on, grinning at Dick's back. Usually I was the one who did the clown act. And Dick always called me "Cyclone" when he was a bit upset, a silly nickname given me by the Abos around the Rossville tinfields because I was so slow-going, always shying clear of work when I could dodge it. I'd have to keep quiet then or smoodge a bit until he called me "Jack" again. Anyway, this time we were soon laughing, for clumsy Bully the Pup lost his balance with a startled yelp and went rolling down over and over to smack up against a rock and stare up at us most stupidly.

"I told you so!" laughed Dick. "You clumsy ass! Your fat backside should be the place your head is, then you might look where you're going!"

We were still laughing when we plunged into the scrub where the dish had vanished. I almost believed it was the laugh, or else because we just *had* to be lucky that day, that caused Dick to stretch up his arm and heave on the one huge, looping liana vine, the only one that counted to us among all those thousands. For we heard a distinct tinkle as of a tin dish tapping against a branch high above. Dick threw up his other arm and pulled down his weight as men would haul down upon a block-and-tackle rope. And we heard it coming down as now we both swung on the living cable; it was looped in its elastic strength among the branches high up there, and with us levering down upon it it was making the branches sway, which kept the dish dropping through the foliage until we saw it coming down just there above us.

In good humor now, we pushed our way through this jungle patch, and had to push Bully as well, for the big, overgrown pup was clumsily scared. This was his first jungle patch, he was not used to the gloom and dense, entangling vegetation, which was now dark as night, for it was towards sundown. It was quite a time before we thankfully saw the first filtering of light brightening the green gloom. As always, it was glorious to step out on an open creek bank bathed in that glorious sunlight beating down from above. And then—we stood and just stared and stared and stared.

The "unknown" creek had been freshly worked! The now so clean blue of the bare slate bottom shone under its crystal-clear water as if freshly scrubbed and polished. Down its centre ran the narrow, beautifully clean head-and-tail race where the good gold had been concentrated and cleaned up; one glance told us not a speck would have been missed.

"Picked as clean as the bones of a beast in drought-time!" Dick's murmur seemed to come with the sigh in the gorge.

Both narrow edges of the creek before the sides rose precipitously up were gleaming, too, with piles of water-cleaned wash-stones, recently forked out. All this, the creek bottom and wash-stones and cementing gravels, would normally have been the dull, bluish gray of slate that had been lying there undergoing the weathering of a million years among large, almost black wash-stones, partly covered with a furry green and brown, and russet of clinging mosses. But the hand of man—and picks and shovels and long-hangled sluice forks—had toiled and cunningly harnessed rushing water as power to uproot and turn over and wash away and throw out the entire creek-bed's accumulation of ages until now only the bare rock-bottom, the piles of wash-stones to either bank remained.

Dick sat down on a rock, reaching for the pipe at his belt. I half glanced at his face. The boyishness almost seemed to have gone, overcast by a strained, bitterly disappointed stare.

I glanced away, feeling nearly as bad myself. This was so nakedly plain. A hidden creek, missed by the earlier miners who, in such carefree fashion had thought they had worked out the river headwaters some miles away. Bill Bowden and Cairns had found the show. Like all other prospectors they had been looking for another Palmer, had not much time for find that was not extraordinarily rich. All the same, two hundred men had come drifting along to the mulga wire—"Bill Bowden's struck gold at some place called the Starcke!" And they had worked good gold here some ten miles back for three years; this little field, so hidden away from civilization, had kept producing gold for a handful of men for about six or seven years.

All this went through my mind as I sat down beside Dick and pulled out my pipe, too. We were both staring across at the opposite bank. I was giving Dick a little time, for had we arrived here but a very, very few weeks ago all the gold, all the wealth that for a million years had been hidden within the bosom of this unnamed creek would have been ours!

Filling the pipe, I wondered how much gold those three hundred or so miners had dug from the field found by Bowden and Cairns, only a few miles away. For they had not even bothered to report the gold. Little old Cooktown, of course, was the only civilization in the Peninsula north of Cairns, and no one had bothered to report there. Of course, there was a good deal of secrecy, there has to be, at times, in the life of the prospector. But the men who follow the prospector are miners, and even these had not reported anything at all of what they had dug from those golden gullies way back behind us.

And we knew that, apart from the smaller alluvial, a lot of big, solid, heavy, gleaming, russet-red nuggets had been dug up. Nuggets are "sweeteners," lumps of solid gold.

How many had been dug out of this unknown creek? I wondered.

From the original find Bowden and Cairns had long since ridden away, of course, leaving fortune behind them in that lifelong search to find another Palmer, another Golden Hundred-mile. Bowden would find a bit more gold, too, then he and Bill Lakeland and John Dickie found wolfram away up on the Pascoe River, only recently proclaimed as the Bowden Wolfram Field. It would prove of little use to Bill Bowden, very soon again he would saddle up and ride away, seeking his dream field. If only he had found that wolfram in the wretched war years so nearly upon us he would have made a fortune. Everything rockets up in price in wartime, everything increases phenomenally in value—except human life and happiness.

My mate Dick and I were to find this out, alas!

Bruce Chatwin

In Patagonia

Bruce Chatwin's Patagonia is a mysterious land of exiles, outlaws, legends, violence, maté, gauchos, Indians, and the bones of dinosaurs he had dreamed since boyhood of finding. The following is from his 1977 book, In Patagonia.

*   *   *

I slept in the peons' quarters. The night was cold. They gave me a cot bed and a black winter poncho as a coverlet. Apart from these ponchos, their maté equipment and their knives, the peons were free of possessions.

In the morning there was a heavy dew on the white clover. I walked down the track to the Welsh village of Trevelin, the Place of the Mill. Far below in the valley, tin roofs were glinting. I saw the mill, an ordinary Victorian mill, but on the edge of the village were some strange timber buildings with roofs sloping at all angles. Coming up close I saw that one was a water-tower. A banner floated from it, reading *"Instituto Bahai."*

A black face popped over the bank.

"¿Que tal?"

"Walking."

"Come in."

The Bahai Institute of Trevelin consisted of one short, very black and very muscular negro from Bolivia and six ex-students from the University of Teheran, only one of whom was present.

"All men," the Bolivian sniggered. "All very religious."

He was making a makeshift spinner from a tin can and wanted to go fishing in the lake. The Persian was dousing himself in the shower.

The Persians had come to Patagonia as missionaries for their world religion. They had plenty of money and had stuffed the place with the trappings of middle-class Teheran—wine-red Bokhara rugs, fancy cushions, brass trays, and cigarette boxes painted with scenes from the Shahnama.

The Persian whose name was Ali, swanned out of the shower in a sarong. Black hairs rippled over his unhealthy white body. He had enormous syrupy eyes and a drooping moustache. He sank back on a pile of cushions, ordered the negro to do the washing up and discussed the world situation.

"Persia is a very poor country," he said.

"Persia is a bloody rich country," I said.

"Persia could be a rich country but the Americans have robbed her wealth." All smiled showing a set of swollen gums.

He offered to show me over the Institute. In their library the books were all Bahai literature. I noted down two titles: *The Wrath of God* and *Epistle to the Son of the Wolf, Bahai Ullah*. There was also a *Guide to Better Writing*.

"Which religion have you?" Ali asked. "Christian?"

"I haven't got any special religion this morning. My God is the God of Walkers. If you walk hard enough, you probably don't need any other God."

The negro was delighted to hear this. He wanted to walk to the lake and go fishing.

"How you like my friend?" asked Ali.

"I like him. He's a nice friend."

"He is *my* friend."

"I'm sure."

"He is my very good friend." He pushed his face up to mine. And this is *our room*." He opened a door. There was a double bed with a stuffed doll perched on the pillow. On the wall, strung up on a leather thong, was a big steel machete, which Ali waved in my face.

"Ha! I kill the ungodly."

"Put that thing down."

"English is infidel."

"I said put that thing down."

"I only joke," he said and strung the machete back on its hook. "Is very dangerous here. Argentine is very dangerous people. I have revolver also."

"I don't want to see it."

Ali then showed me the garden and admired it. The Bahais had set their hand to sculpture and garden furniture, and the Bolivian had made a crazy-paving path.

"And now you must go," Ali said. "I am tired yet and we must sleep."

The Bolivian did not want me to go. It was a lovely day. He did want to go fishing. Going to bed that morning was the last thing he wanted to do.

The tenant of the Estancia Paso Roballos was a Canary Islander from Tenerife. He sat in a pink-washed kitchen, where a black clock hammered out the hours and his wife indifferently spooned rhubarb jam into her mouth. The house was all passage and unused rooms. In the salon a settee flaked patches of gilding to the floor. The optimistic plumbing of half a century had collapsed and reeked of amonia.

Homesick and dreaming of lost vigour, the old man named the flowers, the trees, the farming methods and dances of his sunlit mountain in the sea.

Hailstones battered the currant bushes of the garden.

The couple's son-in-law was the gendarme, his occupation to guard the frontier and detain sheep-smugglers. He had a magnificent athlete's body, but the accordion of his forehead whined a story of immobility and repressed ambition.

His head swam with migrations and conquests. He spoke of Vikings in the Brazilian jungle. A professor, he said, had unearthed runic inscriptions. The people of Mars had landed in Peru and taught the Incas the arts of civilization. How else to explain their superior intelligence?

One day he would return his wife to her father. He would drive the police *camioneta* north, over the Paraná, through Brazil and Panama, and Nicaragua and Mexico, and the *chicas* of North America would fall into his arms.

He smiled bitterly at the mirage of an impossible dream.

"Why do you walk?" the old man asked. "Can't you ride a horse? People round here hate walkers. They think they're madmen."

"I can ride," I said, "but I prefer walking. One's own legs are more reliable."

"I once knew an Italian who said that. His name was Garibaldi. He also hated horses and houses. He wore an Araucanian poncho and carried no bag. He would walk up to Bolivia and then orbit down to the Strait. He could cover forty miles a day and only worked when he wanted boots.

"I haven't seen him for six years," the old man said. "I suppose the condors have got him."

Next morning after breakfast he pointed to a terrace high on the mountain opposite.

"That's where the fossils come from."

The Welshwoman in Sarmiento found mylodon bones here and the mandible of a macrauchenia. I climbed up, sheltered behind a rock from the driving sleet, and ate a can of stale sardines. An ancient seabed had been thrust up here, littered with fossil oysters, wet, glinting, and many millions of years old.

I sat and thought of fish. I thought of *portugaises* and Maine lobsters and *loup-de-mer* and bluefish. I even thought of cod, my stomach rebelling against the diet of greasy lamb and old sardines.

Stumbling about and getting knocked flat by the blasts, I found some obsidian knives along with the armour plating of a glyptodon, Ameghino's *Propalaeohoplophorus*. I congratulated myself on a discovery of importance: no artefacts had yet been found with a glyptodon. But, later, in New York,

Mr. Junius Bird assured me my glyptodon had fossilized before men came to the Americas.

From Paso Roballos I walked east—or rather ran before the gale—my leather rucksack heavy with bones and stones. The sides of the track were littered with empty champagne bottles, thrown away by gauchos riding home. The names on the labels were Duc de Saint-Simon, Castel Chandon, and Comte de Valmont.

I crossed back to the coast, arriving at Puerto Deseado, in the first days of February.

Peter Fleming

Brazilian Adventure

In 1932, at the age of twenty-four, the literary editor of The Times *of London joined a ludicrous, three-thousand mile expedition across central Brazil in search of a missing English adventurer. The literary editor and his mutinous companions hoped to solve the mystery in or near the Serra do Roncador, the Snoring Mountains.*

The humorous, self-conscious way in which the literary young man tells his tale—he talks as if he and his friend Roger merely played at being explorers—scarcely disguises the fact that Peter Fleming himself could easily have disappeared in the Matto Grosso.

In the following excerpt the two young Englishmen, abandoned by the group's leader, make a vain final attempt to walk upriver to the Snoring Mountains to solve the mystery of Col. P. H. Fawcett's disappearance. They are accompanied by a local Man Friday with whom they can scarcely communicate.

Brazilian Adventure (1933) reminds me that the phrase "muddling through" is probably the expression most characteristically British in our common language. At the end of his quixotic water and foot journey across the Matto Grosso, Peter Fleming concludes that the earlier expedition of Col. Fawcett had "perished in the summer of 1925, probably at the hands of Indians."

Plagued by shortages and uncertainties, "all the paraphernalia of tropical mumbo jumbo," Peter Fleming murmurs that, "the hardships and privations which we were called on to endure were of a very minor order, the dangers which we ran were considerably less than those to be encountered on any arterial road during a heat wave."

* * *

The next day we changed once more our plan of operations. And here I must digress to explain one of the difficulties which beset our enterprise, and which I have not so far mentioned.

It was a linguistic one. Roger and I had arrived in Brazil knowing no word of Portuguese, though I had a little bookish and erratic Spanish. On the way up country we had picked up a little of the language, and coming down the Araguaya we had perfected a kind of rudimentary patois, sufficient for the purposes of badinage with the men. The prop and mainstay of this dialect was the word *Tem*, which corresponds (at least I think it does) to the French *Il y a* and the Spanish *Hay*. This was almost our only verb, and on it devolved the onerous duty of vitalizing an extensive though inaccurate vocabulary of nouns; it bore the burden of all the persons and all the tenses. On the part of the natives it required a great deal of intuition to set the Tems on fire with meaning.

Our patois was adequate for the simple contingencies of camp life. But when it came to discussing the merits of some elaborate and not easily definable plan of action, and comparing them with the merits of two or three alternative plans, its deficiencies were painfully evident. Queiroz was a rapid talker and only a fairly good guesser; and at our councils of war we could never be certain whether we had interpreted his wishes rightly, or he ours. So many of the factors which helped to form our plans were imponderable—there was so much supposition and guesswork, so many combinations of possibility—that in the absence of an effective *lingua franca*, generalship was a difficult business. Queiroz's opinions, though not those of an expert, were at least based on a wider experience than ours; unfortunately, we were rarely able to make the most of them. Our ignorance of Portuguese, like our lack of a fish-hook, was a constant source of irritation.

Though it was possible to outline a course of action to Queiroz, we could not explain our reasons for adopting it, or elicit his views on its potential modification. There was a sense of frustration, of incompleteness, about our discussions: just as there would be about the intercourse of two deaf men trying to expound to each other the theory of relativity in the middle of Piccadilly.

Anyhow, this is how we changed our plans on the day after we had waded up the river.

It was obvious that we should not make much more progress up the river bed itself, for it was getting more and more overgrown, with deep pools between the tangles; we had exhausted the benefits of amphibianism. The open country which Roger and I had spied the day before looked promising; but I was still determined not to lose touch with the river by striking away from it at a venture. Moreover, we were now in, or at least very near, Indian territory; to cover distance was no longer our first concern, the crow's flight no longer the sole criterion of our efforts. For it was idle to pretend that we should get much further towards the Kuluene without guides and fresh supplies; even barring accidents (a bit of grit in the action of the .22 would have crippled us altogether), I knew that we should have to acknowledge defeat at any moment. Our only hope of postponing that moment lay in getting in touch with these invisible Indians and finding (a) that they were friendly, (b) that they had with them more food than they needed, and (c) that they would come with us towards the Kuluene. It would have been difficult to find three more remote contingencies than (a), (b), and (c).

All the same, it was worth trying, if we could only find out how to try it. I decided to take all our gear to the edge of the open country, a mile upstream; to leave it there in charge of Queiroz; and to make an unburdened reconnaissance with Roger. Apart from keeping a look out for Indians, we would aim at finding an easily accessible camping ground further up the river; if we did, we would return to Queiroz, bring up the stuff along our tracks, and make camp before nightfall. The advantage of this scheme, theoretically, was that it left Roger and me active and mobile without our packs, which by this time were reducing us to the level of oxen, able merely to plod forward, without enterprise, without curiosity, hoping only for a valid excuse to lie down. I looked forward to a certain amount of the eagle eye business.

An hour later we were saying good-bye to Queiroz on the edge of the jungle. He fired the scrub there, to make a landmark for us, and went back to our base, 400 yards away on the river bank. Roger and I struck across the campo in a westerly direction.

It was a hot, bright morning. The country looked somehow more exciting, promised more, than usual. Perhaps it was the knowledge that we were close to Indians, that at any moment a string of little black figures might debouch across the blank yellow grass between two distant clumps of trees. Perhaps it was the lie of the land, the disposition of the solitary or clustered trees which picketed its desolation, that lent it a fortuitous attraction: just as, at a shoot where all the coverts are new to you, one irrationally arouses higher hopes than the others. But I think that really it was I, and not that immutable plateau, who was different on that blazing morning, still acrid with last night's smoke.

Hitherto my imagination had not been fired by the thought that we were in a place never before visited by white men. There were several reasons for this. I abhor labels, and I am not impressed by records. If you tell me that a thing is the largest, or the oldest, or the newest of its kind in the world, I feel no awe: I am not conscious of that sense of privilege which the mere fact of being in its presence ought by rights to arouse in me. I am, if anything, rather prejudiced against it. For by that braggart and fortuitous superlative the thing seems to me to be laying claim to a respect which has nothing to do with its essential qualities. The phrase "to go one better" has come to be very loosely used; it is too often forgotten that to exceed is not necessarily to excel.

In my mind the thought of the word Untrodden aroused some shadow of this prejudice. I looked at those plumed expanses, aching in the heat, at the inviolable murmurous reaches of our river, and I did my very best to feel like stout Cortez. But it was no good. Common sense strangled at birth the delights of discovery, showing them to be no more than an unusually artificial brand of snobbery.

After all, common sense pointed out, the things you see would look exactly the same if you were not the first but the twenty-first white man to see them. You know perfectly well that there is for practical purposes no difference between a place to which no one has been and a place to which hardly anyone has been. Moreover it is quite clear that your visit is going to be entirely valueless; for all the useful data you are capable of bringing back the Great Unknown will be the Great Unknown still. You will have made a negligible reduction in that area of the earth's surface which may be said to be Untrodden; that is all. On your return you will write a book in which you will define at some length the indefinable sensations experienced on entering territory never entered before by a white man; but you know perfectly well that these sensations are no more than the joint product of your imagination and literary precedent—that at the time you were feeling only tired and hungry, and were in fact altogether impervious to whatever spurious attractions the epithet Untrodden is supposed to confer on a locality.

So far common sense had had things all its own way. But on this fiery golden morning, plodding across those decorative and enigmatic wastes, I became suddenly converted to the irrational, the romantic point of view. I felt all at once lordly and exclusive. After all, nobody *had* been here before. Even if we found the spoor of no prehistoric monsters, even if we brought back no curious treasures and only rather boring tales, even if we were unable to give more than the vaguest geographical indication of where exactly it was that we had been—even if these and many other circumstances branded our venture as the sheerest anti-climax—Roger and I would have done a thing which it is becoming increasingly difficult to do—would have broken new ground on this overcrowded planet. As an achievement it was quaint rather than impressive: like being married in an aeroplane, or ringing up Golders Green from San Francisco. But as long as one recognized it as freakish rather than creditable, as long as one never forgot how little it was really worth, it would be to one for ever a source of rather amused satisfaction.

In this comfortable though childish frame of mind I stumbled through the long grass beside Roger. We were making for a distant clump of very tall trees, which was as good a goal as our aimless purpose required, and a better landmark than most of the scenery on this empty stage provided. We were expecting—at this date, so long after disillusionment, it is odd to remember how confidently we were expecting—to sight at any moment a range of mountains: the Serra do Roncador, no less, the Snoring Mountains. Hardly a map of those which we had seen—from the most cautiously non-committal to the most recklessly chimerical—but had stamped those words across the country before us, the country between the Araguaya and the

Xingu. But our horizon remained empty; we might as well have searched it for the Angels of Mons. The Serra do Roncador does not exist; or exists elsewhere. One of the first things I read on my return to London was the statement of Mr. Petrullo, of the Pennsylvania University Expedition, who flew over some of the Kuluene country, that "the supposed range of mountains does not exist."

But we could not know this at the time. We could not know that the Serra do Roncador was a figment of the fevered imagination of Brazilian cartographers, a stage property in the unauthenticated legends of Indians. Somewhere at the far end of the shimmering, unnumbered miles in front of us we looked for mountains.

We came at last to the clump of very tall trees. We passed the cordon of indolent palms which fringed it. We crossed the hard cracked bed of a dried up pool which had given the trees their extra cubits. On the far side we found one which looked as if it could be climbed. We piled our equipment at its roots and went up.

Climbing trees made us realize how far we were from being in the best of condition. The last few days had geared us for solid unrelenting endurance: not for frantic acrobatics, which told on us more than they should have. In physical emergencies we discovered alarming weakness.

All the same, we followed the branches as far as they would take us and clung, sweating, to the last tapering forks, sixty or seventy feet above the ground. All round us the heads of palms nodded in gracious, slightly ironical condescension. We had a magnificent view of the Great Unknown.

To us it looked familiar. Open country, quilted with the tops of close-set clumps of trees, stretched as far as the eye could reach: and doubtless farther. We cursed the visibility, which was bad; last night's smoke lingered as a tenuous haze. We had hoped from here to see those mountains.

It is always pleasant to be higher than one's surroundings; sky-scrapers have contributed materially to American self-confidence. We hung there, cooling, as our tree swung slowly to and fro. I ran my eyes along the river's carapace of jungle, searching for a break.

Then something happened that changed all the values of that spacious but unresponsive scene. From beyond the river's guardian belt of trees— here at its narrowest—a yellowish club-shaped cloud of smoke rose slowly and began to spread. We watched it. We were too far away to hear the ravening of the flames. We could see only the smoke, a sudden, bulbous, and significant growth above the green wall of trees less than a mile away: laborious but dramatic in its rise, like the beanstalk in a pantomime. We were indeed close to Indians; and they knew it.

Looking back along the way we had come, we saw the smoke from Queiroz's fire, a diffuse brackish stain across the blue sky. It was being answered.

"Come on," said Roger.

We were both rather excited. We swarmed down the tree, to the ominous but unregarded sound of tearing. Then we picked up our equipment and the rook rifle and made for the jungle.

For once, the jungle did us a good turn (though we did not feel like that about it at the time). It tripped us up on the threshold of what would probably have been disaster. Forced to scramble and make detours, cut off by the enclosing trees from the irresistible beckoning of that pillar of smoke, our forlorn hope lost impetus. By the time we reached the river, sanity, sponsored by exhaustion, had returned; and the smoke had thinned and spread, so that you could no longer trace its original source. Moreover, the river was deep here, too deep to be crossed without stripping: a thing we were loath to do while we stood a good chance of being attacked. Also the jungle on the further bank was inordinately thick; it would be folly to cut our way through it when our only hope lay in silence.

We were disappointed. Anti-climax, as usual. Our high hopes withered. Our excitement, like the smoke, was dissipated. We began to drop down-stream along the river, searching for a clearing on the opposite bank. Vestiges were plentiful. I wondered if the Indians had marked us down, or if they thought of us as being out on the campo, near our smoke.

We had only the river bank to march by, and that led us on a twisting course. It was a long time before we found the place we wanted: a good and strategically strong camping ground, with only a thin fringe of trees on the opposite, the Indian bank, between the river and the campo.

But it was past noon. If we were to get back to Queiroz and bring up the gear before nightfall we had no time to reconnoitre the opposite bank now. We marked the place and went on working our way down stream.

The going was bad, but we hesitated to strike back on to the campo, where it was better. Queiroz's fire, lit with such forethought for our guidance, had exceeded its terms of reference, spreading swiftly over a huge tract of country and making a holocaust of all our landmarks. It was better to play for safety and stick to the river bank, which must eventually lead us back to our base, by however maddeningly tortuous a route. We had a strenuous, groping afternoon.

Queiroz received the news that Indians had answered our smoke with his usual impassivity. We ate a partridge which I had shot, a particularly well-knit bird, and shouldered our loads. We got back to the chosen camping ground with an hour to spare before nightfall. It was a good place, sandy and secret and backed by thick cover which made the distant possibilities of night attack even more remote. The river here had altogether changed its nature. It was no longer swift and shallow and much overgrown, but ran in a deep and very nearly stagnant channel between steep and sometimes rocky banks. Though we were a stage nearer its source it seemed to have grown rather than diminished.

* * *

There was some talk of crossing to the other bank after dark and taking compass bearings on anything that looked like a camp fire, so that in to-morrow's reconnaissance we should have some clue to work on. I wanted to have a look at the lie of the land; so while Queiroz was making a fire I stripped and tied a pair of trousers round my neck and waded across. The water came up to my neck; the river was deeper here than we had known it since we had left Saō Domingo.

As usual, the open country on the other side was less open than it looked. The scattered trees and the tall grass made a screen which the eye could not penetrate to any great depth. About 400 yards inland there was a thickish belt of low scrub, and on the edge of it stood a tree with a broad but curiously twisted trunk. This I climbed.

I stayed up it for half an hour, and in that half hour the world below me changed. A wind began to sing in the sparse leaves round my observation post. The sky darkened. Massed black cohorts of clouds assembled in the west and came up across the sky under streaming pennons. The wind rose till its voice was a scream; great weals appeared in the upstanding grass, and in the straining thickets the undersides of leaves showed pale and quivering in panic. My tree groaned and bent and trembled. The sky grew darker still.

The earth was ablaze. That fire which the Indians had lit raced forward under the trampling clouds, and behind me, on the other side of the river, a long battle-line of flames was leaping out across the campo we had fired that morning. Huge clouds of smoke charged down the wind, twisting tormented plumes of yellow and black and grey. The air was full of fleeting shreds of burnt stuff. The fall of sparks threw out little skirmishing fires before the main body of the flames. A dead tree close beside me went up with a roar while the fire was still half a mile away.

There was something malevolent in its swift advance. The light thickened and grew yellow; the threatening sky was scorched and lurid. If there could be hell on earth, I thought, this is what it would look like. I remembered with a curious distinctness a picture which had made a great impression on me as a child: a crude, old-fashioned picture of a prairie fire, in a book of adventure. Swung to and fro among the gesturing branches of my tree, I saw again in memory every detail of that picture: the long grass flattened in the wind, the fierce and overstated glare of the approaching fire: and in the foreground a herd of wild horses in panic flight. I remembered that they were led—inevitably—by a grey: that a black horse in the right hand corner of the picture had fallen and would be trampled to death. I even recalled the place and time when I had first seen this picture: the dark winter afternoon, the nursery in which I was recovering from illness, the smooth brass rail on top of the high fender gleaming in the firelight, the shape of the little tree outside the window where half a cocoanut always hung for the tits. I realized with surprise how near the distant image in that picture had been to the reality now before me, and how curiously the fascination exerted by the image had foreshadowed the fascination exerted by the reality.

There was indeed a kind of horrible beauty in the scene. A fury had fallen upon the world. All the sounds, all the colours, expressed daemonic anger. The ponderous and inky clouds, the flames stampeding wantonly, the ungovernable screaming of the wind, the murky yellow light—all these combined to create an atmosphere of monstrous, elemental crisis. The world would split, the sky would fall; things could never be the same after this.

The fire was almost on me now, but my retreat to the river was open and secure. Flames flattened and straining in the wind licked into the belt of scrub beside my tree; great gusts of heat came up from below and struck me. Little birds—why so tardily, I wondered—fled crying to the trees on the river bank. Two big kites warily quartered the frontiers of the fire, though I never saw either stoop. Presently one of them came and sat on a branch below me, so close that I could have hit him with a stick. He stayed there brooding majestically, with his proud eyes, over the work of desolation. Every now and then he shrugged himself and fluffed his feathers: for fear, I suppose, that he might entertain a spark unawares. I felt oddly friendly towards him, as one might to a coastguard in a storm; his imperturbability, his air of having seen a good deal of this sort of thing in his time, were comforting. But a spark stung my naked back, and I swore. The kite looked at me in a deprecating way and dropped downwind to the next tree.

Then the storm broke. It opened first a random fire of huge and icy drops. I saw that we were in for worse and scrambled down the tree: not without regret, for I had seen a fine and curious sight and would willingly have watched for longer, the cataclysmic evening having gone a little to my head. But shelter of a sort was essential, and I found the best available under the trees on the river bank.

On the opposite side Roger and Queiroz had bundled our belongings into a hole between the roots of a tree and were sitting on them, to keep them dry. It was a hopeless task, though. There began such rain as I had never seen before. It fell in sheets and with ferocity. It was ice-cold. It beat the placid river into a convulsive stew. The world darkened; thunder leapt and volleyed in the sky. From time to time lightning would drain the colour and the substance from our surroundings, leaving us to blink timidly at masses of vegetation which had been suddenly shown up as pale elaborate silhouettes, unearthly, ephemeral, and doomed. The rain beat land and water till they roared. The thunder made such noise in heaven as would shortly crack the fabric of the universe. The turmoil was almost too great to intimidate. It could not be with us that Nature had picked so grandiose a quarrel; her strife was internecine. Dwarfed into a safe irrelevance, dwarfed so that we seemed no longer to exist, we had no part in these upheavals. Roger and I smiled at each other across the loud waters with stiff and frozen faces.

The thunder drew slowly off. The rain fell still, but no longer with intolerable force. I slipped into the river, on my way across, and found it so warm that I wished that I had gone to it for shelter from the numbing rain.

The trees had done something to protect our fire, but it was almost out. Shivering like pointers, Roger and I knelt over it in curious heraldic attitudes; our bodies sheltered the last dispirited embers and kept the fire alive. We were so cold that we could hardly speak.

But presently the rain stopped, and the fire was coaxed out of its negative frame of mind into a brisk assertiveness. We thawed, and began to cook a meal and to review the situation.

It was not so much a situation as a predicament. Everything we had with us was soaked. It is true that in this circumstance there was no cause for immediate alarm. We should no doubt survive a night spent in clothes which were after all not much wetter with the rain than they normally were with our sweat. The little that was left of our food was not in a form which could be spoilt even by what corresponded to total and prolonged immersion. As for the films and cameras, their ruin would not prejudice our chances of survival. As far as our possessions were concerned, the storm had left us virtually unscathed.

There were, it is true, our weapons: the little rifle and the revolver. We depended on the one for food, and we might have to depend on the other for defence. Both were wet; they were rusting before our eyes, for lack of a dry stitch to wipe them with. Their never very reliable mechanism would be in a horrible condition by the morning.

But there was more to it than the certainty of an uncomfortable night and the danger of a partial disarmament. We had good reason to feel daunted as well as draggled. For we could not afford to look on this storm as an isolated phenomenon, an unlucky fluke, a source only of easily bearable inconvenience. We had to admit that it looked very much as if we had seen the beginning of the rains.

We knew what it meant if we had. We should have to turn tail and run for it, guzzling quinine as we went; even if all turned out for the best there were at least five hard weeks of travel between us and the nearest roof. If this was really the rains, we should be lucky if we all three got down to Pará with our skins.

The worst of it was, there was every reason to suppose that it was the rains, or at any rate that they were almost upon us. Local opinion set their advent for early September; and these were the last days of

August. The two storms in the last week were the first rain we had seen in Brazil.

All through the night the sky was threatening. It was too cold to sleep very much; Roger and I, huddled over the hissing fire, drowsily debated the merits of retreat and advance. In the end we put off a decision till the morning.

Evelyn Waugh

Ninety-two Days: A Tropical Journey

British novelist Evelyn Waugh (1903–1966) was by nature snobbish,
melancholy, and acerbic. He cannot have been the most pleasant of
companions. Yet he was a man for whom travel was "simply part of
one's life." In travel he found the grist for his writing. In travel he
sought "distant and barbarous places, and particularly . . . the bor-
derlands of conflicting cultures and stages of development, where
ideas, uprooted from their traditions, become oddly changed in
transplantation."

Evelyn Waugh's 1933 journey by horse, foot, and boat across
British Guiana was often made in the company of priests, a reminder
of Waugh's conversion to Roman Catholicism three years earlier. A
host of other characters flicker across this narrative of the savannah,
jungle and rivers but it is the travel itself that dominates.

To his credit this sour fellow had the gumption to travel "in the
manner of the country, taking horses or cars where possible, walking
when necessary, getting rations and labour where one can . . . and
fitting out expeditions of one's own where no facilities exist. . . ."

In the following excerpt from Ninety-two Days *(1934), Evelyn*
Waugh treks with an Irish missionary along the hilly route of a much
earlier survey team. Father Keary was, "a tall, ex-army chaplain, with
the eyes of a visionary, a large grizzled beard, an Irish brogue, a
buoyant and hilarious manner."

* * *

We set out on foot next morning across the Tipuru, walking one behind
the other in a single file which presently spaced out until we straggled a
good half-mile from first to last. The organization was in Father Keary's
hands and I had been witness to some of the difficulties that attended it, so
I was not critical; there did seem, however, to be more people in our party
than our needs warranted. First there was a sturdy gnome-like woman of
great age, who, since she was a slow walker, always set off alone an hour
before the rest of the party, was passed half-way and finished a constant but

undismayed last. She carried nothing except her own belongings, a slab of meat, and a few cooking pots; her interest in coming seemed to be change of air, healthy exercise and the pleasure of observing two foreigners in discomfort; also the half-dollar a day in trade goods, which she received in common with the more heavily burdened members of the expedition. Then followed Antonio who as guide and interpreter was too proud to carry anything except a gun and a cutlass; behind him plodded his wife bowed double with his luggage, her own, and a fair share of the general rations; she was one of the few attractive Macushi women I saw, stocky and drab but with a very sweet, childlike face and long loose hair which blew round her head on the hilltops. Then came Father Keary and myself, and behind four other droghers and Eusebio. He showed a clear aversion to taking a load and usually escaped without anything heavier than the things I needed on the road—hammock, towel, change of clothes, rations for the next meal, and the rapidly depleted bottle of Lisbon brandy which I had bought from Figuiredo. Even so he started reluctantly, looked pathetic all day, and often ended only a few paces ahead of the old woman. The heavy stuff, Father Keary's altar equipment and the farine rations, were borne by two brothers, very large and muscular for their race, shock-headed, with lowering caveman brows and loud, unexpected laughs; they were more untamed than their companions, whom they seemed to despise, and ate apart from them.

They all went barefoot except over the rocks when they would produce flat sandals of palm bark. Father Keary and I wore rubber-soled canvas boots. There is no satisfactory alternative to my knowledge, for we were in a country where one is wading streams five or six times a day and then rapidly becoming dry in direct tropical sun, but the softness of the soles, though it prevented blistering to some extent, made the feet easily bruised on loose stones and the trellis of root in the bush.

We walked for about five hours with a ten-minute rest half-way at a village of five houses named Shimai, and finally made camp by the Maripakuru creek, a short distance from its confluence with the Ireng; there we found a solitary skeleton house, half built and then deserted, and slung our hammocks under the thatched section of its roof. Our day's progress seemed discouraging for the trail had wound in and out of the bush, up creeks to find suitable fords, over steep passes and round spurs, climbing all the way, so that though we had covered a lot of ground and were thoroughly tired, our actual distance from Tipuru seemed negligible.

The cabouri fly here were unbearable so that though we wrapped our hands in handkerchiefs—gloves were one of the highly desirable things it had not occurred to me to bring—and swathed our necks and faces in towels, there was no sleep and little real rest until sunset. We had no lamp with us, so it was necessary to eat by daylight, and even the small amount of uncovering necessary to enable us to handle spoon and knife, made meals, hungry as we were, wholly unwelcome. The bath was delicious so long as one remained submerged, but any limb that appeared over the surface of the water was instantly covered with voracious flies. Cabouri will not attack one so long as one is in motion, and I found it on the whole more agreeable to walk up and down, in spite of stiffness and soreness of feet, than to lie tormented in the hammock. Antonio went out with his gun but came back empty-handed, but we still had fresh meat from the kill at Tipuru so this did not worry us. The truth became clear later, when we were in some need of food, that he was a thoroughly incompetent hunter; moreover the moment he was out of his own country he became timid, and made excuses to avoid leaving the party.

The life of every Indian in these parts is overshadowed by an ever-present, indefinable dread, named *Kenaima*. I met plenty of people, from a self-confident woman graduate in Trinidad to a less certain mineralogist who had lived half his life among Indians, who were willing to explain Kenaima to me and each told me something different. All the books on the country mention Kenaima, many at some length. Its existence and importance cannot be doubted; baptism and even continual contact with Europeans do little to dispel its terror; it is as deep-rooted in the belief of the clothed, English-speaking Indians who work timber at Batika and Mazaruni, as of the unsophisticated people in the Pakaraima Mountains, but no one has yet discovered what exactly constitutes it. All unexplained deaths are attributed to Kenaima, certain places are to be avoided on account of Kenaima, strangers may be Kenaimas, people can set a Kenaima on you, you are in danger of Kenaima if you associate with men of another tribe. Various ceremonial acts are necessary to propitiate Kenaima. It is certainly something malevolent and supernatural, that is all that can be said certainly of it.

It is as well to be highly sceptical of all statements made about primitive beliefs, particularly at the present moment when so much information is being confidently doled out to the public at third hand in the innumerable popular "Outlines" of culture. These are usually *précis* with the qualifications omitted, of weightier books which for the most part are collections of untravelled scholars; the authority ultimately depends on evidence of explorers and travellers and only those who have some acquaintance with the difficulties of obtaining this evidence know what sort of value to attribute to it. At least two-thirds of it is derived from interrogations conducted either through interpreters (the most unsatisfactory form of conversation even on the simplest matters) or with an incomplete knowledge of the language. In any case the languages do not as a rule possess a vocabulary or syntax capable of accuracy, being devoid of abstract terms. And even were it possible for the primitive man to express what he believed—it is hard enough for the highly educated—he is invariably reluctant to do so. Even in the practical questions of direction—as appeared when I asked the Indian at Takutu ford whether I had reached the Sauriwau creek—his natural inclination is to tell the enquirer what he thinks he wishes to hear. This is still more the case in dealing with intimate and embarrassing questions about his private beliefs.

I encountered a very clear instance of this fallability of opinion in the case of Kenaima. Two Europeans, who had exceptional opportunities of studying Indians, had earned their confidence, and had certainly devoted most of their life to them, gave me completely contradictory explanations of the belief. One said that it was the power of evil, the abstract malevolent and destructive principle in life, working for its own end, sometimes in concrete form either human or animal, in order to injure and kill; the other, that it was the art by which a human enemy was able to develop supernatural advantages, become a beast, like the leopard men, werewolves, etc., of universal reputation, travel immense distances instantaneously, go without food, become invisible, and so on, in order to accomplish his revenge. I can imagine either of these statements finding its way into a text-book and becoming part of the material for anthropological hypothesis. Both cannot be wholly true and probably neither is. Possibly Kenaima is supernatural evil, always present and active, which can on occasions be canalized by magic and used for a human motive, in which case the revenger is possessed by evil to such an extent that for the time being he is Kenaima. That is merely a guess. I quote the two confidently definite explanations as being noticeable contributions to the general scepticism that is one of the more valuable fruits of travel.

Another rather more arduous march left us still depressingly close to the point of our departure; as on the day before, we scrambled up and down, through bush where the trail was almost lost and had to be cleared step by step with cutlasses, turning on our tracks, and wading through creeks—one of them the Echilifar, deep and very fast so that it was hard to keep our feet. As before, whenever we attempted to rest we were beset with cabouris. At half-past eleven we reached a hut inhabited by a negress who had been brought up by one of the servants of the Boundary Commission and left there. She gave us fresh milk and four addled eggs. We put up our hammocks in her house and the shade and swaddlings of handkerchiefs and towels gave us some respite from flies. After an hour and a half we resumed the march; at half-past four Antonio gave a loud holler, which was taken up by the following men, and we came in sight of a village of three huts, apparently nameless; there was a fourth partially ruinous hut which we were offered for our camp and unwisely accepted; unwisely because the place was alive with fleas, djiggas and ticks.

We seemed popular here for the people greeted us with unusual cordiality, and besides the ceremonial bowl of cassiri laid out for us on the ground a great dish of cassava bread (not unlike oat cake) and earthenware bowls of peppers and stewed leaf (not unlike spinach). I was intensely thirsty and, seeing Father Keary drink some of the cassiri, did so too. It was agreeable and enormously refreshing, so that always after this, when it was offered, I drank a pint or more with increasing appreciation.

Attempting to check our position on the map by enquiries from Antonio, I found that we were even nearer Tipuru than I had thought, for the two mountains Yewaile and Tawaling, marked several miles apart, are, according to Antonio, two humps on the same spur of hill, and our whole afternoon's march had been merely to encircle this. Father Keary did not share the geographical interests of the early missionaries of his Society and was wholly oblivious to his position or direction. It was his habit to spend most of the day's march telling his beads, quietly following Antonio from one sphere of his true activity to the next. Before supper that evening he baptized a child and married the parents.

We were able to purchase two cocks here with Woolworth bracelets, one of which we killed for supper and the other carried on alive for the next day. It is a curious fact that, though most Indian households keep a few fowls, they do not use them or their eggs for food; indeed the birds, which live frugally on what they can pick up round the houses, are barely eatable. They are kept because the Indians find the crowing of the cocks at night a comforting sound, likely to scare away Kenaimas, and also as measure of time, for they crow pretty regularly at an hour's interval from midnight until dawn.

The night was one of exceptional discomfort, for the moonlight streamed through the ruined roof of the hut, brightly illuminating the interior, with the result that the cabouris kept awake; there were also mosquitoes in fair numbers (I was not using my net at the time and did not wish to disturb the boys to find it among the baggage) and they, with the fleas already mentioned, made sleep difficult; the djiggas and ticks were also at work but did not cause immediate pain. All that was needed to complete the discomfort of night was rain, and this began in a steady downpour some hours before dawn, just when the setting of the moon offered some relief from the cabouris. The boys crowded into the hut but were little better off, for there was no roof of any consequence; so we lit a small fire and sat scratching and shivering until daylight. Father Keary said Mass in the smoky gloom of one of the houses, and we set out again in the rain, scarcely at all refreshed by our night's rest.

That day's march was three long and steep climbs, with two small descents, one to cross the Yowiparu creek, and the other to a bush valley beside the Kowa River where we made camp. We stopped to eat some bananas at the summit of one of the hills but were too tired to trouble about having a meal prepared before supper; then we killed our own cock and ate it in the inevitable swarm of cabouris. But the bush where we camped was tall and dense so that the moonlight did not penetrate to us; the flies disappeared at sunset and we got ten hours' undisturbed sleep.

Next day, for the first time, we seemed to make real progress; the line lay more or less straight, mounting all the way, mostly through open country. We left camp at 6:45 and, taking an hour and a half's rest between 11 and 12:30, reached Karto, the first of the Patamona villages, at 4:45. The last few hours were very painful, first climbing a hillside of sharp pebbles in the full glare of the afternoon sun, and then crossing a dead flat tableland of hot, iron-hard earth.

There were three houses at Karto and an open shelter where we slept. The people were cheerful and hospitable, bringing out, as before, cassiri, peppers, cassava bread and vegetables. Here, for the first time, we met women wearing no clothes except their little bead aprons. There were no cabouris or mosquitoes here, but there was little sleep, for the old bites were continuously at work; we were at a considerable height and it was bitterly cold after sundown; also the djiggas, inflamed by the day's walk, began to make themselves felt.

These djiggas are small insects which live in and around houses; they work their way through one's boots to the soles of one's feet where they drill holes and lay their eggs, preferably under the toe-nails or any hard piece of skin; the process is painless or at least unnoticeable among the numerous other bites that torment one. In a day the eggs have begun to grow; they continue to do so at great rapidity, raising a lump which is at first irritating and later painful. If allowed to remain they hatch out into maggots in the foot and serious poisoning sets in. Their removal is a perfectly simple process if performed by someone native to the place; the eggs are in a little, onion-shaped envelope and it is essential that this shell be removed unbroken, otherwise an egg remains and hatches out. People who live in places liable to djiggas usually have their feet examined by their servant every evening after their bath. He opens up the hole with a pin and dexterously picks out the bag of eggs intact. I had seen Antonio and his wife attending each other in this way several times during the journey. I felt two or three djiggas during the night and asked Antonio to get them out next morning. When he came to do so he found a dozen more and got them all out without difficulty; the operation was practically painless.

It had painful consequences, however, for when I came to walk I found that what with the bruising of the day before and the several small punctures, I was exceedingly lame in both feet. Fortunately we had not far to go and with the help of numerous swigs of brandy, and two sticks, I was able to hobble along at about half the usual pace and four times the usual effort, and just made Kurikabaru, the next village, before giving out, feeling that I had in some measure atoned for whatever suffering I had inflicted on the town clerk's horse on the journey from Boa Vista.

We spent two nights at Kurikabaru; a little hut was at our disposal, built of bark and divided into four minute cubicles, dark and draughty. I spent most of the time there, lying in my hammock. It was a bleak village, thirteen huts scattered on a desolate hilltop, and the people were impoverished and dour. There was rain some of the time and a continuous, raw wind; the height by the aneroid was a little under three thousand feet; I slept with shirt, trousers, and stockings over my pyjamas, but even then was cold at night under the blanket. There was dust and refuse blowing about all day when the rain did not keep it down. The people kept to their houses, huddled in the wood-smoke. The Macushi droghers were ill at ease there and my three wished to go home; loads had grown lighter—in fact we were now uncomfortably short of provisions—and they could easily be spared. Eusebio stayed on and I engaged a Patamona man to carry what was left of my things.

Paying the droghers was a complicated process as it had to be done in powder, packed in little red flasks, shot, gun caps and necklaces; in the end I had not enough to go round for I had been frivolously open-handed at the beginning of the journey, making presents to anyone with an amiable manner. The droghers had to take dollar notes for some of their wages; they accepted them with the apparent lassitude they maintained in all their dealings and tucked them away in their loincloths, from which cache, if they had not disintegrated, as seemed probable, during the journey, they would no doubt pass from hand to hand from the hills to the savannah until eventually they reached Mr. Figuiredo.

I also sent a messenger ahead to find Mr. Winter with a note warning him of our approach, and throwing myself on his kindness for provisions and transport down the Potaro.

Provisions were running short. When I had given the droghers rations for their return journey, we were left without meat and barely enough farine to last the boys four days. Of the personal stores of Father Keary and myself, there was a fair amount of coffee, some rapidly coagulating sugar, two cupfuls of rice, one-eighth of a bottle of brandy, a tin of sardines and a tin of salmon. There was nothing to be got in Kurikabaru except a few bananas. In these circumstances it was impossible to stay on there so we set out again on the second day. On the last evening a hunter came in with a small deer, of which we were able to secure a leg.

It was hunger rather than restored fitness that decided us on the march. The holes from the djiggas were now mostly healed over, but I was suffering from an inflamed toe where one of them had become slightly poisoned. It was astonishing and slightly ludicrous that so small a disability could affect one so much—a single minute limb, shiny, rosy, and increased by half of an inch at the most in girth, made one dead lame; walking was acutely unpleasant; not only was every step very painful but the effort to the rest of the body was absurdly magnified so that an hour's march exhausted one as much as four hours of normal progress. It was annoying too for the rest of the expedition who were obliged to adapt their pace to my limp, for it is every bit as distressing to be held back on a march as to be pushed on.

Fortunately the next stage was a very short one, and by cutting the side out of my boot to ease the swelling, I was able to make it in four hours. We left the open hills now and entered the forest which stretches from there, unbroken, to the coast; there were no more invigorating changes of view, prospects of river and mountain suddenly disclosed and as suddenly shut out as though the curtain had fallen on the act of a play; no shifting of horizon, five miles distant at dawn, fifty miles distant at noon; no confidence, no possibility of surprise, that urged one up the steepest and most fiery hillside with eagerness to see what was beyond; instead there was a twilit green tunnel, leaves on each side and overhead, leaves in front that had to be cut clear as we advanced, and underfoot slippery leaf-mould or a cruel network of bare roots.

We were still crossing Amazon waters; the creeks we crossed and recrossed were tributaries of the Tumong, which in its turn ran into the Ireng, and so by the Rio Branco past Boa Vista into the Rio Negro, the Amazon, and the South Atlantic. During the next two days we passed the continental divide where the waters start flowing towards the Carribean, feeding the Potaro and Essequibo, but there was no clearly defined watershed; the streams dovetailed into one another, the source of the Kowa, which is Amazon water, being north of the source of the Murabang which runs eventually to the Essequibo; the official map of this river system was wildly inaccurate, and what with my complaints about the complexity of the geography, and my lameness, I must, I think, have proved a very tiresome travelling companion to Father Keary.

Peter Matthiessen

The Cloud Forest

*In 1960 Peter Matthiessen and some Peruvian friends made an im-
pulsive decision to search for fossils and archaeological ruins in Peru's
flat rain forest near the Brazilian frontier. The mountain journey down
from the Andes into the* selva, *described in* The Cloud Forest *(1961),
began in late March when the rivers would be navigable. The men set
out on foot to reach a point on the Urubamba River where they could
begin their quixotic thousand-mile canoe and balsa raft trip.*

*This was the misty cloud forest region where legends of jungle
rulers, lost tribes, Inca ruins, prehistoric creatures, and deadly rapids
(such as the dreaded Pongo de Mainique) will probably always attract
adventurers. There in the continent of "magic realism," fact and fiction
blend together like the foliage of the jungle itself.*

* * *

APRIL 15. ARDILES.

Last night I slept badly on a hard cane mat on the mud, beset by chicken
lice, small flies, and mosquitoes: Andrés, who had no sleeping bag, was
given a kind of mattress, an ironic reward, I thought, for his improvidence,
but one which came at a fortunate time, as he needed all the rest he could
get. I awoke this morning rather low in my mind and taped a growing boot
chafe on my ankle.

Our faithful Zacharias and his valiant Tarzan had departed in the early
hours, bearing with them, as it turned out, the greater part of our emergency
ration. Tired before we started, we soon set off ourselves, accompanied by
two fresh bearers lent us by Rodriguez, and bound for the hacienda of César
Lugarte—no relation, it was said, of the César Lugarte upriver. This Lugarte
lived "three hours away, *señores*, walking slowly."

We reached our destination early in the afternoon. The march had
required five or six hours over a path infinitely more tortuous than that of
the previous day; once we paused to fire the .44 in vain at a *pava*, or guan,

of which we saw several during the morning. Our feet were giving out, and we slumped exhausted on the bank while Lugarte peons on the opposite shore waved us back upstream; they were trying to indicate that they had no canoe and that we should cross at a point farther up where, an hour previously, we had been waved downstream. This latter intelligence, of course, was impossible to convey across the roar of the river, and so we simply slumped there, for reasons which were becoming psychological as well as physical.

At last two young men came across the river on a small balsa to talk to us. One of them, called Ardiles, claimed to have a larger balsa farther downriver; to our surprise and pleasure, he agreed to take us down to the Pereiras'. He departed immediately on the trail upstream, to return in less than an hour with a *canoa*, in which he transported us to the Lugarte clearing across the way. One of our bearers, Alejandro, came along with us; he had decided to run away from Señor Rodriguez. In return for his services, we agreed to see to it that he got eventually to Lima.

Tomorrow we walk again, the usual *"cuatro o cinco kilómetros, señores, nada mas,"* but at the end of this walk, whatever its distance, there is at least a balsa. Ardiles claims that he is willing to take us into the jaws of the Pongo itself, and Andrés, who would now willingly risk his life rather than walk even one mile farther on this jungle trail, is all for it. (He may feel, of course, that walking is more dangerous for him, for his heart, than the Pongo could possibly be, and after yesterday I can scarcely blame him.) Though he feels better today, his legs are swelling badly, and he will soon reach the point where courage will not be enough.

We still have a few hours of daylight, and I have taken a bath in the river and washed out both sets of clothes. I am sitting now in the mud yard, observed by the silent Indian peons; their huts, surrounding us, are characteristic of the Machiguengas, high-peaked and closely made, with mud floor, thatch roof, and a kind of straw wall from floor to chin level. Chickens and dogs pick through the huts, and swarms of guinea pigs.

On both sides the mountain ridges hem us in, as if we were trapped in some sort of chute. And of course we are, for there is no turning back: we will soon have the Pereiras and the Pongo to deal with, and after that the open jungle, the unknown.

Of the Pongo de Mainique we have had only dark reports, and Ardiles himself, despite his avowed willingness to take us through it, speaks excitedly of enormous waves and falls and whirlpools, or *remolinos*. As for the Pereiras, they are as much a legend in the *montañas* as they were in the era of Mrs. Cox, and the truth is hard to come by. This much is probably fact: the patriarch, Fidel Pereira, is the mestizo, or half-caste, son of a Portuguese slaver and a Machiguenga woman. He was sent to the university in Cuzco, where he was a brilliant student, and was studying to be a lawyer. But during this period, for reasons disputed, he murdered his father and, fearing reprisal or the law, or both, he fled back into the upper Urubamba. There, in a wilderness to which he held no title, he has established a huge domain, and has gained control of virtually all of his mother's people above the Pongo, even the wild Machiguengas of the tributary rivers. The law has not cared to follow Pereira into Pangoa, as his home grounds are known, and Pereira himself, a single visit to Quillabamba excepted, has not left the jungle in nearly forty years. Some of his holdings he has parceled out among three sons, and there are several other children recognized as well. It is said on the upper Urubamba that his children by Machiguenga women number more than fifty, and that after his return from Cuzco he committed many other murders among his people, but these reports are as doubtful as the one that attests that the old man maintains potency to this day with a secret potion made of monkey milk.

APRIL 16. CASIRENI.

Rudi Ardiles is a well-made young man with no front teeth and a thin mustache; under the circumstances, the mustache cannot be said to do very much for his appearance. Lugarte's *capitaz*—Lugarte himself is absent—dislikes Ardiles and says he is a liar of sorts and that on no account should we risk our lives by going with him through the Pongo; while it is hard to put one's finger on the liars in these parts, it must be said that Ardiles has a wild and shifty eye.

He appeared in mid-morning, and we set off immediately into the jungle. Toward noon we arrived at the clearing of our second *boga*-to-be; after a short argument this man was conscripted, and we celebrated the agreement over a bowl of *caldito*, the watery jungle soup in which, from time to time, one comes upon a piece of chicken. In the yard before us a large butterfly hunched along the ground, black as a burned cinder; it raised its wings suddenly, and the undersides were vivid yellow.

In a few minutes we were off again, Ardiles and the new man, Julio, forging ahead up a very steep jungle trail—at one point that afternoon the river was more than a mile below. Since Julio, was if anything, even less clean-cut in appearance than Ardiles, and since they had with them a good part of our gear, I attempted to keep up with them. It was impossible: the endurance of these people is subhuman. I got far ahead of Andrés and our faithful Alejandro, however, and for the next two hours, the difficult ascents and occasional cliff-hanging excepted, enjoyed myself very much. It was a sunny afternoon and, while humid, not uncomfortable in the shade, and I was able to absorb the atmosphere of mountain jungle as I went. As we descend the river the palms increase in variety and number—there are said to be over one hundred species of palms in the Peruvian jungles alone—

and in one of these the ten to twelve thorny roots merge to form the trunk at least fifteen feet above the ground. There is also a tree with roots crimson in color; these roots are frequently exposed along the trail. The dominant tree, however, is still the tall white *leche-leche*.

There were new bird calls and many butterflies, a huge emerald and mauve cricket, and the largest black ant I have yet seen: this beast, an inch long, looked capable of killing one outright. The flowers, more scattered now, are nonetheless numerous and pretty: there is a violet-like species, and a blue-flowered vine, and a lovely orange bell flower. Some of the epiphytes and parasitic plants are starting to appear—one has clusters of tomato-colored berries. At the end of the trail, on the cliff overlooking the river, I came on a stone incribed with a curious design, like a poised spider. Though not large, it was too heavy to add to our sacks, and I left it behind with regret.

The trail ended in the papaya grove of a Señor Olarte, presently away in Quillabamba; I was offered a papaya and a lemon by a peon and ate them greedily. Ardiles and Julio, with a boy from the Olarte hacienda, were repairing the promised balsa and have cut three new logs for it. The logs are trunks of the balsa tree, a species common on these upper rivers and the one from which the very light wood of children's model airplanes and other toys is derived: the trees are stripped of their green bark and lashed into place with liana vines. The machete is the only tool used by these people to construct what can be a very large and able craft. Ours is somewhat less than that, having a certain fly-by-night air about it: the poles of a first-class balsa are pegged together with hardwood spikes, cut usually from the black cortex of the chonta palm, while our poles are unpegged. Julio, in fact, made no secret of his contempt for our craft, which seems to me a rather unhealthy attitude.

I photographed the building process—the first photographs I have taken in some days, as the camera has been tied into a rubber bag while travelling, because of the frequent stream and river crossings and the rain. Unlimbering it has been more trouble than I have cared to take, perhaps because I dislike carrying a camera: it seems to me that one misses a great deal of *seeing* and *feeling* through thinking of one's experience in terms of light and angle.

The photographic duties done, I washed myself in the river, which was cold and roiled. Then, sitting on a rock, I washed out my socks and shirt, both in a state of dire emergency. After this, naked in the sun, I devoured a second papaya I had brought along. I rarely exult over food, which does not fascinate me unduly, but the excellence of this papaya can scarcely be appreciated by anyone who has not subsisted for a week on the white mealiness of boiled yuca.

When my shirt was dry I visited the balsa-builders: they were not finished, and we decided to put off our departure until morning. I returned to the hacienda, climbing up through large banana groves. There Andrés and Alejandro had arrived at last, and both of them were prostrate. I gathered that Andrés had had a bad time of it on the trail, and feel very guilty about it. Poor Andrés expected a calm journey by canoe, surrounded by all his beloved gear, and instead he has spent the last three days stumbling up and down these steep jungle valleys, with nothing certain at the end of it but another dirt floor and more yuca. His clothes are torn and his legs are swollen, and he carries with him a secret dread about his heart. But he scarcely complains, and, as the saying goes, I hope I am half the man he is when I reach his age.

We have now marched from above the Sirialo to well below the Casireni, a negligible distance on the river but a formidable route overland, burdened with gear. Actually we have walked little more than fifteen hours in the past three days, not counting delays and rests, but anyone willing to try this goat path in its present condition for five hours in the heat of a jungle day—anyone, that is, who is not of Quechua extraction and equipped with Quechua lungs, as all these mestizos appear to be—is welcome to do so, with my blessings. I can only say that Andrés Porras Caceres, a very durable man, will not walk another step if he has to go through the Pongo de Mainique on a papaya rind.

It seems, at last, that our days on foot are over. I am tired myself, and my impressions of our route are blurred, for most of the time, trudging and clambering and sliding onward, I stared at the ground in order to find my footing. But there were some fine moments as well as painful ones—the cold water drunk face down in white mountain streams, the mysterious cries and bird calls, the light-dappled forest stretched high above the roaring river, the scarlet macaws—*bolivars* or *papagayos*—which followed us with their raucous screeches, the long files of leaf-cutting ants swaying along with their burdens, like an endless thin green snake, the perched wood butterflies with the strange "cye" on the underside of their lifted wings, and the "eyes" themselves, staring owlishly from the jungle shadows. These details I shall remember longer than the muddy hillsides, the dry, rasping canebrakes, the palm thickets and thorns, the fierce humidity.

Michel Vieuchange

Smara: The Forbidden City

This is a case where curiosity killed the cat.

The settled confines of bourgeois life were as stifling to 26-year-old Michel Vieuchange as they were to his heroes, Walt Whitman, Rimbaud, and Nietzsche. Eager to experience life, young Michel wrote,

> I have every hunger and every thirst.
> I stay only with that which enlarges my youth.
> Nothing is near to me save all appetite.
> I am shaken by all things.
> I am heedless.
> Everything pleases me, draws me.

After military service in Morocco, what most drew Vieuchange was the lost city of Smara in the Anti-Atlas Mountains. His quest had a nineteenth-century Stanley and Livingston flavor. Unpacified tribes. Rumors. Romance. Danger. The ruins of the ancient, walled city.

In September 1930, disguised as a Berber woman, he left the French-pacified north, and travelled by foot and by camel some 900 miles across the desert to Smara and back. His journey, like his life, was long on enthusiasm and courage but short on practicality. He knew neither Arabic nor Berber. His guides were untrustworthy. His thin slippers were no protection from the desert's rocks, heat, and cold.

[On November 30, 1930 Michel Vieuchange died of dysentery shortly after his agonizing return from "the forbidden city." In order to escape detection he had only been able to spend three hours in Smara. He had once written,

"I have wrestled with the futile restriction of old ideas,
And in the succession of joy and grief I have found
    the tree of knowledge."]

* * *

THURSDAY, SEPTEMBER 11.

The start. Heelless slippers. From the outset I found much discomfort, screwing up my toes in vain. The road: *bled* [prairie-like open country] on either side, in the moonlight. We covered two, three miles. I kept as close to the women as I could. We left the track for a sort of ditch in the *bled*, into which we dropped and lay down. I was between El Mahboul and Larbi. Slippers under my head. Fatigue. I was soon asleep.

Awoke about five a.m. We took the track again, like a nice little family on the road. Camel drivers, whose line we crossed. I was uneasy, because my ankles were too white.

Four hours on the road. Very hard going. Sometimes it seemed that I could go no farther. Feet swollen, little patches where the skin had chafed. Then, the pain overcome, it left me a little calmer.

We crossed Ahl Madher, a small hamlet.

I walked. That is my only objective—to keep going. There is no longer day or night for me. One single thing to do: to arrive. I will sleep anywhere, suffer anything.

Tiznit could be seen, a little over a mile away. Scrub palms standing out from a group of houses with flat roofs and walls of earth. Cactus hedges. The *bled* all round, flat and stony.

We left the track, an awful moment! and crossed little gullies, full of stones. Faint trails, almost parallel, hardly defined, save by stones kicked out of the way in the course of years by the feet of men and beasts. Still, the going was better there.

I thought of Jeannie, of Jean, of Perros. I sang inaudibly "I kiss your little hand, Madame," so that I might forget my feet. But my feet insisted. Then, a phrase of the song awoke sweeter thoughts.

After a time, El Mahboul came to my side and indicated a row of buildings whose walls looked like the earth of the *bled*. A souk, [market] still a long way off. I was afraid to ask them to stop for a while. Luckily, we came to a grove, nearer, surrounded by crumbling low walls of earth. A gap. I went in with El Mahboul and Larbi. El Mahboul talked the whole time we were on the move. Scheming.

In the grove, they made me change my clothes. No longer the red tunic. A large haik, blue, like those of the Dra. I got my miserable feet out of my slippers.

(Immediately, they brought me tea. I could have shouted for joy. I heard the bubbling of the saucepan over a fire between three stones at the foot of a young palm-tree. A few yards away, my guides drank also, exchanging comments and inhaling noisily.

How good it was!

I had forgotten that it was so good to drink.)

In new clothes. They made me go farther into the grove, where I lay down, bare feet on the cool earth. Poor feet, how they hurt! I did not know where to put them so that I should no longer feel them.

El Mahboul made me understand that he was going to Tiznit with Chibani, and that I could sleep while they were gone. I stretched myself out, slippers under my head, and I slept . . . not soundly; but each time I awoke was conscious of less pain in my feet.

I roused completely. I saw the elder of the women hunting for twigs here and there in the orchard. I heard her blowing her fire. I smelt the marvellous, sumptuous perfume of mint, when Larbi put it into the hood of his burnous to ward off the flies. And I rejoiced greatly. I thought of water, but I knew that soon I should drink. I welcomed my thirst. Larbi took a slice of a sort of pumpkin, cleaned it, cut it into small pieces. I saw also, appetising bits of meat on the twigs.

Then I changed my clothes again, with the help of Larbi. Over my white tunic, a black one. Then I lay down again. Immediately my foot or my hand (too white) became uncovered, Larbi hid them with a rough and rather surly pull at my clothes.

I find that he rather overdoes this covering business: blue haik, and then thick white haik. I suffocate, the more because my veil comes almost up to my eyes, above my nose. It seems pretty hard.

Still, when I asked him for writing materials, he obeyed. . . .

El Mahboul and Chibani returned with provisions. They left me in peace, and while I wrote, El Mahboul brought me the first cup of tea, then a second, and the young girl brought me a third. My writing was further interrupted while we ate.

We sat around a sort of stew, in which everybody hunted for his portion with his fingers, Arab fashion: then a drink of water—discoloured water, drawn from the goatskin, with a strong taste of the skin and a sediment of black dust. But it was water. It was good: cool.

Then I withdrew a little farther, to write this.

I shall try to take one or two photographs. But El Mahboul has gone again. Shall I make a bloomer? We shall see.

FRIDAY, SEPTEMBER 12.

(Continuing from where I left off yesterday.)

Lying drowsily beside Larbi, he touched me, and, showing me the half of a pomegranate, peeled off the yellow skin and gave me a handful of the seeds, which I took in the palm of my hand. Lying flat on my face, I ate from my hand, taking the seeds in a single mouthful and chewing them. The juice spurted into my throat.

. . . To the last moment the juice is good, and, at the end the pulp of crushed seeds leaves a pleasant tartness which lasts for a long time. . . .

Impatiently I awaited every move of Larbi, who gave me more seeds. Not one of them was wasted. I eyed them lovingly before putting them into my mouth. They were of a pale rose colour at one end, changing imperceptibly to a translucent white: a colour as fresh as the juice is good.

Larbi cut my fingernails to his liking, with his knife.

Then I rested. I was drowsing when El Mahboul and Chibani came back from the souk with two asses.

While they were getting things together to make a fresh start, I took a few photographs.

We moved on about 3.30 or 4 o'clock.

El Mahboul, without my knowing it, took my slippers to the souk. He had two small pieces added to the sides which grip the heel, so that now I can walk very easily. My feet are still sore; but, taken altogether, I am not in pain.

I rode one of the donkeys, like a horsewoman, across the panniers. Ahead of me, on the other donkey, rode El Mahboul. Like mine, it also carried a pannier on either side. A water-skin in one of the hampers. The teapot near the rump.

The women always walk. What energy they possess, these Arab women. As soon as we make a halt, it is they who gather the wood, build a fire between three stones . . . and often they have to blow a long time to get it going.

We skirted Tiznit. The plain littered with stones. Larbi and Chibani left us, going alone into Tiznit to buy barley for the beasts, to catch up with us later in open country. We continued across the stony plain.

On the right, Tiznit, with its ramparts and flat roofs, its sea of verdure, and, a little higher, the crowns of the palms.

Enclosing the plain, to the left and ahead: the djebel [mountain] not very considerable, at least seen from where we were.

We travelled until sunset, Larbi and Chibani not yet having caught up. Tiznit always in sight. Even the seven o'clock prayer of the muezzin was audible, followed by a French bugle call—farewell to the West—then silence. To-morrow, we shall finally lose contact with the conquered territory.

The sun still shone on the mountains beyond Tiznit: pale green sky above; but, to the left, the mountains and sky were darkening. How the sun caresses the earth here.

Bored by the slow going, El Mahboul called a halt in the middle of a vast plain. I took the chance, and shaved my legs. The shaving-cream worked like a charm.

El Mahboul left me with the two women and the asses, and went off to look for Larbi and his companion, but returned without having found them.

Carefully, I stained my legs, arms, and hands with permanganate of potash, but the solution was too weak, so the result was not too good.

Fed-up with waiting, El Mahboul decided to move on without the others.

As we went, I was afraid to ride the donkey. It grew dark, and the ass stumbled so often; but I stumbled myself, wrenching my feet. Still, I did not suffer as I did this morning . . . and last night.

We kept going for a while. I opened my blue veil slightly, in the gloom, so that I could breathe. I was ahead, leading one of the donkeys, when I heard voices in the rear: Larbi and Chibani, who had overtaken us.

How could they find us in the dark?

They argued vociferously with El Mahboul, who flung his arms about: obviously in a bad humour. Discussing the missed rendezvous undoubtedly.

Still we continued. It began to be hard going. I was just about to get on to the donkey when we stopped for food. The journey had swollen my feet again and, stretched on a sack, my feet bare, it was a real delight to feel the cool air on them. I was absolutely flat on my back—the magnificent sky above—the cool wind on my feet (so that I found their pain almost agreeable)—my face entirely uncovered.

But the pleasure of the moment was utterly spoiled by the smoke of two fires the women started, and which was blown into my eyes by the wind. I was forced to get up: my eyes full of tears, my nose running.

The Arabs breathed the smoke without so much as a frown.

Dinner. Stew, as usual. I was not very hungry; but, how good the mint tea seemed! El Mahboul told me it came from Tiznit, the best in Morocco —in all the world. I took a leaf of mint and crushed it in my hand. I put one in my nostril. Never have I breathed so rich, so refreshing a perfume. What is the mint of France . . . or of anywhere else?

I understood that we were to go no farther during the night. Lying near to El Mahboul, Larbi passed me another djellaba. It was very cold. Everybody suffered because of it. I heard the women shivering, their teeth chattering, complaining, when I awoke in the middle of the night under a brilliant moon.

Larbi was the only one to say his prayers before going to sleep.

Benedict Allen

Who Goes Out in the Midday Sun?

About sixty years from now, if he lives that long, Benedict Allen will be able to rest on his laurels as a classic English explorer. What, a real explorer, in this twenty-first century, they will say. Yes! At the age of twenty-two he made a solo trip alone across a thousand miles of South American jungle between the Orinoco River and the Amazon River. His savoir faire in living and surviving with Indians, renegades, and wild animals would have done credit to a seasoned jungle veteran. Along the way he learned about the rain forest from Indians, he escaped from dangerous prospectors, and he made a seventy-five mile forced march without food through jungle wilderness.

While escaping the predatory gold seekers, Allen took to the jungle in a frail canoe with a dog named Cashoe, who soon capsized it. The canoe broken, his supplies lost, he set off into the Amazon selva in the perhaps hopeless attempt to cross about eighty miles of darkness to the nearest road (which he remembered having seen on a map). Along the way, delirious with fever, he constructed a mental castle complete with keep, parapets, and moat. Before the ordeal was over he had to kill and eat his only friend to keep from starving to death.

The following is from Who Goes Out In The Midday Sun? An Englishman's Trek Through The Amazon Jungle *(1986).*

* * *

JULY 8TH. 6:00 P.M.

Fruit, fruit, fruit! Plenty of it. Marajá berries. I'm camping by a small icy water brook in the mosquito clouds, mashing up those juicy, purple berries, each one like a grape. My neck must be crimson from the wasp bites of yesterday, but for the first time my stomach is full and bloated.

Why did Tautau tell me to bring that dog along with me? Why? Everything might have been fine. I was so near to success. Haven't I got the right to feel angry? Maybe the dog lived. Maybe it is trotting downriver to Mendez, and will live happily ever after.

I will take enough berries for many days. 4½ miles done today.

JULY 9TH.

My stomach cannot take the diet. The stronger half of me shouts in my ear: "Don't be so damn soft!" But have crippling stomach pains. These helped by chewing charcoal from my camp fire, an Eddie McGee and SAS trick. He would be pleased with me, and I can see him now, grinning. 2½ miles completed today, 35 miles total. Must be almost half-way, but my pace is slower today. *Poco a poco* I will get there, Peña said. But now I know *poco a poco* I am packing up.

JULY 10TH. 5:00 P.M.

Stomach pains continuing as I walk. Today I felt weak and light headed. Is it alcohol in the marajá berries, or am I fading away through lack of sugar in my blood? Today I came across a splash of daylight on the forest floor. Yes, it's that rare. A capybara had spotted it as well, and was dozing on some bark chippings. I stalked it clumsily and wanted to cry when it bolted off into the forest. The jungle is my larder. I see it as an Indian does now. Not for its majesty, or beauty, but for its food. Strange that it has taken deprivation by force to bring me close to them spiritually. And though I am not well enough to think clearly, I sense the spirits they talked of. Whatever God is, he is here, and he is not the person that Jorge, and the other Godmen, are worshipping.

Sometimes, even under this hardship, I have moments of utter inner peace. With no company or possessions I am close to God. The Indians had a better idea all along! God is not manlike. He is everything: the stones, the water, the brazil nuts, the parrots. If you have to picture him as a human, see him as a woman. Maternal. God is Mother Nature.

Collected some andiroba nuts, much like brazil nuts, crunched them for my stomach ache, just as Tautau showed me.

Three miles done. 38 total. No water near camp today and passed only two (pathetic) streams. You should see the castle now. The walls are soaring up! The moat is being dug. I'm almost up to the battlements. Stone by stone it's coming along. 2 . . . 3 . . . 4 . . . 5. . . .

JULY 11TH. NOON.

Not at all well. Slept in. Just cannot make myself move camp. I've therefore broken a resolution. I know I will regret the weakness. It just cannot be helped. It is stupid to try and move. Slight fever. Headache. Thoroughly tired. Just unwell. *Can you imagine what it feels like to be slowly winding down like this? To know you are petering out?* My life seems like the flame of a candle. The wind is growing stronger. Now I am flickering. Soon I'm going to be snuffed out. I cannot see my castle, or hear the scrape of the bricks slotting into place today. The forest is silent. Every now and again in that deep silence I hear the dull wine of bluebottle flies—'zzzzzzzzzz'— droning in my ears. They are swarming in the trees. The leaves are heavy with them. If only I could run away from the flies. To stop them jumping over my face I have to bury my face in the earth. No miles done.

Made tea from *quina-quina* bark to lessen the fever. Took two aspirin. Feel so weak.

JULY 12TH. 6:30.

Help in the form of Cashoe! He's with me again. Is it a dream? No, he really is warm in my arms.

Last night, I knew I was being tracked by an animal. I thought I was going to come face to face with a jaguar, and with only a machete. Never mind Maipuri's pig! A jaguar, with claws and teeth! In the darkness, I slid from my shelter, crouched in its entrance with my boots covering my face and fired off two of my three explosive flares into the bushes. Pow! Pow! I blasted away the bush ahead of me. The air clouded with a grey sulphur. The forest burned yellow. Then silence, and nothing but jabbering monkeys, which were grabbing at branches and rolling through the branch limbs, making a run for it.

I stoked the fire, waited five minutes, and then heard a whimper. An emaciated Cashoe, with his white tail high but his ribs jutting out so far they cast shadows in the fire-glow. Twelve days after the capsize he has found me. How? I don't know.

He ate a little of the cooked marajá, but not much. I think he thinks I have more decent food. His poor condition makes me feel strong. But "tomorrow and tomorrow and tomorrow" I creep on with my petty pace. Will I be stronger with the dog? He knows the jungle like an Indian.

Once, Pim told me *I* did. "I have learnt more since."

5 P.M.

I'm up and about again, back in the race. Did three miles. Cashoe following. Clearly he isn't the world's greatest hunting dog, to my disappointment. He is slow and easily exhausted. I refuse to wait for him. "Be bloody bold and resolute." The stronger half of me is in the ascendant, I almost march through the greenery now, 1 . . . 2 . . . 3 . . . 4 . . . whisking my boots through the ground creepers, kicking off those that try and hold me back, tinging my machete through the lianas, carving the jungle up. For the first time I'm convinced I'm coming out of the hill range. But today I had not a dribble of water since this morning's camp. Yet I'm sweating gallons of it. I suck pebbles to keep saliva in my mouth. I lick my arms for salt. I no longer wash my exposed skin. I cannot afford to wipe off the stinking tobacco. I have to fend off those mosquitoes somehow. That, and sleeping in the wood-smoke, is the only way.

So my shirt and trousers are greasy and squidge against my skin because of the algae, but with the dog to chat to I am happier than ever. We both hope for water tomorrow.

Cashoe, as I write this, looks into my eyes and pleads with me for water. He pleads with the same face as the convicts by the roadside in El Callao, wagging their tongues in the dust of my car, as I passed. I know now how they suffered, and wish I had stopped for them.

JULY 13TH.

My tongue swelled up in the night, and almost choked me. But later the rain came in torrents, and I laid my head out from my shelter and let it splash in my eyes. Then I lapped it up from puddles like Cashoe.

5 P.M.

Only about two miles done. Wallowed in the forest stream. That water tasted so sweet. Cashoe drank furiously. But he can't keep up. He is dying. I'm sure of that now. He came to me as a last hope. The stronger half of me, still strong, whispered in my ear, "Of course he's a walking refrigerator." A thought I cannot dismiss. The meat on him could make all the difference. . . . If I spend a while smoking it on the fire, I could have perhaps four days' good supply. I have had no decent protein for two weeks. I am wasting away. I cooked up my last packeted soup, I did not share it. I must be firm about this. Have I the right to do this? Is it so inhumane? I'm not going to weaken my resolve. We would both die. He caused the whole mess. Yet I feel a traitor writing this.

Did only two miles again. Yes, if things don't get dramatically better, he is for the chop. Wonder if he is waiting for me to die? He looks at me, and his look is so hurtful. I saved him from agony once—saved his life—now he looks to me for further help. I'm trying not to become a friend again. It will only make it harder. 43 miles done total.

JULY 14TH. 5:30 P.M.

Continuing without deviation on a NE bearing. I'm sure this obstinacy will pay off. My rhythm is strong. 1 . . . 2 . . . 3 . . . 4. . . . I can last two hundred paces now, before notching them up on my stick. And the notches are not gashes any more, they are neat nicks. The castle is coming along well. The moat complete, crocodiles installed, and underfed so as to appreciate trespassers. The arrow slits are there; the battlements. I am working on the tower for the damsel in distress. I think, I will chose a girl like Yimshi with long straight Indian hair, as thick as thread; but a girl less like a jaguar—she wouldn't surrender herself to imprisonment anyway—though with the same satiny skin. Maybe Zorola of the Orinoco delta, with the long nimble fingers. I wonder if she has been married off yet? 1 . . . 2 . . . 3. . . .

Today I came across a clearing. Daylight! The sun. A burning sphere, instead of putrid stuffy air. It is so good to feel my clothes baking, the water percolating away in steam. To smell the jungle burning to a frazzle, the leaves suffering under the sun's rays.

This is a small patch of neck-high grassland only the size of a tree crown. I can't think why it's here. Not man-made. No tree stumps, burnt-out settlements, or scruffy man-spoilt vegetation. The greatest excitement is that there are locusts here. Big juicy fat things. Tomorrow I may have the strength to go after them.

Four miles done, and for long stretches Cashoe was out of sight. He still manages to smell me out, and now limps in pursuit of the locusts.

JULY 15TH. 6:00.

The locusts are massive and slow. Forefinger length, vivid green jobs, with red/orange-tinged bellies. They flash as bright as beetroot when they fly, and edge round the other side of branches when you approach. Clobbered 15 with a stick. Netted 16 more with my shirt. I packed mud on my shoulders the way that Narru and Camahu showed me that day we spent hunting in the grey mud delta. But my back is still cracking open, red and blistered with the sun. The oil of my andiroba nuts should help smooth them. This evening I fried the last of the locusts on a stick. For the first time I shared food with Cashoe. I gave him the three biggest ones. I value his company so much. Why didn't I listen to the Sicilian in El Callao? Why did I ever come through the gold zone? I think it couldn't have been avoided. That is my comfort, but I broke my promise.

I ought to have a celebration. 50 miles done! Three today. I'm in better-than-should-be-for-circumstances spirits. But why, oh why, didn't I hang around the clearing? I could have scrounged some more food. Now it's back in the darkness, with the cobwebs in my eyes and skin raw with fungi. 1 . . . 2 . . . 3 . . . 4. . . .

JULY 16TH. 5:00 P.M.

The dog seems to have picked up in spirits. I have a sneaking feeling he found some food today. Maybe a rat. I feel weak again. My lips are puffed out and chafed. They feel like tyre treads.

My cheeks have been slashed with a poisonous spiky palm. The dog licked the cuts clean. The only water nearby was black and stagnant. It smelt of tarmac. I filtered it with a trouser pocket, and boiled it. I shared some boiled palm stems with the dog. We are companions again. I share my food with him nowadays. Having him here is uplifting. This jungle is his home. He knows the ropes.

I tapped a banana tree for water today, and remembered Fritz doing the same. Chico, *his* dog, was a source of strength to him, as Cashoe is to me. But Cashoe as well reminds me of the times when I was with the Indians. In those days I could live off the jungle. *That* is why having him here makes me feel stronger.

D. H. Lawrence

Mornings in Mexico

Mornings in Mexico (1927) describes the period in Oaxaca when novelist D. H. Lawrence (1885–1930) was writing his Mexican novel The Plumed Serpent *(1926).*
The following excerpt is titled "Walk to Huayapa."

* * *

Curious is the psychology of Sunday. Humanity enjoying itself is on the whole a dreary spectacle, and holidays are more disheartening than drudgery. One makes up one's mind: On Sundays and on *fiestas* I will stay at home, in the hermitage of the *patio*, with the parrots and Corasmin and the reddening coffee-berries. I will avoid the sight of people "enjoying themselves"—or try to, without much success.

Then comes Sunday morning, with the peculiar looseness of its sunshine. And even if *you* keep mum, the better-half says: Let's go somewhere.

But, thank God, in Mexico at least one can't set off in the "machine." It is a question of a meagre horse and a wooden saddle; on a donkey; or what we called, as children, "Shanks' pony"—the shanks referring discourteously to one's own legs.

We will go out of town. "Rosalino, we are going for a walk to San Felipe de la Aguas. Do you want to go, and carry the basket?"

"*Como no, Señor?*"

It is Rosalino's inevitable answer, as inevitable as the parrot's "Perro!" "*Como no, Señor?*"—"How not, Señor?"

The Norte, the north-wind, was blowing last night, rattling the worm-chewed window-frames.

"Rosalino, I am afraid you will be cold in the night."

"*Como no, Señor?*"

"Would you like a blanket?"

"*Como no, Señor?*"

"With this you will be warm?"

"*Como no, Señor?*"

But the morning is perfect; in a moment we are clear out of the town.

Most towns in Mexico, saving the capital, end in themselves, at once. As if they had been lowered from heaven in a napkin, and deposited, rather foreign, upon the wild plain. So we walk round the wall of the church and the huge old monastery enclosure that is now barracks for the scrap-heap soldiery, and at once there are the hills.

"I will lift up my eyes unto the hills, whence cometh my strength." At least one can always do *that*, in Mexico. In a stride, the town passes away. Before us lies the gleaming, pinkish-ochre of the valley flat, wild and exalted with sunshine. On the left, quite near, bank the stiffly pleated mountains, all the foot-hills, that press savannah-coloured into the savannah of the valley. The mountains are clothed smokily with pine, *ocote*, and, like a woman in a gauze *rebozo*, they rear in a rich blue fume that is almost cornflower-blue in the clefts. It is their characteristic that they are darkest blue at the top. Like some splendid lizard with a wavering, royal-blue crest down the ridge of his back, and pale belly, and soft, pinky-fawn claws, on the plain.

Between the pallor of the claws, a dark spot of trees, and white dots of a church with twin towers. Further away, along the foot-hills, a few scattered trees, white dot and stroke of a *hacienda*, and a green, green square of sugar-cane. Further off still, at the mouth of a cleft of a canyon, a dense little green patch of trees, and two spots of proud church.

"Rosalino, which is San Felipe?"

"*Quien sabe, Señor?*" says Rosalino, looking at the villages beyond the sun of the savannah with black, visionless eyes. In his voice is the inevitable flat resonance of aloofness, touched with resignation, as if to say: It is not becoming to a man to know these things.—Among the Indians it is not becoming to know anything, not even one's own name.

Rosalino is a mountain boy, an Indian from a village two days' walk away. But he has been two years in the little city, and has learnt his modicum of Spanish.

"Have you never been to any of these villages?"

"No, Señor, I never went."

"Didn't you want to?"

"*Como no, Señor?*"

The Americans would call him a dumb-bell.

We decide for the farthest speck of a village in a dark spot of trees. It lies so magical, alone, tilted in the fawn-pink slope, again as if the dark-green napkin with a few white tiny buildings had been lowered from heaven and left, there at the foot of the mountains, with the deep groove of a canyon slanting in behind. So alone and, as it were, detached from the world in which it lies, a spot.

Nowhere more than in Mexico does human life become isolated, external to its surroundings, and cut off tinily from the environment. Even as you come across the plain to a big city like Guadalajara, and see the twin towers of the cathedral peering around in loneliness like two lost birds side by side on a moor, lifting their white heads to look around in the wilderness, your heart gives a clutch, feeling the pathos, the isolated tininess of human effort. As for building a church with one tower only, it is unthinkable. There must be two towers, to keep each other company in this wilderness world.

The morning is still early, the brilliant sun does not burn too much. Tomorrow is the shortest day. The savannah valley is shadeless, spotted only with the thorny ravel of mesquite bushes. Down the trail that has worn grooves in the turf—the rock is near the surface—occasional donkeys with a blue-hooded woman perched on top come tripping in silence, twinkling, a shadow. Just occasional women taking a few vegetables to market. Practically no men. It is Sunday.

Rosalino, prancing behind with the basket, plucks up his courage to speak to one of the women passing on a donkey. "Is that San Felipe where we are going?"—"No, that is not San Felipe."—"What, then, is it called?"— "It is called Huayapa."—"Which, then, is San Felipe?"—"That one"—and she points to her right.

They have spoken to each other in half-audible, crushed tones, as they always do, the woman on the donkey and the woman with her on foot swerving away from the basket-carrying Rosalino. They all swerve away from us, as if we were potential bold brigands. It really gets one's pecker up. The presence of the Señora only half reassures them. For the Señora, in a plain hat of bluey-green woven grass, and a dress of white cotton with black squares on it, is almost a monster of unusualness. *Prophet art thou, bird, or devil?* the women seem to say, as they look at her with keen black eyes. I think they choose to decide she is more of the last.

The women look at the woman, the men look at the man. And always with that same suspicious, enquiring, wondering look, the same with which Edgar Allen Poe must have looked at his momentous raven:

"Prophet art thou, bird, or devil?"

Devil, then, to please you! one longs to answer, in a tone of *Nevermore.*

Ten o'clock, and the sun getting hot. Not a spot of shade, apparently, from here to Huayapa. The blue getting thinner on the mountains, and an indiscernible vagueness, of too much light, descending on the plain.

The road suddenly dips into a little crack, where runs a creek. This again is characteristic of these parts of America. Water keeps out of sight. Even the biggest rivers, even the tiny brooks. You look across a plain on which the light sinks down, and you think: Dry! Dry! Absolutely dry! You travel along, and suddenly come to a crack in the earth, and a little stream is running in a little walled-in valley bed, where is a half-yard of green turf, and bushes, the *palo-blanco* with leaves, and with big white flowers like pure white, crumpled cambric. Or you may come to a river a thousand feet below, sheer below you. But not in this valley. Only the stream.

"Shade!" says the Señora, subsiding under a steep bank.

"*Mucho calor!*" says Rosalino, taking off his extra-jaunty straw hat, and subsiding with the basket.

Down the slope are coming two women on donkeys. Seeing the terrible array of three people sitting under a bank, they pull up.

"*Adios!*" I say, with firm resonance.

"*Adios!*" says the Señora, with diffidence.

"*Adios!*" says the reticent Rosalino, his voice the shadow of ours.

"*Adios! Adios! Adios!*" say the women, in suppressed voices, swerving, neutral, past us on their self-contained, sway-eared asses.

When they have passed, Rosalino looks at me to see if I shall laugh. I give a little grin, and he gives me back a great explosive grin, throwing back his head in silence, opening his wide mouth and showing his soft pink tongue, looking along his cheeks with his saurian black eyes, in an access of *farouche* derision.

A great hawk, like an eagle, with white bars at the end of its wings, sweeps low over us, looking for snakes. One can hear the hiss of its pinions.

"*Gabilan,*" says Rosalino.

"What is it called in the *idioma*?"

"*Psia!*"—He makes the consonants explode and hiss.

"Ah!" says the Señora. "One hears it in the wings. *Psia!*"

"Yes," says Rosalino, with black eyes of incomprehension.

Down the creek, two native boys, little herdsmen, are bathing, stooping with knees together and throwing water over themselves, rising, gleaming dark coffee-red in the sun, wetly. They are very dark, and their wet heads are so black, they seem to give off a bluish light, like dark electricity.

The great cattle they are tending slowly plunge through the bushes, coming up-stream. At the place where the path fords the stream, a great ox stoops to drink. Comes a cow after him, and a calf, and a young bull. They all drink a little at the stream, their noses delicately touching the water. And then the young bull, horns abranch, stares fixedly, with some of the same Indian wonder-and-suspicion stare, at us sitting under the bank.

Up jumps the Señora, proceeds uphill, trying to save her dignity. The bull, slowly leaning into motion, moves across-stream like a ship unmoored. The bathing lad on the bank is hastily fastening his calico pantaloons round his ruddy-dark waist. The Indians have a certain rich physique, even this lad. He comes running short-step down the bank, uttering a bird-like whoop, his dark hair gleaming bluish. Stooping for a moment to select a stone, he runs athwart the bull, and aims the stone sideways at him. There is a thud, the ponderous, adventurous young animal swerves docilely round towards the stream. "*Becerro!*" cries the boy, in his bird-like, piping tone, selecting a stone to throw at the calf.

We proceed in the blazing sun up the slope. There is a white line at the foot of the trees. It looks like water running white over a weir. The supply of the town water comes this way. Perhaps this is a reservoir. A sheet of water! How lovely it would be, in this country, if there was a sheet of water with a stream running out of it! And those dense trees of Huayapa behind.

"What is that white, Rosalino? Is it water?"

"*El blanco? Si, agua, Señora*," says that dumb-bell.

Probably, if the Señora had said: Is it milk? he would have replied in exactly the same way: *Si es leche, Señora!*—Yes, it's milk.

Hot, silent, walking only amidst a weight of light, out of which one hardly sees, we climb the spurs towards the dark trees. And as we draw nearer, the white slowly resolves into a broken, whitewashed wall.

"Oh!" exclaims the Señora, in real disappointment. "It isn't water! It's a wall!"

"*Si, Señora. Es panteón.*" (They call a cemetery a *panteón*, down here.)

"It is a cemetery," announces Rosalino, with a certain ponderous, pleased assurance, and without afterthought. But when I suddenly laugh at the absurdity, he also gives a sudden broken yelp of laughter.—They laugh as if it were against their will, as if it hurt them, giving themselves away.

It was nearing midday. At last we got into a shady lane, in which were puddles of escaped irrigation-water. The ragged semi-squalor of a half-tropical lane, with naked trees sprouting into spiky scarlet flowers, and bushes with biggish yellow flowers, sitting rather wearily on their stems, led to the village.

We were entering Huayapa. *Iª Calle de las Minas*, said an old notice. *Iª Calle de las Minas*, said a new, brand-new notice, as if in confirmation. *First Street of the Mines*. And every street had the same old and brand-new notice: 1st. Street of the Magnolia: 4th Street of Enriquez Gonzalez: very fine!

But the First Street of the Mines was just a track between the stiff living fence of organ cactus, with *poinsettia* trees holding up scarlet mops of flowers, and mango trees, tall and black, stonily drooping the strings of unripe fruit. The Street of the Magnolia was a rocky stream-gutter, disapearing to nowhere from nowhere, between cactus and bushes. The Street of the Vasquez was a stony stream-bed, emerging out of tall, wildly tall reeds.

Not a soul anywhere. Through the fences, half deserted gardens of trees and banana plants, each enclosure with a half-hidden hut of black adobe bricks crowned with a few old tiles for a roof, and perhaps a new wing made of twigs. Everything hidden, secret, silent. A sense of darkness among the silent mango trees, a sense of lurking, of unwillingness. Then actually some half-bold curs barking at us across the stile of one garden, a forked bough over which one must step to enter the chicken-bitten enclosure. And actually a man crossing the proudly labelled: Fifth Street of the Independence.

If there were no churches to mark a point in these villages, there would no nowhere at all to make for. The sense of nowhere is intense, between the dumb and repellent living fence of cactus. But the Spaniards, in the midst of these black, mud-brick huts, have inevitably reared the white twin-towered magnificence of a big and lonely, hopeless church; and where there is a church there will be a *plaza*. And a *plaza* is a *zocalo*, a hub. Even though the wheel does not go round, a hub is still a hub. Like the old Forum.

So we stray diffidently on, in the maze of streets which are only straight tracks between cactuses, till we see *Reforma*, and at the end of *Reforma*, the great church.

In front of the church is a rocky plaza leaking with grass, with water rushing into two big, oblong stone basins. The great church stands rather ragged, in a dense forlornness, for all the world like some big white human being, in rags, held captive in a world of ants.

On the uphill side of the *plaza*, a long low white building with a shed in front, and under the shed crowding, all the short-statured men of the *pueblo*, in their white cotton clothes and big hats. They are listening to something: but the silence is heavy, furtive, secretive. They stir like white-clad insects.

Rosalino looks sideways at them, and sheers away. Even we lower our voices to ask what is going on. Rosalino replies, *sotto voce*, that they are making *asuntos*. But what business? we insist. The dark faces of the little men under the big hats look round at us suspiciously, like dark gaps in the atmosphere. Our alien presence in this vacuous village, is like the sound of a drum in a churchyard. Rosalino mumbles unintelligibly. We stray across the forlorn yard into the church.

Thursday was the day of the Virgin of the Soledad, so the church is littered with flowers, sprays of wild yellow flowers trailing on the floor. There is a great Gulliver's Travels fresco picture of an angel having a joy-ride on the back of a Goliath. On the left, near the altar steps, is seated a life-size Christ—undersized; seated upon a little table, wearing a pair of woman's frilled knickers, a little mantle of purple silk dangling from His back, and His face bent forward gazing fatuously at His naked knee, which emerges from the needlework frill of the drawers. Across from Him a living woman is half-hidden behind a buttress, mending something, sewing.

We sit silent, motionless, in the whitewashed church ornamented with royal blue and bits of gilt. A barefoot Indian with a high-domed head comes in and kneels with his legs close together, his back stiff, at once very humble and resistant. His cotton jacket and trousers are long-unwashed rag, the colour of dry earth, and torn, so that one sees smooth pieces of brown thigh, and brown back. He kneels in a sort of intense fervour for a minute, then gets up and childishly, almost idiotically, begins to take the pieces of candle from the candlesticks. He is the Verger.

Outside, the gang of men is still pressing under the shed. We insist on knowing what is going on. Rosalino, looking sideways at them, plucks up courage to say plainly that the two men at the table are canvassing for votes: for the Government, for the State, for a new governor, whatever it may be. Votes! Votes! Votes! The farce of it! Already on the wall of the low building, on which one sees, in blue letters, the word *Justizia*, there are pasted the late political posters, with the loud announcement: Vote For This Mark ⊕. Or another: Vote for This Mark ⊖.

My dear fellow, this is when democracy becomes real fun. You vote for one red ring inside another red ring and you get a Julio Echegaray. You vote for a blue dot inside a blue ring, and you get a Socrate Ezequiel Tos. Heaven knows what you get for the two little red circles on top of one another ∶. Suppose we vote, and try. There's all sorts in the lucky bag. There might come a name like Peregrino Zenon Cocotilla.

Independence! Government by the People, of the People, for the People! We all live in the Calle de la Reforma, in Mexico.

On the bottom of the *plaza* is a shop. We want some fruit. *"Hay frutas?* Oranges or bananas?"—"No, Señor."—"No fruits?"—*"No hay!"*—"Can I buy a cup?"—*"No hay."*—"Can I buy a *jicara*, a gourd-shell that we might drink from?" *"No hay."*

No hay means *there isn't any,* and it's the most regular sound made by the dumb-bells of the land.

"What is there, then?" A sickly grin. There are, as a matter of fact, candles, soap, dead and withered chiles, a few dried grasshoppers, dust, and stark, bare wooden pigeon-holes. Nothing, nothing, nothing. Next-door is another little hole of a shop. *Hay frutas?—No hay.—Qué hay?—Hay tepache!*

"Para borracharse," says Rosalino, with a great grin.

Tepache is a fermented drink of pineapple rinds and brown sugar: to get drunk on, as Rosalino says. But mildly drunk. There is probably *mescal* too, to get brutally drunk on.

The village is exhausted in resource. But we insist on fruit. Where, *where* can I buy oranges and bananas? I see oranges on the trees, I see banana plants.

"Up there!" The woman waves with her hand as if she were cutting the air upwards.

"That way?"

"Yes."

We go up the Street of Independence. They have got rid of us from the *plaza.*

Another black hut with a yard, and orange-trees beyond.

"Hay frutas?"

"No hay."

"Not an orange, nor a banana?"

"*No hay.*"

We go on. *She* has got rid of us. We descend the black rocky steps to the stream, and up the other side, past the high reeds. There is a yard with heaps of maize in a shed, and tethered bullocks: and a bare-bosom, black-browed girl.

"*Hay frutas?*"

"*No hay.*"

"But yes! There are oranges—there!"

She turns and looks at the oranges on the trees at the back, and imbecilely answers:

"*No hay.*"

It is a choice between killing her and hurrying away.

We hear a drum and a whistle. It is down a rocky black track that calls itself The Street of Benito Juarez: the same old gent who stands for all this obvious Reform, and Vote for ⊙.

A yard with shade round. Women kneading the maize dough, *masa*, for *tortillas*. A man lounging. And a little boy beating a kettledrum sideways, and a big man playing a little reedy wooden whistle, rapidly, endlessly, disguising the tune of *La Cucuracha*. They won't play a tune unless they can render it almost unrecognisable.

"*Hay frutas?*"

"*No hay.*"

"Then what is happening here?"

A sheepish look, and no answer.

"Why are you playing music?"

"It is a *fiesta.*"

My God, a feast! That weary *masa*, a millstone in the belly. And for the rest, the blank, heavy, dark-grey barrenness, like an adobe brick. The drum-boy rolls his big Indian eyes at us, and beats on, though filled with consternation. The flute man glances, is half appalled and half resentful, so he blows harder. The lounging man comes and mutters to Rosalino, and Rosalino mutters back, four words.

Four words in the *idioma*, the Zapotec language. We retire, pushed silently away.

"What language do they speak here, Rosalino?"

"The *idioma.*"

"You understand them? It is Zapoteca, same as your language?"

"Yes, Señor."

"Then why do you always speak in Spanish to them?"

"Because they don't speak the *idioma* of my village."

He means, presumably, that there are dialect differences. Anyhow, he asserts his bit of Spanish, and says *Hay frutas?*

It was like a *posada*. It was like the Holy Virgin on Christmas Eve, wandering from door to door looking for a lodging in which to bear her child: Is there a room here? *No hay!*

The same with us. *Hay frutas? No hay!* We went down every straight ant-run of that blessed village. But at last we pinned a good-natured woman. "Now tell us, *where* can we buy oranges? We see them on the trees. We want them to eat."

"Go," she said, "to Valentino Ruiz. He has oranges. Yes, he has oranges, and he sells them." And she cut the air upwards with her hand.

From black hut to black hut went we, till at last we got to the house of Valentino Ruiz. And lo! it was the yard with the *fiesta*. The lounging man was peeping out of the gateless gateway, as we came, at us.

"It is the same place!" cried Rosalino, with a laugh of bashful agony.

But we don't belong to the ruling race for nothing. Into the yard we march.

"Is this the house of Valentino Ruiz? *Hay naranjas?* Are there oranges?"

We had wandered so long, and asked so often, that the *masa* was made into *tortillas*, the *tortillas* were baked, and a group of people were sitting in a ring on the ground, eating them. It was the *fiesta*.

At my question up jumped a youngish man, and a woman as if they had been sitting on a scorpion each.

"Oh, Señor," said the woman, "there are few oranges, and they are not ripe, as the Señor would want them. But pass this way."

We pass up to the garden, past the pink roses, to a little orange-tree, with a few yellowish-green oranges.

"You see, they are not ripe as you will want them," says the youngish man.

"They will do." Tropical oranges are always green. These, we found later, were almost insipidly sweet.

Even then, I can only get three of the big, thick-skinned, greenish oranges. But I spy sweet limes, and insist on having five or six of these.

He charges me three cents apiece for the oranges: the market price is two for five cents: and one cent each for the *limas*.

"In my village," mutters Rosalino when we get away, "oranges are five for one cent."

Never mind! It is one o'clock. Let us get out of the village, where the water will be safe, and eat lunch.

In the *plaza*, the men are just dispersing, one gang coming down the hill. They watch us as if we were coyote, a zopilote, and a white she-bear walking together in the street.

"*Adios!*"

"*Adios!*" comes the low roll of reply, like a roll of cannon shot.

The water rushes downhill in a stone gutter beside the road. We climb up the hill, up the Street of the Camomile, alongside the rushing water. At one point it crosses the road unchannelled, and we wade through it. It is the village drinking supply.

At the juncture of the roads, where the water crosses, another silent white gang of men. Again: *Adios!* and again the low, musical, deep volley of *Adios!*

Up, up wearily. We must get above the village to be able to drink the water without developing typhoid.

At last, the last house, the naked hills. We follow the water across a dry maize-field, then up along a bank. Below is a quite deep gully. Across is an orchard, and some women with baskets of fruit.

"*Hay frutas?*" calls Rosalino, in a half-voice. He is getting bold.

"*Hay,*" says an old woman, in the curious half-voice. "But not ripe."

Shall we go down into the gully into the shade? No; someone is bathing among the reeds below, and the aqueduct water rushes along in the gutter here above. On, on, till we spy a wild guava tree over the channel of water. At last we can sit down and eat and drink, on a bank of dry grass, under the wild guava tree.

We put the bottle of lemonade in the aqueduct to cool. I scoop out a big half-orange, the thick rind of which makes a cup.

"Look, Rosalino! The cup!"

"*La taza!*" he cries, soft-tongued, with a bark of laughter and delight.

And one drinks the soft, rather lifeless, warmish Mexican water. But it is pure.

Over the brink of the water-channel is the gully, and a noise —chock, chock! I go to look. It is a woman, naked to the hips, standing washing her other garments upon a stone. She has a beautiful full back, of a deep orange colour, and her wet hair is divided and piled. In the water a few yards upstream two men are sitting naked, their brown-orange giving off a glow in the shadow, also washing their clothes. Their wet hair seems to steam blue-blackness. Just above them is a sort of bridge, where the water divides, the channel-water taken from the little river, and led along the top of the bank.

We sit under the wild guava tree in silence, and eat. The old woman of the fruit, with naked breast and coffee-brown naked arms, her under-garment fastened on one shoulder, round her waist an old striped *sarape* for a skirt, and on her head a blue *rebozo* piled against the sun, comes marching down the aqueduct with black bare feet, holding three or four *chirimoyas* to her bosom. *Chirimoyas* are green custard-apples.

She lectures us, in slow, heavy Spanish:

"This water, here, is for drinking. The other, below, is for washing. This, you drink, and you don't wash in it. The other, you wash in, and you don't drink it." And she looked inquisitively at the bottle of lemonade, cooling.

"Very good. We understand."

Then she gave us the *chirimoyas*. I asked her to change the *peso*: I had no change.

"No, Señor," she said. "No, Señor. You don't pay me. I bring you these, and may you eat well. But the *chirimoyas* are not ripe: in two or three days they will be ripe. Now, they are not. In two or three days they will be. Now, they are not. You can't eat them yet. But I make a gift of them to you, and may you eat well. Farewell. Remain with God."

She marched impatiently off along the aqueduct.

Rosalino waited to catch my eye. Then he opened his mouth and showed his pink tongue and swelled out his throat like a cobra, in a silent laugh after the old woman.

"But," he said in a low tone, "the *chirimoyas* are not good ones."

And again he swelled in the silent, delighted, derisive laugh.

He was right. When we came to eat them, three days later, the custard-apples all had worms in them, and hardly any white meat.

"The old woman of Huayapa," said Rosalino, reminiscent.

However, she had got her bottle. When we had drunk the lemonade, we sent Rosalino to give her the empty wine-bottle, and she made him another sententious little speech. But to her the bottle was a treasure.

And I, going round the little hummock behind the wild guava tree to throw away the papers of the picnic, came upon a golden-brown young man with his shirt just coming down over his head, but over no more of him. Hastily retreating, I thought again what beautiful, suave, rich skins these people have; a sort of richness of the flesh. It goes, perhaps, with the complete absence of what we call "spirit."

We lay still for a time, looking at the tiny guavas and the perfect, soft, high blue sky overhead, where the hawks and the ragged-winged *zopilotes* sway and diminish. A long, hot way home. But *mañana es otro dia*. To-morrow is another day. And even the next five minutes are far enough away, in Mexico, on a Sunday afternoon.

Philip Glazebrook

Journey to Kars

Philip Glazebrook's Journey to Kars *(1984) recounts his journey through the lands of the former Ottoman Empire, a region much beloved by English travelers a century or more earlier. Glazebrook's goal was not only to explore the modern Balkans and Anatolia, but also to understand why mid-nineteenth century English travelers left "the company of the race they considered God's last word in breeding, to travel in discomfort, danger, illness, filth and misery among Asiatics whose morals and habits they despised, in lands which, at best, reminded them of Scotland."*

Why indeed? Why has travel—or more accurately tourism—become more and more popular throughout the twentieth century, even when a person on foot is still subject to many of the old privations?

"What was the impulse which drove middle-class Victorians to leave the country which they loved so chauvinistically" and us to turn much of the rest of our world into a tourist resort?

In the following excerpt we find Philip Glazebrook in low spirits in Kayseri in central Turkey.

* * *

In my experience of travelling alone there is no telling when your confidence will evaporate, in face of the most ordinary little everyday dealing, and let you see only the vulnerability of your situation, and your awkwardness in it. This happened to me now.

There wasn't in Kayseri exactly the hostility of Konya, but the town's remoteness, and the busyness of everyone about their own affairs, and the old volcano clothed in snow, gave me a feeling of being very far from home. I saw myself as a curious and outlandish figure wandering about amongst the proper inhabitants of the town. People stared without smiling. I was not welcome in the mosque, where I had gone as any stranger might enter a church in Christendom, to sit quietly at the base of a pillar. The tea-houses were not like cafés, with tables on the street, they were more like dens under the ruinous houses, and I didn't care to enter them. My confidence had gone. Instead of looking out at the world, forgetful of self, I saw my own reflection with all its oddities thrown back at me by the eyes of passers-by. I walked into various *medresse*, and *türbe*, and mosques; and soon walked out again.

I walked, for something to do, far out along a pot-holed street, into regions of crumbling masonry and dust and weeds where the town petered out, in search of the archaeological museum I had been told of. Here at least the road was almost empty, and in places shaded by trees, so I walked slowly and thought about my situation. The more isolated and solitary my position became, particularly in the somewhat threatening atmosphere of this town, the closer I felt I might come to understanding the feelings and ideas it would be interesting to explore in such a character as I proposed to invent for the Traveler in my book, so I did not try to quench, but rather to exaggerate, my twinges of uneasiness.

"No small part of the pleasure of Eastern travel," says Murray briskly, quoting David Urquhart, "arises from sheer hardship and privation." That is quite true, but . . . an element of "danger," too, was a draw. Murray's zestful attitude to the risks of desert travel, in the 1854 Handbook to Turkey, show that they would be an attraction to the traveler: "The sons of the desert, mounted on wild-looking but high-bred mares, come down upon him like a whirlwind, with a loud unearthly yell, shaking their lances over their heads; and the interview is soon over, the tourist finding himself again alone upon the plain, with or without his shirt, as the case may be." All right; the traveler is prepared for that much danger; would he go on to agree with George Hayward, who said in a note smuggled to Shaw whilst both were imprisoned in Tartary, that he was "possessed of an insane desire to try the effect of cold steel across my throat?" Newbolt, in his poem about Hayward's murder in a high pass of the Himalaya, makes of the killing just such a picturesque and romantic incident as most appealed to the reading public. Travelers had a duty to Mudie's patrons occasionally to be murdered.

Hayward was reckless, as no doubt were many who never returned; what is of interest is the attitude of less extreme cases, of the many travelers who survived great dangers, towards fear of death deliberately encountered. "In the long struggle between us," wrote Arminius Vambéry, "fear was finally subdued; but it is this struggle which I blush to remember, for it is marvellous what efforts are required, to grow familiar with the constant and visible prospect of Death." And dear, good Dr. Wolff, who bearded the Emir of Bukhara to ask him what he'd done with Stoddart and Conolly, and feared no man, said of a boating trip he was once obliged to make, "Wolff was so much afraid that he is ashamed to this day to think of it."

Englishmen, of course, don't speak so frankly, but I am sure it was with the intention of calling out and subduing fear that they chose such unsettled regions for their researches. Privation, long days, lean meals, toughened their bodies; danger hardened their nerves. The ordeal proved to the traveler that he possessed the qualities he had been taught to admire. His life might depend on the force of his character to impose its will on superior numbers and strength and arms, just as authority in "old times"— and at beloved Eton, too—had depended on these strengths, rather than on the gradations of society. "In the East," says Robert Shaw, noting the sudden familiarity and rudeness of his captors in Yark and, "want of respect is the precursor of danger." He responded by giving out orders like a drill-sergeant; but how closely he must have watched and waited for the executioner! As Captain Abbott did, night after night, in the tents of the Kuzzauks, amongst whom he had in his mind identified his executioner, a half-mad giant of whom he conceived a horror.

There were plenty of gloomy examples, not only of blackening heads over gateways, but of Europeans who had paid with their lives for an ill-chosen word, or a blow, or just for the misfortune of finding the country disturbed. A chair, or a silver watch, or an English gun, might be spied in the possession of a sheikh in whose territory an Englishman had vanished. The penalties were severe. All had watched the bastinado, many had seen natives executed, or blinded; Vambéry, in the courtyard of a castle in Tartary, watched the executioner kneeling on prisoners' chests to blind them with a knife, knowing that his own fate would be theirs if his disguise was discovered.

Sang-froid was cultivated by these conditions. "G. Fowler, Esquire," faced with a deteriorating situation in Kurdistan, tells us, "Our position now became critical; but I do not know how it is, I can never bring myself to the anticipation of danger, so I lay down on my mat and slept most soundly." Did he really? From the point of view of constructing the character of a traveler, as I mean to do, it is interesting that Fowler should claim for himself such excessive *sang-froid* as is found only in romances, or poems by Newbolt. The narrator, for all his assertions that "pressure of friends" had obliged him against his will to place "these few notes of a rough traveler" before the public—the narrator was very conscious of his reader. There was conscious art. James Fraser (who wrote a number of novels "of Eastern life" or, more accurately, of Victorian life in Eastern costume) says in a book of travels, "In a well-told tale now, as one sits in his snug parlour before the bright fire, a foot on either hob, and a decanter of old port or madeira at his elbow—in such a tale, an incident like this [he was lost at dusk amid the Persian mountains] would bring delight to all the hearers."

The behavior and conduct of the traveller—at any rate the ridiculous degree of "stout heart and cool head" sometimes claimed—were directed by the expectations of the readership. When Alexander Burnes made his journey to Bukhara it is evident that he was cautious and canny as well as brave—in obeying the Emir's edict forbidding infidels to ride in the streets, for instance—but I wonder if his fame as a hero to his readers, which the runaway success of his *Travels* brought him, didn't encourage him in an arrogance and foolhardiness which in the end made him hated by the natives of Kabul? Faced with capture by tribesmen whom he suspected of murdering an earlier traveler, Burnes says, "I will not conceal my feelings at this moment, which were those of vexation and irritability." If those really were his feelings, they were inadequate. The fragments of his body, after he had been torn to pieces by the Kabul mob in 1841, remained hanging in the trees of his garden until the bones dropped out of them.

The archaeological museum at Kayseri, when I eventually came upon it among compounds of a military sort, behind wire defences, wasn't a sanc-tuary at all. The officials were very surprised indeed to receive a visit. Staff scattered to their posts, settling caps on their heads, and holding cigarettes behind their backs, until it was discovered that I wasn't a superior come to vex them, but only a foreign tourist. I bought a ticket from one, had it ripped by another, was directed into the proper traffic-flow by a third; and found myself, at the end of all this administration, in the two small rooms com-prising the whole museum. Battered fragments of marble from the West, a few Assyrian cylinder seals from the East: meagre remains from the empires it lay between testify to the fact that a city so strategically important as Kayseri is sure of total destruction by each invader. Towns built in the wrong place, like Palmyra or Fatehpur Sikri, are the towns which survive whole. In these bare little rooms I was followed and watched by the whole staff until I gave way under their stare, and set out to walk the mile or so back through the glare and dust of the town's outskirts.

Self-consciousness attracts an audience. Boys seeing me pass from a window clattered downstairs and ran into the road to stare, even crossed it to walk backwards just in front of me, looking up with unsmiling black eyes into my face. With a turn of speed I caught up with a woman with a long stick in one hand, and a handbag in the other, who was driving four calves along the road. The woman I overtook, but I couldn't push past the wretched calves without them kicking up their heels and flying in all directions. So a strange race began. Past me ran the cowherd, chivvying scattered calves into order, banging them with handbag or stick; then they would stop to peer into a hole, I couldn't help catching them up, and off they would fly again. I tried crossing the road but they followed me, the nudge of their noses at my back as bad as the boys' stare on my face. In this way our party leapfrogged into the *meidan* once more, where the water-seller was tinkling his bell at the midday crowd.

I looked for somewhere to eat. In the very middle of the town is a little ruinous quarter, a lane, stone hovels with glassless windows and rotten doors, their walls supported on poles bedded in heaps of filth. Nearby I found a greasy eating-shop where men in leather caps scooped meat and juice into their mouths with wedges of bread. There was no rest from the flat, uncivil eyes. I chose food from the cooking pots and sat eating it, when it was slopped out for me, at the corner of a stained table.

I soon found myself on the street again, with four hours to fill before my bus left for Erzurum. I went to the bazaars, which I had saved up until now.

In 1856 one of those controversial figures of the Eastern scene, a British consul, rode into "Kaiseriah" at the head of a cavalcade of horses and pack-animals bought by the British for the Crimea War and now being sold off on a peripatetic auction through Asia Minor. The consul was H. J. Ross, a fiery, touchy individual, who hedged himself in with the defensive arrogance against the contemp which traveling gentlemen had for the commercial gents and half-bred Levantines lording it as consuls in seaports of the Euxine or in provincial capitals of the Turkish empire. Travelers, he wrote, knew nothing of the East or its peoples: "It is astonishing how long it is ere an Englishman can understand the depths of falseness of the Oriental character." Loving his garden and his spaniel and his pheasant-shooting as an Englishman should, Ross prided himself equally on his Eastern ferocity: "I am grown cruel-hearted and watch the bastinado I have ordered as quietly as any Turkish pasha." He loved, too, the trappings of power ceded him in the wild towns of Anatolia. Here he describes his entry into Kayseri:

> Our entry was very grand. Three pairs of kettledrums, the insignia of a pasha, were beaten before me . . . Tufenkjis [musketeers] escorted me through the long ranges of bazaars. I was surprised at their extent—all covered in. They reminded me of Cairo; the same Eastern half-lights, and the same heavy smell of drugs. Some twelve years ago I left Kaiseriah without a single prospect before me, and I return with the pomp and circumstance of an Eastern Pasha.

It may be surmised that the bombast in this, like the fact of the man having been born in Malta, may have made him and his like seem half-bred, not quite gentlemen, to Englishmen on their travels.

But on the bazaars at Kayseri Ross's work is sound. Very wonderful they still are. You walk down long tunnels of stone, shafted through with sunlight which falls in spots of brilliance on the heaps and gaudy piles of goods massed in front of shadowy caverns, and all the echo and bustle and glitter of life fill these stone-arched lanes. Here everyone was too busy to stare at me. I sank back into the anonymity of a pair of eyes to look through. The bazaar leads to the courtyard of an old caravanserai, that central feature in the travels of past times, where merchants put up, and sold or exchanged the goods on their pack-animals, and sat smoking *narghileh* or chibouks on a rug spread before their cell door. Here was great activity in Kayseri. Over cobbles clattered carts, boots, the rattling hooves of sheep—and amongst the bewildered living flocks were pushed iron-shod handcarts heaped with sheepskins still steaming from the knife. The stone square stank with blood and dung. In its quieter corners the sun fell on bales of wool, and on old men in skullcaps seated crosslegged at their work of sorting or scraping the skins.

In coming on this scene I had an instinctive feeling of putting my hand on what I wanted. This is what it was like. Details of clothes and all the little anachronisms in the picture—wires, motors and so on—don't signify in the sudden vivid stroke of light your imagination can receive. This is what it felt like to be there. If you catch that, and keep it, you have a keynote. The essence is in your grasp. From a living fire you take a live coal.

I walked back through the gray stone vaults of the *bedestan*, where carpet dealers were drinking tea gravely together in front of their solemn shops, and crossed a square and busy roads to a small green park by the Kursunlu mosque, where I sat down on a small green bench, and took out my book.

But I was badgered out of all patience by inquisitive Turks. They converged by every path, crowding my bench, picking up my bag to examine it, tapping my arm to make me look up, taking the very book out of my hands to discover what language it was written in. No inhibitions restrained them; every kind of inhibition made them uncomfortable. As with their love of sweets and loud noises, this inquisitiveness makes Asiatics seem to Europeans like children. In Lindos two English children aged four or five used to come and stand in front of me whilst I ate breakfast, and shout "Eat shit!" and "Fuck!" in my face to see how I responded—I shook my head sadly over the bread and honey—and these Turkish youths crowding me off the bench seemed anxious to test me in the same way. In patience they can always outlast a European. But they came closer, and the crowd grew, and my possessions were soon being passed out of the front row for others to see. So eaten up with curiosity to see the Feringhee were the villagers of Feridun that they not only filled the courtyard of Layard's house, they climbed on the roof and peered at him down the chimney. It is part of the Asiatic character; to stare is not rude, but to object to being stared at is taken as offensive behaviour. I got up, and held out my hand for my bag, which was at once given back to me. I put my book into it and walked away, and the young men drifted off in ones and twos as they had come.

I managed to hide myself away pretty well amongst the pillars and shadows in the courtyard of the nearby mosque, and so to observe the Faithful gargling and spitting, and washing hands and feet in the fountain, and laying out to bake in the sun the handkerchiefs they had dried themselves with. The domesticity is appealing. "The Faithful" seems perfectly to describe this ceaseless traffic of people in and out of the holy precincts, fitting devotion into their lives in a matter-of-fact way which makes earth seem nearer heaven. Here is the child-like quality again, but this time in the form found in the Beatitudes "Except ye become as little children. . . ." I didn't follow them into the shadow of the mosque.

Instead I walked away towards the bazaars again, where I had felt myself less noticeable than in other parts of the town, and I thought as I went about the ambiguous attitude towards Islam to be found in Victorian travel books. Condemnation of Muhammad and all his works, and particularly of the Mussulman's eagerness for a paradise full of "profligacy," is expressed in strong terms. But that, you feel, is to establish the writer's orthodoxy as far as the Circulating Libraries are concerned; his real views, which leak out in asides, are more complex. For one thing, the Englishman travelling through Islam found himself, very naturally, attracted towards the powerful rather than towards the downtrodden—towards pasha and sheikh rather than servants and moneylenders—and this partiality led him to associate himself with Mussulmans rather than with Christians. The Syrian or Greek Christian under Ottoman rule was perhaps the most wretched, and most despised, of all inhabitants of the empire. True, Christ himself under the Roman Empire in these lands was wretched and despised; but the nineteenth-century English gentleman based the whole of his outlook on the world upon confidence in his ascendancy, which in England did not conflict with his support of Christian principles as they had evolved in the English context. To find himself confronted with a set of beggars and servants as his natural associates, by faith, in the East, did not suit either him or his readers. Of a village in Kurdistan, Rich says sadly. "It would be a tolerable place except for the extreme dirtiness, which, with the smell of liquor, is, I am sorry to say, the characteristic of a Christian village in these parts." Simply by recording the facts, the traveler moves away from championing Christianity against Islam at all points.

Perhaps due to rough handling by the inquisitive, my second bag, bought at Belgrade, required a stitch or two to secure its strap, so when I reached the bazaars again, I looked about until I found the cobblers' quarter. Showing the first in the row what I needed done, I was passed from booth to booth until, down a couple of steps into a shop like the den of some leather-hoarding animal, I found a quick little shoemaker in a leather apron who possessed a machine which would sew through the material of my bag. All the family was at work. Three sons, besides the father, were busy tapping, stitching, cutting, at their cluttered bench in the half-light amongst a crowd of customers. I sat in a corner waiting my turn. It is strange that there is no strong smell, peculiar to Turkey, which pervades it as the pungent sweetness of India reaches into everything that India touches. In a den like this in an Indian bazaar, that sweet scent would be at its thickest; here the shoemaker's shop smelt of leather, nothing more.

Whilst I waited—glad to rest unstared at in such light as the shoe-cluttered window let in from the covered bazaar—a seller of melons who was passing called down the steps. Work was suspended. A fruit was bought, slices pared off the mighty green sphere and handed about on the point of a cobbler's knife. With great kindness I was provided with a share, which I ate in the usual delicious dissolution of juice and seeds. At last my bag was sewn up for me.

At last, too, the time had come to find a *dolmus* [shared taxi] in the *meidan* [square], where the westering sun lit up evening crowds hurrying past the water-seller's pitch, and to return to the *otogar* [bus station]. I wasn't bored, or particularly tired, but I was surfeited with the restless interest of travel, and I looked forward to a quiet seat in the bus.

Daniel Gavron

Walking Through Israel

Daniel Gavron is an English Jew who moved to Israel and worked as a reporter for the national radio. After eighteen years he had begun to feel stifled by life in Israel's cities. Their congestion made him dream of the simpler life in the "real Israel." There he hoped to find "real enterprise and achievement, pioneering and idealism."

> *The question was how to travel. I abhor driving, loathe buses, and fear taxis. The trains in Israel do not reach most of the places I intended visiting. Cycling in our country is tantamount to suicide. I am ignorant of the ways of donkeys, horses, and camels. I decided to walk.*
>
> *Once I had made the decision, it made more and more sense. I liked the idea of the slow pace. I would be independent of petrol engines and bus timetables, free to dally or to wander over open country. My route would be dictated by my personal inclinations. . . .*

The following is from Gavron's 1980 book, Walking Through Israel.

* * *

On the bus, leaving Jerusalem for the north, I found myself sitting next to an elderly man with a face the color and texture of fine old parchment. He was reading from a small card, which he subsequently handed to me, entitled, appropriately enough, "Prayer to be said when going on a journey." It appealed to God to "direct our steps in peace" and to "deliver us from any enemy, ambush, or hurt by the way." Reading, rather than praying, the ancient Hebrew text, I nevertheless saw it as a fitting start to my expedition.

"It has a particular relevance in Israel these days," remarked the old fellow.

"Yes, indeed," I agreed.

"Aha, a new immigrant!" he declared, spotting the British accent in my Hebrew, still clear after almost two decades.

"Certainly not," I protested. "I have been living in Israel for nearly eighteen years."

"New compared to me," he replied a trifle smugly. "My family has been in Jerusalem for sixteen generations."

I worked it out. More than four centuries, I reckoned. He was a dapper old boy in a smart, off-white linen suit, his straw hat bound with a black band. I was slightly overawed by him and did not feel inclined to contradict, even when he lauded the Jewish talent for making the desert bloom, while pointing to a field of corn that was manifestly being cultivated by Arabs.

I had decided to begin my walk in Metulla, the northernmost settlement in Galilee. The northern part of Galilee, only some six miles in width, is known as Etzba Hagalil, the Finger of Galilee. If northern Galilee is the finger, Metulla is the fingernail, a tiny, isolated village almost entirely surrounded by Lebanese territory.

It was founded in 1896 by men of the first *aliya*, the first wave of modern Jewish immigration to Palestine, which took place in the last two decades of the nineteenth century. During this period, there were repeated outbreaks of anti-Jewish violence in Russia and other parts of Eastern Europe. Far from preventing these pogroms, the authorities often encouraged them and in some cases initiated them.

The Jewish community reacted in a number of ways. Many Jews became active in the revolutionary movements and later played leading parts in the Bolshevik revolution. Enormous numbers left Russia: between 1880 and 1914, more than 2 million Jews migrated to Western Europe and America. A minority were prompted to revive Jewish national and cultural life, and these formed groups called Lovers of Zion. Like the majority, they were determined to leave Russia, but they decided to return to the Land of Israel, the ancient, Biblical homeland of the Jews, then a province of the Ottoman Empire. Their journey to Palestine was regarded as something more than mere immigration; they called it "aliya" (going up). They believed that they were elevating themselves in reviving the Jewish nation.

The Lovers of Zion established a number of villages in Palestine, such as Rishon Lezion, near modern Tel Aviv, and Rosh Pina, in Galilee. They were joined in their pioneering endeavors by young Jews from Jerusalem, the sons of the religious community there, which was supported by charity. Also aiming to establish a self-supporting Jewish community in Palestine, they founded Petah-Tikva. The very names of these early villages give us a clue to the motivations of their founders: Rishon Lezion means "the first in Zion"; Rosh Pina is "the foundation stone"; and Petah-Tikva, "the gateway of hope."

However, because of the swampy or stony nature of much of the land, the villages foundered, and the villagers faced poverty and near-starvation. They were rescued by Baron Edmond de Rothschild of Paris. A member of the rich banking family, he was deeply concerned about the pogroms in Eastern Europe and also aware of the less brutal anti-Semitism in his own country.

Without "the Baron," as he came to be known, the early Jewish villages in Palestine would probably not have survived, yet he was not popular among the pioneers.

As a businessman, he naturally expected to control his ventures and to make his investments pay off, but the villagers fiercely resented the actions of the agents he sent out to run the settlements, which in some instances extended even to interference in the settlers' domestic arrangements. They regarded the Baron as an unfeeling capitalist who did not understand their national aspirations. In fact, there is evidence to the contrary. In 1889 he told the settlers of Rishon Lezion:

> I did not come to your aid because of your poverty and suffering . . . I did it because I saw in you the realizers of the renaissance of Israel and of that idea so dear to us all, the sacred goal of the return of Israel to its ancient homeland.

Metulla was founded on land the Baron bought from an absentee landlord who resided in Sidon, Lebanon. A selected group of farmers, for whom there was no room in the existing villages, was sent there to begin a new village. Almost at once, they had to fight off raids by local Druze, who claimed that the land really belonged to them. More than two decades were to pass before other Jewish settlements were established nearby. Its long isolation has made Metulla distinctive; other Israelis sometimes refer to the villagers as "half-Arabs."

The first sight of Metulla was disappointing. Dull, gray terrace houses, built since my first visit many years ago, straggled down the hillside. But then, as the bus climbed into the village, I found myself, this time as in the past, won over by its tatty charm. Modern hotels rubbed shoulders with rickety stone-and-wattle bulidings dating back to the time of the Baron. I noted at least six hostelries of various standards, three restaurants, a couple of refreshment stalls, a garage, bank, and post office—but no shops. For even the most basic supplies, the villagers must travel to the town of Kiryat Shmona, six miles to the south.

I arrived on the day before the municipal elections, and every wall and blank space was plastered with election posters. Metulla is still a very small community. It has a population of some 600 and an electoral roll of just over 200, but there was enough political activity going on for a metropolis of thousands. Some half-dozen candidates were vying for the position of mayor: leaflets were being handed out, party functionaries hastened to and fro, vehicles plastered with manifestos dashed up and down the only street.

Apart from finding it a natural starting point for my journey, I had come to Metulla to see the "Good Fence,"* across which the Arabs of Lebanon come by the hundred to work, trade, and receive medical attention in Israel.

A border that people cross to visit and work may seem normal enough, but not in Israel, which was hermetically sealed from its neighbors for three decades. The Good Fence, then, is a dramatic break with the past, and, like many of the best things in this country, it was unplanned.

A pregnant woman, wounded in the Lebanese civil war, came to an Israeli army border post. Responding to his normal instincts, a medical orderly bandaged her wounds, little imagining that he was inaugurating a new era. More wounded started coming to the border, and the Israel army made openings in the fence, which had been erected to prevent terrorist attacks. A temporary clinic was set up, and trucks began to bring in supplies of food and water to the Lebanese villagers, who had been cut off from their natural hinterland by the war. Within a few months, what had started as a hastily improvised plan to help a few dozen unfortunates had expanded into a full-scale institution. The Good Fence was born.

Today the welfare aspect is only a part of the story. A permament clinic has been established, supplying free medical services to the Arab villagers (serious cases are sent to hospitals in Israel); agricultural instructors cross the border to help the Lebanese farmers; and the Good Fence has become a trading-post and checkpoint for the hundreds of Lebanese who commute daily to jobs in Israel.

The project has long since ceased to be a news story and has, indeed, become something of a local tourist attraction. The army spokesman in Jerusalem had told me that I would not even have to produce my journalist's card. Just go to Metulla, he said, and see it. However, when I descended from the bus, I found myself in a quandary, for the border in Metulla is north, east, and west. Which direction should I take? Two ancient villagers were sitting on a bench nearby conversing in Yiddish and, approaching them, I asked courteously, "Can you please tell me the way to the Good Fence?"

The two raised their heads, their gaze all hostility. They looked me up and down, taking in my faded jeans, rucksack, water bottle, and camera. Finally, one of them spoke. "Whoever needs to get there, gets there all right," he said with heavy significance. I had met the famous Metulla mentality face to face.

My next encounter was with an army officer. Apparently he felt satisfied

---

* In vain did we pedantic journalists try to have it called the "Good-Will Fence," or the "Good-Neighbor Fence." How, after all, can a fence be "good"? But to no avail: the Good Fence it has remained.

that I was neither a spy nor a saboteur, for he set me on the road without delay.

Proceeding westward, I passed through the newer part of the village, a pleasant street lined with modern houses and well-tended gardens, and soon arrived at the end house on the right-hand side, famous in the media as "the last house in Israel." Its owner, Arik Yaacov (formerly Eric Jacobs of New York), teaches high school in nearby Kiryat Shmona and farms his apple orchards in his spare time. A stocky redhead, Arik was standing on a newly cast section of his roof. Although busy with the extension of his home, he invited me in for a cup of coffee.

Arik is a Metulla enthusiast. He laughed when I told him about the old men and defended their right to be unfriendly to strangers. Things had been tough for many years, he explained. "Oh, yes, I know that if a cow shat on your neighbor's plot in nineteen nineteen, it's a vendetta, but you have to get to know these people. Underneath it all, they're wonderful."

I did, of course, know something of the history, the struggles of the early pioneers to grow cereals and tobacco in the poor soil, their fights with the Druze raiders, the bitter cold they suffered in the winter. I also knew that the first settlers, like most of the first aliya, had exploited the local Arabs. One of the Baron's agents had written in 1905, "The Jew in Metulla is a supervisor, and for the most part a very bad supervisor."

It is easy enough to be critical, but I knew that much of the villagers' land was mountain rock; in 1912 they had suffered a typhus epidemic; in 1920 they had been forced to evacuate the village for almost a year; in 1948 they lost most of the good land they did possess. Following Israel's War of Independence against the Arabs in that year, the Lebanese border, like all the others, was sealed off. Metulla's farmland and its water source had been in the Ayun Valley, now on the wrong side of the border.

Arik told me that he and his wife got on well with everyone in the village. Once the locals realized that they had come to stay, they had been accepted wholeheartedly. It had been difficult, particularly during the intensified terrorist activity that followed the Yom Kippur War in 1973. Like most citizens of Israel, Arik had been in the army for much of 1973 and 1974; his wife, alone with their small children, had faced the *katyusha* rocket attacks on Metulla.

"It was only later that I understood quite how tough it had been," he confessed. "But even then, she never thought of leaving."

I thanked Arik for the coffee and walked out of the village through the apple orchards, finding myself in the company of Lebanese workers on their way home. In my inadequate Arabic, I struck up a conversation with Michael from the village of Kafr Killa, who told me that he was *mabsut* (happy). He came across the border at six o'clock each morning to work in the apple orchards. Now he was on his way home.

By the time I arrived at the complex of huts beside the fence, more and more Lebanese were streaming back to their villages. Elderly Arabs with the traditional *keffiya* headdresses, baggy trousers, and *galabiya* tunics walked beside young men in working clothes who could have passed for Israeli Jews. A party of young women, several of them wearing slacks and sleeveless blouses, licked ice creams and posed cheekily for my camera. Across the fence a line of cars waited to take them all home.

I looked in at the clinic, where an Israeli army doctor was listening patiently to a couple who had brought their baby for treatment. A young soldier was translating from Arabic into Hebrew. The doctor examined the baby carefully before administering an injection.

"Ear infection," he told me, wiping his hands on a towel. After the parents left with the baby, he went on, "They were here this morning also. They're learning from us how to be *nudniks*." (That's Yiddish for those who nag.) Tall and gangling, his nose and chin curving toward each other, a Mister Punch in tinted glasses, he introduced himself as Dr. Guttman. Then, catching sight of my souvenir postcard of the Good Fence, he left the clinic to buy one, saying that he might send it to Rumania. But when he returned with the card, he had decided not to, and he explained why. When he still had been living in Bucharest, Israeli friends had sent him a pound note, and he had been interrogated by the police and forced to deposit the pound in the bank to avoid being charged with currency speculation. He didn't know how the Rumanian authorities might react to a picture postcard of the Good Fence, but he did not want to take the risk of embarrassing his relatives.

In the clinic, he dealt courteously with the stream of patients. Complimenting him on his kindness and thoroughness, I told him a story current in Israel about a Metulla villager who was fed up with his local doctor. Dressing as an Arab, the villager went to the Good Fence and received top-notch medical care for the first time in years. Guttman smiled weakly and noted that in civilian life he too was a health-fund doctor.

"A good doctor is always good," he stated. "I don't behave differently here."

We returned to the village and sat on a wall in the street. Political activity had died down, but the whole community was out for its afternoon stroll. The army was much in evidence, soldiers walking in groups or entering a hotel to phone home. Old men ambled along, assisted by canes, mothers wheeled prams, children shot past on skateboards. A statuesque woman of indeterminate age, impressive teak-colored shoulders rising from her emerald dress, looked us up and down speculatively. The village whore? Surely not, I decided. Metulla would not have one.

On a month's stint of army service, Guttman was hungry for conversation and quizzed me about my work. What was my motivation? Fame, fortune, self-expression? He told me that he had written some chapters of a novel, which he kept in a drawer at home.

"I may go into competition with you one day" was his parting shot.

I sat and thought about the Good Fence, a splendid humanitarian gesture to an enemy country, nonetheless so for being so patently self-serving.

C. S. Lewis

A Friend Revisited

C. S. Lewis (1898–1963) was an author, scholar, teacher, and Anglican apologist. What matters most to me, however, was that he was also a confirmed walker. His long solitary walks in Ulster, Ireland, Surrey, and Oxford became the landscape of the Narnia tales.

In 1930 he wrote to his lifelong friend Joseph Arthur Greeves, after Greeves had just paid him a visit. The term "soaking machine" in this letter means a comfortable place to think or daydream.

This selection is excerpted from C. S. Lewis: Images of His World, *edited by Douglas Gilbert and Clyde Kilby.*

* * *

On the day you left I went our usual walk through Old Headington, past that little isolated house which you admired, the brook, and then over two fields to our soaking machine. . . . I felt that sort of melancholy—you probably know it—which comes from walking through the same scenes through which you walked with a friend a few hours ago, when he has gone. . . . Mixed with this melancholy, however, . . . there was a freshness of solitude which itself on such occasions feels like a friend revisited.

Patrick Leigh Fermor

On Foot to Constantinople: From the Hook of Holland to the Middle Danube

In 1933 eighteen-year-old Patrick Leigh Fermor began a one-and-a-half-year journey, mostly on foot, from the Hook of Holland to Constantinople. His picaresque account of the mountains, castles, farms, monasteries, and Gypsy caravans of central Europe is told in Between the Woods And The Water *(1986).*

Much of what he experienced could not be duplicated today. War, revolution, dams, and social change have altered much of his geographic and social landscape beyond recognition. Yet his youthful quest was, to me, universal and timeless. The details would differ but how I would love to walk on such a journey today!

Imagine, just over the next rise we might fall in with Hungarian swineherds.

* * *

From the path that climbed along the edge of the forest, backward glances revealed swamps and trees and a waste of tall rushes and the great river loosely dividing and joining again round a chain of islands. I could see the waterfowl rocketing up and circling like showers of motes and stippling the lagoon with innumerable splashes when they settled again. Then high ground put them out of sight. Foothills rose steeply on the other side, lesser hills overlapped each other downstream and the fleece of the treetops gave way to cliffs of limestone and porphyry, and where they converged, the green river ran fast and deep.

A village would appear below and storks stood on one leg among the twigs of old nests on thatch and chimney. There were flurried claps as they took to the air, and when they dropped level with the treetops and crossed the river into Slovakia, sunlight caught the upper sides of their wings; then they tilted and wheeled back into Hungary with hardly a feather moving. Landing with sticks in their beaks, they picked their way along the roofs

with black flight-feathers spread like tight-rope-walkers' fingers fumbling for
balance. Being mute birds, they improvise an odd courting-song by leaning
back and opening and shutting their scarlet bills with a high-speed clatter
like flat sticks banging together: a dozen courtships in one of these riverside
hamlets sounded like massed castanets. Carried away by sudden transports,
they would leap a few yards in the air and land in disarray, sliding precariously on the thatch. Their wonderful procession had stretched across the
sky for miles the night before; now they were everywhere, and all the
following weeks I could never get used to them; their queerly stirring rattle
was the prevalent theme of the journey, and the charm they cast over the
ensuing regions lasted until August in the Bulgarian mountains, when I
finally watched a host of them dwindling in the distance, heading for Africa.

It was the first of April 1934, and Easter Day: two days after full moon,
eleven from the equinox, forty-seven since my nineteenth birthday and a
hundred and eleven after I had set out, but less than twenty-four hours since
crossing the frontier. The far bank was Slovakia still, but in a mile or two a
tributary twisted through the northern hills, and the tiled roofs and belfries
of the little tearful-sounding town of Szob marked the meeting place of the
two rivers. The frontier wandered northwards up this valley and for the first
time both sides of the Danube were Hungary.

For most of this journey the landscape had been under snow; icicle-
hung and often veiled in falling flakes, but the last three weeks had changed
all this. The snow had shrunk to a few discoloured patches and the ice on
the Danube had broken up. When this is solid, the thaw sunders the ice
with reports like a succession of thunderclaps. I had been out of earshot
downstream when the giant slabs had broken loose, but all at once the water,
halted by occasional jams, was crowded with racing fragments. It was no
good trying to keep pace: jostling triangles and polygons rushed past, cloudier
at the edges each day and colliding with a softer impact until they were as
flimsy as wafers; and at last, one morning, they were gone. These were mild
portents, it seemed. When the sun reaches full strength, the eternal snows,
the glaciers of the Alps and the banked peaks of the Carpathians look unchanged from a distance; but close to, the whole icy heart of Europe might
be dissolving. Thousands of rivulets pour downhill, all brooks overflow and
the river itself breaks loose and floods the meadows, drowns cattle and flocks,
uproots the ricks and the trees and whirls them along until all but the tallest
and stoutest bridges are either choked with flotsam or carried away.

Spring had begun as at a starter's pistol. Bird song had broken out in
a frenzy, a fever of building had set in, and, overnight, swallows and swifts
were skimming everywhere. Martins were setting their old quarters to
rights, lizards flickered on the stones, nests multiplied in the reeds, shoals
teemed and the frogs, diving underwater at a stranger's approach, soon
surfaced again, sounding as though they were reinforced every hour by a

thousand new voices; they kept the heronries empty as long as daylight lasted. The herons themselves glided low and waded through the flagleaves with a jerky and purposeful gait, or, vigilantly on one leg like the storks, posed with cunning as plants. Flags crowded the backwaters and thick stems lifted enormous kingcups among the leaves of pink and white water-lilies that folded at sunset.

Between the shore and the reddish-mauve cliffs, aspens and poplars tapered and expanded in a twinkling haze and the willows, sinking watery roots, drooped over fast currents. Tight-lacing forced the yellow flood into a rush of creases and whorls and, after my earlier weeks beside the Danube, I could spot those ruffled hoops turning slowly round and round, telling of drowned commotion amidstream.

The path climbed, and as the hot afternoon passed, it was hard to believe that the nearly mythical country of Hungary lay all around me at last; not that this part of it, the Pilis hills, tallied in the remotest degree with anything I had expected. When the climb had let the Danube drop out of sight, hills and woods swallowed the track and sunbeams slanted through young oak-branches. Everything smelt of bracken and moss, sprays of hazel and beech were opening, and the path, soft with rotten leaves, wound through great lichen-crusted trees with dog-violets and primroses among their roots. When the woods opened for a mile or two, steep meadows ran up on either hand to crests that were dark with hangers, and streams fledged with watercress ran fast and clear in the valleys. I was crossing one of them on stepping-stones when bleating and a jangle of bells sounded; then barking broke out, and the three demons that rushed down with bared fangs were called to heel by their shepherd. His sheep were up to their bellies in a drift of daisies; the ewes must have lambed about Christmas and some of them were already shorn. I had been in shirt-sleeves for several days, but a heel-length sheepskin cloak was thrown over the shepherd's shoulders; peasants are slow to cast clouts. I shouted, *"Jó estét kivánok!"*— a quarter of my stock of Hungarian—and the same evening-greeting came back, accompanied by the ceremonious lift of a narrow-brimmed black hat. (Ever since I had come across the Hungarian population in southern Slovakia I had longed for some head-gear for answering these stately salutes.) His flock was a blur of white specks and faraway tinklings by the time I caught sight of a different herd. A troop of still unantlered fallow deer were grazing by the edge of the forest across the valley. The sun setting on the other side of them cast their shadows across the slope to enormous lengths: a footfall across the still acres of air lifted all their heads at the same moment and held them at gaze until I was out of sight.

I had been thinking of sleeping out, and those shorn lambs clinched matters; the wind was so tempered that hardly a leaf moved. My first attempt, two nights before in Slovakia, had ended in brief arrest as a suspected smuggler; but nothing could be safer than these woods high above the hazards of the frontier.

I was casting about for a sheltered spot when a campfire showed in the dusk at the other end of a clearing where rooks were going noisily to bed. A pen of stakes and brushwood had been set up in a bay of the forest under an enormous oak-tree and a swineherd was just making it fast with a stake between two twists of withy, and the curly and matted black pigs inside were noisily jostling for space. The hut next door was thatched with reeds and when I joined the two swineherds, both looked up puzzled in the firelight: who was I, and where did I come from? The answers—"Angol" and "Angolország"—didn't mean much to them, but their faces lit at the emergence of a bottle of *barack* which was parting loot from my friends in Esztergom, and a third stool was found.

They were cloaked in rough white woollen stuff as hard as frieze. In lieu of goads or crooks, they nursed tapering shafts of wood polished with long handling and topped with small axe-heads and they were shod in those moccasins I had first seen Slovaks wearing in Bratislava: pale canoes of raw cowhide turning up at the tips and threaded all round with thongs which were then lashed round their padded shanks till half-way up the calf of the leg; inside, meanwhile, snugly swaddled in layers of white felt, their feet were wintering it out till the first cuckoo.

The younger was a wild-looking boy with staring eyes and tousled hair. He knew about ten words of German, learnt from Schwobs in the neighbouring villages (I heard later that these were Swabians who were settled nearby) and he had an infectious, rather mad laugh. His white-headed father spoke nothing but Magyar and his eyes, deep-set in wrinkles, lost all their caution as we worked our way down the bottle. I could just make out that the deer, betokened by spread fingers for their missing antlers, belonged to a *főherceg* (which later turned out to mean an archduke). Continuing in sign-language, the younger swineherd grunted, scowled fiercely and curled up his forefingers to represent the tusks of the wild boars that lurked in brakes hereabouts; then he twirled them in spirals which could only mean moufflon. The sign-language grew blunter still when he jovially shadowed forth how wild boars broke in and covered tame sows and scattered the pens with miscegenate farrow. I contributed some hard-boiled eggs to their supper of delicious smoked pork: they sprinkled it with paprika and we ate it with black bread and onions and some nearly fossilised cheese.

The swineherds were called Bálint and Géza and their names have stuck because, at this first hearing, they had so strange a ring. The firelight made them look like contemporaries of Domesday Book and we ought to have been passing a drinking-horn from hand to hand instead of my anachronistic bottle. In defiance of language, by the time it was empty we were all in the grip of helpless laughter. Some kind of primitive exchange had cleared all hurdles and the drink and the boy's infectious spirits must have done the rest. The fire was nearly out and the glade was beginning to change; the moon, which looked scarcely less full than the night before, was climbing behind the branches.

There wasn't much room in their stifling den and when they understood I wanted to sleep out they strewed brushwood in the lee of a rick. The old man put his hand on the grass and then laid it on mine with a commiserating look: it was wet with dew. He made gestures of rugging up and I put on everything I possessed, while they dossed down indoors.

When we had said goodnight I lay gazing at the moon. The shadows of the trees lay like cut-out cloth across the clearing. Owls signalled to each other close by and there were sleepy grunts from the sties prompted by dreams, perhaps, or indigestion, and now and then a pig, roused in the small hours by night-starvation, munched in semi-liquid bliss.

Hamish Brown

Hamish's Groats End Walk

One of the surprising aspects of the twentieth century is that the opportunities for foot-powered adventure are not yet over. Anyone could set off today, as Hamish Brown did on May 1, 1979, to walk the most spectacular hills and mountains of Scotland, England, Wales, and Ireland. After five months of exploration with his collie Storm, he quoted famed mountaineer, Reinhold Messner that, "These long marches, day after day, are the surest, if not the only, way to avoid spiritual blindness. They provide the possibility, or rather the necessity, of uniting the active and contemplative components of one's nature. This is never more easily achieved than on a long trek. . . ."

Or as Hamish Brown put it himself, "Much of my youth was spent in tiny Clackmannanshire which had the admonitory motto, 'Look Aboot Ye.' This book [Hamish's Groats End Walk (1981)] if you like is my continuing response to that irrepressible urge."

The following is part of his early spring walk south from Cape Wrath through the northwest hills and mountains of Scotland.

* * *

THURSDAY MAY 10 SANDWOOD BAY

I can think of fewer places where I would like to wake to sunshine glowing golden through the walls of a tent. Perhaps sunrise is more impressive than sunset because it is an older spectacle. It is not very much older but it stands shimmering on the brink of creation. This is earth's oldest wonder. Sunset is too often a Sunday school award for being good boys all day. Sunrise comes out of the pit, as we do, and is a fearsome, tingling marvel, before which we bow in awe. It takes a while for the rising sun to warm flesh and blood and soul. It is a great gesture of faith.

The walk back to Strathan fell into three parts: cliff-walking, sand-strolling and glen-floundering, each attractive in differing ways. What a varied number of birds we saw: bonxies, stonechats, kestrels, eiders, hoodies, wrens, gannets, fulmars, cormorants, wheatears, pipits, redwings, divers, golden plovers, sandpipers—birds of the ocean meeting birds of strath and moor.

The going was strenuous: lots of ups, lots of downs—Keisgaig Bay, Strath Cailleach—deep-cut *geodha*, then a rock scramble down to the first sands which linked with the miles of Sandwood Bay as the tide was out. Boots were kicked off to walk barefoot, I piled the sack with driftwood and played soccer with Storm when we found a ball. The sands ran southwards to end at a square-cut headland from which is detached the 200-foot needle of Am Buachaille, *the shepherd*, and a fine climb for those prepared to swim for their fun. "He that mounts the precipices . . . has a kind of turbulent pleasure, between fright and admiration" as Dr. Johnson declared. Tom Patey, John Cleare and Ian Clough made the first ascent. A Tyrolean traverse is rigged and you have just four hours before the tide covers it.

We turned into a nook which was in the sun yet out of the steadily-growing wind. I had tea and ate every last bit of food, then set off up the glen past Sandwood Loch trying, for interest, to track our outwards route and making a poor job of it. We reached "Home" just before two Londoners staggered in with massive packs. They greeted us with "we have just seen an adder!" The resident member was off to Balchrick and came back with the news that some female had fallen off Clo Mor that afternoon, news picked up in Kinlockbervie via the fishing boat radios and soon passed about the area. *The Scotsman*, at Rhiconich next day, carried details: she had been one of that day's mini-bus party from Keoldale—her body was picked up by the fishing boat *Golden Fleece*, after having fallen 500 feet into the sea off the cliffs near Kervaig.

It became a wild night and the snugness of the sleeping bag was relished. The rain rattled on the corrugated iron roof and the door rattled as the wind tried to bully its way inside. After listening to it for an hour I suddenly remembered I had left my boots up on the roof, to dry.

FRIDAY MAY 11 TO RHICONICH

"A real soaker which had us longing for the simplicity of snow" my logbook noted. We procrastinated but eventually set off into the driving rain, up the hill on a path and then over trackless moors of riven peat, navigating by compass in the featureless landscape and eventually dropping directly down to Kinlochbervie to relax for an hour in the cafe at the Fishermen's Mission. Lunch was eaten in a road workers' hut during another deluge as we walked along above the fjord-like Loch Inchard. It was five-cuckoos-per-mile country.

The Rhiconich Hotel—cum shop—cum petrol station stands just along from a Police Station in one direction and the Post Office in the other. That *is* Rhiconich. The barman was off ill and Mr. McLeod, the elderly owner, and a Canadian lassie (on her third year of wandering) were quietly and efficiently dealing with everything, and still had time to chat over welcome tea. A parcel had been left, the most northerly one of my hectic delivery run, so there was the usual fussing about: parcelling up maps and films I'd finished with, making several phone calls, washing clothes, writing letters, feeding and walking the dog, taking a well-deserved shower, and collapsing into bed. Rest days were far more frantic than simply walking. The old body had fully adjusted by now. There is always some suffering in the beginning but it soon goes. A cuckoo in the garden struck every minute while on the quarters a cuckoo clock in the hall joined in: a sleep-inhibiting combination.

I had half-planned to walk out and visit Ardmore, John Ridgeway's Adventure Centre, but it was a dreich sort of day and a long lie and laziness won over character building and so on. It was pleasant doing nothing and resting afterwards. The Gualin shepherd filled up with petrol but the Canadian lassie had no idea of prices so he simply said, "Ach, I'll pay for it next time." By the bridge some kids left their cycles all day long; with lamps and pumps on them too. All six telephone boxes I had used in Caithness and Sutherland had been in working order. The bar that night was to close at eleven as the lassie wanted to go in to a dance at Kinlock. They would do breakfast for me the next day at six if I wanted it. No wonder Highland hospitality and atmosphere is renowned; what a sad commentary on elsewhere. . . .

The cuckoo gave its usual evening serenade. I hate cuckoos!

SUNDAY MAY 13 LOCH STACK

The Rhiconich River was my route, leading to long narrow lochans, beyond which, framed by crags, lay Arkle, an oddly rounded shape from that angle. The scoured gneiss landscape is as much water as rock, and is as peculiar on the ground as it looks on the map. It can be tricky walking country, even my well-defined line gave one paddle which would have been impossible with the river in spate. I know of several near-drownings among my surviving mountaineering friends. People going on big backpacking trips like the *Ultimate Challenge* should plan with this in mind. It is quite possible to be marooned at the head of Loch Nevis, say, or have to climb 2,000 feet and many miles up streams before being able to cross them.

Storm and I had a delightful picnic under a rowan by one of the larger lochs, Loch a' Cham Altain. In the middle of the meal we were startled by the sound of wild waters. Over the calm loch came a rush of waves. The squall sent the spray flying over us, then all was calm again except for the cackle of laughter from a pair of loons. It was a warning and we camped early, in a wood, rather than up on Ben Stack, and the sounding surge of trees that night showed it had been a wise choice. A parcel, buried in the wood only about two weeks before, was already well nibbled by mice but I had learnt that danger during *"Hamish's Mountain Walk"* so this time the contents were safe in a biscuit tin. The storm was washed off the peaks. It was probably fine midge-incubating weather. The larches in the wood were all sprouting their bright green mini shaving brushes and slowly, very slowly, the dead flats were taking on a sheen as the new grass sprouted.

MONDAY MAY 14 BEN DREAVIE TO GLENDHU

At 5 A.M. it was blowing a great gale so I decided to sleep again. The dog was all for going. Whenever my alarm sounded he would jump up and start trying to dig me out of my sleeping bag, a very effective system when I really did want to rise but having disadvantages if only a false alarm.

We set off at nine by a path which goes over the north-west shoulder of Ben Stack and eventually joins the A894 some miles north of Kylesku. Ben Stack was in boiling cloud so would do some other day, but I was determined to keep in the wilds so we cut over for Ben Dreavie and a path beyond. It was rough going and once in the cloud wild enough to blow my balaclava off and make balance precarious on rocky steps. The lochans were flying up in sheets of spray again. The dog had chased after deer the day before, and had had a thrashing; today he knew better and instead tore round in tight circles and jumped on me after each circuit. The hint was not taken. The ban on deer, as on sheep, stood. Storm was very quick in learning anything and made the perfect hill companion. He was hard to live up to in fact: always cheerful, keen, never complaining—sometimes in contrast to his master. He had a delight in all living things, not to hurt them, but just out of curiosity. A chick held in the hand would be sniffed, not grabbed; and friendship would be offered to any and all dogs and cats, not always to his own good.

The summit of Ben Dreavie, over 1,600 feet was a sandstone plateau, littered with the pebbles which had come from the crumbling rock. If this sandstone is among the oldest rock in the world, what of these pebbles which must have washed into the sea long before that? Most are round and smooth and, with a little tumbling, mount well to make homely jewelry.

I dropped down to pick up stalking paths through this desolation, one of the country's largest uninhabited areas. Miles on, I felt a new wooden hut was an intrusion but it made a welcome lunch spot. I crossed the inflow of a lochan and cut over the hill to angle down to Loch Glendhu, one of the two lochs that fork into this harsh country from Kylesku. I just made out a ferry on its crossing, a tiny beetle of blackness on the silver of the water away in the west. Among the tumbled red crags fragile wood sorrel was flowering. A path took me up to the head of the loch and I camped beyond the empty buildings and their two guardian leafless trees. A bonfire of driftwood was a doucer ending to a wild day, though the smoke pursued me round and round in circles. My clothes reeked of wood smoke for days.

TUESDAY MAY 15 INTO ASSYNT

Rising from Loch Glendhu there is a path to the promontory that separates it from Loch Glencoul, though it is not on maps, and from the top of this neb I noticed a shaft of light striking my camp site. It was really green. Summer was winning—as it must. I lost the path and then climbed to find it again. It was Himalayan in style yet 1,000 feet below lay sea, backed by the barrelled buttresses of Quinag. Dropping dramatically down to Glencoul was like descending to a camp site somewhere in the Rishi Ganga. It was tempting to linger. We went on by Loch Beag where we had camped once before when exploring here. The tide goes well out, exposing sand and mud, and underneath it must be hollow for on the flow the surface bubbles and boils in extraordinary fashion as the air escapes again.

Up the glen I lunched opposite the Eas Coul-Aulin, the highest waterfall in Britain, which is four times the height of Niagara. Conditions were right for taking photographs. It is by no means the most splendid of falls for the vast, open setting gives no idea of scale. It drops in two steps and a slither before braiding away among the screes. The nearest path leads past the top so it cannot be seen well from there, nor is the descent easy. All in all, the fall retains a kingly distance from the casual gaper.

The Abhainn an Lock Bhig, which I was following, is attractive in its own right with many small, utterly charming falls but leading up into ever-rougher and remoter regions, debouching originally from a lost lochan through a black gorge. Beyond this is another of those forgotten uplands, shot with old snow and patched with a thousand pieces of water, edged with ermine-white ridges and muffed in cloud. This is Assynt. The very name has a stony ring to it for *ass* is the Norse for rocky.

We scrambled from loch to crag, to corrie, to settle by Loch Bealach a' Mhadaidh, *the loch of the pass of the fox*. It looked out over the tawny bowl to Beinn Leoid and Meallan a' Chuail, while shivering below the eastern rampart of Ben More Assynt. Beinn an Fhurain, immediately above, was a gigantic fossilised jam roll, the strata curling in massive convolutions. No site for the rest of the journey would so combine loneliness, emptiness, roughness and grandeur.

Gwen Moffat

Space Below My Feet

*In 1953 at the age of twenty-nine, Gwen Moffat was the first British
woman to become a mountain guide. Her autobiography* Space Below
My Feet *(1961) ends with her happy in the high country on the Swiss-
Italian frontier.*

>   *It was eight o'clock when I mantelshelfed on the top of the
> cornice and stood up in the moonlight. Eight o'clock and the
> valleys dark, and the lights of villages gleaming in Italy. We had
> spent twelve hours on the ridge.*
>   *We came straight down the Verra glacier to turn the south-
> ern spur of the Breithorn. Below, in the dimness, we could see
> vague troughs and domes softened by moonlight. It was very cold
> and we were tired. It needed a lot of willpower to concentrate
> on the snow as we walked, watching for the thin lines of hidden
> crevasses.*
>   *We came under the spur and started the long uphill climb
> to the Breithorn Pass. As we gained height the wind increased—
> a north wind, bitterly cold.*
>   *We came to the level ridge and there were not more cre-
> vasses and we walked side by side. Occasionally we stopped to
> examine each other's faces by torchlight, looking for signs of
> frostbite.*
>   *My senses were a little dulled and life held no problems.
> Life was the sound of crampons scrunching the snow, the lights
> of the refuge coming up, and Life was the power and the glory
> of all the mountains I had ever climbed—as I walked along the
> frontier in the moonlight.*

   Gwen Moffat began her career as an alpinist by deserting from
the British Army (in which she had spent four years as a World War
II driver and dispatch rider). She was a feisty twenty-one year old
when the war ended. She was at loose ends, disappointed in love,

frustrated with Army life, and eager for excitement and purpose. She became friendly with a conscientious objector named Tom and set off with him on a ten-day leave, climbing her first mountains. The Welsh peaks and the bohemian life that Tom showed her were irresistible.

When she deserted from the Army it was on foot, with no looking back.

* * *

The cottage stood at the top of a ravine, among the wooded uplands that lie between Cader Idris and the Mawddach estuary.

We came to it one dark night when the stream in the ravine was in full spate. We had no torches. At first the path seemed to be a few hundred feet above the water and Tom warned me to keep away from the edge (with the loads we were carrying, we wouldn't have stopped had we started to roll), then we dropped down the side of the ravine and stumbled along a path only a few feet from the river. The noise was shattering. Speech, of course, was impossible. Once I walked into Tom. He pushed me against the bank and I realized that I was meant to stay on that side; I edged forward unhappily, splashing through water, knowing that there would be no warning if the path collapsed and Tom went with it.

The track swung back on itself, climbing through thick trees just sensed in the darkness, and the noise of the river faded gradually, then dropped to a low murmur as we came out into high open country.

I felt rather apprehensive as we crossed the fields. I had come to know Tom slowly: the long talk in the car back in the summer, the letters, the last ten days' climbing. The man himself tended to overshadow the life he led. When one is in love, the lover is, in one sense, taken for granted; there is no criticism: eccentricities are accepted, perhaps with mild surprise, often with amusement, always with approval. Now, suddenly, I realized that the people only a few hundred yards away in this fascinating cottage were strangers in every sense of the word and there would be no buffer between us. I would see them and their life more objectively than I saw Tom, and I wasn't sure that I was going to like it—and them. Least of all, that they would like me.

Tom had told me a little about them: they were all artists of one kind or another; there were several men and one girl. I had built up a picture of a tall, elegant woman in smart country clothes, beautiful and sophisticated. Her beauty would be of the flawless, mass-produced Hollywood type.

A light showed, a soft yellow square in the darkness, and I smelt wood smoke. Our boots rang on slate, there was an open door, a flagged passage and then a room, seemingly full of men. They were huge, all six footers and over, and they wore enormous fishermen's jerseys, exaggerating their size. They wore beards too, and long hair. They looked like benignant vikings.

And when their welcome was over and they had subsided on to mattresses (on the floor) to sit and beam silently at me, I became aware of Barbara, sitting on a low stool by the fire, very soft and womanly in shabby brown velvet, with red-brown hair hanging long and straight to her shoulders. No make-up, of course, but violet eyes. I think she was Irish. Anyone less like the sophisticated picture I'd had in mind would have been difficult to find. She had been an art mistress in an exclusive girls' school, had met one of the men and given up everything to join him in this strange wandering life between the mountains and the sea (they spent a lot of their time in Cornwall).

They earned their living by felling trees. They lived very cheaply, travelling by road, hitching or walking, carrying only rucksacks and their axes and saws. They rented various cottages in Wales and Cornwall: bases where they kept a few books, blankets and odd tools.

I liked the cottage on Cader best; it was the most comfortable, and it possessed atmosphere: the happy feeling of an old house, much lived in. Tom maintained that when he first came into the kitchen, when they had just rented the place, he saw an old man sitting by the fireplace. After a while he wasn't there. Tom felt no apprehension at all; on the contrary, he said he had the unmistakable feeling that he was being welcomed.

Life at the cottage was very simple. Invariably we talked until late at night or the early hours of the morning, so we never woke up before ten or eleven. There were no beds; we slept on mattresses on the floors, and when we got up we didn't eat but went swimming. On the first morning, with a heavy frost on the ground and January snow lying a few hundred feet above the house, I was too shocked to accompany them. They grinned tolerantly and scampered off like great shaggy dogs—except Barbara, who was like a red setter. When they came back, red-faced and rowdy, their hair was wet, so they *had* swum.

Next morning I went.

There was a small brick reservoir built in a high gorse-filled valley— a kind of hanging combe above the estuary. It was about ten feet deep, deep enough to dive—and I have to dive in winter. If I had to wade, I should never get there. I watched them dive, swim, and emerge gasping and shouting with laughter. Slowly, reluctantly, I took off my clothes, and climbed on the brick parapet. Mad, I thought, utterly mad, as my poor white body, rough with gooseflesh, swayed and shivered in an icy blast. Tom roared at me and splashed. Thinking that the shock might kill me, I dived.

It was cold, but not too bad if you kept your head. I surfaced. There was an aching pain across my forehead.

I thought, you're in water, cold certainly, but still water; swim! I swam to the side of the reservoir and hauled myself out, gasping. Then I joined the others, running frantically up and down the frosty grass between the gorse. When we were breathless, we did exercises and slapped ourselves, until we were dry and shining like a lot of boiled lobsters. We never used towels.

Sometimes we swam in the ravine where a dam had been built across the river and a deep pool formed behind. When the river was in spate, the water poured over the top of the dam and it was hard work to reach the other side without being swept over. Even when the snow was thick on the ground and glassy icicles hung from the banks, the dam pool seemed warmer than the reservoir, possibly because there was more life and excitement here; you thought more about the danger and less of the cold.

After swimming and eating we spent the rest of the day walking, shopping, or getting in fuel. We burnt wood, and there was an old forest of oaks at the back of the cottage which supplied us with logs. Shopping meant walking to Dolgellau and back—about ten miles. "Walking" was less strenuous: a scramble up Cader and along the four tops, or a ramble over the foothills, watching birds or talking. Sometimes people went alone, sometimes they all stayed together. There was no consistency in the arrangements; there were no arrangements.

To me the life was completely absorbing in its simplicity, but as my leave drew to an end I began to feel uneasy. In the evenings the others criticized me gently for my way of life. They had been conscientious objectors during the war. I listened to them and—when I became too bewildered—turned to Tom and he smiled and changed the subject. One night we brought a young naval officer home with us from Dolgellau. They were less tolerant with him and, for the first time, I heard the word "deserter."

One morning they decided to go down to Cornwall, and the next day they were gone. Tom and I walked with them to the foot of Cader, and stood there, watching silently as they scrambled steadily upwards to the skyline. After a while Tom said,

"Go on, go back and get your pack and go with them."

I turned away, remembering the grey fogs and the dirty canals of Stoke. I couldn't speak.

I overstayed my leave by three days, but I went back eventually. I arrived in Stoke early one evening.

When I came into the Nissen hut that was my billet it was empty, except for one girl. She told me I was to report to the sergeant-major. I did this and was asked why I was late back. I said carelessly that the floods were over the railway line. Had I a signed statement from the police to that effect? I hadn't, but I had one from a Welsh Nationalist stationmaster. Inexplicably, even to me, I didn't trouble to produce it. I walked back to the billet and started to pack a few personal belongings. I realized that I was shaking as if I were cold, but I felt nothing: no elation, no fear; my mind was completely blank.

I tied up my parcel, addressed it to my mother and went next door to the pub. There I gave it with ten shillings to a disreputable-looking customer to post. Surprisingly, it reached its destination. I went back to the billet, washed my hair and bathed. I wasn't sure when I would do either again—in hot water. While the other girl was out of the room for a moment I hid my rucksack in the bushes outside the hut.

An hour after I had come back, I nodded casually to the girl, murmured something about a drink, and slipped out of the hut. I scooped up my pack, slunk through the shrubbery to the main road, and started walking.

Anthony Bailey

A Walk Along the Boyne

*Though it is not true that poets are as common as priests in Ireland,
the countryside there is full of the poetry of walking.*

*History is as much a part of that poetry as the thistles, bogs, ruins,
and Wee Fellas.*

*The Boyne River has a symbolic significance in Ireland, north and
south, comparable to a combination Valley Forge/Appomatox in the
United States.*

*In 1979 it also held out the possibility of good fun for Anthony
Bailey and poet Seamus Heaney when they set out along waters whose
name derives from Boann, one of Ireland's pre-Christian goddesses.
Seamus Heaney's newly-bought brogues were soft, white, and emblazoned with the name "Dr. Marten's." "They would be all right," said
the poet, "after he had stepped in a few cowpats."*

"A Walk Along the Boyne" appeared in Bailey's 1986 book, Spring
Jaunts.

* * *

Just after three, Heaney and I sallied forth from [Trim Castle's] precincts, heading east. The rain was holding off. We took one backward look
at the castle against the gray sky and strode forward in the direction of the
riverbank, where a solitary figure stood—a young man, as we saw at closer
range, with a surveyor's tripod. We asked him about walking conditions
between here and Navan. He looked doubtful. There were lots of ditches
and streams coming in to join the river, he thought. It might be better
beyond Navan, where he had heard there was a towpath to Slane next to
the abandoned riverside canal. As for his tripod, which we inquired about,
he was surveying for a new road bridge, which would bypass Trim. The
Board of Works, he added, had recently been dredging the Boyne along
here, getting much silt out of the riverbed and exposing shelves of stone—
an activity that stirred up the water and added oxygen to it, to the benefit
of fish (and fishermen).

The path was blocked by a fence, a garden, and a large "PRIVATE" sign, so we made a detour across a field and walked up the road, which ran parallel to the river. Just before a bridge at a place identified on the map as Newtown Trim, we paused at a gate in a stone wall. "The Echo Gate," the Trim guidebook calls it. From it there was a view across a field and the Boyne to a ruined monastery on the far bank. Newtown Trim was a medieval suburb, it seems, and is now largely ruins. Heaney leaned over the gate and called out across to the monastery, "Go home!" The echo came: "*Go home!*" "Good gate!" called Heaney. A second or so later came the hollow reply: "*Good gate!*" "Cistercians—Trappists—silence!" shouted Heaney, getting into the swing of it. "*. . . silence!*" replied the echo.

I judged that to be a good exit line, and walked on toward the bridge, Heaney following, reluctant to leave this poets' plaything. At the bridge, a fine piece of medieval masonry, a few people were fishing while their children played on an adjacent ruined friary. For half a mile beyond this pile of stones, Heaney and I succeeded in following the riverbank. In the river, there were occasional natural weirs—stone ledges, outcrops of rock, and little islands, among which the silver-green Boyne waters tumbled. We passed a woman fishing from the bank. She had long red-gold hair, and didn't turn her head as we walked behind her swishing through grass, tall nettles, and flopping poppies. I was thinking that this was a fine symbol of woman's emancipation—spending the afternoon fishing—and looked at Heaney. His eyes were narrow slits. I wondered what he was thinking about. Boann, perhaps. She ought to be here.

For a while, the sun almost came out. Yellow-lit gray clouds scudded before a southwest wind, at our backs. We made our way along the edge of a meadow, which a farmer was mowing with a tractor, and clambered down into a gully where a small brook rushed in to join the Boyne. The Knightsbrook River, said my Irish Ordnance Survey map of the County of Meath. The Knightsbrook runs down through Laracor, two miles away, where Swift had a living, and which he made his base from 1700 to 1713. The brook at first seemed impassable, but Heaney spotted a place with far-spaced stepping stones, meant perhaps for Brobdingnagian strides; we made it over. His Dr. Marten's boots were beginning to look less new.

Heaney was brought up on a farm in Derry; his father farmed and dealt in cattle. Heaney learned as a child how to mow and scythe, and how to milk cows. Now, at forty-one, in tweeds, and with a big-featured face, he looks more like a farmer than like a scholar-poet. ("Jaws puff round and solid as a turnip" are his own accurate words, in a poem called "Ancestral Photographs.") I am a generation further away from the land: my grandfather had a dairy and fields rented for his herd on the Isle of Wight, but insisted that my father, who wanted to be a farmer, enter a bank. When Heaney and I matched the names of plants and wild flowers we could see, he came out well ahead. There was mint and gorse, iris and forget-me-not, cow

parsley, and celandine; big oxeye daisies; meadowsweet and charlock; rag-
wort, herb Robert, yellow flat, and marsh valerian. Lovely words! Heaney
told me some local names, such as "boor," which is what in Ulster they call
the elder trees, thick along the riverbanks here, the white flowers on them
looking, he thought, like full plates of meal. Vetch in Ireland is "robin-run-
the-hedge." I thought the sound the river made was "running, running."
And now we began to feel warm. It was still three miles to Bective, the next
settlement. In Dublin, the pubs and bars are by law closed in midafternoon,
the so-called holy hour. Heaney wondered if there was a holy hour in Bective.

We were now forced by wire and brambles and a deep, unbridged
ditch to leave the river again, ascending a steep and overgrown bank and
making our way beside a thick hedge to the narrow road to Bective. And
along here, after half a mile or so of roadwork, we came to a pump—a large
iron pump, with a purposeful-looking curved handle, standing in a little
concrete area at the roadside. We took turns at pumping and at holding our
mouths under the gushing spout—the water cool, with the definite stony
taste of well water. Both Heaney and I were hung over. The previous evening
had begun with a reading by the Irish poet John Montague at U.C.D. and
had continued with drinks at U.C.D., then at a bar, and finally at a bardic
session at the Heaneys', fuelled by wine and whiskey, that went on until
2:30 A.M. Montague and Senator Augustine Martin, a U.C.D. professor,
vied with each other for an hour in a duel of spontaneous chanting—making
up a poetic dialogue of invocation, description, and abuse as they went along.
This was followed by recitation, all present taking turns to speak their favorite
poems of Yeats and Patrick Kavanagh, along with any other verses that came,
fully or partly remembered, to their lips. The authors had to be guessed. I
quoted now to Heaney, as the water splashed over his cheek, some lines
from one of several poems of his that have pumps in them:

> The helmeted pump in the yard
> heated its iron,
> water honeyed

We passed several small houses on this stretch. In the front garden of
one cottage, a man was up a stepladder, cutting roses from a trellis. Everyone
we had passed (save the woman on the riverbank) had given us a nod or a
hello, and this man was no exception. Heaney called out as we ambled by,
"It's keeping up." The gardening man replied, "Oh, yes. You have it at your
backs."

"We do, that," said Heaney.

"Are you going fishing?"

"No," said Heaney. "We're tormenting ourselves by walking."

"Oh. The fish are great in the river."

"Salmon?"

"No, the trout."

I had the feeling that we were upholding a tradition that the Irish—strangely, for such a tradition-bound people—were letting slip; that is, tramping, our possessions on our backs, a few things in our pockets, our heads in the air, and the country at our feet. Patrick Kavanagh, a country cobbler's son who became a farmer and then a poet, once went off tramping during a quiet spell on the farm. He set off in April with five pounds in his pocket and stayed two months on the road, getting back home in time to sow turnips, and cured of wander-lust.

As we came into Bective, we looked out over fields and slowly rising ground to the east and saw, three or four miles away, the Hill of Tara, dwelling place of the Dark Age kings of Ireland—a yellow-green ridge crested with a long clump of trees. But Bective itself at that moment interested us more: half a dozen houses at a road junction a few hundred yards from a bridge across the Boyne, and a general store, the left half selling groceries and the right half housing a bar, which was open. Here we shed our packs; here we sat down on barstools and drank a pint and a half apiece—I of Smithwicks bitter, and Heaney of Guinness stout. Three other customers were in the bar, all agriculturally clothed. One, to my left, was by himself, a taciturn fellow who grunted uninformatively in reply to what I hoped was a friendly remark designed to open a conversation that might leave me wiser in local knowledge, particularly about which bank of the river to choose between here and Navan. On Heaney's right, the two other drinkers were talking quietly together, using occasional words like (Heaney reported) "redolence" and "sensibility." More farmer-poets? While we were there, Heaney used the phone to call a Navan hotel. Success! The Russell Arms would reserve some rooms for us. What was more, they served dinner until 11 P.M. Navan, by the river's bent-elbow route, was seven miles farther on. We ought to be there long before eleven.

It was, according to my watch, six o'clock. I looked at my watch because the electric clock over the bar, which had said a quarter past eleven when we came in, now said twenty to eleven. The second hand, moving counterclockwise, confirmed the fact: time in the Bective bar, if not throughout the Boyne Valley, was moving backward. We grabbed our things and set off quickly, before we found ourselves even further back in the past than we had imagined ourselves to be. We traversed the bridge to the north bank (which looked like being better for the walk to Navan) and headed across a field stretching before the lovely ruins of a twelfth-century abbey: lichen-and-ivy-covered tower, and loopholes, battlements, lancet arches, and the remains of a cloister. The Cistercian monks—obviously monks militant—possessed two hundred and forty-five acres hereabouts, together with a mill and a fish weir on the river and the right of their abbot to sit as a spirtual peer in Parliament. As we walked along the meadow edge, dragonflies darted out of the rushes along the river, ducks took off from the sliding river surface at our approach, and the blue-green reeds bent forward, dipping their heads constantly in the stream. After the open meadow, we came to a narrow bank on which thick woods impinged. The river wound into the distance among trees and fields and plantations, with the glimpse of a great house—Balsoon House, said the map—on the far bank. The map worried us by drawing our attention to the Clady River, a tributary that was due to spill into the Boyne any moment now. Anything called a river might take some crossing. However, when the Clady was reached it proved no more of a hindrance than the Knightsbrook had been. A series of stones, not very evenly spaced, allowed us to hop over. Then the bank widened. There was gravel underfoot and, for a while, the sense of an old riverbank road. Swallows were swooping. I said, "If only they flew more slowly, so that one could see *how* they flew so fast"—a disjointed thought that Heaney fielded neatly, replying to me with Yeats' words, "I meditate upon a swallow's flight." Meditation was the only way of setting about it.

We passed a long-disused stone slip in which a boat had presumably once been moored; hard by was a tumbledown boathouse. Midges in clouds betokened a fine day on the morrow (though it seemed a little soon after the recumbent cows to draw attention to this). Heaney spotted among the elder, alder, ash, and hickory growing along here a clump of bamboo, and cut himself a six-foot pole—something he said he's always wanted as a boy, for a fishing rod. His countryman's acute eye also served me well. I was a pace or two in advance of him, and was just about to step into some thick brush overgrowing the path when he grabbed my shoulder and said urgently, "Look out there!" Prodding with his bamboo pole, he pushed aside the brush and long grass to reveal a crevasse, a foot or so wide, into which I had been just about to walk—perhaps plunging (since no bottom was visible) into the Irish netherworld.

A little after seven-thirty, we reached a high stone bridge spanning the river, which ran through a slight gorge. We decided to climb here and strike north to reach a road. Despite the initial suppleness of his Dr. Marten's boots, Heaney had a blister forming. Navan seemed distant and the evening well advanced, although, thanks to the northern summer twilight, it wouldn't be dark for two more hours. Irish miles had a separate legal existence until 1826 (when they were abolished); one Irish mile was approximately 1.27 British miles. They still feel longer. Perhaps this is so because one consults the Irish Ordnance Survey maps as if they were British maps, with the same scale, whereas the scale of the Irish is half an inch to a mile rather than one inch, as is most common in England. Consequently, what looks like an hour's walk is in fact two hours'. Moreover, when country walking, one finds no paths as straight as the routes that crows fly. One respects crops by walking the long way, round the edge of a field. One follows meandering riverbanks and curving contour lines. And now getting up the embankment of the bridge took some zigzag climbing, which effectively doubled the distance.

On the bridge, we walked out into the middle and sat for a few minutes looking upstream and down before bidding a temporary farewell to the Boyne. A grassed track ran across the bridge, which had once (we conjectured) carried a railway. Its course ran northward in a cutting that had become—as Irish land when left to its own devices often does—a sort of bog. Heaney, despite his blister, was in good spirits, possibly affected by the boggy ground underfoot. He has written a number of poems that have to do with bogs and with their preserving power, whether of food or implements or bodies that sink in them, and bogs have become for him a way of getting at and expressing in poetry the tenacious quality of Irish history— how so much that has happened in it keeps resurfacing, looking much as it did when it first went under. When the ground got too wet, we walked along one edge of the cutting. We noticed that the gateposts to a field were made of old railway ties. Rabbits scattered into the banks. After a mile or so with small farms on either side, we met a road. Under it, through a bridge, ran the former railway line that we had been following, and there, on the far side of the brick arch, was the former railway station, spick-and-span, looking as if—save for the missing tracks—the 7:30 P.M. to Navan were about to come steaming in.

I went a bit astray at this point. I said we must obviously turn right on the road to get to Navan. Heaney said that clearly we should go left. The station (in retrospect seen as having been done up as a house) disoriented me—gave me the feeling of being in another time and in an unexpected landscape. "Going astray" is not uncommon in Ireland. The phenomenon affects the natives, too. Some tell of getting into the middle of a well-known field and wandering around for an hour, maybe, unable to find the way out. Patrick Kavanagh and his mother went astray once while coming home in an ass cart from a visit to friends. All evening, in the rain, they drove around a skein of wet roads near Inniskeen, getting nowhere. "Everything seemed strange," Kavanagh wrote, in his book "The Green Fool." "The folk we saw were not ordinary mortals." Finally, they decided to let the ass choose its own direction, and this worked. When they reached home, other traditional solutions to the predicament were proposed, such as turning one's coat inside out.

"Paddy, ye were with the Wee Fellas," [one listener said].
"Only for the ass we'd never escape," I said.

"Indeed you would not," he supported, "sure the ass is a blessed animal."

After some dithering and discussion on the roadside, we went left, as Heaney had proposed, and soon met the Navan road. Possibly the railway station had been a figment. Perhaps I had been with the Wee Fellas. There was, however, nearly four miles still to go. The sky was darkening as the sun set, and gray clouds came in from the west. A mile along the lonely road, the rain began to fall. Umbrella up, coat collars up, we walked along, Heaney limping from his blister. We sang "It's a long, long way to Tipperary," and Kavanagh's "On Raglan Road," to the tune "The Dawning of the Day," which Heaney's wife, Marie, sings in a way to bring the moisture to your eyes. It wasn't long before the decision was taken, with one barely spoken accord, to try to hitch a ride into Navan.

Cars were infrequent on that road, but the goddess of the river was looking after journeyers that night: the second car stopped. Its driver was a friendly Australian, who dropped us right outside the Russell Arms Hotel in Navan. There the lady behind the reception desk—perhaps unused to guests who arrived with knapsacks and bamboo staffs, looking touched with the Meath greenery—asked to be paid in advance. But neither Heaney nor I reacted huffily to this suggestion. Hot baths and food and drink were in our minds. We paid up.

The Russell Arms: staircases going this way and that; the feeling of being in two or three large Victorian houses knocked together in a period of expansion, and now, that moment passed, in old age propping one another up. In the bathroom I used, there were no light bulbs in the fixtures and no plug in the bath. Fortunately, daylight of a feeble sort persisted. I used the small plug from the washbasin, and added my facecloth to stem the ebb from the tub. In my bedroom one out of three lights worked. However, on the ground floor all was well set up and jovial. The bar was full of early arrivals for a meeting of the local association of Tipperary Men—exiles, it appeared, from that fair county, all of a hundred miles from Navan. Heaney arrived, still hobbling but otherwise restored by hot water. We drank apéritifs of Bushmills whiskey, from the North, and dined off sirloin, from the South. We toasted the Boyne with several carafes of red Spanish plonk. Meanwhile, the river was running a hundred yards off, unseen, past the backs of the houses of Navan, which resolutely look the other way.

We talked about the phrase "the Boyne." Where Heaney grew up and went to school, in Northern Ireland, it was loaded with significance. For Northern Protestants, "the Boyne" connotes the battle in 1690 at which the troops of William III beat those of James II and thus kept all of Ireland firmly under British hegemony for the following two hundred and thirty years. In much of Ulster, to mention the Boyne is to reassert Protestant superiority. We swapped references that we recalled from ballads and folk songs—among others, "The Boyne Water" and "The Green Grassy Slopes of the Boyne," both of which celebrate Orange patriotism and William's victory. And the river's name occurs as symbol or metaphor in modern Irish poetry as often as blackbirds do in medieval Irish lyrics. The Boyne figures in the specifically Irish section of Louis MacNeice's long poem "Autumn Journal," where the poet (born in Belfast) evokes the yearly celebrations in Ulster on the anniversary of the Battle of the Boyne: "The voodoo of the Orange bands drawing an iron net through darkest Ulster." That section of the poem begins with a memorable ironic passage:

> Nightmare leaves fatigue:
>   We envy men of action
> Who sleep and wake, murder and intrigue
>   Without being doubtful, without being haunted.
> And I envy the intransigence of my own
>   Countrymen who shoot to kill and never
> See the victim's face become their own
>   Or find his motive sabotage their motives.

He wrote those lines in 1938 or 1939, and it would be harder now, since the renewed Troubles and the many deaths caused by terrorists in the past ten years, to use the word "envy" in that way—even though a sardonic tone comes through.

Tramping also leaves fatigue. Heaney and I retired before the bar called for last orders. I slept profoundly, and failed to hear the boisterous departure of the Tipperary Men, which Heaney next day reported as having taken place sometime after two. He might have recalled a line of his own: "Drunk again, full as the Boyne."

James Matthews

Frank O'Connor, Poet

Frank O'Connor (1903–1966) grew up in rustic Ireland as Michael O'Donovan. His accounts of Irish country life eventually propelled him into the ranks of the world's best short story writers. Although often in exile from his homeland, he believed that only in Ireland could one truly enjoy a good walk.

Wherever he was, he was sure to be walking. In 1953 his new American wife said of the dear groom who was more than twenty years her senior, "The man is a fiend for walking and I'll get to be a fiend for it too or find myself discarded for sure." At the end of his life O'Connor wrote that, "When I agitate for a five-mile walk the surgeon smiles pityingly."

A friend once said that walking with O'Connor was "like listening to an encyclopedia." Those walks must have had some of the intensity of O'Connor's short stories, which he said were designed to "lay bare a person's fundamental character in one moment of crisis." In the early days those walks were most often shared by either a volatile young priest (Tim Traynor) or by a middle-aged historian/physician. During the winter of 1930–31 O'Connor suffered badly from boils until finally his mother persuaded him to overcome his fear of all doctors, and to visit the eccentric neighborhood practitioner.

In Voices: A Life of Frank O'Connor, *James Matthews reports what happened next.*

*   *   *

Richard Hayes was in charge of a crowded dispensary near his house; officially he didn't take private patients, but in fact he looked after nearly everyone in Ringsend on a well-if-it's-that-bad-but-only-this-once basis, generally without pay. Hayes lived in the family house, a modest Georgian redbrick cautiously set back from the road behind a high stone wall. The day Michael first came to call was the housekeeper's day off, so the doctor answered the door himself. Michael ceremoniously announced the reason for the call, and Hayes calmly upbraided his presumptuousness for calling at that hour of the day with no introduction and less grace. He went on to say that he didn't take private patients and knew nothing about boils. He informed Michael that if he wanted an X-ray, a miracle drug, or even, God forbid, a lancing, he would have to go somewhere else. By this time Michael had changed his opinion of the man from impertinent and pompous to delightfully eccentric. Michael distrusted a respectable doctor or lawyer or priest, but a renegade was something else. His protests met further elegant reproach, which, it turned out, was Hayes's way of accepting a patient. Finally, he asked Michael's name and occupation. Rather than calling himself "Michael O'Donovan, Librarian," he pulled himself erect and in grand Yeatsian fashion announced, "Frank O'Connor, Poet." When Hayes asked him to enter, Michael was so disconcerted that he did so at once, following Hayes like a dutiful puppy to a small room off the hall. From that day on they were friends.

It was a ridiculous friendship to everyone in Dublin, including Seán O'Faoláin, who years later gave this fictional description of two men resembling Hayes and O'Connor walking arm in arm like father and son along O'Connell Street.

> The doctor straight and spare as a spear, radiating propriety from every spiky bone of his body, as short of step as a woman, and as carefully dressed from his wide–brimmed bowler hat to the rubber tip of his mottled, gold–headed malacca cane; the poet striding beside him, halting only to swirl his flabby tweeds; his splendid hydrocephalic head stretched behind his neck like a balloon; his myopic eyes glaring at the clouds over the roofs through the thick lenses of his glasses; a waterfall of black hair permanently frozen over his left eye; his big teeth laughing, his big voice booming, he looked for all the world like a peasant Yeats in a poor state of health.

By all accounts O'Faolain's description was hardly invention at all.

Tim Traynor scoffed at them and gave the association less than a year. Traynor's obsession at the time was psychoanalysis, and he was quick to pontificate that the two eccentrics, the urbane doctor and the provincial writer, had invented each other. As with every problem he faced, Traynor reduced the friendship to sex, though he knew Michael better than to call his friendship with Hayes a homosexual relationship. What he meant was that they both needed encouragement to continue a bachelor life, for they both detested celibacy. Traynor was right but for the wrong reasons. O'Connor invented Hayes (and vice versa) but only insofar as he invented any friend or father or lover—to offset his terrible feeling of loneliness. Almost every evening they walked the broad streets of Ballsbridge or along Sandymount Strand. Michael drew furiously on one cigarette after another, his head cocked back in strutting celebration of some line of poetry, while Hayes smoked thoughtfully on his slender pipe and saluted gracefully every person he knew, bending "his long frame in two like a jack-knife, his walking stick thrust out from behind his back like a tail and his punchinello face distorted with amiability." For several years this was Michael's "dearest friend": "the man," he wrote, "who replaced Corkery in my affections, to whom I went in every difficulty and who gave me advice that was always disinterested and sometimes noble."

Richard Hayes was not a very public person, preferring the quiet of his study to the hubbub of medical practice or the swirl of committee rooms. Medicine consumed less of his time and interest than did history, more precisely the history of Franco–Irish relations. One of the reasons he stayed in his modest position at the dispensary was the time and privacy it afforded his research on France. He even declined an offer to be made governor-general, a titular representative of the British Crown in Ireland. The day the rumor of the nomination broke in the Irish press, Hayes and O'Connor walked and talked as usual along the strand. Michael argued that if Hayes did not accept, then some "bloody government eejit" would get himself appointed. Hayes remained adamant for some time. Then something struck him about the whole affair and he began to laugh, not his usual sedate chuckle but a hearty O'Connor roar. Michael was stunned. He saw nothing funny about it. The only thing he saw was a man so vain that he would not lower himself to mere civil responsibility. Reading Michael's mind, Hayes said, "And you're right, of course. I am mad with vanity." They toasted their mutual arrogance with fine French brandy that night.

Hilaire Belloc

The Path to Rome

At the turn of the century Catholic convert, Hilaire Belloc, decided to make a pilgrimage to the Holy See. Alsace-Lorraine's heavy armaments and pre-World War I social mores have changed as much as the word "driving" (which Belloc used in the sense of driving a horse and carriage). But even if motorcars had been common in 1900, Belloc would have certainly made his pilgrimage on foot. The following passage is from The Path to Rome *(1902).*

* * *

Above these fields the forest went up steeply. I had not pushed two hundred yards into its gloom and confusion when I discovered that I had lost my way. It was necessary to take the only guide I had and to go straight upwards wherever the line of greatest inclination seemed to lie, for that at least would take me to a summit and probably to a view of the valley; whereas if I tried to make for the shoulder of the hill (which had been my first intention) I might have wandered about till nightfall.

It was an old man in a valley called the Curicante in Colorado that taught me this, if one lost one's way going *upwards* to make at once along the steepest line, but if one lost it going *downwards,* to listen for water and reach it and follow it. I wish I had space to tell all about this old man, who gave me hospitality out there. He was from New England and was lonely, and had brought out at great expense a musical box to cheer him. Of this he was very proud, and though it only played four silly hymn tunes, yet, as he and I listened to it, heavy tears came into his eyes and light tears into mine, because these tunes reminded him of his home. But I have no time to do more than mention him, and must return to my forest.

I climbed, then, over slippery pine needles and under the charged air of those trees which was full of dim, slanting light from the afternoon sun, till, nearly at the summit, I came upon a clearing which I at once recognized as a military road, leading to what we used to call a "false battery," that is, a dugout with embrasures into which guns could be placed but in which no guns were. For ever since the French managed to produce a really mobile heavy gun they have constructed any amount of such auxilliary works between the permanent forts. These need no fixed guns, to be emplaced, since the French can now use one such parapet, now another, as occasion serves, and the advantage is that your guns are never useless, but can always be brought round where they are needed, and that thus six guns will do more work than twenty used to do.

The false battery was on the brow of the hill, and when I reached it I looked down the slope, over the brushwood that hid the wire entanglements, and there was the whole valley of the Moselle at my feet.

As this was the first really great height, so this was the first really great view that I met with on my pilgrimage. I drew it carefully, piece by piece, sitting there a long time in the declining sun and noting all I saw. Achettes, just below; the flat valley with the river winding from side to side; the straight rows of poplar trees; the dark pines on the hills, and the rounded mountains rising farther and higher into the distance until the last I saw, far off to the southeast, must have been the Ballon d'Alsace at the sources of the Moselle—the hill that marked the first full stage in my journey and that overlooked Switzerland.

Indeed, this is the peculiar virtue of walking to a far place, and especially of walking there in a straight line, that one gets these visions of the world from hill-tops.

When I call up for myself this great march I see it all mapped out in landscapes, each of which I caught from some mountain, and each of which joins on to that before and to that after it, till I can piece together the whole road. The view here from the Hill of Archettes, the view from the Ballon d'Alsace, from Glovelier Hill, from the Weissenstein, from the Frienzer Grat, from the Grimsel, from above Bellinzona, from the Principessa, from Tizzano, from the ridge of the Appenines, from the Wall of Siena, from San Quirico, from Radicofani, from San Lorenzo, from Montefiascone, from above Viterbo, from Roncigleone, and at last from that lift in the Via Cassia, whence one suddenly perceives the City. They unroll themselves all in their order till I can see Europe, and Rome shining at the end.

But you who go in railways are necessarily shut up in long valleys and even sometimes by the walls of the earth. Even those who bicycle or drive see these sights but rarely and with no consecution, since roads also avoid climbing save where they are forced to it as over certain passes. It is only by following the straight line onwards that anyone can pass from ridge to ridge and have this full picture of the way he has been.

So much for views. I clambered down the hill to Archettes and saw, almost the first house, a swinging board, "At the sign of the Trout of the Vosges," and as it was now evening I turned in there to dine.

Two things I noticed at once when I sat down to meat. First, that the people seated at that inn table were of the middle-class of society, and secondly, that I, though of their rank, was an impediment to their enjoyment. For to sleep in woods, to march some seventy miles, the latter part in a dazzling sun, and to end by sliding down an earthy steep into the road, stamps a man with all that this kind of people least desire to have thrust upon them. And those who blame the middle-class for their conventions in such matters, and who profess to be above the care for cleanliness and clothes and social ritual which marks the middle-class, are either anarchists by nature, or fools who take what is but an effect of their wealth for a natural virtue.

I say it roundly; if it were not for the punctiliousness of the middle-class in these matters all our civilisation would go to pieces. They are the conservators and the maintainers of the standard, the moderators of Europe, the salt of society. For the kind of man who boasts that he does not mind dirty clothes or roughing it, is either a man who cares nothing for all that civilisation has built up and who rather hates it, or else (and this is much more common) he is a rich man, or accustomed to live among the rich, and can afford to waste energy and stuff because he feels in a vague way that more clothes can always be bought, that at the end of his vagabondism he can get excellent dinners, and that London and Paris are full of luxurious baths and barber shops. Of all the corrupting effects of wealth there is none worse than this, that it makes the wealthy (and their parasites) think in some way divine, or at least a lovely character of the mind, what is in truth nothing but their power of luxurious living. Heaven keep us all from great riches— I mean from very great riches.

Now the middle-class cannot afford to buy new clothes whenever they feel inclined, neither can they end up a jaunt by a Turkish bath and a great feast with wine. So their care is always to preserve intact what they happen to have, to exceed in nothing, to study cleanliness, order, decency, sobriety, and a steady temper, and they fence all this round and preserve it in the only way it can be preserved, to wit, with conventions, and they are quite right.

I find it very hard to keep up to the demands of these my colleagues, but I recognize that they are on the just side of the quarrel; let none of them go about pretending that I have not defended them in this book.

G. K. Chesterton

Hilaire Belloc Meets Henry James

How many walkers have had the experience of returning to civilization, dirty and bedraggled, only to meet the glares of proper stay-at-homes? In the following example from James Sutherland's Oxford Book of Literary Anecdotes, *G. K. Chesterton recalls the unannounced meeting of his footloose friend, Hilaire Belloc, just back from a long walk on the Continent, with the august American expatriate, Henry James.*

Gilbert Chesterton (1874–1936) was the author of the Father Brown series of mysteries. Like his friend Belloc he became a Roman Catholic convert; he contributed regularly to Belloc's Eye-Witness, *later the* New Witness, *and edited it from 1925 until his death. G. K. Chesterton and Hilaire Belloc also collaborated on some books satirizing Edwardian society.*

Henry James (1843–1916) was born in New York, schooled there and in Europe, and settled permanently at Lamb House, Rye, England in 1898 where he wrote his three great later novels contrasting American and European sensibilities. At the end of the Edwardian era he finally became a British subject—just when the onslaught of World War I was to break apart the world he had sought and to elevate the American model he had escaped.

The nineteenth century lingered on in Henry James until his death in 1916. By then the Edwardians' sense of freedom and frisson was being replaced by the horror of the trenches.

In his Catholic longings Belloc was perhaps as much a traditionalist as Henry James, but the following scene at G. K. Chesterton's house hints at other breaks with convention later in the century. I like to imagine Hilaire Belloc hitting the by-ways with Henry Miller and some Dharma Bums, *"ragged, unshaven, shouting for beer, shameless above all shades of poverty and wealth."*

* * *

One summer we took a house at Rye, that wonderful inland island, crowned with a town as with a citadel, like a hill in a medieval picture. It happened that the house next to us was the old oak-panelled mansion which had attracted, one might almost say across the Atlantic, the fine aquiline eye of Henry James. For Henry James, of course, was an American who had reacted against America; and steeped his sensitive psychology in everything that seemed most antiquatedly and aristocratically English. In his search for the finest shades among the shadows of the past, one might have guessed that he would pick out that town from all towns and that house from all houses. It had been the seat of a considerable patrician family of the neighbourhood, which had long ago decayed and disappeared. It had, I believe, rows of family portraits, which Henry James treated as reverently as family ghosts. I think in a way he really regarded himself as a sort of steward or custodian of the mysteries and secrets of a great house, where ghosts might have walked with all possible propriety. The legend says (I never learned for certain if it was true) that he had actually traced that dead family-tree until he found that there was far away, in some manufacturing town, one unconscious descendant of the family, who was a cheerful and commonplace commercial clerk. And it is said that Henry James would ask this youth down to his dark ancestral house, and receive him with funereal hospitality, and I am sure with comments of a quite excruciating tact and delicacy. Henry James always spoke with an air which I can only call gracefully groping; that is, not so much groping in the dark in blindness as groping in the light in bewilderment, through seeing too many avenues and obstacles. I would not compare it, in the unkind phrase of Mr. H. G. Wells, to an elephant trying to pick up a pea. But I agree that it was like something with a very sensitive and flexible proboscis, feeling its way through a forest of facts; to us often invisible facts. It is said, I say, that these thin straws of sympathy and subtlety were duly split for the benefit of the astonished commercial gentleman, while Henry James, with his bowed dome-like head, drooped with unfathomable apologies and rendered a sort of silent account of his stewardship. It is also said that the commercial gentleman thought the visit a great bore and the ancestral home a hell of a place; and probably fidgeted about with a longing to go out for a B and S at the *Pink 'Un*.

Whether this tale be true or not, it is certain that Henry James inhabited the house with all the gravity and loyalty of the family ghosts; not without something of the oppressive delicacy of a highly cultured family butler. He was in point of fact a very stately and courteous old gentleman; and in some social aspects especially, rather uniquely gracious. He proved in one point that there was a truth in his cult of tact. He was serious with children. I saw a little boy gravely present him with a crushed and dirty dandelion. He bowed; but he did not smile. That restraint was a better proof of the understanding of children than the writing of *What Maisie Knew*. But in all relations of life he erred, if he erred, on the side of solemnity and slowness; and it was this, I suppose, that got at last upon the too lively nerves of Mr. Wells; who used, even in those days, to make irreverent darts and dashes through the sombre house and the sacred garden and drop notes to me over the garden wall. I shall have more to say to Mr. H. G. Wells and his notes later; here we are halted at the moment when Mr. Henry James heard of our arrival in Rye and proceeded (after exactly the correct interval) to pay his call in state.

Needless to say, it was a very stately call of state; and James seemed to fill worthily the formal frock coat of those far-off days. As no man is so dreadfully well-dressed as a well-dressed American, so no man is so terribly well-mannered as a well-mannered American. He brought his brother William with him, the famous American philosopher; and though William James was breezier than his brother when you knew him, there was something finally ceremonial about this idea of the whole family on the march. We talked about the best literature of the day; James a little tactfully, myself a little nervously. I found he was more strict than I had imagined about the rules of artistic arrangement; he deplored rather than depreciated Bernard Shaw, because plays like *Getting Married* were practically formless. He said something complimentary about something of mine; but represented himself as respectfully wondering how I wrote all I did. I suspected him of meaning why rather than how. We then proceeded to consider gravely the work of Hugh Walpole, with many delicate degrees of appreciation and doubt; when I heard from the front-garden a loud bellowing noise resembling that of an impatient fog-horn. I knew, however, that it was not a fog-horn; because it was roaring out, "Gilbert! Gilbert!" and was like only one voice in the world; as rousing as that recalled in one of its former phrases, of those who

> Heard Ney shouting to the guns to unlimber
> And hold the Beresina Bridge at night.

I knew it was Belloc, probably shouting for bacon and beer; but even I had no notion of the form or guise under which he would present himself.

I had every reason to believe that he was a hundred miles away in France. And so apparently, he had been; walking with a friend of his in the Foreign Office, a co-religionist of one of the old Catholic families; and by some miscalculation they had found themselves in the middle of their travels entirely without money. Belloc is legitimately proud of having on occasion lived, and being able to live, the life of the poor. One of the ballades of the *Eye-Witness*, which was never published, described tramping abroad in this fashion:

> To sleep and smell the incense of the tar,
> To wake and watch Italian dawns aglow

And underneath the branch a single star,
Good Lord, how little wealthy people know.

In this spirit they started to get home practically without money. Their clothes collapsed and they managed to get into some workmen's slops. They had no razors and could not afford to shave. They must have saved their last penny to re-cross the sea; and then they started walking from Dover to Rye; where they knew their nearest friend for the moment resided. They arrived, roaring for food and drink and derisively accusing each other of having secretly washed, in violation of an implied contract between tramps. In this fashion they burst in upon the balanced tea-cup and tentative sentence of Mr. Henry James.

Henry James had a name for being subtle; but I think that situation was too subtle for him. I doubt to this day whether he, of all men, did not miss the irony of the best comedy in which he ever played a part. He left America because he loved Europe, and all that was meant by England or France; the gentry, the gallantry, the traditions of lineage and locality, the life that had been lived beneath old portraits in oak-panelled rooms. And there, on the other side of the tea-table, was Europe, was the old thing that made France and England, the posterity of the English squires and the French soldiers; ragged, unshaven, shouting for beer, shameles above all shades of poverty and wealth; sprawling, indifferent, secure. And what looked across at it was still the Puritan refinement of Boston; and the space it looked across was wider than the Atlantic.

Vladimir Nabokov

Butterfly Walks

The passion for science has never been more widespread than in the twentieth century. For the devotee its pleasures are intense and deep-rooted. Walking, however, is not likely to play much of a part unless the science be something outdoorsy like geology or ecology or unless walking be equated with creative stimulus.

Novelist Vladimir Nabokov (1899–1977) was not known primarily as a scientist but his love of "Butterfly Walks" was both passionate and poetic. "Butterfly Walks" is excerpted from his 1966 autobiography Speak Memory.

*   *   *

On a summer morning, in the legendary Russia of my boyhood, my first glance upon awakening was for the chink between the white inner shutters. If it disclosed a watery pallor, one had better not open them at all, and so be spared the sight of a sullen day sitting for its picture in a puddle. How resentfully one would deduce, from a line of dull light, the leaden sky, the sodden sand, the gruel-like mess of broken brown blossoms under the lilacs—and that flat, fallow leaf (the first casualty of the season) pasted upon a wet garden bench!

But if the chink was a long glint of dewy brilliancy, then I made haste to have the window yield its treasure. With one blow, the room would be cleft into light and shade. The foliage of birches moving in the sun had the translucent green tone of grapes, and in contrast to this there was the dark velvet of fir trees against a blue of extraordinary intensity, the like of which I rediscovered only many years later, in the montane zone of Colorado.

From the age of seven, everything I felt in connection with a rectangle of framed sunlight was dominated by a single passion. If my first glance of the morning was for the sun, my first thought was for the butterflies it would engender. . . .

I have hunted butterflies in various climes and disguises: as a pretty boy in knickerbockers and sailor cap; as a lanky cosmopolitan expatriate in flannel bags and beret; as a fat hatless old man in shorts. . . . Incredibly happy memories, quite comparable, in fact, to those of my Russian boyhood, are associated with my research work at the Museum of Comparative Zoology, Cambridge, Massachusetts (1941–1948). No less happy have been the many collecting trips taken almost every summer, during twenty years, through most of the states of my adopted country.

In Jackson Hole and in the Grand Canyon, on the mountain slopes above Telluride, Colorado, and on a celebrated pine barren near Albany, New York, dwell, and will dwell, in generations more numerous than editions, the butterflies I have described as new. Several of my finds have been dealt with by other workers; some have been named after me. . . .

Few things indeed have I known in the way of emotion or appetite, ambition or achievement, that could surpass in richness and strength the excitement of entomological exploration. From the very first it had a great many intertwinkling facets. One of them was the acute desire to be alone, since any companion, no matter how quiet, interfered with the concentrated enjoyment of my mania. Its gratification admitted of no compromise or exception. Already when I was ten, tutors and governesses knew that the morning was mine and cautiously kept away.

In this connection, I remember the visit of a schoolmate, a boy of whom I was very fond and with whom I had excellent fun. He arrived one summer night—in 1913, I think—from a town some twenty-five miles away. His father had recently perished in an accident, the family was ruined and the stouthearted lad, not being able to afford the price of a railway ticket, had bicycled all those miles to spend a few days with me.

On the morning following his arrival, I did everything I could to get out of the house for my morning hike without his knowing where I had gone. Breakfastless, with hysterical haste, I gathered my net, pill boxes, killing jar, and escaped through the window. Once in the forest, I was safe; but still I walked on, my calves quaking, my eyes full of scalding tears, the whole of me twitching with shame and self-disgust, as I visualized my poor friend, with his long pale face and black tie, moping in the hot garden—patting the panting dogs for want of something better to do, and trying hard to justify my absence to himself.

Let me look at my demon objectively. With the exception of my parents, no one really understood my obsession, and it was many years before I met a fellow sufferer. . . .

It is astounding how little the ordinary person notices butterflies. "None," calmly replied that sturdy Swiss hiker with Camus in his rucksack when purposely asked by me for the benefit of my incredulous companion if he had seen any butterflies while descending the trail where, a moment before, you and I had been delighting in swarms of them. It is also true that when I call up the image of a particular path remembered in minute detail but pertaining to a summer before that of 1906, preceding, that is, the date on my first locality label, and never revisited, I fail to make out one wing, one wingbeat, one azure flash, one moth-gemmed flower, as if an evil spell had been cast on the Adriatic coast making all its "leps" (as the slangier among us say) invisible. Exactly thus an entomologist may feel some day when plodding beside a jubilant, and already helmetless botanist amid the hideous flora of a parallel planet, with not a single insect in sight; and thus (in odd proof of the odd fact that whenever possible the scenery of our infancy is used by an economically minded producer as a ready-made setting for our adult dreams) the seaside hilltop of a certain recurrent nightmare of mine, whereinto I smuggle a collapsible net from my waking state, is gay with thyme and melilot, but incomprehensibly devoid of all the butterflies that should be there.

I also found out very soon that a "lepist" indulging in his quiet quest was apt to provoke strange reactions in other creatures. . . . On a path above the Black Sea, in the Crimea, among shrubs in waxy bloom, in March 1918, a bow-legged Bolshevik sentry attempted to arrest me for signaling (with my net, he said) to a British warship. In the summer of 1929, every time I walked through a village in the Eastern Pyrenees, and happened to look back, I would see in my wake the villagers frozen in the various attitudes my passage had caught them in, as if I were Sodom and they Lot's wife. A decade later, in the Maritime Alps, I once noticed the grass undulate in a serpentine way behind me because a fat rural policeman was wriggling after me on his belly to find out if I were not trapping songbirds. America has shown even more of this morbid interest in my retiary activities than other countries have—perhaps because I was in my forties when I came there to live, and the older the man, the queerer he looks with a butterfly net in his hand. Stern farmers have drawn my attention to NO FISHING signs; from cars passing me on the highway have come wild howls of derision; sleepy dogs, though unmindful of the worst bum, have perked up and come at me, snarling; tiny tots have pointed me out to their puzzled mamas; broad-minded vacationists have asked me whether I was catching bugs for bait; and one morning on a wasteland, lit by tall yuccas in bloom, near Santa Fe, a big black mare followed me for more than a mile.

When, having shaken off all pursuers, I took the rough, red road that ran from our Vyra house toward field and forest, the animation and luster of the day seemed like a tremor of sympathy around me.

Very fresh, very dark Arran Browns, which emerged only every second year (conveniently, retrospection has fallen here into line), flitted among the firs or revealed their red markings and checkered fringes as they sunned themselves on the roadside bracken. Hopping above the grass, a diminutive Ringlet called Hero dodged my net. Several moths, too, were flying—gaudy sun lovers that sail from flower to flower like painted flies, or male insomniacs in search of hidden females, such as that rust-colored Oak Eggar hurtling across the shrubbery. I noticed (one of the major mysteries of my childhood) a soft pale green wing caught in a spider's web (by then I knew what it was: part of a Large Emerald). The tremendous larva of the Goat Moth, ostentatiously segmented, flat-headed, flesh-colored and glossily flushed, a strange creature "as naked as a worm" to use a French comparison, crossed my path in frantic search for a place to pupate (the awful pressure of metamorphosis, the aura of a disgraceful fit in a public place). On the bark of that birch tree, the stout one near the park wicket, I had found last spring a dark aberration of Sievers' Carmelite (just another gray moth to the reader). In the ditch, under the bridgelet, a bright-yellow Silvius Skipper hobnobbed with a dragonfly (just a blue libellula to me). From a flower head two male Coppers rose to a tremendous height, fighting all the way up—and then, after a while, came the downward flash of one of them returning to his thistle. These were familiar insects, but at any moment something better might cause me to stop with a quick intake of breath. . . .

Let me also evoke the hawkmoths, the jets of my boyhood! Colors would die a long death on June evenings. The lilac shrubs in full bloom before which I stood, net in hand, displayed clusters of a fluffy gray in the dusk—the ghost of purple. A moist young moon hung above the mist of a neighboring meadow. In many a garden have I stood thus in later years— in Athens, Antibes, Atlanta—but never have I waited with such a keen desire as before those darkening lilacs. And suddenly it would come, the low buzz passing from flower to flower, the vibrational halo around the streamlined body of an olive and pink Hummingbird moth poised in the air above the corolla into which it had dipped its long tongue. Its handsome black larva (resembling a diminutive cobra when it puffed out its ocellated front segments) could be found on dark willow herb two months later. Thus every hour and season had its delights. And, finally, on cold, or even frosty, autumn nights, one could sugar for moths by painting tree trunks with a mixture of molasses, beer, and rum. Through the gusty blackness, one's lantern would illumine the stickily glistening furrows of the bark and two or three large moths upon it imbibing the sweets, their nervous wings half open butterfly fashion, the lower ones exhibiting their incredible crimson silk from beneath the lichen-gray primaries. "*Catocala adultera!*" I would triumphantly shriek in the direction of the lighted windows of the house as I stumbled home to show my captures to my father.

The "English" park that separated our house from the hayfields was an extensive and elaborate affair with labyrinthine paths, Turgenevian benches, and imported oaks among the endemic firs and birches. . . . On a picturesque boulder, a little mountain ash and a still smaller aspen had climbed, holding hands, like two clumsy, shy children. Other, more elusive trespassers—lost picnickers or merry villagers—would drive our hoary gamekeeper Ivan crazy by scrawling ribald words on the benches and gates. The distintegrating process continues still, in a different sense, for when, nowadays, I attempt to follow in memory the winding paths from one given point to another, I notice with alarm that there are many gaps, due to oblivion or ignorance, akin to the terra-incognita blanks map makers of old used to call "sleeping beauties."

Beyond the park, there were fields, with a continuous shimmer of butterfly wings over a shimmer of flowers—daisies, bluebells, scabious, and others—which now rapidly pass by me in a kind of colored haze like those lovely, lush meadows, never to be explored, that one sees from the diner on a transcontinental journey. At the end of this grassy wonderland, the forest rose like a wall. There I roamed, scanning the tree trunks (the enchanted, the silent part of a tree) for certain tiny moths, called Pugs in England—delicate little creatures that cling in the daytime to speckled surfaces, with which their flat wings and turned-up abdomens blend. There, at the bottom of that sea of sunshot greenery, I slowly spun round the great boles. Nothing in the world would have seemed sweeter to me than to be able to add, by a stroke of luck, some remarkable new species to the long list of Pugs already named by others. . . .

On my butterfly hunts I always preferred hiking to any other form of locomotion (except, naturally, a flying seat gliding leisurely over the plant mats and rocks of an unexplored mountain, or hovering just above the flowery roof of a rain forest); for when you walk, especially in a region you have studied well, there is an exquisite pleasure in departing from one's itinerary to visit, here and there by the wayside, this glade, that glen, this or that combination of soil and flora—to drop in, as it were, on a familiar butterfly in his particular habitat, in order to see if he has emerged, and if so, how he is doing.

There came a July day—around 1910, I suppose—when I felt the urge to explore the vast marshland beyond the Oredezh. After skirting the river for three or four miles, I found a rickety footbridge. While crossing over, I could see the huts of a hamlet on my left, apple trees, rows of tawny pine logs lying on a green bank, and the bright patches made on the turf by the scattered clothes of peasant girls, who, stark naked in shallow water, romped and yelled, heeding me as little as if I were the discarnate carrier of my present reminiscences.

On the other side of the river, a dense crowd of small, bright blue male butterflies that had been tippling on the rich, trampled mud and cow dung through which I trudged rose all together into the spangled air and settled again as soon as I had passed.

After making my way through some pine groves and alder scrub I came to the bog. No sooner had my ear caught the hum of diptera around me, the guttural cry of a snipe overhead, the gulping sound of the morass under my foot, than I knew I would find here quite special arctic butterflies, whose pictures, or, still better, nonillustrated descriptions I had worshiped for several seasons. And the next moment I was among them. Over the small shrubs of bog bilberry with fruit of a dim, dreamy blue, over the brown eye of stagnant water, over moss and mire, over the flower spikes of the fragrant bog orchid (the *nochnaya fialka* of Russian poets), a dusky little Fritillary bearing the name of a Norse goddess passed in low, skimming flight. Pretty Cordigera, a gemlike moth, buzzed all over its uliginose food plant. I pursued rose-margined Sulphurs, gray-marbled Satyrs. Unmindful of the mosquitoes that furred my forearms, I stooped with a grunt of delight to snuff out the life of some silver-studded lepidopteron throbbing in the folds of my net. Through the smells of the bog, I caught the subtle perfume of butterfly wings on my fingers, a perfume which varies with the species—vanilla, or lemon, or musk, or a musty, sweetish odor difficult to define. Still unsated, I pressed forward. At last I saw I had come to the end of the marsh. The rising ground beyond was a paradise of lupines, columbines, and pentstemons. Mariposa lilies bloomed under Ponderosa pines. In the distance, fleeting cloud shadows dappled the dull green of slopes above timber line, and the gray and white of Longs Peak.

I confess I do not believe in time. I like to fold my magic carpet, after use, in such a way as to superimpose one part of the pattern upon another. Let visitors trip. And the highest enjoyment of timelessness—in a landscape selected at random—is when I stand among rare butterflies and their food plants. This is ecstasy, and behind the ecstasy is something else, which is hard to explain. It is like a momentary vacuum into which rushes all that I love. A sense of oneness with sun and stone. A thrill of gratitude to whom it may concern—to the contrapuntal genius of human fate or to tender ghosts humoring a lucky mortal.

Loren Eiseley

The Star Thrower

Loren Eiseley (1907–1977) was that rare scientist whose domain was as much metaphysics as the merely physical. Of his many essays, with titles like "Science And The Sense Of The Holy" or "The Inner Galaxy," my favorite is about man as "the homeless and unspecified one." Think of this excerpt from The Star Thrower *(1978) the next time you go for a walk along the beach.*

* * *

It has ever been my lot, though formally myself a teacher, to be taught surely by none. There are times when I have thought to read lessons in the sky, or in books, or from the behavior of my fellows, but in the end my perceptions have frequently been inadequate or betrayed. Nevertheless, I venture to say that of what man may be I have caught a fugitive glimpse, not among multitudes of men, but along an endless wave-beaten coast at dawn. As always, there is this apparent break, this rift in nature, before the insight comes. The terrible question has to translate itself into an even more terrifying freedom.

If there is any meaning to this book [*The Unexpected Universe*], it began on the beaches of Costabel with just such a leap across an unknown abyss. It began, if I may borrow the expression from a Buddhist sage, with the skull and the eye. I was the skull. I was the inhumanly stripped skeleton without voice, without hope, wandering along upon the shores of the world. I was devoid of pity, because pity implies hope. There was, in this desiccated skull, only an eye like a pharos light, a beacon, a search beam revolving endlessly in sunless noonday or black night. Ideas like swarms of insects rose to the beam, but the light consumed them. Upon that shore meaning had ceased. There were only the dead skull and the revolving eye. With such an eye, some have said, science looks upon the world. I do not know. I know only that I was the skull of emptiness and the endlessly revolving light without pity.

Once in a dingy restaurant in town I heard a woman say: "My father reads a goose bone for the weather." A modern primitive, I had thought, a diviner, using a method older than Stonehenge, as old as the arctic forests.

"And where does he do that?" the woman's companion had asked amusedly.

"In Costabel," she answered complacently, "in Costabel." The voice came back and buzzed faintly for a moment in the dark under the revolving eye. It did not make sense, but nothing in Costabel made sense. Perhaps that was why I had finally found myself in Costabel. Perhaps all men are destined at some time to arriving there as I did.

I had come by quite ordinary means, but I was still the skull with the eye. I concealed myself beneath a fisherman's cap and sunglasses, so that I looked like everyone else on the beach. This is the way things are managed in Costabel. It is on the shore that the revolving eye begins its beam and the whispers rise in the empty darkness of the skull.

The beaches of Costabel are littered with the debris of life. Shells are cast up in windrows; a hermit crab, fumbling for a new home in the depths, is tossed naked ashore, where the waiting gulls cut him to pieces. Along the strip of wet sand that marks the ebbing and flowing of the tide, death walks hugely and in many forms. Even the torn fragments of green sponge yield bits of scrambling life striving to return to the great mother that has nourished and protected them.

In the end the sea rejects its offspring. They cannot fight their way home through the surf which casts them repeatedly back upon the shore. The tiny breathing pores of starfish are stuffed with sand. The rising sun shrivels the mucilaginous bodies of the unprotected. The seabeach and its endless war are soundless. Nothing screams but the gulls.

In the night, particularly in the tourist season, or during great storms, one can observe another vulturine activity. One can see, in the hour before dawn on the ebb tide, electric torches bobbing like fireflies along the beach. This is the sign of the professional shellers seeking to outrun and anticipate their less aggressive neighbors. A kind of greedy madness sweeps over the competing collectors. After a storm one can see them hurrying along with bundles of gathered starfish, or, toppling and overburdened, clutching bags of living shells whose hidden occupants will be slowly cooked and dissolved in the outdoor kettles provided by the resort hotels for the cleaning of specimens. Following one such episode I met the star thrower.

As soon as the ebb was flowing, as soon as I could make out in my sleeplessness the flashlights on the beach, I arose and dressed in the dark. As I came down the steps to the shore I could hear the deeper rumble of the surf. A gaping hole filled with churning sand had cut sharply into the breakwater. Flying sand as light as powder coated every exposed object like snow. I made my way around the altered edges of the cove and proceeded on my morning walk up the shore. Now and then a stooping figure moved in the gloom or a rain squall swept past me with light pattering steps. There was a faint sense of coming light somewhere behind me in the east.

Soon I began to make out objects, up-ended timbers, conch shells, sea wrack wrenched from the far-out kelp forests. A pink-clawed crab encased in a green cup of sponge lay sprawling where the waves had tossed him. Long-limbed starfish were strewn everywhere, as though the night sky had showered down. I paused once briefly. A small octopus, its beautiful dark-lensed eyes bleared with sand, gazed up at me from a ragged bundle of tentacles. I hesitated, and touched it briefly with my boot. It was dead. I paced on once more before the spreading whitecaps of the surf.

The shore grew steeper, the sound of the sea heavier and more menacing, as I rounded a bluff into the full blast of the offshore wind. I was away from the shellers now and strode more rapidly over the wet sand that effaced my footprints. Around the next point there might be a refuge from the wind. The sun behind me was pressing upward at the horizon's rim— an ominous red glare amidst the tumbling blackness of the clouds. Ahead of me, over the projecting point, a gigantic rainbow of incredible perfection had sprung shimmering into existence. Somewhere toward its foot I discerned a human figure standing, as it seemed to me, within the rainbow, though unconscious of his position. He was gazing fixedly at something in the sand.

Eventually he stooped and flung the object beyond the breaking surf. I labored toward him over a half-mile of uncertain footing. By the time I reached him the rainbow had receded ahead of us, but something of its color still ran hastily in many changing lights across his features. He was starting to kneel again.

In a pool of sand and silt a starfish had thrust its arms up stiffly and was holding its body away from the stifling mud.

"It's still alive," I ventured.

"Yes," he said, and with a quick gentle movement he picked up the star and spun it over my head and far out into the sea. It sank in a burst of spume, and the waters roared once more.

"It may live," he said, "if the offshore pull is strong enough." He spoke gently, and across his bronzed worn face the light still came and went in subtly altering colors.

"There are not many come this far," I said, groping in a sudden embarrassment for words. "Do you collect?"

"Only like this," he said softly, gesturing amidst the wreckage of the shore. "And only for the living." He stooped again, oblivious of my curiosity, and skipped another star neatly across the water.

"The stars," he said, "throw well. One can help them."

He looked full at me with a faint question kindling in his eyes, which seemed to take on the far depths of the sea.

"I do not collect," I said uncomfortably, the wind beating at my garments. "Neither the living nor the dead. I gave it up a long time ago. Death is the only successful collector." I could feel the full night blackness in my skull and the terrible eye resuming its indifferent journey. I nodded and walked away, leaving him there upon the dune with that great rainbow ranging up the sky behind him.

I turned as I neared a bend in the coast and saw him toss another star, skimming it skillfully far out over the ravening and tumultuous water. For a moment, in the changing light, the sower appeared magnified, as though casting larger stars upon some greater sea. He had, at any rate, the posture of a god.

But again the eye, the cold world-shriveling eye, began its inevitable circling in my skull. He is a man, I considered sharply, bringing my thought to rest. The star thrower is a man, and death is running more fleet than he along every seabeach in the world.

I adjusted the dark lens of my glasses and, thus disguised, I paced slowly back by the starfish gatherers, past the shell collectors, with their vulgar little spades and the stick-length shelling pincers that eased their elderly backs while they snatched at treasures in the sand. I chose to look full at the steaming kettles in which beautiful voiceless things were being boiled alive. Behind my sunglasses a kind of litany began and refused to die down. *"As I came through the desert thus it was, as I came through the desert."*

In the darkness of my room I lay quiet with the sunglasses removed, but the eye turned and turned. In the desert, an old monk had once advised a traveler, the voices of God and the Devil are scarcely distinguishable. Costabel was a desert. I lay quiet, but my restless hand at the bedside fingered the edge of an invisible abyss. "Certain coasts"—the remark of a perceptive writer came back to me—"are set apart for shipwreck." With unerring persistence I had made my way thither.

Ronald W. Clark

Sigmund Freud's Alpine Walks

*Sigmund Freud (1856–1939), the founder of psychoanalysis, was also
an avid walker. Until late in life his summer holidays in the Austrian
Alps were his personal prescription for mental health.*

In Freud: The Man and the Cause *Ronald Clark described the
great psychoanalyst's love of walking.*

* * *

The [Freuds'] annual holiday followed a pattern which changed only
slightly over the years. Martha and the children would leave Vienna in
advance for a cottage already rented in one of the more picturesque parts
of the Alps. Freud would follow later, arrangements often being made by
Alexander so that his brother could travel in comfort and in solitary state.
His arrival, always the highlight of the summer holiday according to his
eldest son, Martin, marked the start of rambles, scrambles, mushroom-
hunting and the search for flowers.

These pursuits were enjoyed in an Alpine landscape uncluttered by
funiculars, chair-lifts or the trappings of tourist resorts, a landscape not so
different from that which only a century earlier had seen the first ascent of
the Gross Glockner, the highest peak in the Austrian Alps, by the Bishop
of Gurk. Freud showed that he was by no means the townsman turned
pseudo-countryman, dependent on others in a different habitat and helpless
in an emergency. Martin remembered his father's reaction to the torrential
floods that swept the Aussee district one year, washing away mountain tracks,
cutting off villages and endangering supplies. "When father came down from
his room one morning shouldering his biggest knapsack and dressed in the
Norfolk jacket, knickerbockers, thick stockings and boots he used for forest
expeditions, we were surprised," he has written. "No plans had been made
for a family expedition; but when we were told that he was about to begin
a foraging expedition over the mountain road, in the hope of finding villages
not affected by the flooding and with shops open, we decided that he was
the most efficient, the wisest and most knowledgeable hero in the world."

He was also a connoisseur of scenery with an eye for the niceties of a great view, and embedded deep within his psyche there was a compelling need for intimate contact with nature. The need had to be regularly assuaged. "At about this time of year," he wrote one June, "I acquire a notable similarity to Columbus. Like him, I long for land"—the German word also meaning "country." The longing stands out clearly from his correspondence, and it lasted all his life. In his late seventies, already eaten into by cancer, and staying in the Alps on one of his last visits, he impressed his doctor by an "enthusiastic appreciation of nature, of flowers, a meadow, the view of the mountains. It was obvious that all the suffering did not substantially impair his capacity for such enjoyment." Later still, able only to reach the suburbs of Vienna, his eye was as sharp as ever when he wrote to Arnold Zweig: "I am sitting in my room in Grinzing, in front of me the glorious garden with its fresh green and reddish brown leaves (copper beech) and I note that the snowstorm with which May came in has stopped (or paused), and that a cold sun dominates the climate."

In the 1890s lack of money had sometimes restricted the family to the Belle Vue, where he had experienced the dream of Irma's injection, and in April 1898 he had written despondently, "I should love to go to our lovely Italy again this year, but earnings have been very bad. I must economize . . ." Yet even from the Belle Vue he could write that, "the evenings and mornings are delightful; the scent of acacia and jasmine has succeeded that of lilac and laburnum, the wild roses are in bloom, and everything, as even I notice, seems suddenly to have burst out."

But it was the mountains that he most enjoyed. "The first climb of the season is not easy," he wrote to the family from Waidbruck, in the south Tyrol, where he was staying with Alexander, "but the new boots proved a great success. I feel so at home in them I might have been born in them. So long as the people in the Furichgasse sell boots like this they may so far as I am concerned stick their tongues out at their customers before and after the deal."

The limitations imposed by his heart during the 1890s had been a cause of constant nagging regret. "I have given up [mountain] climbing 'with a heavy heart,'" he had written to Fliess, ". . . how meaningful colloquial usage is!" But eventually he had seemed to be fighting his way back. "Monday morning I climbed the Rax with my brother-in-law H. as in the good old days," he was able to write. "3½ hours going up, 2½ coming down. Only, the Rax has gotten much higher since I climbed it the last time, at least 500 meters. My heart took it splendidly."

All this was essential to his *Weltanschauung*, in which enjoyment of fine scenery was an essential to human life. What really pleased him was the "delightful solitude—mountain, forest, flowers, water, castles, monastery, and not one human being," as he wrote. "Yesterday," he recorded at the age of fifty-three, "after dragging my weary bones to a mountain slope, where nature achieves such a magnificent effect with the simplest props, white rock, red fields at Alpine roses, a patch of snow, a waterfall, and lots of green, I hardly knew myself."

Freud did not climb in the modern meaning of the word, but he walked and scrambled strenuously, had gone up to the 6,000-foot Raxalp three times in some weeks—once meeting the Katharina of *Studies on Hysteria* on the way—and when forced by circumstances to take a holiday in Holland could not think of anything much to do on a flat beach. There is, moreover, some indication that he might have developed as a genuine mountaineer—like his son Ernst—had he seriously taken to the sport in his youth. In 1891, when visiting Schladming, he traversed the Dachstein from south to north, climbing alone. The direct route up the south face of the 9,830-foot mountain, the second highest of the northern linestone Alps, was described by the Baedeker of the period as fit for "proficients" but only when accompanied by a guide. Fixed wire ropes and stanchions had to be negotiated, and while only just a rock climb in the mountaineer's sense of the phrase, the ascent demanded freedom from vertigo and strength of wind and limb.

However, as Martin has written:

"Although father loved climbing and had a flair for it, it would not be true to say that he was a good mountaineer: he started too late in life, too late to appreciate what might be called the rigor of the game; and he showed the faults of all eager beginners, notably that optimistic attitude of mind towards snow-bridges, towards hidden crevasses in glaciers, to exposed ravines upon which rocks can crash and towards shrubs growing out from steep rock faces."

Second only to mountains as a holiday attraction there were the mushrooms that feature so often in his letters. At Berchtesgaden he and his children collected them daily. At Ausee he recorded finding "a wonderful wood full of ferns and mushrooms," while his report on Reichenhall, visited on a carriage outing from Thumsee, says that he had lost his heart to the place, with its "Alpine roses coming right down to the roadway, a little green lake, magnificent woods all around, as well as strawberries, flowers and (we hope) mushrooms." Although all the family was trained in the tricks of mushroom hunting, Freud himself usually found the best. When he had discovered a perfect specimen, Martin Freud remembered, "he would run to it and fling his hat over it before giving a shrill signal on the flat silver whistle he carried in his waistcoat pocket to summon his platoon. We would all rush towards the sound of the whistle, and only when the concentration was complete would father remove the hat and allow us to inspect and admire the spoil."

The obsession lasted. During the First World War he and his family spent one holiday in the Tatra mountains along which there today runs the Polish–Czech frontier. Here there grew *Herrenpilze*, among the most tasty of all mushrooms, and here Freud instituted a competition, with finders of the best and the second-best specimens winning twenty and ten heller respectively. But, his friend Hanns Sachs reported, only one member of the family ever won the money: Freud himself always got both prizes . . .

The three-month summer break was a very necessary counterpart to the previous nine months of concentrated effort. It helped to keep Freud in balance as he began slowly to convince first one, then another of his Viennese colleagues that there might, after all, be something in what were still regarded as extraordinary ideas.

Herbert Kubly

A Parade in Zurich

In Native's Return *(1981), a fourth generation American Swiss visits Zurich's springtime Sechselauten festival as an "honored guest" of the guild of tailors.*

These tailors are no more likely to be true tailors than Odd Fellows are necessarily odd. "Today's guild members," says Herbert Kubly, "are the social aristocrats of the city, its bankers, professors, and business and professional leaders. Guild houses are palaces containing some of the best restaurants in Switzerland. There is a story that the haughty Constaffell *[a guild of "Renaissance princes"] has for more than a century accepted only sons of members into its brotherhood and that a newly rich industrialist offered a contribution of a million francs in exchange for membership and was refused."*

In socially-conservative Switzerland the festival's colorful processions of bearded, inebriated men on foot is an extraordinary "chauvinist celebration of maleness and is a temporary cease-fire in Switzerland's battle of the sexes." Just as Swiss women's role in voting has been strictly circumscribed throughout the twentieth century— women only got the vote in 1971—so, too, is their role limited in the spring festival to the throwing of flowers and to "the gathering up of incapacitated celebrants."

* * *

It was time to assemble for the parade. We clattered down two flights of stairs to the street where woman again pelted us with flowers. I was carrying a bright red umbrella from the Tessin, using it as a cane. All the tailors had them; they blended very well with our costumes. We followed the blaring band across the Urania bridge to Löwenstrasse, where we joined a dazzling medieval panoply. Each of the twenty-five guilds had fifty or more men bearing flowers, a band, and a float, and many had a cavalry of mounted horses and a children's cortege. The *Constaffel* were Renaissance princes, the *Saffran*—spice merchants—were dark Bedouins, the *Widder*—butchers—wore aprons and carried cleavers. When the time arrived to fall into line the sun burst forth and this, after two weeks of miserable weather, was hailed as a heavenly benefaction.

The dazzling procession backtracked on Bahnhofstrasse so that it appeared to be going two ways at once. Sidewalks were jammed with women bearing baskets of flowers, which they ran out to present to the men with a kiss. The marchers slyly gauged one another's popularity by the quantity of flowers each carried. There was an air of heart-touching absurdity about the solemn men, some old, others fat, laden with flowers, treading like walking wreaths.

Each guild had its identifying emblem. The carpenters' was a wooden bridge mounted on a lorry almost a block long; the boatsmen carried baskets of fish, which they threw at screeching ladies. The most unruffling symbols were our own five-foot-long gleaming scissors with which our "sons," weaving in and out of the crowd, cut neckties and beards and ladies' scarves and ribbons. Their leader was my godfather who, leaping about like a goat, measuring with his tape the busts of shrieking ladies, seemed demented by pagan ecstasy. One popular ploy was a scene from *commedia dell'arte*. A youth approached a gentleman in the crowd with his opened scissors and the gentleman, backing away, had his hat seized from behind by the scissors of another youth, who running across the street, placed the hat on the head of a screaming woman.

We marched four kilometers. Several of the brothers carried canisters of wine with which faltering members, drinking from a spout, were restored. Twice ladies ran out from the crowd to bring me a stein of beer. The well-timed procession ended a few minutes before six o'clock on Bellevue Square where the *Böögg* [the bogeyman of winter] was mounted on a great pyre of logs that men were soaking with gasoline. The square was a sea of people; on the lake boats were filled with viewers and choppers circled overhead.

The crowd silenced to wait for the striking of the clock in the tower of St. Peter's Church. On the sixth knell a torch was put to the pyre and the flames swooshed up. Firecrackers in the pyre exploded like an artillery charge. A black column of smoke rose into the skies.

As the flames leaped, cavalrymen shouting like Cossacks raced their horses around the conflagration. Watching the robed horsemen whirling about the fire, I felt a strange and inexplicable thrill, and I tried to understand what it all signified. Bells were ringing over the town and bands blared everywhere. The exploding firecrackers scared the horses, which leaped like crazed Pegasuses in and out of the smoke. Two riders were thrown and one had to be taken away in an ambulance, its siren adding to the clamor. A brother explained that the way the *Böögg* burned and the manner with which its head exploded would indicate the summer's weather and fruitfulness. The *Böögg* took fourteen minutes to burn and its leaping flames, reflecting in the glass vestibule of the opera house, made the theater glow as if it also were burning. Cecil B. DeMille could not have staged a more ostentatious Apocalypse.

Quite suddenly it was over. The multitudes dispersed and we marched behind our band back to the King's Chair [the tailors' clubhouse and restaurant]. Another banquet had been prepared and because everyone was exhausted its mood was subdued. Sitting across from me was the famous brother from Brazil whose name was Hans August Schweitzer. He was a tall, lean man who spoke of his coffee plantation and cattle farm. His two sons were doctors in Brazil. "But only in the afternoons. In the forenoons they are ranchers," the old man said. He added that he needed periodically to return to his Zurich townhouse to experience Switzerland's northern climate. "I'm sick of sunshine," he said. "I long for clouds, for rain and snow."

It was time for the Master's annual message. He began by reviewing with rhetorical flourishes the glories of the tailors. In what seemed a curious non sequitur he moved into an attack on protesting students in Paris, Germany, America, and Switzerland. He called the students "mentally disturbed anarchists, a discredit to human society, who would destroy everything you saw today, everything in which we believe." He concluded on a cheering note, "Today you saw youth of Zurich participating in traditions which glorify our history, perpetuate our ideals, and preserve our bourgeois society."

After the meal the tailors, like every other guild in the city, split into two groups. Senior brothers remained in the King's Chair to hold court for visiting bands of young guildsmen, and the younger tailors set out to visit other guilds. Since my godfather was a leader of the rovers I chose to accompany them.

The evening was mild and the city was like a Medician fête, with spotlights glowing on churches and public buildings. Instead of one great parade there were now twenty-five small ones moving through the streets, each choosing its own spontaneous course. Flowers were abandoned for lanterns with flickering candles and the covert movements of lanterned groups through the old city were strange and wonderously mysterious. Bands played everywhere and streets were filled with dark clusters of witnessing women.

We commenced our night journey by boat, making our first visit to the Riesbach Guild, which had its headquarters on the shore of the lake. Chugging softly up the Limmat and onto the lake, we met other flotillas of lantern-lit boats. At the Riesbach dock we disembarked in the same moment as young visiting wine merchants emerged and reembarked in their own water procession. A herald went inside to announce us and returned in a moment with a summons to enter. Like young knights visiting a foreign court we stalked in and were met by girls bearing trays of wine-filled goblets. There were toasts of *"Hoch! Hoch!"* and glasses were refilled. The hall was resplendent with banners and tapestries; the Riesbach seigneurs wore red, gold, and black robes, and gold chains about their necks.

My godfather gave an account of our journeys that turned into a paraphrasing of Homer's *Odyssey* with imaginary perils and sirens repulsed en route. Odysseus had remained in the court of Nestor for a year, he said, but we, unfortunately, did not have the time to stay as long.

The Riesach Master responded jocularly, saying that he hoped we hadn't too much difficulty embarking—a reference to our drinking—and he congratulated us "for getting your billygoats around the fire" in the afternoon. Polite insults were delivered in Biblical-sounding rhetoric and gifts were exchanged.

It was four guilds later and after 2 A.M. when we marched around Grossmünster Cathedral to prove to ourselves we were still mobile, and like errant knights, returned to our home castle. When we arrived we were required to give a detailed account of our night's journey to our stay-at-home brothers. Emil, our spokesman, began, "We return refreshed in spirit and joyful at being reunited with our fathers and brothers . . ." Shouting with excitement, the veins throbbing on his forehead, he summarized our wanderings, naming all the streets through which we had passed, abstracting all speeches made and heard. He enumerated the glasses of wine we drank and the girls whose clothing we assailed with scissors and he embellished his report with fantastic details of pursuing sirens and evil witches and "a Spanish lady with a fabulous measurement" whom we had rescued in a sea battle with pirates.

Our elders invited us to be seated and listen to their account of everything that had occurred in our absence in the King's Chair. When that was finished there was a communal partaking of *Mehlsuppe*, the sobering creamed soup of scorched flour, served at the conclusion of drinking orgies.

At 3:30 A.M. some of the older men began to totter away and I slipped out with them. The Niederdorf was still roaring. I met two women supporting a tottering drunk and one of them was sing-songing baby talk like a lullaby, saying, "The poor little Rudi, so bad in the stomach, so dizzy in the head."

My manhood, so manifestly celebrated, was completely spent. Creeping wearily home, I continued to wonder what it all meant.

Ernest Hemingway

A Moveable Feast

If the "man in the street," however illiterate, were asked to name one twentieth-century writer, the choice would probably be Ernest Hemingway. No other person in modern times has so captured the public's imagination with his writing-as-lifestyle.

Papa, as he was called, was, at the time he committed suicide in 1961, a literary superstar, a macho avatar, part hunter, bullfighter, warrior, tippler, cocksman, penman. The legends about Hemingway have continued to grow since his death.

Part of the rich lore about Ernest Hemingway (1898–1961) is that he began as an unknown Michigan scribbler, was wounded in an ambulance crew in World War I, and spent the Roaring Twenties living and writing in Parisian garrets and cafes. Many penniless writers have since been consoled by the thought of Hemingway hungrily walking the streets of Paris. "I was always hungry with the walking and the cold and the working," Papa wrote almost four decades later.

But A Moveable Feast (about his Paris years, 1921–26) is a joyous book full of rich Bohemian pleasures. "It was wonderful to walk down the long flights of stairs," wrote Hemingway, "knowing that I'd had good luck working."

* * *

You got very hungry when you did not eat enough in Paris because all the bakery shops had such good things in the windows and people ate outside at tables on the sidewalk so that you saw and smelled the food. When you had given up journalism and were writing nothing that anyone in America would buy, explaining at home that you were lunching out with someone, the best place to go was the Luxembourg gardens where you saw and smelled nothing to eat all the way from the Place de l'Observatoire to the rue de Vaugirard. There you could always go into the Luxembourg museum and all the paintings were sharpened and clearer and more beautiful if you were belly-empty, hollow-hungry. I learned to understand Cézanne much better and to see truly how he made landscapes when I was hungry. I used to wonder if he were hungry too when he painted; but I thought possibly it was only that he had forgotten to eat. It was one of those unsound but illuminating thoughts you have when you have been sleepless or hungry. Later I thought Cézanne was probably hungry in a different way.

After you came out of the Luxembourg you could walk down the narrow rue Férou to the Place St.-Sulpice and there were still no restaurants, only the quiet square with its benches and trees. There was a fountain with lions, and pigeons walked on the pavement and perched on the statues of the bishops. There was the church and there were shops selling religious objects and vestments on the north side of the square.

From this square you could not go further toward the river without passing shops selling fruits, vegetables, wines, or bakery and pastry shops. But by choosing your way carefully you could work to your right around the grey and white stone church and reach the rue de l'Odéon and turn up to your right toward Sylvia Beach's bookshop and on your way you did not pass too many places where things to eat were sold. The rue de l'Odéon was bare of eating places until you reached the square where there were three restaurants.

By the time you reached 12 rue de l'Odéon your hunger was contained but all of your perceptions were heightened again. The photographs looked different and you saw books that you had never seen before.

"You're too thin, Hemingway," Sylvia would say. "Are you eating enough?"

"Sure."

"What did you eat for lunch?"

My stomach would turn over and I would say, "I'm going home for lunch now."

"At three o'clock?"

"I didn't know it was that late."

"Adrienne said the other night she wanted to have you and Hadley for dinner. We'd ask Fargue. You like Fargue, don't you? Or Larbaud. You like him. I know you like him. Or anyone you really like. Will you speak to Hadley?"

"I know she'd love to come."

"I'll send her a *pneu*. Don't you work so hard now that you don't eat properly."

"I won't."

"Get home now before it's too late for lunch."

"They'll save it."

"Don't eat cold food either. Eat a good hot lunch."

"Did I have any mail?"

She looked and found a note and looked up happily and then opened a closed door in her desk.

"This came while I was out," she said. It was a letter and it felt as though it had money in it. "Wedderkop," Sylvia said.

"It must be from *Der Querschnitt*. Did you see Wedderkop?"

"No. But he was here with George. He'll see you. Don't worry. Perhaps he wanted to pay you first."

"It's six hundred francs. He says there will be more."

"I'm awfully glad you reminded me to look. Dear Mr. Awfully Nice."

"It's damned funny that Germany is the only place I can sell anything. To him and the *Frankfurter Zeitung*."

"Isn't it? But don't you worry ever. You can sell stories to Ford," she teased me.

"Thirty francs a page. Say one story every three months in *The Transatlantic*. Story five pages long makes one hundred and fifty francs a quarter. Six hundred francs a year."

"But, Hemingway, don't worry about what they bring now. The point is that you can write them."

"I know. I can write them. But nobody will buy them. There is no money coming in since I quit journalism."

"They will sell. Look. You have the money for one right there."

"I'm sorry, Sylvia. Forgive me for speaking about it."

"Forgive you for what? Always talk about it or about anything. Don't you know all writers ever talk about is their troubles. But promise me you won't worry and that you'll eat enough."

"I promise."

"Then get home now and have lunch."

Outside on the rue de l'Odéon I was disgusted with myself for having complained about things. I was doing what I did of my own free will and I was doing it stupidly. I should have bought a large piece of bread and eaten it instead of skipping a meal. I could taste the brown lovely crust. But it is dry in your mouth without something to drink. You God damn complainer. You dirty phony saint and martyr, I said to myself. You quit journalism of your own accord. You have credit and Sylvia would have loaned you money. She has plenty of times. Sure. And then the next thing you would be compromising on something else. Hunger is healthy and the pictures do look better when you are hungry. Eating is wonderful too and do you know where you are going to eat right now?

Lipp's is where you are going to eat and drink too.

It was a quick walk to Lipp's and every place I passed that my stomach noticed as quickly as my eyes or my nose made the walk an added pleasure. There were few people in the *brasserie* and when I sat down on the bench against the wall with the mirror in back and a table in front and the waiter asked if I wanted beer I asked for a *distingué*, the big glass mug that held a liter, and for potato salad.

The beer was very cold and wonderful to drink. The *pommes à l'huile* were firm and marinated and the olive oil delicious. I ground black pepper over the potatoes and moistened the bread in the olive oil. After the first heavy draft of beer I drank and ate very slowly. When the *pommes à l'huile* were gone I ordered another serving and a *cervelas*. This was a sausage like a heavy, wide frankfurter split in two and covered with a special mustard sauce.

I mopped up all the oil and all of the sauce with bread and drank the beer slowly until it began to lose its coldness and then I finished it and ordered a *demi* and watched it drawn. It seemed colder than the *distingué* and I drank half of it.

I had not been worrying, I thought. I knew the stories were good and someone would publish them finally at home. When I stopped doing newspaper work I was sure the stories were going to be published. But every one I sent out came back. What had made me so confident was Edward O'Brien's taking the "My Old Man" story for the *Best Short Stories* book and then dedicating the book for that year to me. Then I laughed and drank some more beer. The story had never been published in a magazine and he had broken all his rules to take it for the book. I laughed again and the waiter glanced at me. It was funny because, after all that, he had spelled the name wrong. It was one of two stories I had left when everything I had written was stolen in Hadley's suitcase that time at the Gare de Lyon when she was bringing the manuscripts down to me to Lausanne as a surprise, so I could work on them on our holidays in the mountains. She had put in the originals, the typescripts and the carbons, all in manila folders. The only reason I had the one story was that Lincoln Steffens had sent it out to some editor who sent it back. It was in the mail while everything else was stolen. The other story that I had was the one called "Up in Michigan" written before Miss Stein had come to our flat. I had never had it copied because she said it was *inaccrochable*. It had been in a drawer somewhere.

So after we had left Lausanne and gone down to Italy I showed the racing story to O'Brien, a gentle, shy man, pale, with pale blue eyes, and straight lanky hair he cut himself, who lived then as a boarder in a monastery up above Rapallo. It was a bad time and I did not think I could write any more then, and I showed the story to him as a curiosity, as you might show, stupidly, the binnacle of a ship you had lost in some incredible way, or as you might pick up your booted foot and make some joke about it if it had been amputated after a crash. Then, when he read the story, I saw he was hurt far more than I was. I had never seen anyone hurt by a thing other than death or unbearable suffering except Hadley when she told me about the things being gone. She had cried and cried and could not tell me. I told her that no matter what the dreadful thing was that had happened nothing could be that bad, and whatever it was, it was all right and not to worry.

We would work it out. Then, finally, she told me. I was sure she could not have brought the carbons too and I hired someone to cover for me on my newspaper job. I was making good money then at journalism, and took the train for Paris. It was true all right and I remember what I did in the night after I let myself into the flat and found it was true. That was over now and Chink had taught me never to discuss casualties; so I told O'Brien not to feel so bad. It was probably good for me to lose early work and I told him all that stuff you feed the troops. I was going to start writing stories again I said and, as I said it, only trying to lie so that he would not feel so bad, I knew that it was true.

Then I started to think in Lipp's about when I had first been able to write a story after losing everything. It was up in Cortina d'Ampezzo when I had come back to join Hadley there after the spring skiing which I had to interrupt to go on assignment to the Rhineland and the Ruhr. It was a very simple story called "Out of Season" and I had omitted the real end of it which was that the old man hanged himself. This was omitted on my new theory that you could omit anything if you knew that you omitted and the omitted part would strengthen the story and make people feel something more than they understood.

Well, I thought, now I have them so they do not understand them. There cannot be much doubt about that. There is most certainly no demand for them. But they will understand the same way that they always do in painting. It only takes time and it only needs confidence.

It is necessary to handle yourself better when you have to cut down on food so you will not get too much hunger-thinking. Hunger is good discipline and you learn from it. And as long as they do not understand it you are ahead of them. Oh sure, I thought, I'm so far ahead of them now that I can't afford to eat regularly. It would not be bad if they caught up a little.

I knew I must write a novel. But it seemed an impossible thing to do when I had been trying with great difficulty to write paragraphs that would be the distillation of what made a novel. It was necessary to write longer stories now as you would train for a longer race. When I had written a novel before, the one that had been lost in the bag stolen at the Gare de Lyon, I still had the lyric facility of boyhood that was as perishable and as deceptive as youth was. I knew it was probably a good thing that it was lost, but I knew too that I must write a novel. I would put it off though until I could not help doing it. I was damned if I would write one because it was what I should do if we were to eat regularly. When I had to write it, then it would be the only thing to do and there would be no choice. Let the pressure build. In the meantime I would write a long story about whatever I knew best.

By this time I had paid the check and gone out and turned to the right and crossed the rue de Rennes so that I would not go to the Deux-Magots for coffee and was walking up the rue Bonaparte on the shortest way home.

What did I know best that I had not written about and lost? What did I know about truly and care for the most? There was no choice at all. There was only the choice of streets to take you back fastest to where you worked. I went up Bonaparte to Guyenemer, then to the rue d'Assas, up the rue Notre-Dame-des-Champs to the Closerie des Lilas.

I sat in a corner with the afternoon light coming in over my shoulder and wrote in the notebook. The waiter brought me a *café crème* and I drank half of it when it cooled and left it on the table while I wrote. When I stopped writing I did not want to leave the river where I could see the trout in the pool, its surface pushing and swelling smooth against the resistence of the log-driven piles of the bridge. The story was about coming back from the war but there was no mention of the war in it.

But in the morning the river would be there and I must make it and the country and all that would happen. There were days ahead to be doing that each day. No other thing mattered. In my pocket was the money from Germany so there was no problem. When that was gone some other money would come in.

All I must do now was stay sound and good in my head until morning when I would start to work again.

Anaïs Nin

Paris Diary

Anaïs Nin (1903–1977) is remembered as one of the greatest diarists of our century. In the Bohemian Paris of the 1930s many artists fell in love with her classic beauty, but her heart belonged to her dairy and, occasionally, to someone like Henry Miller (Tropic of Cancer). The emotions of her long, impassioned walks through the City of Love are as fresh today as if we had just returned from a walk with her.

* * *

APRIL 1932

What do I feel when I see Henry's cold blue eyes on me? My father had icy blue eyes.

Henry talks beautifully to me, in a cool, wise mood.

"Sunday night after you left us, I slept a while and then I went out for a walk. I realized a terrible truth: that I don't want June to come back. At certain moments I even feel that if June should come back and disappoint me, and if I should not care for her any more, I would be almost glad. Sunday night I wanted to send her a cable telling her I did not want her any more. What I have discovered with you is that there can be friendship between men and women. June and I are not friends."

We were walking to the Place Clichy, Fred, Henry and I. Henry makes me aware of the street, of people. He is smelling the street, observing. He shows me the whore with the wooden stump who stands near the Gaumont Palace. He shows me the narrow streets winding up, lined with small hotels, and the whores standing by the doorways, under red lights. We sit in several cafés, Francis Carco cafés, where the pimps are playing cards and watching their women on the sidewalk. We talked about life and death, as D.H. Lawrence talked about it, the people we know who are dead, those who are alive. Henry said, "If Lawrence had lived and known you, he would have loved you."

JUNE 1933

I meet Artaud in a café, and he greets me with a tormented face. "I'm clairvoyant. I see you did not mean anything you said the other day. Right after our talk in the garden, you became aloof, your face impenetrable. You eluded my touch. You took flight."

"But there was no question of a human love . . . as soon as I spoke, I felt you had given my words a human interpretation."

"Then what was it a question of?"

"Affinities, friendship, understanding, imaginitive ties."

"But we are human beings!"

I forget the order of our phrases. All I knew was that I did not want a physical tie with Artaud. We walked. When he said, "We walk in step. It is heavenly to walk with someone who walks with the same rhythm . . . it makes walking euphoric," then I began to feel it all to be unreal. I was no longer within my own body. I had stepped out of myself. I felt and saw Artaud watching me with delight. I saw him looking at my sandals; I saw my light summer dress trembling, ebbing back and forth to every breeze; I saw my bare arm and Artaud's hand on it; and I saw the momentary joy on his face, and felt a terrible pity for the sick, tormented madman, morbid, hypersensitive.

At the Coupole, we kissed, and I invented for him the story that I was a divided being, could not love humanly and imaginatively both at the same time. I expanded the story of my split. "I love the poet in you."

This touched him and did not hurt his pride. "That is like mine, like me," he said. "Human beings appear to me as spectral, and I doubt and fear life, it all seems unreal to me; I try to enter it, to be a part of it. But you, I thought you were more earthy than I, your glidingness, your vibrancy. I have never seen a woman look so much like a spirit, yet you are warm. Everything about you frightened me, the enormous eyes, exaggerated eyes, impossible eyes, impossibly clear, transparent; there seemed to be no mystery in them, one thought one could look through them, through you immediately, and yet there are endless mysteries under that clarity, behind those naked, fairy-tale eyes . . ."

I was stirred, and Artaud pleaded: "Whom do you love? I know Allendy loves you, Steele, and many others, but whom do you love?"

APRIL 1934

Paris. I walk the streets. I tease Henry for filling my head with streets, names of streets. I say, "In place of thoughts now, I carry the name of a new street. I think about streets. Riding in the bus, I watch them. I have no ideas. I just watch, and look, and listen. Rue du Faubourg du Temple.

Square Montholon. What do you have when you have the name of a street?"

"Nothing," said Henry.

My head is empty now, it is full of streets.

One may have nothing when one has the name of a street, but one possesses a street in place of a thought; and slowly the earth, the street, the rivers, gain ground, fill the mind with noise, odors, pictures, and the inner life recedes, shrinks. This advance of life, this recession of meditation, was my salvation. Every street displaced a futile yearning, a regret, a brooding, a self-devouring meal. The Square Montholon triumphs over the long hours I spent constructing an imaginary, ideal communion with my father. Smells, automobile horns, and the eddies of traffic dispel the ghosts. I am letting myself live, I eat in all the restaurants of Paris. I go to all the movies, to all the theatres, I want to know many people, possess a map of realities as Henry possesses his map of Paris and of Brooklyn.

A devouring passion for reality, because my imaginary world is so immense it can never be annihilated. Only it must not be allowed to devour me.

Out. I am always out. With everybody. Last night, I did get sad in the beautiful Scheherazade night club with the wrong people. I pinch myself. *Allons donc*, streets, you're on the street at last, walking along, along the crowded streets of Henry's crowded books. External and internal, to be balanced, nurturing each other, or else the internal eats me, like rust. Introspection almost devoured me. Henry saved me. He took me down into the street. It is enough that a few hours ago I was obliged to think about my father in order to write about him. It is enough, enough. Come Square Montholon, Boulevard Jean Jaurès, Rue Saint-Martin, like merry dice dancing in my empty head. It is I who taught Henry that streets in themselves were of no interest. He accumulated descriptions but I felt they needed to be the décor for some drama, some emotion. It is I who awakened the man who walked through the streets. No more anonymous maps, but maps of both form and content, matter and significance, streets and the men who walk through them.

Restless. Looking again for intensity, fever, turmoil. Everything seems to move too slowly . . . slowly.

H. V. Morton

A Traveller in Italy

It might be said of Britain's H. V. Morton (1892–1979), as it was said of an expatriate English novelist, that "she wrote in English with an Italian heart." A Traveller In Italy *(1964) is like an enchanting stroll through the provinces and palaces of Italian history. H. V. Morton was an unhurried, civilized chronicler of sunsets, cheeses, wines, foibles, and walks.*

* * *

When I walked out into Mantua that night, a full moon was transforming the city into the backcloth of an opera. The moonlight, accentuating the shadows, made each colonnade a scene for drama, and every street corner had the appearance of a romantic trysting-place. Towers and domes, rising from immense shadows, shone in a green wash of light, and most striking of all was the rambling palace of the Gonzaga, the open beaks of its merlature touched by moonlight as it stood upon the edge of a lake, crouched in profound darkness. One looked at the rows of windows and imagined behind them the empty palace with its silent marble staircases and its deserted audience chambers, the moonlight falling in angles and bars across the floor; and I looked up half expecting to see a white face glancing down to the moonlit square. Unfortunately the orchestra which this scene demanded was absent; instead, as if Satan were running his pitchfork across the railings of hell, young men mounted upon red motor-cycles raced each other through the streets, and every colonnade multiplied and echoed the hideousness of their passing. Sometimes I could hear them a long way off and so prepare myself to meet the approaching explosions, but often they would arrive suddenly, in full pandemonium, sending their deafening racket into every nook and crevice of the ancient town.

While I was seated in a cafe, loathing the motorists and admiring the moonlight, a sad little Italian whose melancholy face looked as though it had witnessed every conceivable disaster, came to my table and said he could tell I was an American. When we had straightened that out, he explained that he had been an interpreter with the American army. I invited him to

my table and ordered an *espresso* for him. He was a pleasant little man and
knew a great deal about the history of Mantua.

He told me that there is still a Count Castiglione, who lives in the
Castiglione Palace in Mantua and who possesses the manuscript of his ancestor's work, *Il Cortegiano*. The book, he said, was kept in a velvet-lined box
in a bank, and he had seen it, beautifully written in Renaissance script.

Passing to more mundane things, he said how rich and prosperous life
was outside Italy. If only he could get to America, even at his age. He told
me that his salary ran out on the fifteenth of every month and he was always
on the look-out for temporary jobs to keep him going until the next pay
packet arrived. Quite bluntly he conveyed that he would not be too proud
to accept a few lire for showing me round Mantua. I hinted that I should
much like to see the manuscript of *The Courtier*, but he thought that would
be difficult as the Count was not in Mantua at that moment. Changing the
subject hastily, he asked if I knew of a distinguished Englishman named
Signor Giacomo Critonio who had died in Mantua. I said it was not a common
English name, but he insisted that I must have heard of the man and offered
to take me to the church and show me his tomb. It was already fairly late,
but I thought it would be interesting to wander around Mantua, and so we
were soon strolling through silent back streets which, with the coming of
darkness, appeared to have retreated beyond the Renaissance to the Middle
Ages. We came at length to the church of S. Simone which was, as I had
expected, closed and locked for the night. This did not worry my acquaintance, however, and, asking me to wait for a moment, he vanished into the
darkness.

We were in a shabby little back street where the lamplight fell upon
ancient shuttered houses and upon an arcade whose shadows were impenetrable. I felt that in some preposterous way I had been cast for a minor part
in a Shakespearean comedy. Some absurd character like Gobbo, I reflected,
might open one of the shuttered windows with a "God bless your worship."
Almost as if in answer to my mood, the little Italian appeared under a lamp
at a near-by turning and motioned dramatically for me to follow him. We
crossed a stretch of waste land and came to the backyard of a house where
an old woman was standing with a bunch of keys. She opened a heavy old
gate and we entered an icy darkness fragrant with incense. We had come
into the church by a back door. My friend led the way, grasping a lighted
taper, which he held above an inscription let into the wall. I read:

> To the Memory of
> James Crichton of Eliock and Cluny
> From the Splendour of his talents and the universal
> range of his accomplishments known to history as
> the Admirable Crichton

He expired in early manhood already renowned
For scholarly and courtly attainments,
for ideals of knighthood and honour
combined with wide erudition and skill in arms,
and eloquence and powers of reason.
Born at Eliock, Dumfriesshire,
Scotland, 19 August 1560
Died at Mantua 3 July 1582.
His remains were buried in this church.

"You see," he said, holding the taper an inch from the name, "Giacomo Critonio."

"Yes," I replied, "I have heard of him. How did he die?"

"In a duel," he replied, "about a woman."

I do not know if this is the true explanation. I do know, however, that a young Scotsman named James Crichton arrived in Italy in the late sixteenth century and dazzled everyone by his gift of tongues, his ability to turn out Latin odes at a moment's notice, and his skill in debate. He had everything, it seemed, but money. He caused a sensation in Venice, it was said, by vanquishing the local dons in public argument, and from Venice he arrived at the court of Guglielmo Gonzaga, third Duke of Mantua. Crichton made an instant conquest of the Duke, who was a clever, sour little man who had inherited the Gonzaga curse, a spinal defect which made him almost a hunchback. He detested his son and heir, Vincenzo, who was a gay and handsome young man with a straight back, and only slightly younger than Crichton. While the Duke persecuted his son for his extravagance and his gallantries, he made Crichton one of his councillors and enjoyed long discussions with him on learned subjects.

On the night of July 3, 1582, Crichton left the palace, accompanied by a servant, for a walk through the deserted streets. It was a night of the full moon. As the two men entered a narrow lane they saw two cloaked figures approaching who, as they passed, jostled Crichton so insultingly that he drew a dagger and plunged it into the back of the man nearest to him. His friend drew a sword and ran Crichton through the body. As he fell, the Scotsman recognized the prince, Vincenzo. He staggered to an apothecary, in whose house he died. Crichton's servant, who could have described what happened, disappeared and was never heard of again. Whether Crichton's death was an accident or a planned assassination due to jealousy, who can tell? It will probably never be known. The Duke threatened to have his son tried for murder, but the affair blew over. About twenty years afterwards, when Vincenzo was Duke of Mantua, he wrote a letter to a friend in which he mentioned the Admirable Crichton's death. "It was a case of pure misadventure," he wrote, "and if I had been dealing with anyone but a 'barbarian' so much harm would not have followed."

As we walked back through the same lanes and arcades, lit by the same green wash of moonlight, my acquaintance pointed out to me the Piazza Sordello, the thirteenth-century palace which the Castiglione family still inhabit. We found the cafe open and sat down at a table.

"It must be a fine thing," said the Italian, "to live in an affluent society."

But I was conscious that something even finer had happened to Mantua. The motor-cyclists had gone to bed.

Susan Chitty and Thomas Hinde

From Santiago to Lake Trasimeno

Many walkers dream of escaping the rat race and hitting the trail to distant horizons. This article from Quest/77 *magazine (original title: "Making Each Day Extraordinary: How To Multiply Your Memories"), is an account of such a dream come true.*

Susan Chitty and Thomas Hinde are an English husband-and-wife team of writers who decided to walk across southern Europe to Izmir, Turkey. The following account tells of their 1975 adventures walking with donkeys to Lake Trasimeno, Italy. [In 1976 they continued their walk eastward, now following the route of the First Crusade to Salonika, Greece where illness halted their trip.]

* * *

What were we doing anyway, trying to walk from Santiago, Spain to Izmir, Turkey, a distance of 2,000 miles even by the most direct route? Basically, we were in search of adventure, a chance to come down off the feather bed of civilization and feel the natural world around us once more. In our centrally heated house in Sussex, we had all too successfully insulated ourselves against our environment. Moons waxed and waned unheeded outside the double glazing. Even when we traveled, we went by car, content to let the world pass by us on what was little better than a television screen. For a period, at least, we wanted to feel the wind in our faces and watch the night sky.

This was not the first time such a yearning had hit us. Fifteen years earlier we had driven a Land-Rover from Nairobi to Cape Town, camping every night of the 2,500-mile safari. Andrew had been six at the time, and Cordelia four. Since then we had begun to form vague plans for a journey on a larger scale, which might last many months, if not years.

Unlike most people, we had no jobs to tie us down. We both earned a living of sorts as writers. But our children had to be educated, and for years preparation for O and A levels kept us rooted in the vicinity of schools. Then, when Cordelia was 12, Miranda was born, followed four years later by Jessica, and we had another reason for putting off the journey. Yet we were anxious not to postpone it too long. A start must be made before the serious education of the new pair of children began and, incidentally, before we ourselves were too decrepit for adventure.

Thomas's 50th birthday seemed right. Cordelia was established at university, Miranda was seven and Jessica was three. Andrew had come down from Oxford and was ready to share the adventure with us. But we had yet to decide what form it should take. Thomas had always wanted to buy a boat and sail around the world. When feeling particularly trapped by a job at an American university, he had even taken out a subscription to *Yachting,* and used to scan the small ads for secondhand fishing smacks suitable for conversion. I, however, had no faith in the sea and was bored by photographs of families waving good-bye over the taffrail at Falmouth. It was the land I cared for, not the sea, and best of all, the wild, lonely places where people still lived as they have lived from time immemorial. I wanted the children to see these people before they were swallowed up by the progress machine. Thomas agreed, but pointed out that the only way to see the wilder parts of Europe would be on foot. Only by keeping away from the main roads and taking footpaths could we penetrate the true backwaters. There remained the problem of how to transport the children and the baggage. Then we had the inspiration about donkeys.

It only remained to decide where our journey should take us. While looking at a family tree, Thomas came across an 18th-century ancestor named Joseph Chitty, of Smyrna (now Izmir) and Dagenham. It seemed that Joseph had made a modest fortune trading goat's hair and carpets in Smyrna before returning to a country seat in the Thames-side village of Dagenham. We decided that we would go to Izmir and see if we could find any remains of Joseph.

Santiago was chosen as the starting point for our journey because we had wanted to visit it ever since Thomas, as an assistant public relations officer for Shell in the mid-fifties, had helped produce a sumptuous book on the symbolism of the scallop shell. The book had given us a romantic longing to follow the pilgrim route all the way to the Pyrenees and into France. We were vague about where we would go after that, but hoped to winter in Tuscany, near Lake Trasimeno, where we could use an abandoned farmhouse in which we had previously spent the summer holidays. The next summer we would journey eastward again, toward Izmir.

It was a neighbor in Italy, Livingston Pomeroy, who suggested that we should follow Hannibal's route from France to Italy. After all, he pointed out, Carthaginians slaughtered 15,000 Romans beside Lake Trasimeno—their burial pits there, incidentally, are the only *archaeological* evidence for his whole 15-year campaign in Italy. Pomeroy also recommended Sir Gavin de Beer's biography of Hannibal, a book that discards most earlier theories about the Alpine pass over which Hannibal led his 37 elephants and argues convincingly that he used either the Col de la Traversette or the Col de Mary. Neither pass is crossed by a motor road, but our map showed a good mule track over the Col de Mary. We decided to take it.

On April 29, 1975 the great day came, and we set sail from Liverpool on the Spanish liner S.S. *Umbe*. "And what will your donkeys be called?" one of a bevy of reporters asked us as they fed us whiskey in the ship's lounge. The problem had never occurred to us. "Hannibal and Hamilcar," we said on the spur of the moment. This is what they became.

But to find Hannibal and Hamilcar was another problem. Not only have donkeys almost disappeared from northern Spain as work animals, but those that remain command high prices because they can be sold to France for meat. Eventually we found two at Santiago's annual Ascension Day fiesta, a huge agricultural fair. But even there, the competition was so hot and the supply so limited that we had to buy them the moment they left their trucks, before they had even reached the pavilion. Never again do I want to have to spend £250 on two untried animals before breakfast, animals on which the next 18 months of our lives entirely depended.

That afternnoon, our beasts saddled and shod, we took the pilgrim route from Santiago to the east. All our worldly needs for a year and a half, except for food, were being carried along on the eight furry legs of Hannibal and Hamilcar. Four years and four months after the idea had first occurred to us, we were on our way.

The donkeys minced along sedately, taking not the least notice of the continuous market traffic. Thomas and I each led one and Andrew brought up the rear with our dog, Iago, who walked at heel, as befitted a graduate of the West Hoathly Dog Obedience Class. Miranda sat proudly on Hamilcar while Jessica, seated behind her, clung to her waist. Nobody cried. It was a proud moment.

That first day with Hannibal and Hamilcar was long in the way that days are long that are filled with new experiences. I still remember vividly every hour of it, in the way one remembers the first day of a holiday or, for that matter, of a new job. This heightened awareness is, surely, one of the best arguments in favor of travel. Days at home pass pleasantly enough, but one is very like another, and they leave little mark behind. By traveling, you make each day extraordinary and cheat time into giving you more than your share of memories.

The first full day of our walk took us through rolling, cultivated country. Family processions were harrowing on both sides of the road. The wife would go in front, leading a pair of oxen, while the husband was dragged along behind, standing on a wattle hurdle. He in turn led a horse with a metal harrow at its tail. As each little procession went over the horizon, it disappeared in a cloud of pink dust.

If hunger is the best sauce, then so is fatigue a feather bed. That night, although Andrew soon abandoned the thankless task of cutting broom, we seemed to float above the hard ground in delightful slumber. One of the nicest discoveries we made during the journey was the pleasure to be derived from savoring simple things to the full. After a hard day's walk, we had as much enjoyment from a glass of rough country wine as, at home, we might have derived from a bottle of Bollinger. We looked forward as eagerly to our half hour of reading aloud by candlelight as we might have to an evening at Covent Garden.

Walking with donkeys, we discovered, is a slow and exhausting business. Unlike ponies, they do not appear to enjoy their work. They would rather walk than trot, and rather stop than do either. Unless you constantly urge them forward, they will turn onto the verge and start eating, which is their main preoccupation in life. Hamilcar went best if he had the undivided attention of two of us. Thomas would walk behind, poking him periodically with a stick and shouting, "*Arre.*" I would walk in front giving him a lead, which he seemed to like. This arrangement worked well, because I too was developing some donkey characteristics. If allowed to bring up the rear, I lagged farther and farther until the little party had disappeared around the next bend. Then I was only too liable to sit in a ditch and light a cigarette. I now well understand why, in the Middle Ages, travel was considered a penance not a pleasure; a punishment for criminals rather than a way of getting even with the Joneses.

Soon we started to invent games on donkeyback. Mental arithmetic was popular with Miranda, and before long Andrew was setting her shoppings lists of formidable length to tot up in her head. Jessica preferred the flower game, the winner being the child who spied 20 different specimens first. In Galicia this was no problem. The variety of heathers alone was amazing, ranging from giant white ones through all shades of mauve and purple to a dwarf variety of the deepest blue. Andrew insisted that the flowers be given their proper names. "You can't just say 'Dat yellow one,' " he would tell Jessica, who was trying to score a point with a wild vetch. Stories of course were popular, as long as the energy and invention of the teller would last. But nothing helped the miles pass faster than singing. Luckily we had an extensive repertoire of folk songs collected in Sussex.

While Andrew taught the children, I wrote my diary. I was the chronicler of the trip, and it was essential to describe the places we passed through each day before the memory of them either vanished or became a jumble in my mind. Often we were to ask each other questions like, "Where was the camp where the one-eyed shepherd warned us of wolves?" Only the diary could tell. I used to write it some distance from the camp, so that I could not hear the children quarreling. The packsaddle served me for a backrest, and Iago and Felipe II, a cheap brandy, kept me company.

I've often been asked if we formed warm, friendly relationships with our donkeys. I can only say that occasionally my feelings came close to something of the sort, especially for Hannibal. He labored with a heavy, brainless courage that I had to admire. When he stopped on slopes, panting for breath, his chest and shoulders sodden with sweat, I knew that he really did need to pause for new energy and wasn't being lazy. There was something heroic about his character. If donkeys can be said to have personality types, he was a plump, willing sort, Hamilcar a mean, spinsterly kind, continually glancing out of the corner of his eye to catch you not watching him so that he could slow down or begin to graze.

But though I admired Hannibal's strength and dumb persistence, his stupidity and unteachableness were profound and maddening. Five months of heaving at his head whenever he walked on tarmac in preference to a soft, grassy verge entirely failed to teach him this elementary lesson, and each morning I would have to begin again. Equally maddening, he would never stand still when halted and invariably chose the moment when I was struggling with some rain-sodden knot to lurch forward, pulling it out of my hands, at the same time often setting a heavy, iron-shod hoof on my toe. I certainly began to sympathize with those brutal peasants I seem to have been seeing my whole life cursing and beating their asses instead of showing them some kindness.

I began to notice that when something irritating happened—another piece of equipment got left by the roadside, or we were lost for the second time in a morning—I would use a heavy whack on Hannibal's arse to relieve my feelings. And I once heard Andrew call absentmindedly to Jessica, "Walk up there," in exactly the words and tone he used to Hamilcar, though both of them quickly noticed with surprise what had happened.

I suppose I should have found their desire to be near us rather than grazing sensibly on some distant and more nourishing fodder an appealing trait. Unfortunately, as soon as our backs were turned they would pick out a fresh loaf of bread from a knapsack, or nose open a bag of oranges and stand smugly munching them, the juice streaming from their clumsy mouths.

They were at their most likeable when they were unsaddled after a day's march and would find a piece of dry earth to roll on. There was a fine abandon about this rolling, and I could understand just how they felt as they squirmed their uncluttered backs into the dust, the two together often raising a great drifting cloud of it. But Hamilcar, if given the slightest chance, would roll *before* we had removed his saddle bags, and I spent several evil-minded hours picking out wet groceries and anoraks from crushed cartons of milk.

We developed some affection for, but more a sense of inevitable partnership with, our donkeys. We were necessary to each other, and knew that we must endure each other's more infuriating habits.

Of the many different provinces of the three countries we crossed that summer, the very first, Galicia, in the northwest corner of Spain, was by far the most primitive and, to us, the most romantic. At times it seemed that we were walking through a living museum of rural life.

When we turned onto the cart track to the remote villages of Lestedo and Ligonde, we left the 20th century behind and plunged instantly into the 15th. It was market day at Palas de Rey, and we met a succession of people on their way there. First came an old woman with a pig, then a man with two sheep walking primly in front of him like poodles, and finally a whole family in an oxcart spread with shawls. Everyone was wearing his or her best clothes in spite of the mud and the mist.

At the top of the pass of El Poyo (which means stone bench and which leads from Galicia, with its damp Atlantic climate, into Spain itself), the sun burst gloriously upon us, turning the ecstatically circling Iago the color of flame. We were at a height of 5,000 feet, and all around us peaks rose from a boiling caldron of mist. Somewhere among them was Cebrero, the show-piece of the mountain route, where the monks of Aurillac had built a hospice for pilgrims in the 10th century. Cebrero is off the main road, and its streets are of mud and cobble, patched in places with gorse. The Holy Grail is said to be preserved in its solid Romanesque church, where a miracle occurred 500 years ago. A peasant from a neighboring village, who had struggled to mass through a thunderstorm, saw the Host turn to tender meat and the wine in the chalice to boiling blood. The children were disappointed that there were no longer monks in the monastery refectory, but there *was* ice-cream *gâteau* (at a price).

Round the church at Cebrero cluster the famous *pallosas*, stone huts with thatched conical roofs, no chimneys, and portholes for windows. The Spanish government is said to pay the peasants to stay in them for the sake of the tourist trade. One hopes that their lives are not as hard as those of their ancestors during the Napoleonic invasion. A German officer described the interior of one of these hovels:

The fireplace was in the middle and the smoke went whither it listed, up to the roof or out of the door. The fuel consisted of moist heath; they did not burn any light throughout the long winter nights; but illumined their huts with their heath fires, the smoke of which made the eyes smart horribly. The family in this particular hut consisted of a tall, old, black-and-yellow witch with three ugly children, of whom two were suffering from a hectic fever. Everything was extremely dirty; their hair was matted together, and they seemed never to have washed since the day of their birth. Round the woman's neck hung a rosary in three strands, ornamented with sacred medals, and she wore two huge earrings. She did nothing except sit over the fire and shake with cold and misery. The whole place presented a picture of the most appalling wretchedness.

Of many Spanish adventures, one which occurred soon after we left Villa-franca stands out most clearly in my mind. As soon as it was light we set off down a gorge of the Rio Valduerzo by a footpath Andrew had discovered. Broom, gum cistus, and lavender wet with dew had drenched our trouser legs in five minutes. In places the undergrowth was so high that Hamilcar, who was ahead of me, appeared to be swimming. Sometimes they closed over him completely. The smell of lavender was so strong that Jessica looked back suspiciously over her shoulder and inquired who was eating candy.

It was about halfway down that we came within an inch of losing donkey and children. The path, which clung perilously to the almost vertical slope, was barely wider than a human foot at the best of times, but at this point it was completely blocked by a large broom bush which had grown right across it. While attempting to get around it, Hamilcar allowed his hind legs to slip over the edge. For several ghastly moments he scrabbled frantically in the loose earth while the children were suspended over the abyss. Then, somehow, he managed to get back onto the path. I don't think either Miranda or Jessica knew what had happened, and I, for some reason, didn't have hysterics.

It was a relief to come down, after a night on those rain-swept mountains, to the sun-warmed plain where Astorga lies. Astorga is one of the five famous Spanish cathedral towns on the pilgrim route, and we planned to take a day off to visit it. We were within sight of its twin towers by the unprecedentedly early hour of 11 A.M., and I decided to carry on into the town alone, eager for an afternoon of sightseeing and, better still, solitude. My first port of call was not the cathedral but the hairdresser, where for 40 pesetas (50 cents) I enjoyed the luxury of a wash. For the first time in three weeks I was able to study my face in a mirror more than two inches across. It was dirty but shamelessly healthy. To my disgust it betrayed nothing of the toils and difficulties of the summer.

Three and a half months of steady walking followed. They took us all across northern Spain, past the magnificent cathedral cities of León and Burgos, through the wine town of Haro, and brought us by the first week of July to the Pass of Roncesvalles, where Roland blew his horn and where three out of four pilgrim routes crossed the Pyrenees. Turning northeast, still on the pilgrim way, we set off across France, visiting such famous places as the 12th-century cloisters at Moissac and Conques, with its treasure and its golden image of Saint Foy.

Here at last we left the pilgrims and turned east toward Montélimar and Hannibal's route, which we would pick up at the Rhone. Always the Alps, which we would have to cross, lay ahead, and we moved toward them through a broiling French summer with no small sense of urgency. Every day beyond mid-September increased the chances that we might find the passes blocked by snow.

Midmorning of September 8 saw us swinging briskly up the valley of the Ubaye. We were by now averaging 15 miles a day. The road we were following would soon reach a dead end. It led only to the French Alpine Club's refuge at Maljasset and our mule track over the Col de Mary. It was at this moment that Thomas let go of Hamilcar's leading rein and bent to pick up a particularly useful-looking stick with which to urge him forward. Hamilcar had other ideas. Leaving the road, he began to trot down a steep bank, tossing Miranda and Jessica off as he went. They lay in a weeping pile, and when we disentangled them we realized from the pain she was in that something was seriously wrong with Miranda's elbow.

Ten hours later she was in the operating theater of a clinic at Gap, 60 miles away. Her arm was broken and her elbow dislocated. There was no question of any donkey riding for two months. For these two months I must take her home to England to convalesce, leaving Thomas, Andrew, Jessica, and our two loyal donkeys to continue our unfinished task. It is Thomas who continues the story.

Presently our climb led us to even more gentle upland country and we saw ahead an unmistakable dip in the mountain skyline, the Col de Mary. It was the barrier which had lain ahead of us all summer, and there was nothing now between us and it. True, we had still to make the descent "of great difficulty" on the Italian side, but I nevertheless found it scarcely believable that we were going to arrive at this climax of our journey with such ease. And 10 minutes later we did indeed arrive there. The track ran straight over the summit, with nothing but a simple wooden board to mark the point where it began the descent into Italy.

The big hurdle that had stood ahead all summer was now behind us, and we could coast easily home. Autumn was coming but the weather was warm and sunny; in Italy it would surely remain fine for the next six weeks, which was the most we needed. So the three of us set off on what, for me, was probably the most spectacular and certainly the most energetic part of that summer's walk. Spectacular because the mountains of northern Italy are some of the most beautiful and remote that I have seen, and energetic because now at last, away from the ubiquitous tarmac of France, we would walk for day after day on little-used footpaths and nearly vertical mule tracks.

But in one way the fantastic mountain scenery was the least important part of the experience. The Grand Canyon, the Black Canyon of the Gunnison, the High Sierra of Yosemite had all been more remarkable sights, and no doubt I shall see others which are equally superior. Far more important was that we were out in this landscape, a part of it, feeling its rock and earth under our feet as we walked and below our hips as we slept, breathing its cold morning air and hot midday winds, brushing through its bushes and eating its wayside fruits. And not merely a part of this intense and total physical experience but a marvelously healthy part. The physical act of living seemed no longer just a neutral background for mere titillating sensations, but a positive pleasure in itself. Our well-regulated diet now seemed almost pointless, since our health triumphed over whatever we ate, our splendidly active metabolisms burning up the lot in one glorious crackling bonfire.

We found it restful to be without the exact time. There seemed little need to know, since we were usually in agreement about when the stages of our walk had gone on long enough and we needed a rest.

The romantic idea that the watchless man learns to tell the time by the sun is true only in a sense in which it is not usually meant. The time he learns doesn't have numbers attached to it but events or phases of his day, which as a result fall into a more natural pattern. We often noticed after our first timeless crossing of the Alps that, not being artificially prompted to need a meal, our lunch had been late in the afternoon, since it was quickly followed by darkness.

I came strongly to support the idea that the key technological advance, leading to all that is most neurotic about Western civilization, was the mechanical clock. One has only to imagine an office day without clocks to realize that they are essential for its most disagreeable features.

I remember the blackberries at La Crocetta, more luscious and abundant than I had ever seen (we ate them raw, stewed them, turned them into jam, and made delicious hot blackberry tea from them), the figs at Adelano, and the grapes, apples, pears, and chestnuts everywhere. That autumn these last became our staple food, and we contrasted the Italian passion for fungi with their total neglect (at least in the north) of chestnuts. Perhaps these are too closely associated with their peasant past. Day after day we began by collecting them keenly as they lay in glistening brown clusters all over the track, then gave up because we could carry no more. Night after night we filled ourselves with them, baked, fried in butter and garlic, curried, or made into a crude version of *crème de marrons*. That winter in Tuscany, we collected seven sacks of them (here there was local competition) and made chestnut bread, three-fifths flour and two-fifths mashed chestnuts, and baked it under red-hot ashes; also a dish we named Tuscan Delight consisting of a tart case made of chestnuts mashed with butter and sugar and a filling of "Japanese strawberries," the round, red fruit of an arbutus bush that also grew in profusion around us.

Our wayside morality had at first been a problem; we were inhibited by our childhood conditioning. Apples and chestnuts presented no difficulty because they lay everywhere unwanted—there were days when I calculated we munched through 15 apples each during our three marching stages. Nor did such things as juniper berries, fennel seeds, or mint for our daily mint tea. We had brought real tea from England, but when this was exhausted we needed no more the whole summer. Mint tea, even with condensed milk, is the most refreshing drink I know. But actual crops like tomatoes, beans, and sweet corn we began by picking only occasionally and with guilt. Long before the summer was over, we had become bold gypsies picking from fields wherever we could, refraining only from raiding domestic gardens.

The first stages of our daily walks were always the best; the tedious packing complete, rested and energetic, as the sun rose over valley or mountaintop I would feel an optimism I hadn't felt since childhood. Unknown adventures were ahead and, good or bad, I had the strength to meet them. Just to walk through such beautiful and remote country when the rest of the world was asleep was a delight in itself.

This early euphoria corresponded for me to the excitement of writing the first chapters of a novel; and indeed each day formed a parallel, with its tedious second stage when I would count kilometer posts, just as I counted my daily quota of words, enthusiasm only gradually returning when we reached the halfway point. So too, of course, was our whole summer's walk a parallel: the steady building up of tiny daily achievements into something which amazed us by its size; the early excitement of Galicia; the slogging in Castile and France; the climax of the Alps; and now the relaxed cruising to the end.

Though it was less relaxed than I had hoped. Soon after we had turned south beyond Genoa, the glorious autumn sun turned to days of torrential rain. From here onward we almost literally ran for our winter quarters. The final day's walk was the longest of the whole summer—24 miles—and it was after 10 at night when at last, Jessica lolling drunkenly in the saddle from tiredness, we climbed the hill to our farmhouse. A full moon emerged from the clouds to welcome us and there, below on the plain, we caught our first glittering sight of Lake Trasimeno, on the shore of which Hannibal had won his victory more than 2,000 years before.

John Waite

Mean Feat

John Waite was a young Cambridge University graduate when he set off on foot across the south of Europe, from Lagos in southwest Portugal to Brindisi in southeast Italy. What I especially like about his account of that 1981 journey is his happiness at meeting local people. His farm and village folk were often the last generation of their families to be maintaining the old traditions of European peasantry.

Of course, John Waite's trek has its share of difficulties. But the thrill of the adventure made him feel alive in every pore. Every day brought charming new adventures, such as when he came across a woman in Calitri, Italy who was about to walk out to the fields to plant garlic.

> *She made me a cup of tea, chatting away happily, after which we set off into the valley together, working our way down through the complex network of alleyways that often ran over the tops of the houses below, the arching buttresses so solid no earthquake could shift them. She was on her way to plant garlic. Before we parted she gave me two heads of garlic and a bunch of grapes.*
> *"Take them. Go on with you now. Buone cose."*
> *"Good things": it was a nice way of saying goodbye.*

The following excerpt from Mean Feat: A 3,000-Mile Walk Through Portugal, Spain, France, Switzerland and Italy *(1985) finds John Waite approaching the Appenine Mountains from near St. Francis's town of Assisi.*

* * *

First stop in the morning was the gates of the Sassovivo mineral water bottling plant, which blocked the track that I was following up into the mountains. The gates were made of wrought iron about two metres high, tipped with nasty spikes and barbed wire, an obstacle that I got over without many problems, throwing my pack over first, thus burning my boats. As it was Sunday, everything was locked and the source itself imprisoned in the bottling factory, the outlet choked with rubbish and plastic cups. On Sunday, women go to church and men follow their own ritual in the woods, hunting down and shooting anything that moves, from sparrow to hare, sometimes even each other. Above the woods the mountain tops were bare: it was good to see where I was going. I cut across country, over the close-cropped pasture, towards the downy, rounded flanks of Monte San Stefano dotted with juniper bushes, passing a little chapel surrounded by the cars of hunters, dedicated to the memory of Brigata Garibaldi V, 3 February 1944.

The countryside was more inhabited than I had thought from looking at the map and supported a mass of tiny villages. In Morro three old men gathered round on the wall overlooking the valley and pointed out the best way to reach Visso, hidden behind Monte Cavallo where a distant flock of sheep was grazing peacefully. Rasiglia was a lovely place nestling in the valley beside the river Menadre, which flows down to Foligno and on to the Tuscan Sea. I drank a little too much wine on a bench in the sun and floated off to Verchiano. Here, I bought an ice-cream to sweeten the after-taste of the wine while half the village men gathered round to discuss ways and means of getting to Visso, curious to gaze at the maps, saying surely such maps were top secret? The women kept away, peeping from doorways and windows. It was decided by general consensus that I should go via the Piano Grande. I liked the name: it is a former volcanic crater, the eastern side forming the backbone of the Appenine ridge, Monte Vettore rising to 2476 metres, the plain itself at about 1400 metres.

I took the dirt road out, past peasants collecting acorns for their pigs. In Civitella they were holding a village fete, the people all in their best suits and printed cotton dresses, standing around the streets that were decorated with strings of coloured lights and flags. A brass band passed in dark blue uniforms and peaked caps, playing a solid marching tune. The man next to me said there would be a candlelit parade later from the church, but I did not stay, moving on to San Martino, Forcella, just names along the road. The countryside was well husbanded in the traditional way, a mixture of oak trees, pasture, orchards and the smooth curve of ploughed fields. Black and white cows were being brought in to the village, their udders full and swaying gently, hoofs ringing on the concrete as they headed for the water trough where I was busy with domestic chores. The cowman had lost an arm in a combine four years before, on 2nd August, he told me.

"Really! That's my birthday. I was in Bolivia at the time."

"Mine's on 7th March, you know."

It had been a good day, full of contact with the people, the walking interesting, tiring but worthwhile. I camped. The sun set, the sky a warm pink brushed with pastel blue, the clouds golden, the crescent moon up, the stars twinkling, I was asleep in seconds.

My back felt stiff in the morning: so much sleeping on the ground was giving me rheumatism, the ground cooling down after the summer, the sun often not hot enough during the day to dry the sweat from my back when I stopped to rest. I remember Fematre for a beautiful eleventh-century church of white stone and the smell that pervaded the village: a healthy aroma of farm and cow. Villages of this type have nearly all been abandoned in France and Spain. The atmosphere was one I hadn't sensed since the north of Portugal. There it was very much a way of life, but here I sensed the beginning of decay, the gradual abandoning of the village. The empty, shuttered houses and tumbled walls were not there but were, perhaps, lurking in the near future. A large white cow suddenly came out onto the road in front, just fitting through the low, arched doorway under the farmhouse.

At Croce I found a shop, interrupting an angry exchange between the owner and the local representative from the Electricity Board. They glared sullenly at each other as I bought provisions, their voices joining battle again as I worked my way down into the gorge that would take me to Visso. The sun beat down directly overhead, the river classified "Category A," was called the Nera and ran west to Spoleto. The avenue leading into Visso was tree lined, reminiscent of similar scenes in the south of France. The crumbly white crags hung above the little town grimly. Everything was shut. I had a look around and rested on a wall beside the madly rushing mountain river, listening to its different voices. Birds twittered in the branches of a willow nearby, the ground was alive with tiny red and blue grasshoppers. I decided I would walk the last few miles up river to Castelsantangelo and camp the other side. There were willows, ash, alder and walnuts and clouds of gnats dancing in the twilight as the valley cooled. It was dark when I left the cafe in Castelsantangelo, but as I was well fortified with wine, the hill up to Glauco was no great effort. Here I stopped, cocking my ears for the sound of water, following the sound in the pale moonlight to a fountain and roofed washing house, settling down happily on the grass away from the wind. This would do nicely.

I was pottering around in the dark making myself comfortable when a shadowy figure appeared at the fountain, carrying a bucket. The figure froze.

"*Buona sera*," I said.

"What are you doing here?" a gruff voice replied.

"Making supper."

"There's a restaurant up the road."

"Is there? I don't have enough money to eat in restaurants."

"You can sleep there, too."

"I don't have enough money to sleep in hotels either. Anyway, I'm quite happy here: I have water, it's out of the wind and there's a roof if it rains."

"You'll get cold."

"No, I have a good sleeping bag."

"It's very humid in the mornings, you know."

Neither of us had moved. We argued stubbornly for another few minutes, going round in circles, covering the same ground.

"Look," he said at last, "as Christian to Christian, I invite you to my house."

It was a strange expression to use, but the rural Italians seem to divide the world into Christians, meaning Catholics, and Pagans or Saracens if you want to be rude, which embraces all others. When they say "We poor Christians" they mean simply "We poor people." After all, to be a person is to be Catholic.

I accepted his invitation, packed up hurriedly and followed him up a little alley to his house, where we went through a dark, arched doorway into a room lit by a single naked bulb. The unboarded ceiling was blackened by smoke from the wide chimney place, the walls of paint once white were now peeling and brown. Various plastic bags were hanging from hooks in the beams. The floor was tiled and clean swept, and a gas cooker stood over against a wall in the corner. Next to it was a table with two chairs and a washbasin. It was his kitchen.

He put his bucket down. We looked at each other for a moment, then shook hands and introduced ourselves. His name was Gian Battista. He had grizzly white hair, black eyebrows arched above heavy, rather bloodshot eyes, a scar on his broad nose and a Laurel moustache beneath. In stature he was short and thick-set, coming up to my chest. He motioned me to a chair and set about preparing a steaming hot soup. We sat at a table facing each other, breaking bread into the soup, which was peppered and full of onion and garlic. He made an incredible noise slurping it which made me feel positively genteel as I just puffed and blew. This was followed by a slice or two of cold mutton and some cheese, which he took out of one of the bags hanging from the beams. Then we talked.

He was a shepherd and had lived most of his life alone. He would be off to the Roman Campagna soon with the sheep. They had walked when he was a boy, but now they were all taken in cattle trucks. He said that no one stayed there during the winter, it was much too cold and thick with snow. His boss let him have a cottage on the plains and they returned in June.

He lit a cigarette, inhaled deeply, then shook the walls with his coughing, hawking and spitting on the floor, rubbing it in with the leather soles of his boots. He had been alone too long. He had a habit of getting up, walking around and talking with his arms outstretched for emphasis, his body bent forward slightly. He kept repeating himself unknowingly, chasing his tail in an argument over the relative values of the pound and the lira.

He made a cup of coffee after we had been for a walk under the stars, into which he tipped an inch or so of sugar.

"Is it sweet enough?" he asked.

On the mantelpiece was a photograph of him as a young boy soldier during the Second World War. He had been an A.A. gunner, stationed in Sardinia.

"I never did understand what was happening. First the Germans were friends and then we were told they were the enemy."

He made a mattress of greatcoats on the floor and after seeing me into the sleeping bag, turned out the light and left the room. It was a late night for both of us.

I was surprised at the speed with which I reached the lip of the Piano Grande, the bare Sibillini rising to the left, Monte Vettore squatting on its stomach like a huge, tired grey elephant, its sides covered with a patchy moss of trees. The plain is famous for the production of lentils, which had long been harvested, leaving the sheep and cows to graze the parched grass. The village of Castelluccio overlooked the plain from a crag beneath the western edge of the crater. It was a sad place: everyone seemed short-tempered, aware of another harsh winter on the way when those who stayed behind would be isolated from the rest of the world for months. Dogs wandered the streets uncared for, the buildings were never quite finished off, the whole place breathed an air of hopelessly tired third world dilapidation. I was crossing the line between Northern and Southern Italy, entering what is really another country, the *Mezzogiorno*, the *Midi* in France. There had been signs already in the attitudes of the people, their way of life, the questions they asked, their inability to understand why anyone should wish to walk when they could go by public transport.

The differences between the two Italies are marked, though there has been substantial progress in some areas. A glance at some statistics bears this out: in 1951 only 28 per cent of houses in the south had inside drinking water, whereas 43 per cent did in the north. By 1971, the figures were 82 and 87 per cent respectively. In 1951 only 19 per cent of the south had inside lavatories, while by 1971 it was 83 per cent, a higher figure than the north. The figures for literacy are interesting: in the south, in 1951, 48 per cent of the population was illiterate or at least lacked the elementary certificate of education, whereas the north had a figure of 20 per cent. By 1971 the south had improved: only 35 per cent were illiterate, but the figures in the north had increased to almost 30 per cent—the southerners had been emigrating to the large industrial towns in the north, like Milan and Turin. The overall reduction in illiteracy was thus quite small. Net income over the same period increased twofold, but it also doubled in the north, making sure that a worker there continues to earn up to six times as much as his fellows in the south.

I left Castellucio after a glass of wine in a cafe, cutting across the grassland, up out of the bowl, arriving exhausted at Forca Canapine, where there was a water trough next to which I rested and ate lunch. I had grown to distrust my maps, for the paths marked were often non-existent, so I was happy to find the one along the next ridge actually did exist, for it marked the watershed between the Tyrrhenian Sea and the Adriatic. The views on both sides were magnificent, the track perfect for walking, sometimes through scrubby woods, at others over grass, the sun warm and bright. At heights over 1600 meters autumn had arrived. It is my favourite season when the weather is kind, a time for reflection, for looking back on the things one has done during the year. It seemed incredible that I had walked all the way, or nearly all of it, from the south of Portugal. The walking was often hard, an endurance test, but the life was so simple, the cares so few and the taste of complete freedom that it gave so sweet I was certain now of the value of the journey. The soft evening light was crystal clear, the multiple autumn colours sharp, lemon yellow, lime green, orange, brown, red and russet playing one against the other. Time seemed meaningless. I felt a surge of spontaneous joy and exhilaration, happy as I had not been happy for many years, a bubble of contentment floating lightly over the mountains. It was all the compensation that I needed. The villages on either side of the divide were scattered among forest, the peaks of the Gran Sasso d'Italia, the highest in the Apennine range at almost 3000 metres, were clearly visible to the south. The setting sun rose again as I climbed the flanks of Monte Utero, finding a hollow at the summit where I curled up away from the wind, disturbing the birds who had already gone to roost.

Eric Shipton

Dreams of Distant Treks

How does a man become an explorer? How does someone go from the vague wish for distant adventure that most routine-bound people experience at least once in their lives to actually leading a life of expeditions, pilgrimages, and crusades? English explorer Eric Shipton (1907–1977) wrote books with names like Blank On The Map, Upon That Mountain, Mountains Of Tartary, Nanda Devi, The Mount Everest Reconnaissance Expedition 1951, Land Of Tempest, Mountain Conquest, Tierra del Fuego and That Untravelled World (1969) from which this piece comes. He explored the Himalayas at a time when they were largely terra incognita.

Eric Shipton was born in 1907 to a Ceylonese tea planter who died before Eric was three years old.

> For several years after my father's death we were constantly on the move, travelling between England and Southern India and Ceylon, where my mother retained close ties: and also in France, where she had many friends and where her mother had a house on the South Coast. We were never in one place for long and had no settled home, which is generally thought to be essential for the psychological welfare of children. So far as I remember, I found this nomadic existence wholly delightful; I revelled in the thrill of train and ship travel and in each change of scene. One of my earliest recollections is of arriving somewhere after a particularly exciting journey and asking eagerly how long it would be before we set off again; I was told that we would be staying a fortnight. Four nights seemed an awful long time to wait; and when I discovered that the word meant two weeks I wept bitterly.

This nomadic early life set the course for Eric Shipton's later adventures. Fortunately his complete failures as a student and later as a Kenya farmer left him free to pursue his dreams of distant treks. Though he was eventually best known for his participation in five

Everest expeditions, his wanderlust at the age of eighteen focused nearer to home, in France's Dauphiné region.

Eric Shipton ended his autobiography That Untravelled World with this statement:

> There are many ways of finding those moments of delight which come from a sense of complete harmony with wild surroundings. Some of us seek them through the mastery of difficult terrain or stormy seas, by quickening our awareness in contest with the elements. Others, more sensitive perhaps, can discover the same magic in quieter pursuits. Certainly it is not only to be found in unknown lands: my journey over the Karakoram trade route made as deep an impact on me as any through unexplored ranges; a sunrise seen from the top of Stromboli or a distant glimpse or the Cuillins can be as stirring as the view from a nameless peak in the Tien Shan.
>
> The springs of enchantment lie within ourselves: they arise from our sense of wonder, that most precious of gifts, the birthright of every child. Lose it and life becomes flat and colourless; keep it and
>
> all experience is an arch wherethro'
> Gleams that untravell'd world, whose margin fades
> For ever and for ever when I move.

* * *

Now, more than anything, I longed for a reasonably long spell in the summer Alps. The main difficulty, which seemed insuperable, was the cost of hiring guides. I had a little book called *Swiss Mountain Climbs*, by A. D. Abraham, which listed the guides' tariffs for all the Swiss mountains. These seemed prohibitive, and it was obvious that I could not possibly afford more than a couple of climbs in a holiday; particularly since my book made it clear that a guide would not usually venture on a difficult climb alone with an inexperienced amateur, and that it would be necessary also to hire a porter (an unqualified guide, employed not so much to carry loads as to assist his senior). Obviously I could not climb alone, and even if I had been able to find someone to go with, it had been repeatedly impressed upon me that to climb in the Alps without guides was the height of folly. In those days there were no youth organisations to help youngsters to learn the techniques of mountaineering; and even if there had been, my highly developed dislike of communal activities might well have prevented my joining it.

I had already decided to spend part of the next summer holidays (1925) walking through the Auvergne, mainly with the object of looking at the extinct volcanoes and crater lakes of that region (for volcanoes still intrigued me). This plan had my mother's approval, partly because it would help me to learn French, and partly because she had an old friend living in Cleremont-Ferrand who, she supposed, would be able to keep a fatherly eye on me. But I intended to spend the second half of the holidays visiting the scenes of Whymper's early exploits in the Dauphiné. Though the very name made me dizzy with excitement, I thought it better to keep this part of my programme to myself until I actually got there.

The old-fashioned walking tour seems to be a thing of the past. Perhaps, in a way, this is a good thing, for even in the overcrowded holiday Europe of today there is still a lot of country which can hardly be reached except on foot, and thus remains untouched by the ravages of tourism. In 1925 tourists were a great deal easier to avoid. There is no better way of becoming intimately acquainted with country than by walking over it, as I had already discovered in Norway, and soon I was so absorbed in exploring the Massif Central that I almost forgot my eagerness to reach the Dauphiné. I found that there were advantages in being on my own: not only the freedom to do just as I pleased but also a heightened impact of scenes and situations induced by solitude. Certainly I felt a bit lonely at first, particularly as, being stupidly diffident about airing my school French, I kept my human contacts to the minimum necessary for my survival.

One day, having started very early to cross a wild, unpopulated region, I reached a little *auberge* at 2 o'clock, hot, parched and ravenous. There I ordered an omelette; the girl serving me asked, 'Two eggs?' to which I replied, 'No, six, please.' She looked a little surprised, but went off to prepare it. In those days it was the custom in France for even the poorest inns to supply their customers with free wine. There was a large carafe on the table, and as my thirst was even more pressing than my hunger, I drank most of the contents while I waited. The acid *vin ordinaire* acted rapidly on my empty stomach, and by the time my monster omlette appeared I was feeling horribly sick. I paid at once and departed as casually as I dared, leaving the dish untasted and the girl to reflect upon the eccentricities of foreigners. I just managed to get out of sight in time; then, too embarrassed to return for my abandoned meal, I walked sadly on. Gradually, however, the universal kindness I met from the country people dissolved my shyness, and I began to delight in my daily encounters. Once I met a young Greek at an inn, and together we hired a punt which took us down the rapids of the gorges du Tarn. Apart from this one extravagance (and the six-egged omelette), I managed, eating frugally but adequately, to live on little more than a shilling a day. This was well below my budget, so that by the end of my three weeks' trek through the Auvergne and Cevennes I had saved a fair sum of money.

I went by train to Grenoble, where I stayed for a day to buy maps and plan the next part of my programme. I had intended to walk from there into the high mountains (in those days I had never heard of hitch-hiking), but in the windows of the tourist bureaux I saw pictures of the great ice peaks of the Dauphiné, whose names, Mont Pelvoux, Les Ecrins, La Meije, were already enchantingly familiar from Whymper. Swept by a fever of impatience, I booked a seat on a bus which left early the following day for La Bérarde. It was a dismal morning; rain was falling when the bus started, and when, after a couple of hours, it turned into a narrow valley leading into the heart of the range there was nothing to be seen but mist. I listened to the despondent talk of my fellow passengers, who were all, it seemed, making a day trip. Never, they said, had there been such a summer; the sun had not appeared for weeks; it wasn't really worth visiting the high valleys, as there was nothing to be seen. I was rash enough to admit that I proposed to stop in La Bérarde to climb. This evoked an outburst of cynical witticism which made me feel foolish and profoundly depressed. Then, as we approached St. Christophe, a miracle happened. The rain stopped; the clouds retreated up the mountainsides; a window opened to frame a sharp white peak which seemed to be hanging almost over our heads, glistening like a huge diamond; another appeared and another, and soon the valley was filled with sunlight.

We stopped at Les Etages, a small hamlet a few miles below La Bérarde, and while the driver refreshed himself and the other passengers photographed each other I enquired at the inn for a guide. I was promptly introduced to a bandy-legged little man, barely more than five feet tall, a beret cocked over one eye, who was sitting at a table drinking wine. His name was Elie Richard. Yes, he was free to act as my guide; it had been a terrible summer, very little climbing had been possible in August, and the peaks were deeply laden with fresh snow; but now, I would see, the weather would change and we would climb. Several weeks of unemployment during his short professional season (in those days one did not ski in the Dauphiné) had made Elie as eager as I to start. The very next day, he said, we would climb Pic Coolidge, which for all its 12,000 feet was easy enough to be possible in the worst of snow conditions; after that we would go for bigger game. His enthusiasm took my breath away; but how much would it cost? I told him I had very little money. He brushed this aside as lightly as he had dealt with the weather and the snow; he would charge me sixty francs (seven shillings) a day, or less if I couldn't afford it; we would climb every day if I wished, as we would live in huts which were free, and the cost of our food, which we would carry with us, would be small. It was settled; Elie would meet me in La Bérarde at 1 o'clock the following morning; the whole transaction had taken barely ten minutes. I climbed back into the bus in a daze of happiness, scarcely able to believe my good fortune.

At La Bérarde there were few people staying at the inn, and nearly all were climbers. For supper we sat together at one table. From their talk it was clear that the others were mostly experts, and I sat in awed silence listening to a discussion of their lofty ambitions, which could not be attempted until several days of fine weather had removed or settled the new snow. One of them was Nea Barnard, a girl of nineteen, already in her third Alpine season and soon to become one of the most distinguished women climbers of her generation. A warm-hearted extrovert, she was not slow to notice my shyness and to draw me gently into the company of the gods. Later, it was through her that I first made the acquaintance of other British climbers.

The ten days that followed were beyond my wildest dreams. Hitherto I had regarded the climbing of mountains as isolated experiences and had not conceived the idea of linking them together in a continuous mountaineering journey by travelling from place to place over the ranges and even by crossing the peaks themselves. Elie was as good as his word, and his optimism regarding the weather was justified; every day we climbed a peak or crossed a high pass; each night was spent in fresh surroundings. At that time he was a *Guide de Deuxième Classe,* and anxious to attain first-class status, which partly accounted for his willingness to do as much as possible in the time, and to climb on peaks that were new to him; but I believe this was also due to his sympathetic awareness of my delighted response. Luckily, my trek in the Auvergne had left me very fit, or I would not have been able to stand the pace; even so, I was often more tired than I had ever been before, and the prospect of yet another 2 A.M. start seemed intolerable. In the valleys Elie was the mildest of men; often on a mountain, particularly when descending a difficult passage of rock or snow-covered ice, his placid, retiring demeanour would undergo a violent change. He would curse and bawl at me in a mighty voice, while his small stature seemed to grow by several cubits; *"Enfoncez vos talons—Bon Dieu, regardez la corde—Ah, nom de nom de nom!"* At first I thought that these outbursts were due to his fear that my clumsiness would result in our destruction; later I began to suspect that they were an expression of joy at his own mastery. In moments of relaxation he was not grudging in his praise, which helped to restore my shattered self-esteem.

I rediscovered, with greater poignancy than before, the harsh truth that a strenuous pursuit cannot be undertaken without some suffering, and there were many times that I wished myself in softer circumstances: being woken at 1 A.M. from a deep sleep of physical fatigue to face a bleak world of stale bread, hard boots, stiff joints and cracked lips; the endless trudge up a slope of soft snow under a broiling sun with nothing to divert my attention from aching thighs and a raging thirst. There were moments, too, of clumsy fear which made me feel abysmally helpless and foolish. But these things were a minor part of the symphony of varied emotions that composed the experience of a mountaineering day, the sombre background to the contrasting highlights: the quickening of life at dawn after the dead weariness of the night approach; the sheer joy of controlled, rhythmic movement on steep rock and ice; the moment of attainment on the summit; the bliss of relaxation after tensed effort; in whole, the profound satisfaction of achieving a small measure of mastery, and with it a sense of belonging, in a majestic and enthralling environment.

I was surprised and a little shocked to find that I was not greatly impressed by the views from the tops, particularly of the highest peaks. I had supposed that one of the chief delights of climbing was to be found in such views; in fact, I found that the surrounding mountains seemed sadly dwarfed and, by their very profusion, tended to lose their splendid individuality and become shapeless masses in an untidy jumble of snow and rock. Since every climbing book that I had read continually stressed the magnificence of summit views, I assumed that there must be something wrong with me. It took me some time to realise that, for me at least, the aesthetic appreciation of scenery cannot be turned on like a tap; that it comes unbidden, usually at unexpected moments, when the mind happens to be attuned to the realisation of the subtle interplay of form and colour, light and shadow. Views from summits are usually seen in the harsh glare of the noonday sun when this component is notably lacking.

Our last mountain was Les Ecrins, the highest in the Dauphiné and the scene of one of Whymper's more dramatic, if less credible, adventures. My financial resources were now almost at an end, and as in any case I had arranged to spend the last part of the holidays with my mother and sister in Paris, it was time to go. So I set off on the long trek back to Grenoble, too thrilled with the fabulous success of my first real Alpine season to have any regrets. Moreover, Elie and I had agreed to climb together the following summer, and for a far longer time.

Jo Tourte

On Foot Around the World

On Foot Around The World (1947) tells the story of a young French couple's three years of worldwide camping and walking. Jo Tourte had grown up roaming the hills of Burgundy with her sisters. When she met Roger Tourte in Paris he explained his grand plan of walking around the world after he had completed his architectural studies. "Immediately our interests coincided," she later wrote. "We trained together for the hike. Each Saturday, packs on our backs, we hiked throughout Paris."

The couple intentionally did not tell their parents that they were leaving on a walking tour of the world. And no one worried, knowing their love of hiking, when they said that they were going off on a hike in the Midi and in Italy.

We catch up with them here at the Italian border.

* * *

For us, there are no borders. The Midi crossed, the countryside changes, and here it is called Italy. A stamp (the first) in our passport and we pass through.

What makes for strangeness is a sharp contrast between two ways of living. We go so slowly that we assimilate gently to customs and we are not shocked. Here they speak another language. With three books we learn it poorly. A word in the air teaches better. But necessity teaches best.

Genoa, Mantua, Marmirolo, Marengo, the Lake of Garda, Venice, Ferraro, Ravenna, Lucca, Pisa and we arrive at Florence.

All ties weren't yet broken. We were not yet totally isolated and September 1 Roger's sister and three friends arrived to camp with us for fifteen days, their vacation, and to accompany us from Florence to Rome on foot.

When they arrived we understood the distance which four months of separation and this different life had made. Our life for four months had been made only of simple things: the horizon when we got up; the fruits gathered; the sand or pebbles of the roads. Our distractions were: ants which we made fight each other in our hands; the tastes of waters which we began to distinguish; all the little things, the little daily events, the fruits filched, the springs discovered—this great unremarkable happiness.

Rome in our eyes had the importance of Paris. Where to camp? After our long journey in the open air, after having lived freely, without cares about city elegance, with the security of finding each night a place more or less "campable," far from settlements, our arrival in cities posed a real problem. The Coliseum, with its enormous carcass, was unanimously chosen. Thanks to nightfall we slipped in without noise and slept all lined up at the top of the stairs. No one saw us. For three nights we did the same thing without ever being disturbed. In the morning, after a refreshing shower in the establishment where we stored our packs, we visited the city.

Then our friends returned to Paris. Our last tie was broken. We were alone. Completely alone. We continued on.

That night, camped in the rolling and deserted Roman countryside . . .

Tivoli, Subbliaco, Tarento, we arrived in sight of the Adriatic. Brindisi: another frontier with policemen, customs agents, visas. We will take a boat to Corfu, then another to the Greek coast, and we will try to reach Athens on foot. It will be winter and we will need to stop to earn our living.

Adam Nicolson

The Alps, On Foot

Adam Nicolson is an English hiker who wrote two excellent books, The National Trust Book Of Long Walks In England, Scotland and Wales *and* Long Walks In France. *These books are partially guides to the long trails in Britain and France, but they are also much more. Adam Nicolson has an eye for nature, people, history, weather, and the charms and vagaries of life on the trail.*

In the following adventure, which first appeared in the New York Times Magazine, *we join him in hiking from France to Italy across the great divide between the valleys of the Durance and the Po.*

* * *

"If you are ready," Henry David Thoreau wrote at the end of his life, "to leave father and mother, and brother and sister, and wife and child and friends, and never see them again—if you have paid your debts, and made your will, and settled all your affairs, and are a free man—then you are ready for a walk."

I found this invitation in a London bookshop, spoke to my bank manager on the telephone and left for France the next day. It was to be an adventure: crossing the great divide of Europe, where 40 million years ago Italy, pushed up by the block of Africa, had collided with the Continent and built the Alps. It was to be a high crossing, from the valley of the Durance to the valley of the Po, four days' walk across the watershed between the rivers running into the Golfe du Lion and those flowing to the Adriatic. It was to be four days away from the ease of life on the plain, an exposure, a mild rejection, "une évasion," to use that exact French term describing something less than an escape but more than a simple journey. It was to be a turning aside from more mundane occupations by exposing oneself to the shape of Europe, to the great buckle in the surface of the continent.

"Now you know, I just love the idea of a little adventure," a woman on the train between London and the Channel told me, unclipping the jaw of her fox fur from its dangling legs on the other side. "Crossing the Alps. Well," she said, and patted my corduroy thigh. Her husband chewed the sodden end of his cigar and looked out at the Weald of Kent. They too were bound for Italy. "We thought the Orient Express was just a lovely idea for a little adventure," she continued. "Right past all those mountains and then out you come and there you are—the Grand Canal and Cipriani's." The image of these two oozing round the Alps, in their strange created world of rognons à la russe and blue-and-gold stewards with shaved necks and a solicitous air, haunted me at every exhausting pass and at each exhausted nightfall. It was something to envy and to leave behind.

We parted ways at Calais—they to their allotted compartment and I to the night train through Paris to Mont-Dauphin in the valley of the Durance. It arrived early the next morning. There was no ceremony; the guard simply announced that the train would stop for less than a minute. Most of the passengers stayed rolled up in their couchettes. A nervous Parisienne in a white suit descended, was collected by a farmer and drove off somewhere to a warm breakfast. The doors of the train banged shut and I was left alone with my rucksack, the prospect of four days' walk to the Italian frontier, of 15,000 feet of climbing and the dominant third dimension on either side.

The valley was cold and still in shadow. The frost had tightened the gravel on the roadside and the water in the braided streambed of the Durance was peppermint green. The light from the sun over Italy began to creep down from the summits of the Tête de Fouran and the Tête de Clotinaille onto the first of the high pastures, warming and coloring them. This is the moment when you feel both excited and absurd, when all you can do is look up, twist your neck, gaze at mountains and dream of balloons.

The prospect of the first climb is terrible: straight to the summit of le Cugulet, 5,000 feet above the valley floor. But there is no need for any rush. Delay. Drink some cups of coffee in the little market town of Guillestre, on the edge of mountain and plain. Buy oranges and slices of tomme, the rather lardy local cheese, and an apple turnover or two. Jettison as many of your belongings as you dare, as nothing serves better than a long climb in identifying the essentials of life. And explore Guillestre, where hay sticks out of unlikely windows and dead chickens hang upside down by one leg, their feathers fluffed outward and their heads dark with the fallen blood. And realize that this is the land where gravity is king.

There are few pleasures like the reluctance at the beginning of a walk. It is a wonderful teetering sensation as your attachments to comfort slowly ebb away, as you gradually accept that despite all the balm of little cafes, of sitting half-reading a paper for hours, of ordering another cup of coffee and smoking another cigarette—those sedentary joys of not adventuring— there comes a time when there is no alternative but to begin.

On the edge of the town I began to rise above the valley, and the rational, deadeye geometry of Vauban's fort at Mont-Dauphin became clear, coolly designed without romance to control the routes over the mountains into Italy and up the Durance. I met a woman coming down from the mountain. She was perfectly dressed, sweatless in sandals, carrying a pale basket lined in gingham and full of flowers. "You know it's four hours to the top?" she asked casually. "Oh yes," I said, meaning "No," and walked on with as much nonchalance as 25 pounds of rucksack and a 45-degree slope would allow. *Four* hours? A jolt of adrenaline. I had reckoned on two and a half and had wasted all that time with dead chickens and apple turnovers in the fond belief that I would be in Ceillac, on the far side of the mountain, by some early, easy time in the afternoon.

It was not to be; the climb did indeed take a few minutes over four hours. The path zigzagged neatly up past the birch trees and then through the larches, their needles just turning a perfect Japanese lacquer-yellow. To the northwest the glaciers in the high mountains of the Ecrins looked, in that extraordinary phrase Byron used in his journal, "like *Frozen* hurricanes" with the rock black and unapproachable around them. Nearer at hand there was nothing of the thick, lush damp that one associates with Alpine pastures. There was neither softness nor welcome, but an extreme, exposing clarity, tough and definite.

As you climb, a strange process begins to overtake both mind and body. It may be something to do with the obviousness of the enterprise— from one valley over a mountain to next—and something about the simple, one-foot-in-front-of-the-other sweat of it, but the sensation is of growing purity, of uninvolved, hard purity. It is no wonder that the people in the part of the Alps called the Queyras adopted as early as the 13th century a stripped-down sort of Christianity, abandoning anything to do with the mass, the cult of the Virgin, the saints, purgatory or the authority of pope or clergy. Even one morning's exposure to this place makes any sort of complication appear irrelevant. It is a simple world on top of a mountain. That much I realized as I sat on the summit of le Cugulet, eating another apple turnover, surveying the valleys, away from the world, disoriented by heat, altitude and the "evasion" of it all.

It was late in the afternoon, but I didn't mind. Gradually the evening began to squeeze the light back up the slopes. The larches were now back-lighted and the limestone cliffs were streaked orange and black like a sunset. As the dark came I lost the path and found myself in a sharp ravine, trying to feel a way to the lights of Ceillac in the valley below. But it was too far and I was too tired, and I simply unrolled the sleeping bag, took off my boots and lay down on the slope, lodged up against a boulder with my face pointing at the wide stripe of the Milky Way, hoping that adventure and incompetence were part of the same thing. As the Plow swung down under the Pic de Guillestre and Cassiopeia climbed up over it, I fell into a dewy sleep, waking up every few hours through the night to find the stars revolved above me.

In Ceillac the next morning, over a cup of coffee, I told M. Fournier, guardian of the refuge, or hostel, about the beauty and closeness of the Queyrassien stars. He knew all about them. This, he said, is "le pays où les coqs picorent les étoiles," the country where the cockerels can peck at the stars.

It is easier from Ceillac to St. Véran, no more than five hours, with a climb of only 3,500 feet to the col that separates the two valleys. It is an old route, used by the Romans and, until the 1950s, by mule trains. In the valley of the Cristillan River above Ceillac, tiny broken hamlets survive along either side of the track. Tioure is completely defunct, destroyed by an avalanche a few years ago. The stubs of houses stand near a cascading stream, half a sundial in the plaster of one of them, soaked in a desolate romance. Chalky blue butterflies and marbled skippers flounce on the sterile remains of a Sabot de Vénus and you begin the long ascent to the pass. As you climb, the years gather around you, a decade every thousand feet, a lifetime a mountain, so that you reach the col aged and slow, counting the steps, remembering the motto on tens of sundials in the villages of the Queyras: "Every hour wounds; the last one kills." That is the tone of the mountain mind.

You reach the pass, tip the balance and begin to move down to the valley of the Aigue Blanche. Each col is itself a sort of frontier between the sunny and the shady, between the south-facing pastures and the north-facing pelt of larches and pines, between a slope that is silent except for the crickets and one that is heavy with the noise of falling water, an invitation to descend.

St. Véran is on the sunny side, 500 feet up from the stream in the bottom of the valley. Each house is encrusted with balconies, where the hay is dried facing the sun, and everything above the ground floor is made entirely of wood. In the vaulted stone basements, even until the 1960s, the people lived in the same room as their animals; the cows used to be stalled between the beds as the sweetest-smelling space heaters ever known. The main room of the house is still called "the stable," but nobody lives like that now.

St. Véran is famous as the highest village in Europe—more than 6,600 feet above sea level—and many thousands of people come to see it for that reason alone. The place is "denatured," as the guidebook says. The village has become little more than an exhibit; it is full of bars and hotels that are open only in the season. The valley and its ways of thinking have sidled up the road to engulf St. Véran. It is somewhere to leave behind on the path to Italy.

One can walk over the Col de St. Véran and down to Chianale, the first village in Italy, all in the space of one day. But to do that is to miss something. One must go slowly here and spend time in the frontier zone itself. So from St. Véran walk up the valley of the Aigue Blanche, past the abandoned copper mine and marble quarry, the rock stained green, and over the Col de Chamoussière, short of the frontier, to the Refuge Agnel, alone in its circle of mountains just under 8,500 feet.

Like two streams diminishing to drought at the crest line, the national identities on either side have become exhausted, and the frost-ruined landscape of the frontier zone is left unadorned, without gloss, more of a wilderness because it is literally in the middle of nowhere, at the stub-end of two worlds. I have never known a more ghostly place. The horizon is notched and chipped in a crabbed hand. The mountains are in ruins, broken by frosts into thousands of acres of slithered dark slate. This is a place that has always been crossed, and quickly. It has never been cared for or fought over. There could be no competition for territory here.

I spent the night alone in the refuge. The roof creaked in the wind from Italy. Nothing diluted the dark or the creaking, the silence hissing like a gas jet in my ears. I left as soon as the sun came over the Col Agnel, yellowing the bumps in the high meadows, and climbed to the frontier at the Pic de Caramantran, the highest point on the walk, just a few feet under 10,000. As I reached the top over the shaly rock, the whole of Italy appeared in front of me, submerged beneath a layer of cloud with only the dark mountains breaking through it like a school of sharks in a gassy sea. The weightless, effervescent blanket spread to the distant horizon, where it curved down over the round edge of the earth.

Then downhill into Italy: the first trickle of a stream, the first cricket, and then into the mist. The mountains acquired faint bodies where they had been only heads and shoulders before. I met a young shepherd in a thick jersey who spoke twangy French. He had lost three sheep two months back. Had I seen them? I had passed a carcass, picked virtually clean. I told him where and continued down. The valley was deep and wide, a straight exit from the mountains.

I made a wide detour around a sheepdog and came to Chianale. The Torrente Varaita ran straight through it and from there to the Po. It was beautiful, and poor. Women washed clothes at the side of the stream. The roads were rough and muddy, the ground floors half-underground for winter warmth. But it was practically empty. An old man with a twisted leg told me that all the people had gone to work in France, as ever. Hence the vacuum. They would be back in the winter. He too, before his accident, had crossed the pass to cut hay and oats in St. Véran. Things had not changed. It was one people on both sides of the mountain. They were more like each other than the people in St. Véran were like Parisians. "Because in Paris they are much more. . . ." He looked for the words. "Much more. . . ." He looked at me. "More *English*," he said, and clapped me on the back as well as he could.

*   *   *

It was 11 in the morning. We drank wine and I ate noodles in the cafe. The old man told me I had crossed over from the country where everyone thinks he's Napoleon to one where everyone thinks he is the pope. I was beginning the second plate of noodles when the street outside filled with cows, jostling and bellowing, and the cafe filled with their herdsmen, excited, creased men with bunched faces. We all drank to each other's adventures. I had made my crossing. The water in the stream outside would go to the Adriatic. Four honey buzzards floated over the village and the herdsmen began to speak among themselves. "What are they talking about?" I asked my old friend. "Cows," he said. "As ever. Cows, the mountains, next year. As ever. It's always the same."

The Orient Express was on another planet.

Michael G. Harman

The Arizona Limited

Nowadays cross-America walks or bicycle trips are a common occur-
rence, especially to Washington, D.C., where the marchers deliver
petitions for worthy causes or collect contributions for miles walked.
These were not the purposes of Michael Harman in the first decade of
this century when he walked from San Francisco to New York City.
He wished merely to go East and to observe what lay along the way.
With his friend Tim he set out walking beside a burro-drawn cart or
"schooner," the Arizona Limited (which was also the name of his 1909
book).

His chapter about Kansas is called "Mud-Mud-Mud-We Were In
A State Of Mud." It begins with an encounter with "a credulous rube."

* * *

June twenty-eighth we arrived near Newton, Kansas, but how we got
there is a muddy story, sure. For the week previous we were in mud and
the mud in us; the Limited fairly revelled in mud—slept in mud—walked
in mud—and ate in mud. There was mud in the blankets—mud in the cart,
and Tim and I were cakes of mud.

We could no more avoid it than could the Egyptians escape from their
plagues. What kind of mud was it? Kansas mud; the very stickiest, nastiest
and blackest in the world, and why the State wasn't named mud I don't
know. We met a man, who had mud in his head instead of brains. No? A
fact, nevertheless. While slushing through the rain one afternoon, we met
Steve Peppercorn driving west in a buckboard. He was so astonished at
seeing such an aggregation on the highway, that he stopped and asked:

"Where are you going, partner, with them little asses?"

"We are travelling," answered I, "overland to St. Petersburg, in Russia,
from Japan."

"Gosh!" exclaimed Steve, "that's furdern K. C. ain't it?"

"Yes," I continued, "about five hundred times as far. You know these
are among the rarest animals in the world—Japanese mules they are, from
the private stud of the Emperor of Japan. We are taking them as a present
to the Czar."

"By Gosh!" ejaculated Steve.

We left him standing in the road with his mouth agape, swallowing Kansas rain, and trying to assimilate it all. Guess he'll be talking and telling his neighbors, "bout them Japanese mules what he saw," for the next decade.

Since Mark Twain had taken his unexpected departure for mule heaven we decided to replace the tongue in the schooner with a pair of shafts, and work the burros three abreast. Soon after we left Hutchinson we came to a grove of saplings opposite a farm. We pitched the camp, went into the woods and cut two saplings, and worked faithfully on the job the entire day, finishing at nightfall.

One night was passed in a man's corncrib where we afforded the rats and mice quite a diversion, for they were running and hurdling us all night long. June twenty-ninth the Limited managed to cover seventeen miles in ten hours, camped near a farm house where, as usual, the couch was made in the hay loft. Supposed when New York was reached, from continuous habit, I'd seek out a livery stable instead of a hotel. On the road west of Florence the schooner sank in mud holes up to the axles three times. We sat on the roadside, patiently waiting for a team of horses to come along and extricate us. The burros are as game animals as ever looked through a collar, but because they are so diminutive, and possessed of such small feet, they'd sink right up to their bellies. We would unhitch them, one would grab the burro by the ears and the other catch him by the tail, and thus pull him out.

At this stage of the journey a good deal of time was consumed in repairing breakdowns. The schooner and harness were not made to withstand the many hard pulls and jerks to which they were subjected. We expected three or four repair jobs a day, but when it came to mending the strenuous Ted's trace or Carrie's breast yoke a dozen times, more or less, in a day's journey, it grew monotonous. We would never have gotten through without the baling wire and wire pliers—both were indispensable. The latter is the most useful little implement imaginable, not only for all kinds of repairing to both schooner and harness but also around the camp fire while cooking a meal it was a very handy tool to lift pots, pans and kettles on and off the fire.

One afternoon, after a hard day's travel, we hove in sight of a very beautiful place called "Clovercliff." It is an immense alfalfa ranch of many thousand acres. We found the people cultured and refined; they appreciated the novelty of the trip, and the whole family exerted themselves to make the Limited comfortable for one night at least.

While the "chief cook and bottle washer" made a fire preparatory to cooking supper the male member of the family, together with twenty or more farm hands, gathered to see how the trick was done.

We received donations of eggs, bread, milk and cake, and they seemed to enjoy the novelty hugely while we enjoyed the cake et cetera.

After supper Tim and I took a scout to see how the burros were faring. What do you think? In the first stall Teddy Roosevelt was occupying, mind you, a great big box stall alone, wrapped in the solitude of his own originality and chewing away at a bale of alfalfa about the size of himself. Carrie and her son Epaminondas were ensconced in the next, and the old lady was going for a bale as though her very life depended on its being consumed before morning. Epaminondas was rendering slight assistance by occasionally nibbling a few choice straws which ever and anon he'd wash down with a drink of milk. And what of old dame Grover? Had she upon entering her apartment with Joan lapsed into innocuous desuetude?" Not much. They were industriously engaged on a bale of the same brand.

July third, after accomplishing eight miles, a heavy rain set in, and on arriving at a schoolhouse where the fuel house was found open with an abundance of dry wood, we decided to spend the remainder of the day in placing a covering over the water-soaked schooner. Besides my ankle needed a rest; it was not conducive to its improvement to have carried along several pounds of Kansas real estate clinging to each of my rather dilapidated shoes as I had been doing for the past three weeks. To a farmer in the neighborhood a pair of mounted steer horns was given in exchange for some hoops and a piece of canvas, which, together with an old tent we had secured in Trinidad, formed the covering. In the afternoon the sun came out and that night, for the first time in several weeks, the engineer and conductor luxuriated in dry clothing and blankets.

After the organization of the Limited we, once a week, would have wash day; we would camp some afternoon early, make a fire, and put a change of clothing in a pot to boil.

If it was dry weather we'd tie the clothes to a rope attached to the back part of the schooner. If it was rainy weather we would put them on wet; 'twas only an exchange of the clean wet for the soiled wet.

On the glorious Fourth we arrived in Lebo, flying the Star-spangled Banner—the one given us in Los Cerrillos—where quite an ovation awaited us by the celebrators. I gave the crowd one of my choice orations which, while it lacked the eloquence of a Patrick Henry, was well received, and at its termination I sold some souvenirs. No Fourth of July celebration is complete without the usual game of baseball. The "Strong City Giants" were on hand to struggle with the "Lebo Invincibles," for fame, glory and the bright smiles of the rustic beauties who were greatly in evidence, bedecked in their best bibs and tuckers. It was great fun! There is more real, downright enjoyment to be had from a country game of baseball than from a National League contest. As is usually the case in these games, the features were the player by accident catching the ball, and the immense score. The Fickle Goddess of Fortune placed the laurel wreath of victory on the noble brows of the Leboites.

July sixth we camped on a hill overlooking the town of Quenemo where we learned that it would be impossible to cross the river for several days, owing to the high water which was in the streets of the town. Tim and I slept in the schooner in wet blankets, lulled to sleep by the incessant pattering of the raindrops on the canvas.

We woke on the morning of the seventh, the rain still pouring in torrents, wet, hungry and almost despairing. Not one gleam of light marked the horizon. This communing with Nature in fair weather was all right, for what is more alluring than to camp in a picturesque spot, with a bright camp fire burning, and after a good meal to loll around on the blankets, smoking and swapping stories until bed time; and then to seek a luxurious couch of pine boughs with the bright canopy of heaven for a covering? But the communing business through dripping Kansas was "a gray horse of another color."

The Limited, at Quenemo, again suffered the loss of one of its members. The terrible weather had proved too much for Joan of Arc, and the poor little brute died of lung fever. When we first noticed that she was ailing with a bad cough, she was carried to a stable where we worked faithfully over her all one night; but she died the next morning. She was a cute little animal, kind and gentle, and all day long she'd walk contentedly by my side like a big, faithful dog. Joan was never so precocious as Epaminondas who'd be here, there and everywhere. He'd plough through the mud all day long, and when night came would run races with himself and kick your hat off to give himself an appetite for supper.

July ninth the water had fallen sufficiently to allow us to cross the river, and after starting the team on its way I left for Kansas City where I expected to secure an advertisement from some big enterprise for the World's Fair. Tim said he thought he could manage alone for a few days, and we would join forces again in Missouri.

The year previous I had known in Chicago a vocalist of fine attainments who, when on the verge of becoming a great tenor, contracted typhoid fever and died. I walked into his father's store in Shawnee, and both he and my friend's widow were delighted to see me. The following day was passed resting under the big shade trees and talking over old times in Chicago.

The Sunflower State was at my back when the river was crossed into Kansas City, Mo. Why it was so called I'm at a loss to understand, for old King Sol certainly didn't distinguish himself by any lengthy exhibitions while we were traversing it.

Poor old Kansas! Her trials and tribulations have been many. It appears to me as though the Lord takes special delight in chastising her good people— for they are good, kind and hospitable; at least we found them so. Among my earliest recollections are hard-luck stories emanating from Kansas. You may have possibly heard the story of the farmer who had gone bankrupt in the State, back in the eighties. The poor devil was making his exit from Kansas, as rapidly as a poor, worn out, old plug of a horse could travel, with the following sign in large letters on the wagon cover;

"In God we trusted,
In Kansas we busted."

But these Kansans are stickers, and the tenacity with which they cling to their State is most admirable. The Creator has tried blowing them out with cyclones; burning them up with droughts; beating them out with hail; eating them up with grasshoppers; and as a last resort is trying the drowning process. Guess he'll give them up as a bad job if the latter fails. They certainly deserve a few peaceful years, at any rate.

While walking the track, several miles east of Little Blue, Mo., I met an old, old man, with a long white beard, hobbling along with the aid of a walking stick, and carrying a bundle.

"Where are you going, young man?" he inquired.

"I'm on a walk from San Francisco to New York City," I answered.

"Walking from San Francisco to New York," he repeated slowly; "I wouldn't do that for all the money in the world."

"Oh, it's not so hard after one becomes accustomed to it," was my reply.

"Yes, it's true. I guess h—— would be all right after one became accustomed to it," he answered, "but come and spend the night with me in my shack up in the woods, and I want you distinctly to understand, young man, that I'm the only man in Jackson county who would extend you hospitality. They are a bad lot these Missourians, a very bad lot; and I have been here long enough to find them out, over forty years."

The old fellow was quite a character so I decided to accompany him to his lodging up in the hills, situated a mile from the railroad. On reaching his rudely-constructed shack, I planted myself on a bench under a tree after removing my knapsack.

"Will you have a drink?" he called from the interior of his cabin.

"Don't care if I do," was my reply, thinking that a little nip of good old Kentucky Bourbon would do me good.

The old man shortly emerged from the doorway with two tincups, some sugar and a bottle. He placed himself beside me on the bench to mix the drinks. The bottle was labeled "ALCOHOL."

And he rambled thusly: "My name is Albertus Babe Kelly, formerly of Kentucky, and the most serious charge for which I'll be compelled to answer before the last tribunal is that forty years of my life were misspent in Missouri. I came here forty years ago, to escape being drafted for the war, and have never had money enough to return. The very idea of a

Kentucky gentleman having sojourned here so long is alone enough to condemn him to eternal and everlasting punishment."

As he poured the fiery liquid into the cups, he continued:

"A good drink of whiskey cannot be secured anywhere in Jackson county," and, as he handed me the drink he proposed the following toast:

"Here is to dear old Kentucky,
The land of the rich blue-grass;
And to Missouri eternal damnation,
Which is only fit for an ass."

Of course Albertus Babe would have been mortally offended had I balked; so I was game and down went the fiery concoction to the last drop. My, how it burnt!

In reply to the inquiry as to why he lived a hermit's life, he answered:

"I am close to Nature here, far removed from the lying and deceitful world. With the trees, birds and animals for my friends, I am spending my last days contented and happy. I earn with my axe, chopping wood and splitting rails, the necessities of life, and here I will remain until the last call."

Poor, lonely old man! Can you imagine a more pitiful sight than a man eighty years of age quitting this world for eternity without a single friend? I cannot.

The next morning the old fellow insisted on my trying another of his famous Alcohol high-balls, but 'twas nay, nay Pauline—never again for little Willie. Albertus gave me a cane carved from heart oak and it was a peach of a dog stick.

San Francisco, 2,361 miles—1,349 miles New York.

Charles Konopa

The Reason Why

Charles Konopa has been a government courier and a park ranger. But it is as a walker that he would like to be remembered. He has hiked the entire 2,000-plus miles of the Appalachian Trail and has tramped many of North America's most interesting by-ways.

He is a man for whom distance walking is its own reward. "The Reason Why" is previously unpublished.

* * *

I know a man who once walked from Louisville, Kentucky to Cedar Keys, Florida, more or less along the route of John Muir's celebrated thousand-mile walk to the Gulf of Mexico. Whereas Muir made a botanizing expedition with the notes he jotted later becoming a book (*A Thousand Mile Walk To The Gulf*, 1916), this man wished to take a long walk for his own satisfaction only. He admired Muir and thought it would be enjoyable to trace the famous naturalist's footsteps while stretching his legs.

When Muir took his solo walk in 1867 the people he met nearly always treated him with kindness and hospitality. This was as true in the Deep South as it was in the North, though the bitter Civil War had ended just two years before, and though the southern countryside swarmed with brigands and appeared on the verge of anarchy, and though a regiment from Muir's own state of Wisconsin had been on Sherman's town-burning, hog-sticking, skirt-raising march through Georgia. Plant study was virtually a new science then and people nudged one another at seeing the intent young naturalist peer into the throats of wildflowers with a "spy glass." Muir had little trouble gathering all the strange herbs his tote bag could hold.

Now, as this man followed Muir's ghostly track down dusty roads and through villages, people would ask why he walked. When he replied that it was for his own pleasure they reacted as to a hateful thing. Hardly anyone seemed to believe him.

When he said (a little lamely, for it sounded like an excuse) that he was on foot because Muir had been on foot, people frowned and asked why he didn't use a car—or even a motorcycle. Certainly the driver is more efficient at covering territory than the pedestrian. It was clear that his explanations were unsatisfactory.

Thus he discovered that an unconvincing answer is no answer at all. Truth is usually beside the point if it does not fit into daily experience or familiar ideas. "For men," as Pope observed, "never approve any other's sense, but as it squares with their own." The man knew then what must be done; he would copy a page, as it were, from Muir's notebook. At a small college on the way he visited the department of natural history and came away with a plant press and a book on herbs which fitted handily in the pockets of his jacket. In the press he arranged several fine specimens of pennyroyal culled from the roadside.

Thereafter, when the customary question was raised, out would come the press with its pennyroyals squeezed flat and exuding a strong minty smell. He was collecting plants, he told everyone. Where there had been dislike, now there was warmth. People smiled and shook his hand. They invited him into their homes. By the time he reached the gulf whole platoons of chickens had been marched to the chopping stump, rolled in corn meal and fried brown in his honor. He had the memory of happy hours spent in woodsheds over tin cups of homemade bourbon.

Another thing also happened. Before obtaining the plant press this man hadn't known ladyslippers from Jimson weed. But now his interest in an unknown subject was stimulated. Today he is an expert botanist and women's clubs 200 miles distant beg him to lecture in the springtime on the topic "Fragrant Flowers of the Field."

The third day of my own hike on the Appalachian Trail in 1970, I met a young man in Georgia cutting trees and splitting them into fence posts. This is work followed by many hillmen who have no love for supervision and will labor only for their own account. It is as ill-paid as are most healthy and solitary occupations. At my approach the post-splitter shut down his chain saw, seated himself comfortably on a log and lit a cigarette.

"How much do they pay you for walking the trail?" he asked politely. By "they" was meant the federal government. He had noted other strangers on the trail and had come to believe that walking was a new activity of mysterious Washington, D.C. Maybe he could get on. It might be easier than wrestling trees.

Unfortunately, walking as an end in itself results in no saleable product. People who make money from walking are those who make it unnecessary. In fact, the greatest fortunes in history have gone to the Fords, the Firestones, the Rockefellers and the others who have exploited the feeling that the proper way to travel is on one's backside. Only pennies have been made in the other direction.

I was sorry that my answer disappointed the post-splitter. That he didn't believe me was plain. There was a small flash of resentment in his goodbye. I suppose he is at his trade yet, now and again glancing up the footpath in hope of meeting the employer of those who walk the trails. He is young, and the wait will probably be lengthy.

The conviction that the hiker is paid in hard coin for what he wants to do is not uncommon. It owes much to the specious idea that whatever is worth doing should be well worth one's while. Few Americans accept the notion that walking may be a pleasure, much less a hobby. The effort involved is much too strenuous and resists such substitutes as words, slogans, and machinery. It has been forgotten that the human being's natural method of locomotion is shank's mare.

Like the man who followed Muir's route, in time I, too, concocted a story that would please. If he could pass for a plant collector. I could be a tester of trail footgear. So it is that I became an independent, unpaid party of one to judge the qualities, good or bad, of hiking boots. And I still am. None of six pairs of boots have suited me and the vital testing continues apace.

It has been a very satisfactory answer.

E. B. White

A Walk to Fred's Grave

The late E. B. White, essayist and author of Charlotte's Web, *had a very special 13-year-old dachshund, Fred, who died in 1948. In a 1956 essay, titled "Bedfellows," White said that Fred "was intensely loyal to himself, as every strong individualist must be. He held unshakable convictions like Harry Truman."*

In June 1962 E. B. White reminisced about a walk the previous autumn to Fred's grave. This piece is from the Essays of E. B. White *(1977).*

*   *   *

One day last fall I wandered down through the orchard and into the woods to pay a call at Fred's grave. The trees were bare; wild apples hung shamelessly from the grapevine that long ago took over the tree. The old dump, which is no longer used and which goes out of sight during the leafy months, lay exposed and candid—rusted pots and tin cans and sundries. The briers had lost some of their effectiveness, the air was good, and the little dingle, usually so mean and inconsiderable, seemed to have acquired stature. Fred's headstone, ordinarily in collapse, was bolt upright, and I wondered whether he had quieted down at last. I felt uneasy suddenly, as the quick do sometimes feel when in the presence of the dead, and my uneasiness went to my bladder. Instead of laying a wreath, I watered an alder and came away.

This grave is the only grave I visit with regularity—in fact, it is the only grave I visit at all. I have relatives lying in cemeteries here and there around the country, but I do not feel any urge to return to them, and it strikes me as odd that I should return to the place where an old dog lies in a shabby bit of woodland next to a private dump. Besides being an easy trip (one for which I need make no preparation) it is a natural journey—I really go down there to see what's doing. (Fred himself used to scout the place every day when he was alive.) I do not experience grief when I am down there, nor do I pay tribute to the dead. I feel a sort of overall sadness that has nothing to do with the grave or its occupant. Often I feel extremely well in that rough cemetery, and sometimes flush a partridge. But I feel sadness at All Last Things, too, which is probably a purely selfish, or turned-in, emotion-sorrow not at my dog's death but at my own, which hasn't even occurred yet but which saddens me just to think about in such pleasant surroundings.

Joe Malone

Roaming the Streets of Henry Miller, Then and Now

Anaïs Nin said that Henry Miller filled "my head with streets, the names of streets." And no wonder. Miller (1891–1980) was a walker, a chronicler of alleys and avenues, of uptown and downtown. In Black Spring *he said of Brooklyn, "In my dreams I come back to the 14th Ward as a paranoic returns to his obsessions."*

Joe Malone's 1981 article, "Roaming The Streets of Henry Miller, Then and Now" takes readers on a winter walk to thirty Miller locations in Brooklyn, Queens, and Manhattan, as described in Tropic of Capricorn *[TC],* Black Spring *[BS], and the trilogy of the* Rosy Crucifixion: Sexus *[S],* Plexus *[P], and* Nexus *[N]. (Numbers at beginnings of paragraphs refer to the numbered locations.)*

* * *

1. "Day comes when you stand on the Brooklyn Bridge looking down . . . on a spot of foam or a little lake of gasoline or a broken splinter or an empty scow; the world goes by upside down with pain and light . . . Passes through you crazy words from the ancient world, the chinks of the saloon door . . . the gaunt tree against the tin factory . . . One walks the street . . . with the bridge against the sky like a harp." [BS 21f]

Brooklyn Bridge, whose cats-cradled walkway falls like a gangplank tumbling runners and bikers and strollers from Manhattan into the old citadel of Brooklyn. Braids of ancient wire run in loops and strands over the iron-mesh roadway, conjuring the days when the trolleys ran. The oily river runs beneath, and the container ships lean like plastic models against their docks near Buttermilk Channel. Down on the ground, graffiti layer the projects and factories with runes, and the Tree-That-Grows-In-Brooklyn smashes through the tarmac of a playground toward the sky.

2. "I saw a street called Myrtle Avenue, which runs from Borough Hall to Fresh Pond Road . . ."

Used to be, you could climb upstairs above the pawnshops and bars at the very hub of downtown Brooklyn, at Borough Hall and Jay St., and ride the rickety Myrtle Avenue el flush with the rooftops out to Fresh Pond Road and beyond, all the way to the cemeterial quiet of Queens at Metropolitan Avenue. But nowadays you must follow Myrtle Avenue earth-bound from Jay St. under the naked sky until Lewis Ave., where the sawed stump of the old el thenceforth blocks out the sun all the way to Wyckoff Ave. and the Brooklyn-Queens frontier.

2. ". . . Dear reader, you must see Myrtle Avenue before you die, if only to realize how far into the future Dante saw. You must believe me . . . it is not a street of sorrow . . . but of sheer emptiness." [TC 298]

On the lonesome stretch from Lewis Ave. to Broadway there is a junk-strewn lot; also a few ancient tenements, most of them sealed with tin sheeting. However the landscape is primarily faceless low-slung brown buildings

FOR SALE OR LEASE, 25000 SQ FT, SPRINKLER

and people are few and silent. But things change for the better at the intersection with Broadway, where people are rushing around in the cold. Colored streamers dangle from the el to a Chemical Bank; there's a bakery with wedding cakes in one window and cuchifritos in the other; girlie mags in English and Spanish at the newspaper kiosk; Hector's Spanish-American barbershop with Christmas tinsel draped over the potted plants.

3. "Before, Broadway had stuck out like an eye-sore, all ugliness and confusion; now it fell back into its proper place, an integral part of the world, neither good nor bad, neither ugly nor beautiful: *it simply belonged.* [S 308f]

At Brunswick Avenue, in a lull of the cross-traffic, you hear a melodious whine which sounds impossibly like a muezzin calling prayers from a mosque. ("I don't think I caught the words at all, but just the music . . . a kind of sweet, woody music which came through the Algerian wine and the radishes and the black olives" [BS 225].) Wonderously, the droning music is exactly that—an amplified recording of a muezzin's chant broadcast from the muslim community of Ansaru Allah a few blocks off at Suydam St.: a tract of old brownstones refurbished in Islamic style; in fair weather even including an outdoor cafe appointed with indoor couches.

4. "We used to promenade along Brunswick Avenue of a Sunday after-noon, hoping to catch a glimpse of the girls we were in love with. It was

like an Easter Parade every Sunday—from the Little White Church to the reservoir near Cypress Hills cemetery . . ."

There's a lower Bushwick Avenue and an upper Bushwick Avenue, the dividing line being just the bunny-hop of frantic traffic swinging out of Eastern Parkway onto the Interboro for the voyage to Queens beyond the cemeteries. Upper Bushwick Avenue has been well renamed Highland Boulevard, because the backyards of the houses on its western side are on a cliff surveying East New York and Carnarsie and beyond to the Rockaways ("when I say that I was at Far Rockaway I mean that I was standing at the end of the earth" [TC 210]). At the end of Highland Boulevard the Ridgewood Reservoir gleams as always. But it's lower Bushwick Avenue where downhome Brooklyn hobbles or strides on as ever. And though the Little White Church still stands venerable at the corner of Himrod St. under the pastorage of the Rev. Van Der Beek, yet nowadays Easter Parades on Bushwick are Blacker than White. (If only for an emblem of how things ethnic-confessional have shifted, gaze on two churches facing each other over the intersection at Weirfield St.: the small and rundown-looking Prince of Peace Lutheran Church on one side, the jumbo and flamboyant Church of God and Prophecy on the other.)

4. ". . . Midway one passed the lugubrious . . . church of St. Francois de Sales, situated a block or two away from Trommers' beer garden. I speak of a period before the first war, the period when in France men like Picasso, Derain, Matisse, Vlaminck and others were just becoming known. It was still the "end of the century." Life was easy, though we weren't aware of it. The only thought in our head was girls." [P 402]

St. Francois de Sales lives on in name only, in the street sign for De Sales Place, the Trommers' beer garden is now a Burger King on the corner of Conway St. (If you want to frolic in the nearest bastion of contemporary German-American prosperity and Gemutlichkeit, you must turn off Bushwick eastward onto Cooper Street, roam three miles beyond Mutt-and-Jeff's old house at number 316—now a bodega—and finally emerge through a white hole into the solid quiet of Glendale—the home of Archie Bunker as one legend has it—and finally enter an establishment called Zum Stammtish squatting jolly on the corner of Myrtle Avenue.)

5. "A little place called Glendale . . . After all the years which had passed, the sleepy little hamlet still wore a quaint air to me . . . The tavern with its stables, where friends and relatives used to gather of a Summer's evening . . . I could recall running from table to table as a tiny tot, sipping the dregs from the beer mugs, or collecting pennies and dimes from the tipsy revellers. Even the maudlin German songs, which they sang with iron lungs, rang in my ear." [P 74]

(But if prosperity and bürgerlich tranquility are not required, turn off Cooper St. onto Wyckoff Avenue before you reach the white hole at the Queens frontier. Roam down Wyckoff a few blocks to Stephen St., and enter there a sleepy little bar whose sparse White customers are watched by a venerable German shepherd dozing at the windows. Despite the improbable ethnic environs without, within you find a jukebox replete with Teutonic music, loud and unambiguous. Far out of context in space and time, but a genuine afterimage of Trommers for all that.)

6. "Fuchs and Kunz . . . who could be seen drinking every night in Laubscher's Beer Garden near the Fresh Pond Road . . . They talked a bird and skin language over their stinking pots of beer. Ridgewood was their Mecca." [S 80f]

On Myrtle Avenue, east of Zum Stammtisch, the quiet of Queens cemeteries began. But westward, looping back towards Brooklyn, Glendale merges into Ridgewood like Yin into Yang. The emblem of Fresh Pond Road seems no longer to be such as Laubscher's, but perhaps the Glenwood Bowling Alleys and Cocktail Lounge

FREE PARKING IN REAR

German still sounds on the streets, but so do Greek, Italian, Korean. The Kiwanis folk gather on Tuesdays in the Senwood Tavern on Seneca Avenue, not quite in the shadows of the western spur of the old Myrtle Avenue el. You can stand on the el platform and gaze up the back alleys of Seneca Ave. westward all the way to Murray Hill in Manhattan (". . . this book which I used to write every day on my way from Delancey Street to Murray Hill" [TC 50])—just gaze through the tangle of clothesline off the fire-escapes to where the Empire State Building flutes up beyond the gas tanks squatting like bongos on the edge of the English Kills.

7. "Myrtle Avenue was the boundary line . . . The shops were full of nostalgic wares from childhood. I loved . . . the religious shops, the junk shops, the delicatessen stores, the stationery stores . . . The tongues employed had a musical quality, even when it was nothing but an exchange of oaths." [P 388]

On Myrtle Avenue rushing towards the Brooklyn boundary line at Wyckoff Ave., crowds of businesses spring up from door to door under the overarching holiday lights: McDonalds, an OTB parlor, a wig shop, Woolworths and Carvel's, a barbershop, an Army & Navy store, a Chinese restaurant. Dusky faces begin to mingle with the pink and pale of the other shoppers: Spanish vies with English, and even Haitian Creole begins to edge ahead of German. Then the western spur of the elevated line sweeps over

Myrtle again, and you crash into a totally different world, in Brooklyn. The last emblem of the world just gone is in name only, the Ridgewood Clambar (aka Tony's Fish Store) at Gates Ave. Enormous pipes litter the street for a new water main, and ancient trolley tracks seep up through the pavement. There is a live poultry market, a check cashing service, an engine steaming business, a garment factory, an office of the *Partido de Liberación Dominicana*. Social clubs and gas stations abound. And suddenly, near Stockholm St., an old tenement looms alone, its second story ringed with giant stuffed animals like Caryatids on a Greek temple, a place called "Mr. Pushcart's."

8. "It was exactly five minutes past seven, at the corner of Broadway and Kosciusko Street, when Dostoyevski first flashed across my horizon. Two men and a woman were dressing a shop window. From the middle of the upper legs down the mannikins were all wire. Empty shoe boxes lay banked against the window like last year's snow". [BS 23]

Today, at Broadway and Kosciusko Street, a McDonald's reigns supreme.

9. "Always within striking distance were the Navy Yard, fantastic Wallabout Market, the sugar refineries, the big bridges, roller mills, grain elevators, foundries, paint factories, tombstone yards, livery stables, glaziers, saddlers, grill works, canneries, fish markets, slaughterhouses, tin factories—a vast conglomeration of workaday horrors over which hung a pall of smoke impregnated with the stench of burning chemicals, rotting flesh, and seared metals . . . on such walks I thought also of the Middle Ages, and of Breughel the Elder, and Hieronymus Bosch, or of Petronius Arbiter, Lorenzo the Magnificent, Fra Lippo Lippi—to say nothing of the Seven Dwarfs, Swiss Family Robinson, and Sinbad the Sailor." [P 388f]

The old Navy Yard, hard by Willy Sutton's old neighborhood, is now apportioned out to manufacturers of glass and furniture and boxes

FOR INDUSTRY IN THE AMERICAN TRADITION.

Weeds push through its old barbed-wired walls along Flushing Avenue, where trolley tracks still peer up from beneath the tar. Stray dogs sniff in a lot which used to be the site of Battleship Sam's marine clothiers, but at the curb a guy is doing business in charcoal-broiled shish kebab, and Charles Bar is packed with workers at the corner of Adelphi St. The trestle of the Brooklyn-Queens Expressway hangs with black icicles like the spaceship in Alien, and beyond, Wallabout Market lives on linguistically as Wallabout Street. Exhaust pipes adorn a factory like sausages, and inexplicably a strong odor of catsup pervades the air near a junk-strewn lot with an airplane tire at its hub. Across the street is a whitewashed wall studded with air vents configured like hieroglyphs, and the black graffiti at the wall's base glare like Chinese grass writing. Fresh lumber stacked in a shed contrasts with the rotten beams of a devastated tenement, the different wall-paperings of its wrecked apartments showing through like patches of fabric sample.

10. "After a time I am walking the bluff at Columbia Heights . . . Below the bluff lay a street full of warehouses. The terraces of the wealthy homes were like overhanging gardens ending abruptly some twenty or thirty feet above this dismal street with its dead windows and grim archways leading to the wharves . . . Not a soul about. The passageways tunneled through the warehouses gave fascinating glimpses of the river life—barges lying lifeless, tugs gliding by like smoking ghosts, the skyscrapers silhouetted against the New York shore, huge iron stanchions with cabled hawsers slung around them, piles of bricks and lumber, sacks of coffee. The most poignant sight was the sky itself. Swept clear of clouds and studded with fistfuls of stars, it gleamed like the breastplate of the high priests of old." [S 626-8]

Nowadays the bluff is ringed by the Brooklyn-Queens Expressway and topped by that celebrated patio to Brooklyn Heights called the Promenade. Far beneath, at the docks beyond Columbia Street—the turf of "On The Waterfront" not too long ago—lie hundreds of red and blue and orange shipping containers strewn about like animal-cracker boxes. Far above, a police helicopter glides across the river by the new glassy office towers above the financial district. Behind, parallel to the slate sidewalks and wrought-iron copens of the brownstones, two kids skate down Hicks Street. One veers onto Joralemon St., and speeds down the lane of pastel townhouses and on beneath the silhouetted Brooklyn-Queens Expressway to the world of the docks. The other continues down Hicks to the world of Atlantic Avenue. There, a gypsy cab with an I-LOVE-NY sticker is parked at the curb, and a minute later the cabby emerges from Montero's Bar with a drunk fare in tow.

11. "A short walk in any direction brought me to the most diverse districts: to the fantastic area beneath the fretwork of the Brooklyn Bridge; to the sites of the old ferries where Arabs, Turks, Syrians, Greeks, and other people of the Levant had flocked . . . As a boy I had often come here to visit my aunt who lived over a stable attached to one of the more hideous old mansions. A short distance away, on Sackett Street, had once lived my old friend Al Burger, whose father was captain of a tugboat." [P 12]

On Atlantic Avenue, in a bar next to Sahadi's Middle Eastern emporium, a Puerto Rican in a cowboy hat watches *General Hospital* on TV. At the other end of the bar a Syrian-American in a turtleneck sweater reads *People* magazine and listens to Stacy Lattislaw on the jukebox. Half a mile south, on Sackett Street, people are milling in the OTB parlor. Looping back to Atlantic Avenue is the open trench terminating the Brooklyn-Queens Expressway, and along the upper windows of a factory loft overlooking it are still painted in red, white and blue the words:

WELCOME HOME 52 WE LOVE YOU.

12. "Out of the womb of night rises the old Brooklyn Bridge, a torpid dream wriggling in spume and moon-fire. A drone and sizzle scraping the frets. A glister of chrysoprase, a flare of naptha. The night is cold and men are walking in lock-step." [BS 239]

Under the boards of the walkway the traffic sparks and drones like bumper scooters at Coney Island. The Telephone Building shoots up from the twinkling dark near Chinatown. (Hit its bell and win a cigar.)

13. "We sit in a cellar on Allen Street, that dreariest of all streets, where the elevated trains thunder overhead. An Arabian friend . . . ran the restaurant." [P 218]

Dreariest of all streets indeed, the bleak mile of shuttered buildings from Chinatown up to the quantum leap over Houston St. into First Avenue and the East Village. Dreariest of streets, but life still smoulders on the benches along the pathway at the divider where once the el trains thundered above. To find a restaurant of any sort on Allen Street seems hopeless, let alone an Arabian one. But then, just before Rivington St., there is a mirage. On the second story of an ancient building, over a tie factory, a bright crimson sign emblazoned with a black eagle announces the Ali Pasha Albanian Restaurant. Walk through the naked entranceway with the door wired open, pass the tenement mailboxes, climb the stone stairs, and there it is, impossibly out of context: a shining crimson door with a golden peephole.

14. "There are . . . nights in New York when the sky is pure azure, when the buildings are immediate and palpable, not only in their substance but in their essence. That dirty streaked light which reveals only the ugliness of factories and sordid tenements disappears very often with sunset, the dust settles down, the contours of the buildings become more sharply defined, like the lineaments of an ogre in a calcium spotlight. Pigeons appear in the sky, wheeling above the rooftops. A cupola bobs up, sometimes out of a Turkish bath . . ."

Over Houston St. into First Avenue and the East Village, with luck the air being azure, and immediately there's the first of several Turkish baths, albeit without cupola, The Club by name, flush up against the Ortiz Funeral Home. Now well past the drears of Allen Street, things begin to tingle strangely in the next few blocks. As a sentry into these precincts stands a surreal electrical dummy on the sidewalk in front of Brickman's Paints and Wallpaper, eternally splashing the air with his roller. And then a flock of pigeons wheels through the bare girders high above the McDonald's near 6th St., darting between the limp folds of the Golden-Arch flag drooping down.

14. ". . . There is always the stately simplicity of St. Marks-on-the-Bouwerie, the great foreign square abutting Avenue A, the low Dutch buildings above which the ruddy gas tanks loom . . . the triangles which bear the stamp of old landmarks . . ."

At the very hub of this galaxy is the New St. Marks Baths, on St. Marks Place, do-si-do to McSorley's Ale House around the corner. Again no cupola, but there is a triangle landmarking the premises as the last New York home of James Fenimore Cooper. And a triangle of a different sort, a stretch of cobbled pavement strewn with beer cans and pigeons, lies before the ancient fire-scarred dignity of St. Marks-on-the-Bowery at Second Avenue and 10th St., a little triangular plaza whose centerpiece is a World War II monument papered over with the notices to

LEAVE YOUR BODY TO LMO—ARE YOU READY TO ADVANCE YOURSELF?—YES!

Then 10th St. eastward: past another Turkish bath with towels piled high in its steaming windows across from the San Miguel botanica; past Tomkins Square, still foreign and still abutting Avenue A; past high if not low Dutch buildings, like that painted red and yellow at 307 with vines rambling up to the top of its cornice stones—and on towards the river: though the gas tanks are long gone, in their place now impend the science fiction battlements of the Con Ed plant off Avenue D.

14. ". . . the waterfront with the Brooklyn shore so close that one can almost recognize the people walking on the other side." [S 534f]

Nobody can walk on the Brooklyn shore anymore. Piers and machines abound, and factories jut out over the water. And if you gaze downstream beneath the Williamsburg Bridge, you can just make out a pair of burned out wharves on the water-side of a nameless New York City building of red brick which has replaced the old ferry house at the foot of Brooklyn's Broadway.

15. "Surrounding the entrance to the ferry house there were then three saloons which of a Saturday noon were filled with men who had stopped off for a little bite at the free lunch counter and a schooner of beer. I can see the old man . . . his arm resting on the bar, his straw hat tipped on the

back of his head, his left hand raised to down the foaming suds . . . I
remember the way he would dip his hand into the big glass bowl on the
free lunch counter and hand me a few pretzels . . . And perhaps as I ran
out of the saloon . . . a string of cyclists would pass close to the curb, holding
to the little strip of asphalt which had been laid down expressly for them."
[TC 163]

At the foot of Broadway in Brooklyn, the ferry house is gone and so
are the saloons. A tangle of railway tracks threads through the streets and
factory lots. Gulls wing around the smokestacks. A junk truck with a Playboy
sticker pulls into a wrecker's yard. But a few blocks up Broadway, just where
the pedestrian walkway slumps down from the Williamsburg Bridge,
Peter Luger's Bar and Restaurant still thrives after a hundred years. The
lunch is by no means free, but most worthy for all that, served by a crowd
of German waiters. A Latin bartender supervises the taps in the front
room bar where you can drink a good beer and gaze out on the origins
of Driggs Avenue ("I'm from Driggs Avenue—the 14th Ward." [P 31])
An occasional cyclist pedals up the bridge walkway though signs warn
this is illegal. Any strips of asphalt laid down for bikes are gone with the
years.

16. "Riding now along the gravel path under the archway of trees that
runs from Prospect Park to Coney Island, my rhythm one with the machine
. . . only the sensation of rushing through space . . . the landscape to either
side falling away like the leaves of a calendar . . . It was at a place called
Bedford Rest . . . that I experienced the most delicious moments. This spot
. . . was where all the cyclists halted to take a brief rest . . . Here, under
arbors and trellises with a fountain playing in the center of the clearance,
we lounged about." [P 50, 128]

The name of that wonderful trail is Ocean Parkway. There are no longer
arbors or trellises or fountains at the halfway mark, just a green edge of
Washington Cemetery near Avenue K. But no matter; the bicycle path along
Ocean Parkway is one of the few glorious constants in all of Brooklyn. The
gravel path has long since given way to pavement—a pavement moreover
largely free of potholes, and even of debris.

17. "Coney Island on a wintry day. Alone, of course . . . Desolate is
hardly the word for it . . . the bleak, crazy, tumbling edifices, the snarling
piles and planks, the still, empty Ferris Wheel, the noiseless roller coasters,
rusting under a feeble sun . . . There is a shooting gallery open a few doors
away. Not a customer in sight: the owner is shooting at the clay pigeons
himself . . . A drunken sailor comes lurching along . . . I go down to the
beach and watch the sea gulls. I'm looking at the sea gulls and thinking
about Russia. A picture of Tolstoy seated at a bench mending shoes obsesses

me . . . Driftwood lying all about. Fantastic forms . . . I board the train to go home." [P 59f]

Nathan's is open as always, of course; a couple of guys drinking beer from paper cups, a down-and-out old lady crouching by the door with a sign advertising

SKETCHES $1.

Outside, down Stillwell Avenue, wind-swept, piles of dirty snow. Bag folk huddling under the empty boardwalk. The tower of Astroland rises silent like the dead Martian engines at the end of "War of the Worlds." Back on Surf Avenue, thumping music and strobe lights flash from within the Bumping Disco, but the murky glass of its windows makes it impossible to see if anybody is actually riding. Across the street in the Carousel, the owner stands alone amongst his horses, going round and round and round. (And just beyond Coney Island, in Brighton Beach, a Russian copy of *War and Peace* lies in the window of the Black Sea bookstore. Down the block a guy is eating shashlik to the tune of neat vodka at the Tashkent Bar. It starts to snow.)

18. "I lived then, as a boy, close to the boundary line between the north and the south side. The actual boundary was Grand Street . . . but this street meant nothing to me . . . No, North Second Street was the mystery street, the frontier between two worlds. I was living . . . between two boundaries, the one real, the other imaginary—as I have lived all my life . . ."

Nowadays the number streets jump from North First to North Third, Grand Street, real or imagined, continues to be a boundary line. It scoops out the northern tip of Brooklyn like a ball of white ice cream on top of a rich brown sugar cone.

18. ". . . The authorities decided to change the name of North Second Street to Metropolitan Avenue. This highway . . . had been the road to the cemeteries." [TC 215f]

Metropolitan Avenue ultimately crosses Grand Street and passes into Queens out where Brooklyn thins. After that, there's the quiet of the cemeteries. But far before that, amidst the chaos of gas stations and lumberyards, almost in the shadows of the Brooklyn-Queens Expressway, on a wedge of pavement in front of a Lithuanian church, there's a little stone memorial to a Sister Nicodema, its freshly cut flowers stiff in the snow.

19. "Maujer, Conselyea, Humboldt . . . Humboldt particularly. These streets belonged to a neighborhood which was not far removed from our

neighborhood but which was different, more glamorous, more mysterious . . ."

Grand Street cleaves Humboldt into a Latino south of housing projects and live poultry markets and playgrounds, and an Italian-Slavic north of bread shops and narrow two-family houses and bars.

19. ". . . Humboldt Street . . . itself made a most lasting impression on me; why I have not the faintest idea. It remains in my memory as the most mysterious and most promising street that I have ever seen." [TC 152f]

Humboldt Street rises up the slope of the land, all but lost under the broken pavement, from low-lying Broadway on the fringe of Bed-Stuy to the windy top of Brooklyn on the bluff over Newtown Creek in Greenpoint. The TV antennas of the little houses in the north are on eye level with the water towers crowning the huge projects to the south. North and south, there's life behind the walls, and sun and soot pervade both, indiscriminately.

20. "The sight of the gas tanks provoked a sentimental twinge. Now and then a church right out of Russia. The street names became more and more familiar. 'Would you mind stopping in front of 181 Devoe Street?' I asked. 'Sure, why not? Know someone there?' 'Used to. My first sweetheart . . .' "

One old parkie shoveling snow along the entire length of Driggs Avenue through McCarren Park, and the Russian Orthodox Church of the Transfiguration looming onion-domed under its Greek cross towers at the park's southern corner. When the parkie reaches it the setting sun is glowing on its dome, and if you climb up by the cross you can also see the glow on the gas tanks a mile off in the wastelands by the English Kills. Devoe Street lies between.

20. ". . . At 181 I got out, took my hat off (as if visiting a grave) and approached the railing in front of the grass plot. I looked up at the parlor windows; the shades were down as always." [N 251f]

Most of the grass plots on Devoe Street have been paved over. Shades have largely given way to Venetian blinds, and there are Italian-American Civil Rights League stickers in many of the windows. In one areaway a shrine to St. Francis is draped in snow and holly. At the western corner of the block elderly men sit under the Christmas balls in a bar on Graham Avenue across from Frozen Fantasees ice cream shop. In another bar around the eastern corner, on Humboldt Street, a group of beautiful young women are playing pool to the tune of a pitcher of beer.

21. "Perhaps . . . when I got to Humboldt Street and looked upon the new world with astonishment . . . the street itself became the reward.

I remember that it was very wide and that there were high stoops . . . There was snow on the ground but the sun was out strong and I recall vividly how about the bottoms of the ash barrels which had been frozen into the ice there was then a little pool of water left by the melting snow. On the bannisters of the high stoops the mounds of snow were now beginning to slide, to disintegrate, leaving dark patches on the brownstone." [TC 153]

There are no stoops anymore on Humboldt Street south of Grand and those to the north are short and flat against the run-on buildings, and if ever they were brownstone now they're mostly glazed over with stark hues of ceramic paint. The narrow houses sport emblematic eagles on the doors or statues of saints in the areaways, and some window shades have gingerbread men hanging from their tassels. South of the boundary line, just below Grand Street, the windows of the projects are stuffed with potted plants, and in a little plot called "Humboldt Gardens" the blue and yellow bricks of a strolling lane peek up through the snow. Far to the north, life on Humboldt Street ends at a liquor store like a miniature Flatiron Building. Beyond that, it's lifeless warehouses towards Newtown Creek—and out the channel into the East River and across the waters to midtown Manhattan.

22. "I . . . walked instinctively towards the French-Italian restaurant . . . near Third Avenue. It was cool and dark in the back of the grocery store where they served the food. At lunch time there never were many customers. Soon there was only myself and a big sprawling Irish girl who had already made herself quite drunk." [S 509]

A woman, not necessarily Irish, staggers out of Sarge's Restaurant and Delicatessen at Third and 36th, and wheels up the block into the Bagel Nosh at 38th St. After a few minutes she's back on the street towards the Deli Inn at 39th. What she is after is clear to no one, least of all herself. But it is clear that nowadays delicatessens are where the grocery and restaurant businesses cross-pollinate in New York.

23. "It's only a stretch of a few blocks, from Times Square to Fiftieth Street, and when one says Broadway that's all that's really meant and it's really nothing, just a chicken run and a lousy one at that . . . this is the Gay White Way, the top of the world with no roof above . . . The absolute impersonality of it . . . makes you . . . become automatically the personification of the whole human race . . . crackling with a thousand different human tongues, cursing, applauding, whistling, crooning, soliloquizing, orating, gesticulating, urinating, fecundating, wheedling, cajoling, whimpering, bartering, pimping, caterwauling." [TC 97f]

Swish of the buttock in the lamé jeans, flash of the male earring, glare of the strobe light in the hungry eye. "Sportin' tonight?" Purr of the moped, whir of the skate, cluck of the tourist's tongue. *"Gucke mal, Uschi, so'n toller Rollschuh-Oinker!"* Dolly dangling from the Cadillac's visor, here-comes-the-bride on the horn. *"Qué cosa, mariposa!"* Piss in the pants at curb level, ether wafting from the ragged mouth—while up on an upturned trashcan Cousin Cards flashes his game of sting. "Check it out!"

24. "At Forty-Second Street Mona drives into the subway to emerge in a few minutes at Sheridan Square. Here her course becomes truly erratic . . . The Village is a network of labyrinths modelled upon the corrugated reveries of the early Dutch settlers . . . There are alleys, lanes, cellars, and garrets, squares, triangles, courts, everything anomalous, incongruous and bewildering . . . Certain doll's houses, squeezed between somber tenements and morbid factories, have been dozing in a vacuum of time . . . The dreamy, somnolent past exudes from the facades . . . The present announced itself in the strident cries of the street urchins, in the muffled roar of traffic . . . The Americans who have muscled in are off center, whether they be bankers, politicians, magistrates, Bohemians, or genuine artists." [P 129f]

The present also announces itself in signs, whether pasted or painted or welded or tacked. "Erotic Bakery" (VISA ACCEPTED); EAT FOR YOUR HEALTH; "Ramrod"; RENT STRIKE JAN '81; "Duff's Homemade Pasta"; SOLID BRASS FRAMES; "Kiss my cookies"; ARTISTS' MATERIALS & DRAFTING SUPPLIES; "All American Boy Clothiers"; SALUMERIA E LATTICINI; "Bagel And." And "Lion's Head," without a doubt. And some graffiti.

25. "At Fifth Avenue I hopped a bus going north and clambered up to the top deck. Free again! I inhaled a few deep draughts of ozone. As we came alongside Central Park I took a good look at the fading mansions . . . Many of them I knew from having entered through the servants' or trades-men's door." [P 380]

Nowadays Fifth Avenue is one-way, going south, and the double-deckers are long gone. Also mansions alongside Central Park have just about totally faded—though not servants' or tradesmen's doors. (But on the other hand there are now coachwomen alongside coachmen to take you on a horse-and-buggy ride through the Park. And vendors of exotic snacks.)

26. "From Times Square to Fiftieth Street all that St. Thomas Aquinas forgot to include in his *magnum opus* is here included, which is to say, among other things, hamburger sandwiches, collar buttons, poodle dogs, slot machines, gray bowlers, typewriter ribbons, orange sticks, free toilets, sanitary napkins, mint jujubes, billiard balls, chopped onions, wrinkled doil-ies, manholes, chewing gum, sidecars and sourballs, cellophane, cord tires, magnetos, horse liniment, cough drops, feenamint." [TC 98f]

Burger King whoppers, I-LOVE-NY buttons, German shepherds, video games, monogrammed T-shirts, computer print-outs, snowcones, pay toilets, panty-liners, piña colada, pingpong balls, falafel, Ticketron stubs, potholes, sugarless mints, Heinekens and enchilada dip, plastic wrap, power steering, tape decks, Tiger Balm, Listerine, No-Doze.

27. "Passing down Fifth Avenue, cutting through the shoppers and drifters like a wire eel, my contempt and loathing for all that met my eye almost suffocated me. Pray God, I would not have long to endure the sight of . . . these decrepit New World building . . . these parks dotted with pigeons and derelicts. From the street of the tailor shop on down to the Bowery (the course of my ancient walk) I lived again the days of my apprenticeship, and they were like a thousand years . . . of alienation. Approaching Cooper Union, ever the low-water mark of my sagging spirits, passages of those books I once wrote in my head came back . . . They would always be flapping there . . . flapping from the cornices of those dingy . . . shanties, those slat-faced saloons, those foul rescue and shelter places where the bleary-eyed codfish-faced bums hung about like lazy flies . . . Yet it was here that John Cowper Powys had lectured, had sent forth into the soot-laden, stench-filled airs his tidings of the eternal world of the spirit." [N 344]

Down Fifth Avenue and through Madison Square, where guys are lounging against the modernistic sculptures mumbling "smoke? smoke? smoke? . . ."; and further down Fifth Avenue through Union Square where angry people are milling and posters announce that JOHN LENNON'S MURDER WAS A POLITICAL ASSASSINATION; down Fourth Avenue to Cooper Union, where somebody had crowned the statue of venerable Peter Cooper with an old snow tire and painted the words US $TEAL. Two young bums stumble along the Bowery, and it's impossible to tell if they're wearing headbands or bandages. But in the glassed-in terrace of Phoebe's at East 4th Street fashionable women are sipping Pernod, and a guy bikes past with a poodle on his shoulder. And so on down the Bowery, all the way, everything being totally beyond prediction.

28. "It was to the East Side I always came when I wanted to be stirred to the roots . . . Everything was familiar in a way beyond all knowing. It was almost as if I had known the world of the ghetto in a previous incarnation . . . Everything burgeoned and gleamed, just as in the murky canvases of Rembrandt . . . It was the world of my childhood wherein common everyday objects acquired a sacred character. These poor despised aliens were living with the discarded objects of a world which had moved on . . . Their bread was still a good bread which one could eat without butter or jam. Their kerosene lamps gave their rooms a holy glow . . . Many of these unexpected scenes we came upon in the dead of night were like illustrated pages from the Old Testament." [P 29]

A Chinese funeral cortege pulls up in front of St. Theresa's Church on Rutgers Street, the flower car carrying a large portrait of the deceased mounted on a floral piece. A sign on the church tells about masses in Spanish as well as Chinese, and just across the street is a bright multiracial mural called WALL OF RESPECT FOR WOMEN. At the corner of East Broadway a Hassidic family loaded down with groceries blithely cross the street against the bitter wind.

29. "At the Brooklyn Bridge I stand as usual waiting for the trolley to swing around . . . From the tops of the skyscrapers plumes of smoke soft as Cleopatra's feathers . . . The bridge sways over the gasoline tanks below . . . As I take my seat I see a man I know standing on the rear platform . . . His straw hat is just on a level with Chambers Street; it rests like a sliced egg on the green spinach of the bay." [BS 169]

Back on the old plank pathway over the oily waters to the citadel of Brooklyn. Towards the Bay, the orange masts of the old schooners at South Street appear to float out of the sky. Straight ahead in Brooklyn itself, the Watchtower building shines astoundingly like a yellow pleasure palace, and little cars on the steeplechase of the Brooklyn-Queens Expressway are dashing everywhere and nowhere at once.

30. "Dreary, weary, flea-bitten Myrtle Avenue striped down the middle with a rusty Elevated line. Through the ties and the iron girders the sun was pouring shafts of golden light." [N 371]

Alfred Kazin

A Walker in the City

The beauty of walking is often flavored by nostalgia. Writer Alfred Kazin, in A Walker In The City *(1951), said of his native section of Brooklyn that, "Brownsville is that road which every other road in my life has had to cross." He was the child of immigrant Jewish parents in "New York's rawest, remotest, cheapest ghetto."*

* * *

Ahead of me now the black web of the Fulton Street El. On the other side of the BANCA COMMERCIALE, two long even pavements still raw with sunlight at seven o'clock of a summer evening take me straight through the German and Irish "American" neighborhoods. I could never decide whether it was all those brownstones and blue and gray frame houses or the sight of the library serenely waiting for me that made up the greatest pleasure of that early evening walk. As soon as I got out from under the darkness of the El on Fulton Street, I was catapulted into tranquility.

Everything ahead of me now was of a different order—wide, clean, still, every block lined with trees. I sniffed hungrily at the patches of garden earth behind the black iron spikes and at the wooden shutters hot in the sun—there where even the names of the streets, Macdougal, Hull, Somers, made me humble with admiration. The long quiet avenues rustled comfortably in the sun; above the brownstone stoops all the yellow striped awnings were unfurled. Every image I had of peace, of quiet shaded streets in some old small-town America I had seen dreaming over the ads in the *Saturday Evening Post*, now came back to me as that proud procession of awnings along the brownstones. I can never remember *walking* those last few blocks to the library; I seemed to float along the canvas tops. Here were the truly American streets; here was where they lived. To get that near to brownstones, to see how private everything looked in that world of cool black painted floors and green walls where on each windowsill the first shoots of Dutch bulbs rose out of the pebbles like green and white flags, seemed to me the greatest privilege I had ever had. A breath of long-stored memory blew out at me from the veranda of Oyster Bay. Even when I visited an

Irish girl from my high school class who lived in one of those brownstones, and was amazed to see that the rooms were as small as ours, that a Tammany court attendant's family could be as poor as we were, that behind the solid "American" front of fringed shawls, Yankee rocking chairs, and oval da-guerrotypes on the walls they kept warm in winter over an oil stove—even then, I could think of those brownstone streets only as my great entrance into America, a half-hour nearer to "New York."

I had made a discovery; I had stumbled on a connection between myself and the shape and color of time in the streets of New York. Though I knew that brownstones were old-fashioned and had read scornful references to them in novels, it was just the thick, solid way in which they gripped to themselves some texture of the city's past that now fascinated me. There was one brownstone on Macdougal Street I would stop and brood over for long periods every evening I went to the library for fresh books—waiting in front of it, studying every crease in the stone, every line in the square windows jutting out above the street, as if I were planning its portrait. I had made a discovery: walking could take me back into the America of the nineteenth century.

On those early summer evenings, the library was usually empty, and there was such ease at the long tables under the plants lining the windowsills, the same books of American history lay so undisturbed on the shelves, the wizened, faintly smiling little old lady who accepted my presence without questions or suggestions or reproach was so delightful as she quietly, smil-ingly stamped my card and took back a batch of new books every evening, that whenever I entered the library I would walk up and down trembling in front of the shelves. For each new book I took away, there seemed to be ten more of which I was depriving myself. Everything that summer I was sixteen was of equal urgency—Renan's *Life of Jesus*; the plays of Eugene O'Neill, which vaguely depressed me, but were full of sex; Galsworthy's *The Forsyte Saga*, to which I was so devoted that even on the day two years later Hitler came to power I could not entirely take it in, because on the same day John Galsworthy died; anything about Keats and Blake; about Beethoven; the plays of W. Somerset Maugham, which I could not relate to the author of *Of Human Bondage; The Education of Henry Adams*, for its portrait of John Quincy Adams leading his grandson to school; Lytton Strachey's *Eminent Victorians*, for its portrait of Cardinal Newman, the beautiful Newman who played the violin and was seen weeping in the long sad evening of his life; Thomas Mann's *Death in Venice*, which seemed to me vaguely sinister and unbearably profound; Turgenev's *Fathers and Sons*, which I took away one evening to finish on my fire escape with such a depth of satisfaction that I could never open the book again, for fear I would not recapture that first sensation.

The automatic part of all my reading was history. The past, the past was great: anything American, old, glazed, touched with dusk at the end of the nineteenth century, still smoldering with the fires lit by the industrial revolution, immediately set my mind dancing. The present was mean, the eighteenth century too Anglo-Saxon, too far away. Between them, in the light from the steerage ships waiting to discharge my parents onto the final shore, was the world of dusk, of rust, of gaslight, where, I thought, I would find my way to that fork in the road where all American lives cross. The past was deep, deep, full of solitary Americans whose careers, though closed in death, had woven an arc around them which I could see in space and time—"lonely Americans," it was even the title of a book. I remember that the evening I opened Lewis Mumford's *The Brown Decades* I was so astonished to see a photograph of the Brooklyn Bridge, I so instantly formed against that brownstone on Macdougal such close and loving images of Albert Pinkham Ryder, Charles Pierce, Emily Dickinson, Thomas Eakins, and John August Roebling, that I could never walk across Roebling's bridge, or pass the hotel on University Place named Alber, in Ryder's honor, or stop in front of the garbage cans at Fulton and Cranberry Streets in Brooklyn at the place where Whitman had himself printed *Leaves of Grass*, without thinking that I had at last opened the great trunk of forgotten time in New York in which I, too, I thought, would someday find the sources of my unrest.

I felt then that I stood outside all that, that I would be alien forever, but that I could at least keep the trunk open by reading. And though I knew somewhere in myself that a Ryder, an Emily Dickinson, an Eakins, a Whitman, even that fiercebrowed old German immigrant Roebling, with his flute and his metaphysics and his passionate love of suspension bridges, were alien, too, alien in the deepest way, like my beloved Blake, my Yeshua, my Beethoven, my Newman—nevertheless I still thought of myself then as standing outside America. I read as if books would fill my every gap, legitimize my strange quest for the American past, remedy my every flaw, let me in at last into the great world that was anything just out of Brownsville.

So that when, leaving the library for the best of all walks, to Highland Park, I came out on Bushwick Avenue, with its strange, wide, sun-lit spell, a thankfulness seized me, mixed with envy and bitterness, and I waited against a hydrant for my violence to pass. Why were these people *here*, and we *there*? Why had I always to think of insider and outsider, of their belonging and our not belonging, when books had carried me this far, and when, as I could already see, it was myself that would carry me farther— beyond these petty distinctions I had so long made in loneliness?

But Highland Park was different; Highland Park was pure idea. To savor it fully at the end of a walk, I liked to start out fresh from Brownsville. Summer nights that year I was sixteen, I used to meet her on East New York Avenue, at the corner of the police station. Our route was always up

Liberty Avenue, where the old yellow frame houses looked like the remains of a mining town, and the cracks in the pavement opened a fissure that trailed into hills of broken automobile parts littering the junk shops.

The way to the park is north and west, past the Brooklyn line altogether. At the border, the trolley car lines and elevated lines snarl up into one last drab knot; then it is like a fist opening, and the way ahead is clear. We trudged up endless small city hills; except for the rattling of the freight cars in the railroad yards and an occasional watchman's light in the factories, the streets seemed entirely dead. We went past the factories, the freight yards, the hospital, the Long Island Railroad station, an abandoned schoolhouse and an old pottery, its green roof cracked and engraved in thousands of small lines, as if everyone passing that way had knifed his name on it. The way up the hills was always strange, no matter how many times we followed it, for every step took us into the parkway off Bushwick Avenue, with its latticed entrances to the German beer gardens.

At Highland Boulevard the last of the factories vanished below the hill, and the park emerged in its summer sweetness. At every corner along the boulevard there were great trees; as we stopped at the top to catch our breaths, the traffic lights turned red and green on the trees and each leaf flushed separately in the colored light. I used to watch the signals switching red and green on the leaves. The click in the signal box had a humorous sound on the deserted boulevard, and as the light poured on the leaves, green and red, green and red, with a moment's pause between them, I seemed to see some force weary of custom, aroused against the monotony of day and night, playing violently with color in the freedom of the summer evening.

In those days the park lay open along the boulevard. They were always making half-hearted repairs on it that no one ever seemed to finish; we could enter the park anywhere—over the great stone fence above the cemetery; or over planks the workmen had laid between mounds of sand near the basketball court; or up its own hill to the reservoir itself. It was somehow not a real park then, not the usual city park—more like an untended wild growth they had forgotten to trim to the shape of the city. Most people I knew did not care for it; it was too remote, and at night, almost completely dark. It ran past interminable cemeteries where there seemed to be room for all the dead of New York.

But all this made the park more interesting to us. Our favorite way was past the mounds that stood just in from the boulevard. There was something in this I liked—a feeling that we were secretly descending on the park from a great height. I took her hand, and step by step, we went down into the empty park, past the basketball court, the gardens, the bandstand, until we could hear the old rowboat banging against the wire fence and climb up the hill to the reservoir.

From one side of the reservoir hill we could look across the cemetery to the skyscrapers of Manhattan; from the other, to miles of lampposts along Jamaica Avenue. Below us was a wood, then a military cemetery, slope on slope laid out in endless white crosses. We never tired of walking round the reservoir arm in arm, watching the light playing on the water, and going, as it seemed, from one flank of New York to the other. The city was no longer real; only a view from a distance, interrupted by cemeteries on every side. But on a summer night, when we lay in the grass below, the smell of the earth and the lights from the distant city made a single background to my desire. The lampposts winked steadily from Jamaica Avenue, and the YMCA's enormous sign glowed and died and glowed again. Somewhere in the deadness of the park the water gurgled in the fountains. In the warmth and stillness a yearning dry and sharp as salt rose in me. Far away a whistle hooted; far away girls went round and round the path, laughing. When we went home, taking the road past the cemetery, with the lights of Jamaica Avenue spread out before us, it was hard to think of them as something apart, they were searching out so many new things in me.

Lee Gutkind

The People of Penn's Woods West

For those without money, walking is the last resort. In the following true story a young immigrant from Scotland walked from Ohio to a forest in western Pennsylvania where he found something better than riches.

As described in The People of Penn's Woods West *(1984), author Lee Gutkind discovered Scotty's forest inn one night during a Pennsylvania blizzard. Elderly Scotty was "short and wiry with ruddy cheeks and slightly bugged-out eyes that danced as he talked." He had a light dusting of flour on his fingertips when he stepped out of the kitchen. He pretended that Mama, his plump, white-haired wife, would not let him talk with customers until he had finished his baking. Yet within minutes his story was coming as hypnotically as the snowflakes of that Pennsylvania storm.*

* * *

I have hiked the deserts of Texas and New Mexico on hot dry days when the wind suddenly whips up the sand in such a fury that seeing your hand in front of your face is nearly impossible. I have been on a Montana plain and watched at a distance as a tornado inked out the sky. But I have never seen snow and ice come with such sudden ferocity, such compassionless treachery, as it does when it swoops into the mountains of Penn's Woods West.

Luckily, on this particular evening, I sniffed out the warm, soothing smoke of a wood fire. Slipping and sliding, I followed my nose to Scotty's.

First Scotty told me of his comfortable, albeit lonely life in Cleveland, cataloguing and lending books by day and reading those that looked most interesting until late into the night. But when the Great Depression hit, public services were immediately cut back. Eventually, Scotty lost his job.

With no work and a dwindling supply of dollars, he had no choice but to go to the country to look for a livelihood. "I could have stayed in Cleveland, living from soup lines, but a man can't amount to much when he can eat for free. Many of my friends were heading west, but I had often gone camping in Cook Forest during the summer vacations, so I decided to go there, deep into the mountains. After all, California was three thousand miles of dust and Depression away, while Cook Forest was less than two hundred. So," said Scotty, "I started walking."

He paused to light a cigarette, staring out the window and into the snow with distant, fire-reflecting eyes. I watched him carefully. I wasn't certain how much of Scotty's story to believe. The more you hang around in the backwoods, the more you realize that there are those who spend idle hours carefully constructing family and personal sagas which grossly exaggerate real life. But it didn't matter to me right at that moment, for I was completely caught up in the romantic notion of it all. This man had obviously told the story of his life many times before; the tale was well-timed and well-structured. Deep down you could sense, by his force and conviction, that this was more than just a desire to talk or entertain. Scotty may well have been exaggerating here and there, but he obviously felt deeply his every word; he relived with vivid intimacy each scene he remembered and created, "Go on," I said.

"Well, it was tough walking," Scotty continued. "Everywhere you went, people were poor. When I was hungry, I picked berries from bushes, green apples out of trees. Where I could, I chopped wood and performed other odd jobs for my dinner." Sometimes he slept in barns or haylofts, other times concealed himself in the woods, lying down between green sheets of wild rhododendron, on beds of minty fern. "Back then, there were bandits, desperate and forlorn fellows for the most part, but just as dangerous as those in the Old West. Poverty and hunger can make crooks and robbers of us all, one way or another."

It was a long up and down walk across Ohio and into Pennsylvania, heading southeast. He followed approximately the same meandering direction of western Pennsylvania's first toll road, incidentally, the Erie-to-Waterford Turnpike, constructed in 1809, today a part of Route 19. From there, he took the William Flynn Highway, now Route 8, south through Crawford and Venango Counties and into Titusville. Along the way were tiny pockets of Amish settlers, gaunt and ominous in their black suits and hats; unemployed miners, huddling like hobos around meager fires; shoeless children, begging, sometimes stealing, from farmers who themselves could hardly afford feed for horses necessary to harvest even a bare minimum of food. Here too was the site of Colonel Drake's well, the first commercial oil well in the nation. Brown, rusted derricks, dormant for decades, were everywhere back then, silent sentries guarding a failed and senseless past. The Cook Forest-Clarion County area had little oil, but was rich in natural gas, the base of a highly profitable industry in the late nineteenth century but, at the time, no longer in great demand. Pipes, rotting and rusted, extended every which way, spidering miles deep into the woods.

"By the time I got to the forest, not too far from where we're sitting, it was pitch-black in the dead of night," Scotty said, dragging from his cigarette.

"You had nowhere to go?" My voice sounded hollow; it had been a long time since I had said anything.

Scotty nodded. "I walked into the woods and laid my bedroll down. It was comfortable enough, although much too damp. I was in a stand of virgin pine. I remember because the pine needles cushioned the forest more than a foot deep." It was quiet and fairly warm. Scotty couldn't see the moon because the tops of the trees were literally wrapped around one another in an umbrella of darkness.

"I was awed by the power and brilliance of those trees," he said. "Their size and their history were both frightening and exhilirating. Even to this day after having been in the forest now for so long, and always seeing them, I am still awestruck. The feeling never leaves me."

Lying on the forest floor, Scotty closed his eyes and tried to sleep, but he was worn-out from all his travelling and more than a little scared. And now the realization had set in. He was completely on his own. Nothing separated him from absolute poverty except the clothes on his back and the few dollars in his pocket. What friends he had were in another world, hundreds of miles away. Gradually, he drifted into a troubled sleep.

"In the middle of the night, I woke up." Scotty lowered his voice to a whisper and cocked an eyebrow, pausing dramatically in the silent, shadowed room. "I was convinced that I heard the sound of a rich sweet chorus of voices."

"In the woods?" I asked.

"I wasn't sure," Scotty said, pausing briefly once more to tighten the screw of suspense. "So I lay there on my old brown blanket, my eyes tightly closed, my heart thumping, listening until I knew it was true."

"People were singing?"

"It was gospel!" Scotty said.

"But who?"

Scotty slammed his fist down on the table and rolled his eyes in amazement. "Exactly what I wanted to know. Who in their right mind would be singing gospel—or anything else, for that matter—out in the boondocks in the middle of the night?"

Scotty paused to snub out his cigarette. He looked me over carefully to be sure he was commanding my undivided attention. He didn't have to worry. I was hooked.

"I lay there and I listened," Scotty repeated, still whispering, "but the sound didn't go way." The echoing harmony filtered through the forest like a gentle breeze. "I finally opened my eyes and stood up. I could see the faint flicker of a campfire off in the distance, so I gathered up my bedroll and started walking toward it." He paused momentarily to ponder. "Although I had never considered myself a spiritually lost person, I tell you, right at that moment, I quite literally felt saved."

As he told his tale, Scotty had slowly gotten out of his chair and climbed to his feet. He tiptoed, stoop-shouldered, cautiously edging toward the middle of the dining room, just as if he were feeling his way through the forest. I watched him, step by step, and waited, as he went through his lengthy charade. I could picture him hunching behind a tree, parting the leaves and peering out into the darkness.

"It was a midnight gospel service," he announced, his voice filled with wonder. "Even from far away, I could see the congregation, fifty or more, gathered in a circle. I was drawn to them by some mysterious force. I could feel it pulling at me. I began to run," he said, rotating his elbows and knees back and forth slowly, an old man's movement, but with the slightest hint of a steadfast jog. I wondered again, juding by his stiff, awkward motion, if he were in pain. "By the time I made it through the trees, the service was nearly over. But somebody had already caught my eye."

Suddenly, he took two quick steps toward me. Instinctively, I jumped back in surprise.

"A woman." His arm shot up in the air as he raised his voice. "The most glorious and gorgeous woman I had ever laid eyes on in my whole life. I felt the lightning and thunder reverberating from my temples . . ." He paused to look up at the oak-beam ceiling, hesitated, then cast his eyes down to the floor ". . . to my shoes."

"What did you do?"

"I couldn't help myself," Scotty shook his head ferociously. "I walked right out into the middle of the circle of those worshipers and stared at her." He paused once again, and a golden glow crept across his face.

For a long while, I sat back, smiled, and waited, savoring the sauce of suspense. As a storyteller, Scotty's timing was impeccable. "And then?" I finally said.

"I started singing," Scotty said. He straightened his shoulders and plodded over to the window.

"Singing?"

" 'Ah, Sweet Mystery of Life.' "

"What?"

"It's a love song," Scotty answered curtly, looking me up and down with disbelief. "It's the most romantic love song ever written." He rattled off a few bars.

Ah, sweet mystery of life at last I've found you.
Ah, at last I know the secret of it all.

All the longing, seeking, striving waiting, yearning
The burning hopes, joy and idle tears that fall.

"I'm sorry." I shrugged in embarrassment of my ignorance. "It's nice,"
I added.

"You better believe it."

When his song was over, Scotty walked slowly across the circle, made
yellow by the glow of fire, until he stood right in front of his mysterious
lady. I could detect a special glint in Scotty's eye, as if that very night was
right now repeating itself in this room, as if that wonderful woman was
waiting impatiently for him on the other side of the glass.

"Everyone was watching us now, but it didn't matter a bit," Scotty
said. "It wouldn't have mattered if I was in the middle of Carnegie Hall
with thousands of people watching, because I felt completely alone with her
at that moment, and she was obviously completely comfortable with me.
When I finally stopped singing, I reached out and offered her my hand."

"And she took it?"

"Of course." He looked at me suspiciously, but continued. "She took
my hand," Scotty said, "and then she got to her feet and stared right into
my eyes, and I knew—I knew with more certainty than I had ever known
anything in my entire life—that this was the woman I loved and would
marry."

"And did you?"

He rolled his eyes and winked at me. I was getting anxious to hear
the end of the story, but Scotty would not be hurried. It was his story and
he would go along at his own pace, whether I liked it or not.

They spent the rest of the night staring into one another's eyes and
talking. At daybreak, they walked up to Seneca Rock, a jutting rocky shelf
high above the rippling river, to watch the sunrise. Below them, the Clarion
rushed on down toward its eventual union with the Allegheny, blazing with
new morning light.

They ate salmon for breakfast, Scotty said. Right from the can. And
they got to know each other, talking quietly, like old friends. He learned
that she had organized these midnight gospel services all on her own, that
her father was a minister, and that she was here with a girlfriend, on vacation
from Ohio. She loved Cook Forest, she told him, and wanted someday to
live here.

After the narration of the story of his own life, Scotty demonstrated
for the lady the two additional languages he had taught himself over the
years while working at the library—French and Russian. He looked at me.
Grinning, he planted his hands on his slender hips, tilted his head back,
and raised his thick old brush of a brow in the barest hint of pomposity. "I
was brilliant," he announced.

They were married within the year, found jobs, and were eventually able to save and borrow enough money to purchase fifty acres near Cook Forest. "Our first buildings were surplus army Quonset huts, purchased in South Carolina and hauled north in an old truck I had managed to salvage and piece together. We hired some of the local folk to put up the huts, paid them by the hour. The first hut took half a day, the second took three days, and the third one took an entire week to put together. By the time I realized what was going on, we were nearly bankrupt."

Scotty chuckled and shook his head. "I should have known better," he said. Then he laughed right out loud. "After all, these were my own people, just a few generations removed."

Although the eastern part of the state was settled primarily by the English and Germans, the first settlers to take hold in western Pennsylvania were Scotch. Many Irish also made their way over the mountains and into western Pennsylvania—Ulster folk from the north. Presbyterians like the Scotch. The Scotch-Irish were perfectly suited for the wilds of what was then the western frontier. [They were] hard drinkers, tough fighters, cagey traders, and prudent businessmen, a legacy Scotty had obviously carried with him over the ocean and eventually into the woods.

Although he had been cooking and baking for himself and for friends most of his life, he had only started doing it for money when people renting his huts rans out of food or didn't feel much like preparing their own meals. But he was diligent, hard-working, and talented. And so, it didn't take long for Scotty's Restaurant to catch on, not as long as Mama was around, keeping him in line.

"Eventually, we tore down the huts and built these nice cabins behind here, each with its own stone fireplace. Then we put up this lodge, with a fancy, well-equipped kitchen." He stomped his foot, as if to emphasize the solidity of his efforts and investment. Then he paused. "It was a thrill at first; it still is, I guess. But like any other business, it is constantly demanding. Something always comes up."

His voice trailed off right then, as if he suddenly realized that the whole idea of making money doing what you very much liked to do tarnished the fun, if ever so slightly.

Now we both sat, listening to the silence that rang so loudly in the room. For a long time, neither of us moved. The fire had died down to a purring, hissing breath of coals, but Scotty continued to gaze out the window. Out front, at the hitching post, snow blanketed my motorcycle. The round, pale moon made the untouched white of the road look silver. A solitary deer had pressed a ribbon of delicate hoof marks along the side of the building.

A few years later, I learned from a mutual friend that Scotty had been suffering from a long illness. Those bugged-out eyes and painfully difficult movements I had observed were results of a series of small strokes suffered over a period of years, strokes that eventually hampered his ability to move about, to remember past events, or to think clearly. He was not that seriously affected when I met him, although the damage began to take its toll soon after.

Eventually, Scotty and Mama sold their beloved lodge and cabins and went off to Scotland for a long visit. According to mama, who still lives down the road from their old restaurant, Scotty was aware of what was happening to him and was confused and frustrated by his inability to control it. "As time went on, the strokes continued with increasing frequency. He became frightened of being alone. 'Don't ever leave me, Mama,' he'd sometimes cry out. I never did."

In 1977, Scotty died.

These days, Mama works part-time at the Sawmill Craft Center in Cooksburg, the site of John Cook's original mill, now reconstructed—a project for which she raised money and subsequently helped launch. Extraordinarily healthy and ambitious, Mama is now deeply involved in church-related projects, as well as other religious and cultural activities in the forest. Her newest idea is to raise money to build a gigantic amphitheater for dramatic performances under the stars, and to reestablish regular midnight gospel services. As of now, there is an Easter sunrise service at Ridge Camp, drawing thousands of worshipers, but Mama wants religion in the forest year-round. Perhaps she envisions a time and a place when other men and women, lost and lonely like Scotty, might stumble into the light of love.

A decade has gone by since I first met Scotty, but I have never forgotten that night, the wonderful story he told me, and our last few moments together in that silent, shadowed room. He was standing at the window, staring out into the silver bed of snow, watching the moonlight bathe the distant hills and trees. He stood there for so long, and concentrated with such force, that you could almost hear the jangled music of his mind as he relived the previous forty years of his life.

Then we heard a scrape against the floor from the next room. The door of the tiny office into which Mama had disappeared some time before opened a wee crack. "Scotty? Where are you? What are you doing?"

Scotty turned ever so slowly away from the window, but he did not answer. Instead, he padded back toward my table, shoved his old feet into his slippers, and paused to look at me. Fireflies darted and danced in those bugged-out old eyes as he stared. Then he turned and headed into the kitchen, pushing his way through the swinging doors.

"Scotty?" Mama called again.

Instantly, pots, pans, dishes, and silverware began to clatter. I heard water running, cabinets, opening, the thump of a refrigerator closing, and the groan and squeak of an oven door. It was then that he started singing. I knew what the song was going to be before the first word registered. His rich tenor voice filtered into the room, wrapping me in a cloak of reassuring comfort.

Dudley Cammett Lunt

The Woods and the Sea

Maine native Dudley Cammett Lunt says that he is "one who likes to investigate, in any locality where I find myself, the points that are linked with the past."

Like me an exile from New England, his own past is a composite of Maine mountains, coasts, and rivers. In The Woods And The Sea *(1965) he relives an early autumn walk along Maine's Scarborough Beach.*

*   *   *

It was time to go down on the beach. For soon its warm sands would be but the memory of one season and the haunting promise of the next.

After luncheon a breeze sprang up out of the southwest. The afternoons of late summer on the western coast of Maine are often distinguished by this phenomenon, which is known in alongshore parlance as a smoky sou'wester. This will start up at noon after a calm and brilliant morning. In the early afternoon it will freshen, capping with white the rolling waves that it has churned up and suffusing the air with the gray haze that gives it its name. Then the bays, coves, and the open sea will be spotted with triangles of white bent at variant angles, as sailing craft course on different reaches or tacks or run free before the wind. There is no better sailing breeze than a smoky sou'wester.

Thus it was until sundown all of this first afternoon at the shore. Then the wind died, and as I faced westward at the eastern end of the long slow curve of Scarborough Beach in the evening, I felt on my left cheek the gentle caress of a soft southerly. This brought clearly to ear the successive crashing of the cresting waves, and now and again, there mingled with this steady monotone a sharp concussion-like thump as the extended edge of a long wave thumped on the sand. This rote of the sea is a noise at once monotonous and yet never quite the same. It is the endless music of the restless sea.

As I walked, I watched the white crests of the successive waves come gleaming shoreward. It was very dark. There were few stars out, all of them overhead, and a moon, orange against a dark gray sky. This was the effect of the haze of the smoky sou'wester. Through it, the dark line of the dunes and the more distant broken skyline of the black pines were indistinct, shrouded with uncertainty, and on the distant shore of Prouts Neck there were scattered lights, dim and dulled. It was lonely on this deserted beach.

As I walked, I passed through successive layers of air of differing temperatures. This is a phenomenon I have experienced many times on this coast, and I believe the explanation is this. Often on a calm warm afternoon I have noticed the surface of the sea spotted by different cat's-paws. Often also, the long calm slicks and the riffled patches appear for a considerable space in the same locations. Thus it must have been on this beach on this night as I walked first through a calm and then in the midst of the light stirring of air that is known as a cat's-paw.

On the way back I had a new experience. Somewhere out on the dim dark surface of the sea, those who order such things ordained a change of the wind. Suddenly, in contrast to the soft caresses of the warm cat's-paws, I felt the sharp damp chill of a down-east Labradorian breeze. This was an easterly, the harbinger of unsettled weather. The warm soft evening was over.

Then my solitude was broken. I heard the barking of a dog. He was way out ahead, close to the sea. I walked on, and the barking came closer. Then I saw him splashing through the shallow water of the foreshore, barking at the waves. Now he came bounding toward me, and wet and dripping with salt water, inspected me. He was an odd-looking crittur, broad and squat, with long dark ears and a single black spot on his white coat near his vociferously wagging tail. Later I learned that this hound of the Scarborough Beaches was the incongruous product of a basset hound and a St. Bernard. His sniffing soon satisfied his curiosity. Then he was off again, and when I left the beach, he had resumed his barking at the waves. That night the wind hung in the east, and by dawn the fog had rolled in.

Those mornings when little watery rivulets trickling down the mesh of the screen give notice of a thick fog outside are memorable ones. I looked out on a gray-shrouded world. The sea, the beach, the dunes, the rectangle of bathhouses that lined them were all obscured by the fog, and nearer at hand the clump of alders that marked one side of the formal garden was in indistinct outline, and its far edge was lost to sight.

When I emerged there was no one abroad, and after a walk of half a hundred yards, I too was hidden in the fog. This is the way I like it. Privacy, remoteness, detachment—all three are hard to come by, but a good thick fog provides them in abundant measure. And so alone I proceeded down to the beach, the white fog becoming thicker with every step.

The birds of the foreshore were my only companions. In a fog, birds in flight have a spectral aspect. They fly silently, and when first seen, they are a mere motion in the gray air. Then wings and body assume indistinct form. For a short moment the bird, a large herring gull, is overhead. Then silently it begins to merge with the fog. Once again it is a shadowy motion, and a moment later it is lost to sight.

I walked on. This scared up a couple of crows that were feeding amid some thick-strewn kelp. Their startled *cawings* sounded softly, for the fog mutes sound just as it obscures sight. And their soft *caws* ceased when the thick fog shut down between us.

A single shorebird flashed past, uttering as it passed within sudden sight of my alien presence in the fog a single, frightened *tirr-whitt*.

After a plunge into a greasy-looking gray wave, as I retraced my steps to the eastward, I heard from behind and above a sharply whistled cry in a swift sequence of four:

Whir-whir-whir-whir.

Stopping but not turning, I whistled in reply. The bird answered. Then I saw it in toward the dunes, a large bird looming past out of the fog. It whistled. I whistled. Turning, it circled around me, responding to my calling. It did this twice and I saw arched, pointed wings, an oval body, a curved back.

Now with a flare of wide wings it was down, walking on the beach above the wrack of the tide line. An upright stance threw its down-curving beak into clear outline against the soft sand. It was in close, a bare thirty feet from where I stood. Now it was up again in swift flight. Again it circled. Again we exchanged calls in close succession.

Whir-whir-whir-whir.

It went winging out over the dunes. The wingbeats grew indistinct, and then it was lost in depth of the fog. The event of the morning was this encounter with this lone curlew, *Numenius phoeopus hudsonicus*.

This foggy morning ushered in a gray day and a gray sea. In the early afternoon, as I sat before a small open fire, there came from it a low fluttering, interspersed with a faint chuckling. In the wet pine needles of the scrub pine just outside the door, I could hear the soft rustle of the southerly off the sea. The light rain that it was bringing pattered on the roof. A few moments of this, and the lassitude of the sea and the seaside overtook me, and dozing, I fell asleep in my chair.

Later I put on a poncho and walked the beach in the rain. As I emerged from the dunes, three great black crows that had been feeding on the husks and shells of an old clambake arose silently and departed flapping. The sea was steel gray, and broad off in front through the drisk I saw a short white gash that appearing, disappearing, and reappearing, showed that the Old Proprietor was awash. As I walked slowly by the side of the sea, its small surf gave off a low wet wash of sound.

Suddenly I was the lone witness of a piscatorial adventure. Close inshore and just beyond the cresting of the waves, a hell-diver was swimming. I observed the oval, rounding back, the thin reedy neck, and the small head that comes to a sharp point at the end of the beak—a singularly unattractive bird. Of a sudden, in a quick, rolling motion, it dove. Glimpsing this, a gull, hurrying, flew in. It dove and, resting on the surface, gulped up a sand eel. This attracted still another gull, which, gull-like, instead of fishing on its own, went after the prey of the first gull. A shag, scaling just above the water in long, low, curving flight, dropped in. Then out of nowhere three more gulls flew in.

All this time the surface of the glassy sea was being roiled by the swift passage here and there of the school of fish that was the center of this avian attention. After a bit, the school disappeared. The gulls flew off on long errands, the shag departed, and the hell-diver vanished in the volute of the next wave. The gray sea was again completely calm and deserted, and I walked on.

Henry Beston

Northern Farm

One of the century's finest nature writers was Henry Beston (1888–1968), most remembered as the author of The Outermost House, *a memoir of a year spent beside the Atlantic Ocean on Cape Cod.*

Here in a scene from Northern Farm *(1948), the immortal Beston describes spring's first tentative steps across his Maine fields, hills, and woodlots.*

* * *

It has always been our custom to take a stroll before we put the house to bed, merely going to the gate and back when the nights are hostile with a bitterness of cold. Now that nights more mercifully human have come with the slow and dilatory spring, we go beyond the gate for perhaps a quarter mile or even half a mile, walking with miry feet down the farm road and through a sound of many waters.

Tonight under a faintly hazy sky and through a light wind one can feel but not hear, the winter is flowing downhill towards the still frozen and imprisoned pond. Out of the forests and the uplands a skein of rills is pouring, the small streams now seeking their ancient courses, now following an hour's new runnel along the darkness of a wall.

So heavy is the hayfield soil, and so matted down with living roots below and thick dead grass above, that little earth seems to be lost anywhere, and for the moment there is no runnel trying to make its way across ploughed land. But I have had my troubles in the past.

If the opening music of the northern year begins with a first trumpet call of the return of light, and the return of warmth is the second great flourish from the air, the unsealing of the waters of earth is certainly the third. As we walked tonight in a darkness from which a young moon had only just withdrawn, the earth everywhere, like something talking to itself, murmured and even sang with its living waters and its living streams.

Between us and the gate, a torrent as from an overflowing spring, half-blocked by a culvert heaved by frost, chided about our feet, and making another and smaller sound found its way downhill again in the night. Farther on, where woods close in to one side and the ground is stony and uneven, there tinkled out of the tree shapes and the gloom a sound of tiny cascades falling with incessant flow into a pool together with the loud and musical splashing of some newborn and unfamiliar brook.

Cold and wet, the smell in the spring air was not yet the smell of earth and spring. No fragrance of the soil, no mystery of vernal warmth hung above the farmland, but only a chill of sodden earth, water, and old snow. I knew that if I cared to look, I could find to the north of weathered ledges in the woods such sunken, grey-dirty, and gritty banks of ice as only the spring rains find and harry from the earth.

Yet spring somehow was a part of the night, the miry coldness, and the sound of water, a part of this reluctance of winter to break camp, a part of these skies with Sirius and Orion to vanish in the west. The long seige was broken, the great snows were over and gone, the ice was coming down from above tidewater in the current of the great rivers, and the colored twigs of the trees were at last awake.

Walking homewards towards the farm, now listening to the sound of water, now forgetting it as we talked, we both could see that much of the pond was surfaced with open water above its floor of ice. At the foot of our own hayfields a cove facing south and east showed in liquid and motionless dark, whilst beyond, and again above the ice, lay puddles and seas whose reflected quiet of starshine was a promise of the open water soon to come.

Across the pools, at the great farm on the hill, a light suddenly went out. Our own windows shone nearby, but we did not enter, so haunted were we both by the sense of the change in the year and the continuous sound of waters moving in the earth.

When we at length entered the house, using the side door and its tramped over and muddy step, we found ourselves welcomed by something we are very seldom aware of summer or winter—the country smell of the old house.

All old farms, I imagine, have some such rustic flavor in their walls; country dwellers will recognize what I mean. A hundred and fifty years of barrelled apples, of vegetables stored in a fieldstone cellar, of potatoes in the last of the spring, of earth somewhere and never very far, of old and enduring wood and wood-smoke, too, and perhaps the faintest touch of mould from things stored long, long ago in a bin—all these and heaven knows what other farmhouse ghosts were unmistakably present in the neat room with its lamp and books. The cold and humid night had stirred the house as well as ourselves: it had its own rustic memories.

Elizabeth presently brought in two slices of apple pie and two glasses of cold milk, and for a first time I did not bother to build up the fire.

Michael Frome

Strangers in High Places

*Michael Frome is an American journalist specializing in forestry, camp-
ing and wilderness. In the following "Chimney Tops" chapter from
Strangers In High Places (1966), he tells about a day hike with con-
servationist friends in Smoky Mountains National Park near the border
between North Carolina and Tennessee. (The name "Smoky," by the
way, refers to the misty effect produced by this park's great deciduous
forest.)*

*   *   *

It was raining in the Smokies.

Above us in the high places the mist formed, watery molecules arriving
from distant spheres of the oceans and atmosphere, converging briefly before
continuing their long separate journeys. The rain was soft and warm, a
summer spray to cloud one's glasses, or roll down the face like a child's
teardrop, and mix with the perspiration born of a hard climb. It was the
kind of friendly rain to remind you the earth is good, splashing the air with
smells of new life in the woods.

To me the image of the Smokies will always begin with rainfall, whether
a faint fair drizzle or a drenching downpour. "Rain, rain," I said, "Smoky
Mountains is thy name." But Harvey Broome, who had marched in every
conceivable mood of the hills, answered with a laugh. "You don't complain
about weather in the Smokies," he advised. "You just learn to accept it."

My two companions and I were resting on a narrow, rocky ledge,
midway in our climb to the Chimney Tops. It was still early, a cool morning,
alternately brightened with sunlight and darkened with the persistent showers. John Morrell and I were puffing. The climb is steep, almost vertical for
several hundred feet, hand over hand from one rocky perch to the next,
clutching tree roots and raw earth in between; not really a rugged ascent to
anyone accustomed to western mountaineering, but the toughest the Smokies have to offer, and tough enough for me. As for Harvey, he had made
his first trip of the year to the Chimneys in the quiet cold of January and
heaven knows how many more times this grayed eagle would cover this

route, or the scores of hiking trails through the forests and atop the main ridge called Smoky.

When we reached the summit between the Chimney Tops, twin craggy pinnacles of rock, it was a world for dreaming on the manifest mysteries, myths, marvels, and meanings of the Great Smoky Mountains. The rains fell no longer. We sat and spread our lunch on a rocky island, surrounded by rolling haze and, at our fingertips, summer-blooming herbs, mosses, and dwarfed rosy-pink Carolina rhododendron, the "deer laurel" that grows high in the southern mountains and nowhere else. Quiet for a time were the three of us, the older eyes perceiving far more than mine. Harvey Broome and John Morrell—scarcely lustrous names in what we normally consider the big scheme of things. But they epitomize a certain breed of Tennesseans and Carolinians who have given their energies to the Smokies and their love to the earth.

These two were high-school classmates in Knoxville. Both became lawyers. John went to work in the early twenties as a land buyer for the Great Smoky Mountains Conservation Association, acquiring parcels of real estate that would comprise the national park, then for the park itself, and has been more intimately associated with its development than any other person. Harvey entered private practice and made good, which was not quite good enough for him, for in due course he took a job as law clerk to a judge with the understanding there would be ample free time to devote to affairs of the Wilderness Society, a national organization of considerable distinction which he and others founded while on a trip in the Smokies, and which he serves as president. And there we were, wordless for a while, finding ourselves in a breeze-swept aerie, watching and listening to the birds.

A towhee flicked her long, rounded tail while flitting upward toward the spruce and fir, where she builds her summer nest. An ensemble of tiny winter wrens, normally reserved, proclaimed their presence with melodious high-pitched trilling and favored us with their rare antiphonal song—as soon as one uttered the last bubbling *crrrrip*, another began, for round after tuneful round. A flock of fifty swifts, high, fast fliers on tireless wings, swirled in circles, feeding on insects while skimming the air, diving occasionally into deep, dark crevices in the rock which must have been their home. What could be more appropriate than swifts nesting in the natural chimney?

The sound of motorcars drifted up to us, a hollow sound, almost unreal, the muted echo of rubber tires rolling through the tunnel on the trans-mountain highway. It reminded me of how quickly we had removed from our own kind and our own time. As a traveler, I had been acquainted with the Smokies for some years, but merely with their edges, or with the edges of the surface. Harvey Broome, John Morrell, and others were to show me the depths of the Smokies, a distance not readily penetrated. These hills demand time and patience. Entering one must take them on their own terms. They defy the cult of haste, being old and artful and surprising. "There is not a cranny in the rocks of the Great Smokies, not a foot of the wild glen, but harbors something lovable and rare," a man named Horace Kephart once wrote.

From our craggy perch, we looked down on the valley known as the Sugarlands. It became the focus of our attention. It was filled in with growing trees sweeping down toward the mouth of the valley where the park visitors' center and headquarters are clustered. My friends told me how much all this had changed within their recollection. They began coming out from Knoxville as boys, in the teens of the century, when the high places were visited only by herdsmen, bear hunters, and a few venturous hikers who climbed about through brush, briers, and downed timber, often losing their way in torrential rains and heavy fog, without maps, name places, or trails to guide them in many sections. The purple-hazy range was visible from the hills of Knoxville, but barely anyone knew it by name.

In 1913, John Morrell, his father, and two friends came out to camp at the foot of the Chimney Tops. They had first to travel to Sevierville, the county seat, then follow a rough dirt road to Gatlinburg, an inconspicuous mountain village in those days. A guide met them there with a mule to haul their tent and other packs, and up they marched along Fighting Creek and the Sugarlands road, such as it was.

"One morning, while we were camped below," John recollected, "the Chimneys looked so close we started for the top to see if they really had soot in them. Instead, we found a yellow-jacket nest that must have been upset by a bear the night before. We could see the cabins down in the Sugarlands, with their plumes of blue smoke rising over the cornfields and up between the bright, clear green mountainsides. That place could easily have been called Rocky-lands, for the people who settled there were compelled to stack the rocks before they could plant crops, and then had to dig holes between the rock piles to get dirt for covering the seeds."

Horace Kephart visited the Sugarlands, too. He described it as "Blockaders' Glory," or "Moonshiners' Paradise," a country of ill fame, hidden deep in remote gorges, difficult of access, tenanted by a sparse population who preferred to be a law among themselves. He knew his way around admirably—we will in time cross his trail among moonshiners, bear hunters, bourbon tipplers, revenuers, and old-time loggers—but Kephart had an imagination which perhaps was too strong in his picture of the Sugarlands.

The average house had one room and a lean-to kitchen. But those mountaineers, for all their reputed furtiveness and suspicion, rarely turned away a stranger, whoever he might be; instead they gave him a meal and a bed to share with the children. When a boy married, his wife's father was likely to furnish him a little shanty on the farm, or he would simply move in with her family. "My wife and I married when we were both fifteen. It was the usual age," one old Sugarlander told me. "We moved into her house directly. We just waited till everybody was asleep and loved in the dark, kids and all in the same room. That was our honeymoon."

Harvey told how he and his uncle would come out from Knoxville through the sawmill town of Townsend to Elkmont, a logging camp with resort hotel, on the other side of Sugarland Mountain. They came aboard the Little River Railroad, covering the fifty-two miles in two hours, fifteen minutes, with the last portion filled with exciting hairpin turns where they could almost reach out and touch the gorge.

All this changed with the coming of the park. Settlements like the Sugarlands were uprooted from the heart of the Smokies. And so, too, the logging camps and logging railroads and herds of cattle grazing on the grassy mountaintops. Hiking the trails, you still find vestiges of the settlement days, rocky foundations of old houses, vine-shrouded bricks, patches of daffodils and daisies in bloom, gaunt and ghostly fruit trees that refuse to die, graveyards still maintained with paper flowers at the headstones to brighten the shadowy woodlands. But mostly the mountains have reverted to their own, as at the Sugarlands, upward through the natural cycle until the cornfield of three decades ago is a young forest of infinite variety, taking its place alongside older, primitive portions that never were cut or cultivated.

It became time for us to start down. Harvey suggested another course, through a trailless jungle of heath thickets. "Goin' up," as the old native used to say, "you can might' nigh stand up straight and bite the ground; goin' down, a man wants hobnails in the seat of his pants." The steep slopes of Sugarland Mountain were dense with masses of dog hobble, or leucothoe, intertwined with trunks and branches of dripping rhododendron and laurel, an almost impenetrable labyrinth with only an occasional patch of sunlight shining on red partridgeberries. We found ourselves following a bear path but about all that I could do, besides sliding, was to envy the old bear who could take it rolling down. It seemed more practical to step over the rocks of the mountain stream, and when rivulets filled my shoes, my only thought was, Let it rain!

Nearing the foot of the mountain, we joined a rough trail, the old Indian Gap Road. Until 1928 it was virtually the only traversable route between the North Carolina and Tennessee sides of the Smokies. Two centuries ago it was a foot trail trod by Cherokee, connecting their great Warpath down the Valley of East Tennessee with the trail network of North Carolina. It became a route for settlers crossing the divide from Carolina in wagons and on muleback, sometimes in deep snow and cold. It was, in its time, the slim thread of human movement through the hills, but now it was weed-grown, shadowy, lost unless you looked for it.

Suddenly we emerged into the foreground, out of the past, out of the wilderness. Cars rolled along the transmountain road, very slowly, this being the height of the now bright Sunday afternoon. Along the West Fork of the Little Pigeon River, many people had parked their cars and taken to the water. A pair of young lovers held hands on a rock. A father dipped the bare toes of a child into the splashing stream and made him laugh. If a man likes the human race, he would have warmed to the scene.

The Smoky Mountains are the laughter of children and the romance of the young and the music of birds in flight. The Smoky Mountains are the rock that was old when natural life first appeared in the recess of geologic past and the trees, plants, and flowers that sheath almost every cliff and the rain-born streams that flow without end down from the heights in torrents and trickles. The Smoky Mountains are the peaked and spurred ridges, the knifelike edges, the plunging valleys, the splendid solitudes. The Smoky Mountains are the stories of the Eastern Cherokee, whose soul has never died, and of the back-country settlers, who live on the brink of yesterday and tomorrow. The Smoky Mountains are the national park that came into being as a testament of man's faith, and not without sacrifice and struggle. The Smoky Mountains are a composition of endless themes and variations, changing with every season, with every month, in every cove and hollow, on every summit, with every pair of eyes that sees them.

Here is a place where forests bloom and regenerate themselves, where the natural creatures belong, and are wanted. They are no strangers in high places: the modest herbs that flower in spring and by summer have withered and vanished, the woody giants that survive for centuries; the red-cheeked salamander and millepede, the bear, the night-prowling bobcat, the flying-squirrel, and the two hundred kinds of birds that serenade the woods. All of these, the sturdy, the graceful, the exquisite, the puny and humble, the least and lowest. When one enters the hills, as I said, one must take them on their terms.

But also, of course, there is rain. When we came off the mountain from our Sunday climb and drove past headquarters toward Gatlinburg, the skies clouded anew and showers fell. It was the natural blessing.

Lawton Chiles

Diary of the "Walking Senator"

"They all had something they wanted to tell me," wrote Florida Senator Lawton Chiles of the thousands of people he met on his thousand-mile walk to win a seat in the U.S. Senate. The "Walking Senator" celebrated his fortieth birthday on the road, while walking from the Alabama border to the Florida keys. He ate big country meals—as a hard-core distance hiker he lovingly describes all the fried chicken, corn bread and berry pies he downed—and he attracted Southern hospitality like a dog attracts fleas. Reporters often challenged themselves by enduring day-long walks with him, and so the publicity grew.

The walk never degenerated into an empty media event because first, Lawton Chiles was faced with humbling realities such as snarling dogs, violent storms, intense heat, red dust and road sores. And second, his hike was infectiously heartwarming. Its good cheer is evident on every page. This campaign walk took place in 1970; since then many other politicos have taken to the hustings on foot. For some it is a gimmick. But at its best it is reminiscent of Greek leaders and citizens strolling in the agora to discuss issues of the day. I like it. In a century of big bureaucratized government it restores an element of true grass-roots charm to a class of men, politicians, seldom regarded as heroes.

* * *

FROM CENTURY TO JAY: 8 MILES

Well, we started off yesterday morning at 8:30 at Century, Florida. Century is a town that is primarily a sawmill town, and it's on the Florida-Alabama line.

The first fellow that I saw I had to lure down off a power pole. He kept trying to get a word in and I kept talking to him about my running for the United States Senate and finally he got an opportunity to break in and tell me he was from Alabama. I just told him I sure hoped he had some Florida friends to pass the word on to.

We talked with a number of people in Century and had breakfast there. At first they wanted to talk only about the 850-mile plus walk before me, but then everybody started telling me about the Jay hill which lay ahead of me on the way to Jay.

I don't believe it was more than three or four miles but it looked like eight miles when I started up. The word was that if I could make it up the Jay hill, the trip would be coasting the rest of the way to the Keys. I thought I had made it up and stopped to rest. About that time Officer Wood, a highway patrolman who used to be stationed in Lakeland, came by and stopped to see what I was doing there. He broke it to me that I was only half way up the hill. It was kind of a blow 'cause I hadn't realized that when the road curved ahead, I'd have another half of the hill to traverse.

They're breaking ground for their crops up here and the wind is blowing good and hard so everything is red sand and red dust. By the time I walked into Jay I looked like a red man. I met John Pittman at the electric coop here and I think he felt so sorry for me—my hair looking so bad and I had so much dust on my face—he decided to take me home to dinner. I went to his house and we had collard greens and fried chicken and dressing and rice and apple popovers for dessert. I can tell you one thing: I haven't had an appetite like that in a long time. I had all that dinner and then finished up with another piece of chicken for dessert.

I reached Jay about noon and after I had lunch it looked like it was starting to rain, so I went to the livestock auction. That worked out real well because there were some 200 farmers there. By the time I got there, the bottom had fallen out—a real cloudburst. It would have been impossible to walk the streets of Jay and visit with the people.

There was a break in the auction and I was able to get on the microphone and give them a little talk about my campaign, to tell them why I was walking and talking through the state of Florida. And I had a good opportunity not only to talk but to do some listening. I found out a lot about the problems of the row farmer.

The people are trying to raise wheat and soy beans up here and one of them was telling me that of a loaf of bread, the farmer himself gets about two and a half cents; and with their costs of fertilizer, help and tractors and everything going up continually, they're really caught in a squeeze. They're particularly hurt by the high interest rates, having to borrow a lot of money every year to make their crops. They're very disturbed with the government buying wheat and corn in other parts of the country and holding it till they're ready to put theirs on the market. Then the government starts to sell [its] holdings and that breaks the market. It keeps them from being able to make a profit. They don't want to see government controls and yet they feel that is the way they're heading unless they can get together in some kind of co-op and do more to see that the farmer gets a decent price for his goods and that all the profits aren't taken up by the middleman and the people handling the end product.

They had a lot of good-looking livestock—hogs and cattle. Prices for them seemed to be pretty good. The row farmer is the one who's really having a tough time of it.

It's great to have my feet on the ground and to be with good Florida people, to learn from them and to tell them of my ideas. This day has certainly confirmed my belief that there is a crying need to bring more of our government back closer to home to the people it is intended to serve.

FROM JAY TO MUNSON: 18 MILES

We left this morning from Jay about 8 o'clock. I knew we had a long day today to try to go to Munson.

The first people that I saw on the road—a car stopped and out jumped J. Kirby Smith from Bagdad. I had met him at the Milton Kiwanis Club earlier and had also seen him at Milton at a dinner Dick Stone had. He heard at the Gopher Club at Pensacola this morning that I was out on the road so he came out to see me and brought the Chairman of County Commission of Santa Rosa, W. O. Kelly, with him and Clifford Wilson, also one of the commissioners from Santa Rosa County. So we had a nice visit out on the road. Then they took leave and I started on down the road.

The first place that we came to on the road this morning was a place called Crossroads. That's the local name for it. I think it's where the road goes South to Milton and North goes up to Alabama.

I met a couple of mechanics there. Had an interesting visit with them. One of them told me—a hard-working young man—that this year he was paying $3,000 in income taxes, Daniel Sims was his name, and he had the feeling that . . . much of it was being used to give [to] people. He didn't mind helping anybody who couldn't help themselves, but he thought a lot of people were getting his money that weren't working and didn't want to work. He felt there were people that had made more money than he that wouldn't be paying as much taxes . . . that there were too many people that just didn't want to work today. He was also real concerned about a bus driver who had almost lost his job because he had tried to stop the kids from throwing screws with a slingshot. This general permissiveness of our society certainly concerned him. Both of these fellows felt that they had never gotten a chance to see anybody that went to Washington before and they both said they were going to help me and they wanted me to remember them when I got up there.

Then I went on down the road and came to Jay prison. This is actually one of the Dept. of Transportation road camps. This is where 30-something prisoners lost their lives when the fire swept through that building in about a minute. In the Senate we tried to outlaw the use of temporary barracks and also dealt with claim bills in connection with this fire. It was very real, seeing what had happened there as a result of the fire in Jay prison. I had a chance to talk with some people there today—a couple of them were there when the fire occurred.

Again today 3 or 4 people stopped and offered to give me a ride. I had one fellow—Dewell Adams was his name and he heard that I was out on the road—he went to a store and bought a coke and brought it out to me. He stopped and said he knew I wouldn't take a ride but he wanted me to have a coke.

Then I had one of the fellows stop from Independent Life Insurance. He told me that he had seen Rosemary Emmett, who said in Century she was going to sell me a walking policy. So I'm still looking for Rosemary; she's supposed to be getting me an application form. She's got a policy that's going to cost me 50¢ a week, but it's going to insure me as I walk so I think she'll be bringing an application out as I walk here.

Then as I walked up towards Pittman's Grocery which is getting close to the tail-end of my walk for today, two young ladies, Brenda Ellis and Alicia Simmons—these young ladies were 14-years-old—had seen on television last night that I was walking and they told one of the daddys, Mr. Simmons, that they'd like to come out and walk with me a while. So he brought them out to the road and they walked down the road with me a while. Mr. Simmons was in the car along with their sister who was sick and we had a nice visit.

I walked into the Pittman's Grocery store and I got to meet Hank Locklin's mother. Hank Locklin is a country music star and has a home in Milton. His mother lives with him at the home. We had a visit about Hank, who is now in Scotland. His mother is keeping his home while he's gone. Then I visited in Pittman's store and talked with people there. Munson is a couple more miles down the road.

I'm going to make Munson before the end of the evening. I'm a good bit sore today. When I stopped for lunch or a little break, I notice that my legs get kinda stove up like the old race horse and it takes a while before I get loosened up again. At one stretch yesterday I timed myself; and I was walking as much as four miles an hour. Today I was timing it and this morning I think I was making three miles an hour. I stopped for lunch and doctored my feet since I have two blisters on both feet, and after lunch I was walking at a rate down to two miles an hour. It's going to take more hours right now until I get into a little better shape in the legs and get these blisters taken care of.

FROM MUNSON TO BAKER: 13 MILES

We made camp after dark last night because I was a little bit slow getting into Munson and had to walk a little by moonlight. The camper had already gone ahead and they'd located the camp and we camped out by a pool in the Blackwater Forest. I couldn't see it very good that night and we stayed in the camper. We got up this morning about 6 o'clock. It was awfully brisk when we got into the water. We had the camp completely to ourselves so we had sort of a swim in the altogether. That really loosened up my legs a little bit this morning. The sunrise was beautiful at that time.

Then I got out on the road this morning about 7 o'clock. One of my first calls was to the state forest nursery at Munson. They raise thirty million pine seedlings there a year and they sell them at a very low cost, six dollars a thousand I think, to people who'll plant trees. They also raise cypress and cedar trees. . . .

Then I got out on the road and I noticed that we have a pretty good headwind today. You usually think about headwinds when you're flying in an airplane, but I was facing a headwind walking on the ground today. I found that the wind was so brisk that it cut ten steps a minute off my pace. I usually was stepping off at about 120 steps a minute; it cut my pace down to 110. That doesn't seem like too much but the way I was figuring, it was going to add about an hour to my day, so I was a little disgusted with the headwind.

The soil was still damp enough that the dust hadn't started blowing yet, and I was real thankful for that.

I was walking today in some service boots that I haven't worn since I was in Korea. I started thinking back and remembering that it was during the "cease-fire" and we had a Colonel that wanted to keep the troops occupied so that they wouldn't get bored so he had us go on forced marches. I used to lead the column on a twenty-mile forced march wearing these boots. At that time I was a first lieutenant and could step out ahead of the column and slip back to the back and pick up stragglers and see how they were getting along and dog-trot back up to the head of the column and march at a clip that would make twenty miles in a day. I was kinda wondering what was wrong with these boots today 'cause I wasn't making quite that kind of time. Maybe it's the eighteen years in between and not the boots. Lt. Chiles was still at the head of the column today, but he was having a lot of trouble with Sen. Chiles who was a straggler. Sen. Chiles kept looking for a corpsman, and I think he was looking for a stretcher to ride on.

I met two very fine ladies on the road today, Miss Lillian Killam from Bagdad and Mrs. Abbie Carr from Crestview. They said they'd been reading about me in the paper and were delighted to see me. They stopped and we chatted for a long time. They laughed and said I'd made their day 'cause they were hoping they'd get to see me on the road. I really had a great visit with them.

One of the most pleasant surprises I had today was when I met Mr. Nixon on the road. Mr. Nixon stopped and introduced himself to me and I told him I was running for the U.S. Senate and Mr. Nixon pledged his support. It turned out that this was Mr. Perry Nixon, Route 2, Baker, and not Mr. Richard Nixon, but I was delighted to meet Mr. Nixon and get his support.

Baker certainly is a welcome sight!

FROM BAKER TO CRESTVIEW: 10 MILES

Yesterday, my third day of walking and talking in the Panhandle, was the tough one. Every step twinged sore muscles; I think even my bones ached. But today was a new day. When I started off this morning, the spring was back in my legs, and I found I was walking a good bit faster between visits with people.

I left Baker this morning around 8 o'clock with only nine miles to Crestview and a goal of getting there by noon. It was raining a little but this morning—one good shower got me wringing wet and I had to change clothes.

After a four-mile stroll, I came off State Road 4 and onto U. S. 90 at Milligan and headed toward Crestview, the largest town on my route to date.

It had been on the radio quite a bit around here—and in the newspapers—that I was due in Crestview today. It was interesting, and exciting, that at almost every crossroad—or where there was a dirt sideroad—there were people waiting in cars and pickup trucks.

These people had heard that I was coming and that I wanted to talk with people and listen to them, and they all had something they wanted to tell me. About Interstate 10, for example. They have the feeling out here that they're being shortchanged on I-10 and I agree with them . . . I-10 has not been completed. Many people feel . . . that there's some finagling in the funds and that this money is being held for extensions or perhaps other interstates. . . .

Another favorite topic of discussion today was conservation. Up here you find more ardent fishermen and hunters than most anywhere. Many people live in this area because the fishing and hunting has been so good. A number of them are Air Force or Army employees or were servicemen who've chosen to retire here for the outdoor sports. Now, they're really concerned with the pollution problem and what's happening to much of the hunting land up here—that this beautiful country is going to go by the wayside unless something is done to protect it. . . .

Again today, everyone has been most kind to me. Many came out beside the road apparently because they'd heard I was coming by, wanted to see me and wanted a chance to shake hands. They certainly encouraged me in my race.

A lot of people had heard that I had blisters on my feet and that I was sore, so I naturally got a number of home remedies about what to do to toughen my feet. One fellow said soak them in clorox, another gave me a special foot powder to use. We talked about different kinds of boots and how to wear my socks and I got all kinds of remedies. I have been looking in Crestview for some boots; I had a pair that were light and I really liked, but they turned out to be the wrong size.

I got a pleasant surprise when I ran into a Mr. Lance Richbourg waiting on the road for me. He tells me his family has been settlers around Crestview for over a hundred years. He was the school superintendent for a number of years before he retired and now raises cattle. Mr. Richbourg is the father of Nancy Dewey of Lakeland, a good friend, and it was a delightful visit. He told me of his long-time friendship with Senator Holland. They went to the University of Florida together and were fraternity brothers in the same fraternity I was a member of at the university some years later. I mentioned how close Senator Holland had been over the years with my family, and we agreed that the Senator had been a fine public servant for Florida.

When I got into Crestview, I was surprised to find that a group of businessmen there had arranged a luncheon for me. There were about twenty-five people—community and county officials and leading business-men—and I had a chance to talk to them about my Senate campaign. They responded enthusiastically. And I was pleased with Sen. Wig Barrow's public expression of support for me.

Mr. James Lee, who is a former road board member for this area through a couple of governors, was very kind to me and had me to dinner at his home. It gave me a chance to prop my tired feet up and watch Jacksonville University be victorious over St. Bonaventure in the national basketball championship tournament.

This walking-talking effort may be the hardest way to campaign, but I'm convinced it is the best way for me to get to know the people and their problems and for them to get to know me. When I complete this walk, I will have gut knowledge about this state that no other candidate for any office can possibly have.

Vachel Lindsay

Adventures While Preaching
the Gospel of Beauty

Vachel Lindsay (1879–1931) was an American poet and visionary who sang the praises of a rural equality and hope that eluded him in his own life. He was a walker at a time when many destitute men were tramping the countryside in search of work. As a poet he was usually destitute, too, but his reason for setting out on long walks was not transportation or employment. According to biographer Robert F. Sayre, "the walks were an investigation of the quality of provincial life, a means of personal refreshment and renewal, and an application of Lindsay's religion of wandering martyrs."

Lindsay made a Spring 1906 walk from Florida to Kentucky. In April and May of 1908 he walked from New York to Ohio. And in May 1912 he began a walk from his hometown of Springfield, Illinois to Los Angeles, California (giving up, however, in Wagon Mount, New Mexico on September 13). He later said, "The reason my beggar days started talk was that each time I broke loose, and went on the road, in the spring, after a winter of Art lecturing, it was definitely an act of protest against the United States commercial standard, a protest against the type of life set forth for all time in two books of Sinclair Lewis: Babbitt *and* Main Street.*"*

The walks (during which he bartered poems for food and lodging) helped to transform this middle class aesthete into a Middle West populist, a Jeffersonian democrat of a type now almost extinct in our urban world.

There was something both nutty and noble about Vachel Lindsay. How I would like to have met him sauntering along the dirt roads, scorning the newfangled motorcars (yet occasionally accepting rides). Or, faint from the strong Kansas sun, walking behind a harvester shocking new-mown grain. Or, aching with hunger and fatigue, sizing up a farm wife or restaurant owner for a trade of poems for food.

This poet carried no backpack, down bag, camp stove, or the like. His main baggage was his Rhymes To Be Traded For Bread *and his brochures promoting "The Gospel Of Beauty."*

Vachel Lindsay (who had been "Champion Walker" of Springfield High School) followed certain "rules of the road" during his quixotic mission to rural America. They were: "to have nothing to do with cities, railroad, money, baggage, or fellow-tramps." The following is the beginning of the "Walking Into Kansas" chapter of Adventures While Preaching The Gospel of Beauty.

* * *

It has been raining quite a little. The roads are so muddy I have to walk the ties. Keeping company with the railroad is almost a habit. While this shower passes I write in the station at Stillwell, Kansas.

JUNE 14, 1912.

I have crossed the mystic border. I have left Earth. I have entered Wonderland. Though I am still east of the geographical center of the United States, in every spiritual sense I am in the West. This morning I passed the stone mile-post that marks the beginning of Kansas.

I went over the border and encountered—what do you think? Wild strawberries! Lo, where the farmer had cut the weeds between the road and the fence, the gentle fruits revealed themselves, growing in the shadow down between the still-standing weeds. They shine out in a red line that stretches on and on, and a man has to resolve to stop eating several times. Just as he thinks he has conquered desire the line gets dazzingly red again.

The berries grow at the end of a slender stalk, clustered six in a bunch. One gathers them by the stems, in bouquets, as it were, and eats off the fruit like taffy off a stick.

I was gathering buckets of cherries for a farmer's wife yesterday. This morning after the strawberries had mitigated I encountered a bush of raspberries, and then hedges on hedges of mulberries both white and red. The white mulberries are the sweetest. If this is the wild West, give me more. There are many varieties of trees, and they are thick as in the East. The people seem to grow more cordial. I was eating mulberries outside the yard of a villager. He asked me in where the eating was better. And then he told me the town scandal, while I had my dessert.

A day or so ago I hoed corn all morning for my dinner. This I did cheerfully, considering I had been given a good breakfast at that farm for nothing. I feel that two good meals are worth about a morning's work anyway. And then I had company. The elderly owner of the place hoed along with me. He saved the country, by preaching to me the old fashioned high tariff gospel, and I saved it by preaching to him the new fashioned Gospel of Beauty. Meanwhile the corn was hoed. Then we went in and ate the grandest of dinners. That house was notable for having on its walls, really artistic pictures, not merely respectable pictures, nor yet seed-catalogue advertisements.

That night, in passing through a village, I glimpsed a man washing his dishes in the rear of a blacksmith shop. I said to myself: "Ah ha! Somebody keeping bach."

I knew I was welcome. There is no fear of the stranger in such a place, for there are no ladies to reassure or propitiate. Permission to sleep on the floor was granted as soon as asked. I spread out *The Kansas City Star*, which is a clean sheet, put my verses under my head for a pillow and was content. Next morning the sun was in my eyes. There was the odor of good fried bacon in the air.

"Git up and eat a snack, pardner," said my friend the blacksmith. And while I ate he told me the story of his life.

I had an amusing experience at the town of Belton. I had given an entertainment at the hotel on the promise of a night's lodging. I slept late. Over my transom came the breakfast-table talk. "That was a hot entertainment that young bum gave us last night," said one man. "He ought to get to work, the dirty lazy loafer," said another.

The schoolmaster spoke up in an effort not to condescend to his audience: "He is evidently a fraud. I talked to him a long time after the entertainment. The pieces he recited were certainly not his own. I have read some of them somewhere. It is too easy a way to get along, especially when the man is as able to work as this one. Of course in the old days literary men used to be obliged to do such things. But it isn't at all necessary in the Twentieth Century. Real poets are highly paid." Another spoke up: "I don't mind a fake, but he is a rotten reciter, anyhow. If he had said one more I would have just walked right out. You noticed ol' Mis' Smith went home after that piece about the worms." Then came the landlord's voice: "After the show was over I came pretty near not letting him have his room. All I've got to say is he don't get any breakfast."

I dressed, opened the doorway serenely, and strolled past the table, smiling with all the ease of a minister at his own church-social. In my most ornate manner I thanked the landlord and landlady for their extreme kindness. I assumed that not one of the gentle-folk had intended to have me hear their analysis. 'Twas a grand exit. Yet, in plain language, these people "got my goat." I have struggled with myself all morning, almost on the point of ordering a marked copy of a magazine sent to that smart schoolmaster. *"Evidently a fraud!"* Indeed!

"Goin' wes' harvesin'?"

"Yes, yes. I think I will harvest when I get to Great Bend."

JUNE 18, 1912.

Approaching Emporia. I am sitting in the hot sun by the Santa Fé tracks, after two days of walking those tracks in the rain. I am near a queer little Mexican house built of old railroad ties.

I had had two sticks of candy begged from a grocer for breakfast. I was keeping warm by walking fast. Because of the muddy roads and the sheets of rain coming down it was impossible to leave the tracks. It was almost impossible to make speed since the ballast underfoot was almost all of it big rattling broken stone. I had walked that Santa Fé railroad a day and a half in the drizzle and downpour. It was a little past noon, and my scanty inner fuel was almost used up. I dared not stop a minute now, lest I catch cold. There was no station in sight ahead. When the mists lifted I saw that the tracks went on and on, straight west to the crack of doom, not even a water-tank in sight. The mists came down, then lifted once more, and, as though I were Childe Roland, I suddenly saw a shack to the right, in dimensions about seven feet each way. It was mostly stove-pipe, and that pipe was pouring out enough smoke to make three of Aladdin's Jinns. I presume someone heard me whistling. The little door opened. Two heads popped out, "Come in, you slab-sided hobo," they yelled affectionately. "Come in and get dry." And so my heart was made suddenly light after a day and a half of hard whistling.

At the inside end of that busy smokestack was a roaring redhot stove about as big as a hat. It had just room enough on top for three steaming coffee cans at a time. There were four white men with their chins on their knees completely occupying the floor of one side of the mansion, and four Mexicans filled the other. Every man was hunched up to take as little room as possible. It appeared that my only chance was to move the tins and sit on the stove. But one Mexican sort of sat on another Mexican and the new white man was accommodated. These fellows were a double-section gang, for the track is double all along here.

I dried out pretty quick. The men began to pass up the coffee off the stove. It strangled and blistered me, it was so hot. The men were almost to the bottom of the food sections of their buckets and were beginning to throw perfectly good sandwiches and extra pieces of pie through the door. I said that if any man had anything to throw away would he just wait till I stepped outside so I could catch it. They handed me all I could ever imagine a man eating. It rained and rained and rained, and I ate till I could eat no more. One man gave me for dessert the last half of his cup of stewed raisins along with his own spoon. Good raisins they were, too. A Mexican urged upon me some brown paper and cigarette tobacco. I was sorry I did not smoke. The men passed up more and more hot coffee.

That coffee made me into a sort of thermos bottle. On the strength of it I walked all afternoon through sheets and cataracts. When dark came I slept in wet clothes in a damp blanket in the hay of a windy livery stable without catching cold.

Now it is morning. The sky is reasonably clear, the weather is reasonably warm, but I am no longer a thermos bottle, no, no. I am sitting on the hottest rock I can find, letting the sun go through my bones. The coffee in me has turned at last to ice and snow. Emporia, the Athens of America, is just ahead. Oh, for a hot bath and a clean shirt!

A mad dog tried to bite me yesterday morning, when I made a feeble attempt to leave the track. When I was once back on the ties, he seemed afraid and would not come closer. His bark was the ghastliest thing I ever heard. As for his bite, he did not get quite through my shoe-heel.

Caitlin Gareth

Walking My Dog in Montrose Park

Dogs love to walk, too, and Caitlin Gareth's dog Hanus is no exception. When this article was published in 1984, he was one of the "regulars" in Montrose Park in Houston, Texas. He and his owner have since moved to greener pastures and may be walking somewhere near you right now.

This article originally appeared in the Houston Post.

* * *

My dog Hanus and I came to Houston via the scenic route. A year and a half ago we left our home in southern Oregon, drove across Canada, dropped down through New England to stay a while in Boston and New York, then motored southwest until we found ourselves in Houston.

We have covered almost as much ground on foot as we have in our truck. We are indefatigable walkers, Hanus and I.

In Oregon, mountains came right down to the back doors of the town we lived in and every day we roamed the steep dirt roads and the deer-trailed woods that covered them. In autumn when the deer came down for water, Hanus crashed after them, plunging and panting through the woods as they sprang away soundlessly and unconcerned. Across the whole of Canada no rabbit or ground squirrel could rest easy in the evenings when we walked off the weariness of driving. In the big eastern cities, however, Hanus was undone. For the first time he had to take his walks at the end of a leash and he didn't understand third floor apartments. He was not an urban dog. While in New York he committed an unforgiveable social blunder: He killed one of the only two woodchucks in Central Park. Disgraced, we made our way to Texas. Once in Houston we made our way to Montrose.

Dog walking in Montrose is like dog walking nowhere else we have been. Although we probably don't walk much more than a mile in any direction from our duplex, within that radius there is enough variety to rival that found between Oregon and New England.

If we walk six blocks one way we are among groomed estates where gardeners eagle-eye our every move to scotch any sin against the landscaping.

Six blocks the other way, among ragged yards and houses that are folding in on themselves, an elderly woman too frightened to leave her home was amazed when I offered to clean the dog's indiscretion from her parking strip. On Westheimer there are suspiciously tall women with lots of makeup and a strange way of walking who tell Hanus he's "Soooo cute!" while closer to Allen Parkway the Hispanic kids shout, "Hey, Lassie!" Bare-chested boys idling along Avondale run languid fingers through Hanus' fur as he walks by, but up the street where construction workers slap together condos the whistles are for me.

Often we make for the parkway where I turn Hanus loose to play at fetching sticks and to cool off in the unsavory bayou. Along the path, joggers sweat industriously as we amble. Usually the park is as peaceful as a narrow green space between two highways is able to be: Kids splatter about in the fountain, Frisbees are through the air, and the affable Hanus insinuates himself into picnics. But there have been times I was very glad I had a dog and glad the dog was large. Like the time, in a wooded area, I came upon a man whose grin did not disguise the fact that his trousers were around his ankles. Fortunately, Hanus, who had been dawdling along the bayou, suddenly appeared huge and dripping, like something spawned by those unnatural waters.

But there are moments, too, when to be along a bayou at the edge of Montrose is almost like being far away, outside the city. Hanus and I have spent evenings there when he chased rabbits while I watched turtles slide beneath the brown water. I have seen egrets stalking the water's edge, setting their fanned toes softly into the mud, and I once saw a snake slip through the grass, clasping in its mouth a frog whose legs and feet, sticking out on either side, made me think the snake had antlers. In the spring, nesting mockingbirds frequently made reckless assaults on Hanus' tail, but during last winter's freeze there was no one to bother us at all because Hanus and I were the only ones out on those frosted days. Walking alone in the cold air warmed our northern hearts.

We suffer gracelessly, though, when the summer heat curtails our walks, and every day we miss the cool mountains. But not long ago, when my regret over leaving them was deepest, the dog and I walked down a street where we were used to seeing prostitutes—and we met a raccoon instead. Perhaps it is not so bad to trade, for a while, the mountains' serenity for a little something different in every block we pass along. Especially when the something different changes every day. Hanus hasn't found any deer to chase lately, but who knows? From dog walking in Montrose we have come to expect surprise.

Nell Platt

Organized Labor

One of the most important trends of the twentieth century has been that of runaway population growth. From an estimated world total of 1.6 billion in 1900 to 1987's 5 billion, there has been over a three hundred percent population increase within living memory. Famine, chaos, suffering, and violence have often been the result. Clearly there are too many of us.

But Shank's Mare *is not a gloomy book and the following story is about the joy a couple can find in pregnancy and childbirth.*

Even hard-core walkers have probably never considered the possibility of walking into childbirth. Well, meet Nell Platt, a freelance writer in Paris, France. The following story from Walking *Magazine is about the birth of Nell's son Mathieu.*

* * *

One morning before dawn, I went into labor. We fluttered about the apartment entrance: "Toothbrush? Nightgown? Taxi? Car?" Then my husband put the suitcase down, and we looked at one another and laughed. The hospital was less than a mile away and we knew that statistically, at least, our first child had little chance of being born on the sidewalk. "Let's go on foot," I suggested, fully aware that my arms and legs had become uncertain relatives to a body that was no longer entirely mine. Walking— simple, unbroken forward movement—had become a perfect means of integrating the breathing techniques, concentration, and sustained muscle relaxation so important to natural childbirth training.

There are things you don't notice when you're not walking, and other things you never forget when you are. At dawn, the city belonged to bread bakers, garbage pickers, and other kinds of stray cats. A carload of frazzled night owls rolled about. A lone and earnest jogger calculated his pulse. We took giant steps, so as always to get to the next intersection before the onset of the next contraction; that way, if anyone happened by when the contraction came, we could just hang and breathe, waiting for the light to change. We turned a final corner and walked 100 yards to the east; the rooftops at the end of the street released a red and very pregnant sun into the sky.

We received the dressing-down we probably deserved from the hospital staff when it became clear to them that we'd come on our own feet. Following a round of fetal monitors and examinations, we were left to ourselves. Punctuated by visits from the doctor, the morning turned to afternoon. After one examination, the doctor announced that I was still experiencing "ineffective" labor: hard and heavy, but not really advancing the cause. "This is where medication is usually introduced, to speed things up," she said.

"Is that what you're going to do?"

"No. The baby's doing quite well. Why don't you go for a walk?"

We looked at the doctor with stupefaction.

"Within the building, of course." She explained that a change of scenery or some gentle physical exertion often serves as well as any pharmaceutical product to accelerate labor, but that most hospitals, even the most permissive, don't bother to suggest the obvious. "Doctors don't like to run after their patients," she noted. "Just don't go too far away!"

We walked out of the labor room and within moments wondered why we'd stayed there as long as we had. Strolling through the corridors of the maternity wing, we chatted with nurses and orderlies, paused to admire the newborns being changed in the nursery, and scorned the elevator for the stairs. I remained on my feet throughout—standing or squatting through pain, with chairbacks, hospital walls, or handrails for support. Time disappeared. Only the intervals of my contractions and our footsteps were left, to mark off the high drama and the banality of the event taking place within me.

"You only have two centimeters to go," the doctor reported, the next time she examined me.

"Great, shall I go for another walk?"

"Don't you dare!" came the reply—and minutes later, I learned why. Birth comes with the force of an avalanche or tidal wave; you can walk right up to it, but when it arrives there's nothing to do but hunker down, hang on, and ride.

Suddenly it was over. The doctor held our son out to me. As I took him, his tiny feet grazed my skin, and he began taking little steps along my abdomen. "Look, he's walking!" my husband exclaimed. The doctor reminded us that at birth, the motion was every bit as instinctive as breathing, sucking, or grasping—for a day or so the baby would actually be able to support a good part of his own weight. The only difference was that where breathing and sucking would remain reflexive, walking would have to be relearned. With my hands steadying him, I watched our firstborn child step up to my chest. Then I laid him down and held him over my heart, which opened and immediately swelled to twice its previous size.

Gary Snyder

Backpacking with Jack Kerouac

Gary Snyder (born: 1930) is a California poet whose poetry sings with the magic of Zen and of American Indian legends.

Here in a selection from Jack's Book, *the former Northwest logger recalls meeting Jack Kerouac (1922–1969) and other saints of the Beat Generation. Outdoorsman Snyder soon took Kerouac on an October backpacking trip, which the latter described vividly in* The Dharma Bums *(1958):*

> We went on, and I was immensely pleased with the way the trail had a kind of immortal look to it, in the early afternoon now, the way the side of the grassy hill seemed to be clouded with ancient gold dust and the bugs flipped over rocks and the wind sighed in shimmering dances over the hot rocks, and the way the trail would suddenly come into a cool shady part with big trees overhead, and here the light deeper. And the way the lake below us soon became a toy lake with those black well holes perfectly visible still, and the giant cloud shadows on the lake . . . [I]t seemed that I had seen the ancient afternoon of that trail, from meadow rocks and lupine posies, to sudden revisits with the roaring stream with its splashed snag bridges and undersea greenness, there was something inexpressibly broken in my heart as though I'd lived before and walked this trail, under similar circumstances with a fellow Bodhisattva, but maybe on a more important journey, I felt like lying down by the side of the trail and remembering it all. The woods do that to you, they always look familiar, long lost, like the face of a long-dead relative, like an old dream, like a piece of forgotten song drifting across the water, most of all like golden eternities of past childhood or past manhood and all the living and the dying and the heartbreak that went on a million years ago and the clouds as they pass overhead seem to testify (by their own lonesome familiarity) to this feeling. Ecstasy, even, I felt, with flashes of sudden re-

membrance, and feeling sweaty and drowsy I felt like sleeping and dreaming in the grass. As we got higher we got more tired and now like two true mountain climbers we weren't talking anymore and didn't have to talk and were glad, in fact Japhy mentioned that, turning to me after a half-hour's silence, "this is the way I like it, when you get going there's just no need to talk, as if we were animals and just communicated by silent telepathy." So huddled in our town thoughts we tromped on, Japhy using that gazotsky trudge I mentioned, and myself finding my own true step, which was short steps slowly patiently going up the mountain at one mile an hour, so I was always thirty yards behind him and when we had any haikus now we'd yell them fore and aft. Pretty soon we got to the top of the part of the trail that was a trail no more, to the incomparable dreamy meadow, which had a beautiful pond, and after that it was boulders and nothing but boulders.

Later at sundown the young hikers reached a promontory above the valley.

It was beautiful. The pinkness vanished and then it was all purple dusk and the roar of the silence was like a wash of diamond waves going through the liquid porches of our ears, enough to soothe a man a thousand years. I prayed for Japhy, for his future safety and happiness and eventual Buddhahood. It was all completely serious, all completely hallucinated, all completely happy.

In 1969 the American backpacking fad was at its height when Jack Kerouac died at forty-seven. But what the Beat novelist had said of the footloose Gary Snyder character in The Dharma Bums might equally have been true of us Sixties hikers, too. ". . . [w]hat does he care if he hasn't got any money," wrote Kerouac, "he doesn't need any money, all he needs is his rucksack with those little plastic bags of dried food and a good pair of shoes and off he goes and enjoys the privileges of a millionaire . . ."
The real Gary Snyder later remembered it this way.

* * *

When I was a graduate student studying Chinese and Japanese and planning to go to the Orient, in a perhaps excessively orderly fashion I decided I should get my teeth fixed. I didn't realize they had dentists all over the place. Anyway, I signed up with the University of California dental school, and for two years I bicycled from Berkeley to San Francisco once a week and put myself in the hands of a Japanese-American dental student. On one of those occasions I took along *New World Writing No. 7*, and I read the little thing by a fellow named Jean-Louis, which was one of the most entertaining things I'd read in a long time, and it always stuck in my mind. I didn't know anything of Jack or Allen [Ginsberg] at that time, but I never forgot that little piece of prose, "Jazz of the Beat Generation." It was the first time I saw the term Beat Generation. What I liked was the writing, of course, and the energy that was in it, and the evocation of people. Of course it didn't say "Jack Kerouac," it said "Jean-Louis."

Later I met Allen. Shortly after that, I met Jack. When I met Jack, and hearing Allen speak of his projects and hearing Jack speak, I flashed that he was Jean-Louis.

Allen asked Rexroth who was doing interesting poetry in the area. Allen had the idea of trying to put together some kind of poetry reading, and Kenneth mentioned my name as one person he might want to look up. So Allen just turned up at my place when I was fixing my bicycle in the backyard, and said that he had been talking to Kenneth. So we sat down and started comparing who we knew and what we were thinking about.

Jack was, in a sense, a twentieth-century American mythographer. And that's why maybe those novels will stand up, because they will be one of the best statements of the myth of the twentieth century. Just as Ginsberg represents one clear archetypal aspect of twentieth-century America, I think Jack saw me, in a funny way, as being another archetypal twentieth-century American of the West, of the anarchist, libertarian, IWW tradition, of a tradition of working outdoors and fitting in already with his fascination with the hobo, railroad bum, working men. I was another dimension on that.

Like on one occasion I remember we spent a number of hours in which I simply explained to him how logging camps worked and what all the steps in a logging operation are. Now I don't believe he ever used that in a book, but he was collecting that kind of information and enthusiastically digesting it all the time.

If my life and work is in some sense a kind of an odd extension, in its own way, of what Thoreau, Whitman, John Muir, et cetera, are doing, then Jack hooked into that and he saw that as valuable to him for his purposes in this century. . . .

Our interchanges on Buddhism were on the playful and delightful level of exchanging the lore, exchanging what we knew about it, what he thought of Mahayana. He made up names. He would follow on the Mahayana Sutra invention of lists, and he would invent more lists, like the names of all the past Buddhas, the names of all the future Buddhas, the names of all the other universes. He was great at that. But it was not like a pair of young French intellectuals sitting down comparing their structural comprehension of something. We exchanged lore. And I would tell him, "Now look. Here are these Chinese Buddhists," and that's how we ended up talking about the Han-shan texts together, and I introduced him to the texts that give the anecdotes of the dialogues and confrontations between T'ang Dynasty masters and disciples, and of course he was delighted by that. Anybody is. That's what we did. . . .

When Jack came over I was living over on Hillegass, and Philip had come back from the mountains. I had spent the summer up in the Sierra Nevada working on a trail crew and, naturally, we were talking a lot about the mountains. We were just back fresh from it, from the season's work, and I had ruck sacks and climbing rope and ice-axes hanging on the walls around my place. Naturally we talked some about all of that.

I perceived that there was a kind of freedom and mobility that one gained in the world, somewhat analogous to the wandering Buddhist monk of ancient times, that was permitted you by having a proper pack and sleeping bag, so that you could go out on the road and through the mountains into the countryside. The word for Zen monk in Chinese, *yun shui*, means literally "clouds and water," and it's taken from a line in Chinese poetry, "To float like clouds, to flow like water," which indicates the freedom and mobility of Zen monks walking around all over China and Tibet and Mongolia on foot.

With that in mind I said to Jack, "You know, real Buddhists are able to walk around the countryside." So he said, "Sure. Let's go backpacking." I think John Montgomery said, "There's time for one more trip into the mountains before it gets too much colder." It was around the end of October.

So we headed up over Sonora Pass, leaving at night in Berkeley, and went over to Bridgeport, up to Twin Lakes and went in from there, over Sonora Pass.

It was very funny. It's very beautifully described in *The Dharma Bums*, actually. It was very cold. It was late autumn. The aspens were yellow, and it went well below freezing in the night and left frost on the little creek in the canyon we were camped at. There was a sprinkle of fresh white snow up on the ridges and peaks. We made it up to the top of the Matterhorn and came back down again. Actually, Jack didn't. I guess I was the only one that went up there. I was the persistent one.

Herbert Gold

A Zen Hike with Bill Graham

I have often had the fantasy that all the people of the world could solve their problems merely by going for a walk. No matter how hyper or stressed the person is, he or she could come down to earth simply by putting boot to trail.

I once successfully persuaded the well-to-do parents of a truant fifteen-year-old girl that a $2,000 a month wilderness reform school would cure whatever it was that ailed her through a steady diet of hiking, rafting, climbing, ski touring, and winter camping. She would soon exchange her empty youth culture for a deep love of nature and outdoor adventure.

The experiment was a costly failure. Two years later the girl emerged from the backwoods having addicted many of the school's other kids to drugs and having learned to hate wilderness and camping.

Walking is not for everyone.

In the following story, from Walk on the Westside *(1981), Herbert Gold assures Bill Graham, rock music impresario and reluctant hiking partner, that, "Pleasure comes first. Think of this as pleasure."*

"I'm getting a blister," says the rock promoter (who has never worn his boots before this hike).

"Remember, it's a pleasure."

* * *

"A roshi is a person who has actualized that perfect freedom which is the potentiality for all human beings. He exists freely in the fullness of his whole being. The flow of his consciousness is not the fixed repetitive patterns of our usual self-centered consciousness, but rather arrives spontaneously and naturally from the actual circumstances of the present. The results of this in terms of the quality of his life are extraordinary—buoyancy, vigor, straightforwardness, simplicity, humility—"

(Well, I'll have to strike that "simplicity" and "humility" for Bill Graham.)

"—serenity—"

(That one, too.)

"—joyousness, uncanny perspicacity, and unfathomable compassion. His whole being testifies to what it means to live in the reality of the present. Without anything said or done, just the impact of meeting a personality so developed can be enough to change another's whole life. . . . The Extraordinariness we see is only our own true nature . . . a deep flow of being and joy in the unfolding of Buddha mind."

These words, cited by the roshi Richard Baker about the roshi Shunryu Suzuki, of the Zen Mountain Center of Tassajara, California, also apply to Bill Graham, the monster promoter-in-chief of American rock music, proprietor of the Fillmores East and West and of the various Fillmore enterprises, with a few other modifications not usual to advanced roshiness: Bill has made millions of dollars, yells a lot, and now has sore feet. His improvisational language forced an "R" rating on the movie *Fillmore* (in this case, "R" does not stand for Roshi). He is a master of the put-down and the shut-up. He is one of the great telephoners of our time. He has won the Sitting Indoor Desk-Pounding & Telephone Screaming Contest every year since he started competing, and how he has won is with energy, wit, logic, and naked verbal maximum abusive charisma. He knows that the race is to the quick and the heavy; he is a quick and he is a heavy. He also knows how to honor.

How he got the sore feet: I had a vision of hiking with Bill Graham from Arroyo Seco, in the Las Padres Forest, into the Zen Mountain Center, bringing together two California marvels, man and institution. No telephones, no offices, vow of silence optional. I said to him: "It'll be a pleasure." He had nine thousand things to do, by actual count, including the opening of his movie and a Rolling Stones Tour of the United States. His staff pleaded: "Bill, you can't leave us now." His executive assistant called to say: "I'll tell you what, we'll fly you to New York, our expense, you can follow Bill on his rounds, have a lot of fun, get a great story, meet the superstars."

I said: "My heart is set on a Zen hike."

There was a moment of silence. The silence was saying: "What, you'd rather eat peanut butter sandwiches with some shaved-headed freaks than cavort in Manhattan with some long-haired freaks?"

Although I often use words, I know that silence has power. I clung to the gift of silence with both hands.

He said: "Bill can't make it. Nine thousand things to do—"

I said: "Okay, that's all right, I understand. Money and power come first—" (Oh, the gift of sarcasm and hurtie feelings).

"He'll call you back," his assistant said.

Bill called back: "I'll pick you up in the morning. I'm buying my boots and pack now."

He telephoned once more with a threat: "We're gonna walk into the

Zen woods with our vow of silence, my boots, my pack on my back, and in the middle of the forest I'm gonna unzip my pack and up will shoot an aerial and out will come my port-o-phone and I'll start doing business with both coasts. Schmuck."

Oh Lord, won't you buy me a Mercedes-Benz? I thought of his friend Janis Joplin as we got into the successor to Bill's MG, a Jaguar XKE, top down. He hadn't worn his hiking boots before we set out. His feet started to hurt even as we drove south from San Francisco and through the Carmel Valley toward the Las Padres Forest. Foreboding. But I remembered Shunryu Suzuki's description of Zen Mind: "It is wisdom which is seeking for wisdom."

It would have been wise to suggest to Bill that he break in his boots first, or ask his boot assistant to break them in. In the sutra it says, "There are no eyes, no ears, no nose, no tongue, no body or mind . . ." But did the Buddha ever try hiking ten miles across forest, mountain, and streams with stiff new boots? There are feet, Buddha. There is evil in the world, however the wisdom of the East slices it, and in this case, alas, I represented the sin of omission. O Brothers, would *you* have remembered to say: "Bill, listen. So wear the boots a few hours a day for two weeks ahead of time, while you're telephoning the Stones, cursing out Santana, dealing with the police and the presidents of record companies, firing secretaries, hiring assistants, bailing out musicians, entertaining your son, managing your divorce, promoting your film (*Fillmore,* a rock documentary about the closing of the Fillmore, starring Bill Graham), running benefits for the marijuana initiative and free clinics and any other good cause that corners you in a weak moment, brawling with Hell's Angels, cajoling international superstars, and in general, making a new life somewhat similar to your old one?"

I forgot. He put on the shoes that fateful Sunday morning, after one last transatlantic call to Mick Jagger, and off we roared, stopping only for barbecued steaks in Soledad, California, in a beer-and-grill that looked like the place where the families of death-row convicts gather for a moment of communing with scotch, sirloin, and humming fluorescence.

On to the dark and trackless forest.

Bill's Jaguar XKE down dirt and rutted roads to Arroyo Seco, near a diminishing late spring stream and the horsebridge named Horsebridge. We parked. We slipped on our packs. His feet hurt already. We began hiking in the direction of mountain, river, poison oak, unmarked paths which lead to the Zen monastery hidden deep in the forest. The first three experienced hikers of whom we asked directions each gave us a different fork in the trail. The trail was not marked on our map. It seemed as if we were setting out in all three directions. The monks don't need visitors to rip off their peace, and they have planted roaring waters, earth convulsions, and dangerous herbs in the way. *"What is this?"* Bill asked. "I should be on the phone to the Stones. I should be on a talk show in New York."

"Pleasure comes first. Think of this as pleasure," I said.

"I'm getting a blister."

"Remember, it's a pleasure."

We had either six or eleven miles to go, depending on which path we followed. But we didn't know which path we were following.

The Beatles sang that the sun had come, and the Beatles sang that it was all right, it was all right.

It would be sad to die in the forest for mere pleasure. But pleasure, as Bill Graham knows, means to be a winner. Now the task was to hike from mid-noplace to beautiful somewhere, trudging along with packs on back and sweat running down that mighty media-soaked head, and taking note of the fact that the world is a peculiar place. The orphan survivor from Berlin, the streetfighter from the Bronx, the Bronze-Star winner from Korea, the road-building paymaster and hustling character actor, the middle-aged revolutionary rock millionaire were now at one with a fellow whose shoes pinched. Desperation adrenalin spurted, despair muscles clinched, lymph filled the swellings in Bill's new $76.00 plus tax boots. Dear Pushpin Studios: Please design white space to stand for the Vow of Silence.

Which is filled with suffering unalloyed. When the silence is broken, Bill's undaunted face is blue with pain. We stop and lean against volcanic rocks decorated with dull-green, three-leaf vines. He removes his shoes. He will do the rest of the climb barefoot. No, I suggest, wear two pair of socks. Rocks, twigs, vines, brambles, burrs, bugs, and maybe six miles to go.

Okay, we'll talk. Bill reminisces. He was one of eleven Jewish children to survive a wartime hike from Berlin to Paris to Africa; two hundred started. He can't remember anything until he was ten, but his sister tells him he studied the violin from the age of five to nine. His name used to be Wolfgang Grajanka, and he wishes it still were. He learned to be a streetfighter as an adopted child in the Bronx. His ideal was John Garfield: tough, beetle-browed, a smoker, a destroyer of women, His beautiful secretary used to be Otto Preminger's beautiful secretary. If she could stand Preminger, she could surely bear Graham (in fact, like most people who hang out with him, she has fallen into loyalty and fervor, which is better than love for a businessman with a hundred-odd employees, several corporations, enough equipment to furnish the sound system of Purgatory). He started out with Bonnie, his ex-wife, a stapler, and a Vespa putting up Fillmore posters for the first concert in the middle of the night. Oh yes, before that, as a businessman-actor for the San Francisco Mime Troupe, street guerilla pioneers, he had run a benefit which gave him, like, a little idea that something was happening among the kids out there. A few leaves fall from the calendar. Good God, some slick franchise operators are offering him a cool million and a quarter just for his name, and also the Fillmore name, and to open a chain of fifty-seven Fillmores. "All I'd have to do is cut the ribbons and put my papal Graham blessing on it in Cleveland, Denver, Jacksonville, Houston . . . Kosher! I'd be the psychedelic Joe Louis. I'd be Colonel Sanders." He shook his head. "Not for money. No portable Las Vegas, man."

His face was gray. I couldn't carry him, for sure. But he marched on like a psychedelic Sergeant Valley Forge in his bloody socks.

"Tell me more, Bill," I pleaded. I replaced the Vow of Silence with a Vow of Garrulity. As long as we were talking, he would move. It would soon be six o'clock. I thought I saw the caca of wild boar in the dim path. Nothing overhead but hawks, eyeball-eating vultures, and a few Air Force jets practicing to wipe out the enemies of democracy. The trail crossed the stream thirteen or fourteen times. Tension radiated into Bill's body through his tortured wads of feet. Here we were in Downtown Las Padres Forest, no telephones, only small animals, lizards, snakes, and trees, and he couldn't even relieve himself by clobbering me for getting him into this. He had stood up to maddened rock stars, record producers, cops, junkies, Hell's Angels, and now one mild-mannered novelist was causing him all this pain and he couldn't do the necessary: wipe him out. Well, we're friends.

A long zigzag trail up a steep face.

Pushpin Studios, please do another Vow of Silence. I walked ahead to persuade him there was no use stopping. Silence:

End of silence as we cheer ourselves into the monastery. We have done about six hours, nearly nonstop, with two adequate feet between the two of us. Spirits rise as Zen trainees offer us dinner, now being served in the organic dining room from which flies are customarily chased by flapped towels and monks herding them toward the open window. Haha, folks say when we tell of what roundabout trail we followed, how sore the toes, instep, soles. The food is organic, healthy, strong: breads, honeys, veggies, salads. Bill Graham, a celebrity among these monks, generously tells stories. We clap each other on the back. *Made it!*

The Tassajara Zen Mountain Center, gongs, clicks, sitting zazen, the whole smear, is the largest Zen training center outside of Japan, but it's not your ordinary Zen training center. A hundred years ago it was a mountain retreat; before that the Tassajara Indians enjoyed the magic hot springs. Isolated and pure, certain Zen fellow travelers, such as Bob Dylan and Allen Ginsberg, thought to buy the immense and lovely valley, under the auspices of Shunryu Suzuki:

"The sound of running water is his great speech—"

Now, with the death of Suzuki-roshi, the chief priest is Richard Baker-roshi, and the relationship between training monks and visitors in retreat is a sweet one, abetted by vegetarian meals, the swimming pool and the narrows of the stream, the hiking, the talk, and the thermal baths. Many of the monks are married; some are courting. There is much laughter. Although first-time visitors don't expect a lot of monks from Houston and the Lower East Side, they soon accept the pleasures of this odd vocation.

I had three cakes for dessert. Hungry after the day's walk.

Bill and I headed, he limping, for the hot baths. Dear Pushpin Studios: Not necessary to design ahs, ohs, groans of heterosexual male comradeship and pleasure in survival. Bill's blood circulated toward his feet. We lay and swam in the steaming tubs. "Well, it's all worth it, isn't it, Bill?"

"I wanted to hit myself," he said.

"Is that all?" I asked.

"You were walking too far ahead of me. I couldn't hit you," he said.

Next day we would consider purifying our souls by practicing meditation (sitting zazen), chanting sutras, eating in the Zendo, attending lectures, or perhaps just limping back through the forest. ("The color of mountains is Buddha's pure body.") Bill slept the sleep of the just and the suffering. I cranked up the one phone in the monastery to send a signal to the outside world. Good old Bill, he didn't even call his office or the Rolling Stones in London.

For our departure the sweet Zen monks of Tassajara gave us a lunch of health and organic—dates, figs, honest crunchy peanut butter on honest crunchy Zen bread, fruit, non-grass brownies. Bill worried that these good things might ruin his health, since he ordinarily synthesizes chlorophyl and protein from a steady diet of hamburgers and teevee dinners (sometimes he keeps his metabolism going by heating up three teevee foil trays at 2:00 A.M.).

Roshi Dick Baker gave us the V salute (that's V for Vegetarian) as we departed. Half the V for Vegetarian salute is Bill Graham's famous greeting. It only uses one finger, the central and longest one.

Back to Bill's XKE, parked at Horsebridge, and then on down the road to Route 101 and a return to business in San Francisco. We talked about the Rolling Stones' tour of gratitude which culminated in Altamont. "Gratitude? That'd be like I put on a gold lamé suit, hired a plane, and dropped one live chicken on starving Biafra." He was driving in his stocking feet. Melissa Dilworth, the rock critic and hiking expert, had telephoned her advice to keep his feet out of the sun so the flies don't get them. "I hiked through f—ing Pebbleland," he snarled. "I enjoyed my misery so much I didn't even write on my three-by-five cards."

We stopped for donuts and coffee, necessary to save Bill's life after the Zen health menace-food. "Winchell's Donuts are America's Favorites." The millionaire rock producer had to pay three cents extra for a cup of water on Route 101 at Winchell's Donuts. A sign read: "WE ARE PLEASED TO ANNOUNCE THAT THERE HAS BEEN NO INCREASE IN OUR PRICES SINCE THE ESTABLISHMENT OF THE WAGE PRICE FREEZE. WINCHELL'S DONUTS, 'AMERICA'S FAVORITES.' "

The waitress kept a good eye on us. Her pink plastic curlers were set to go off if we made one false move. We looked like desperate characters, scarfing up America's favorites. Bill's normal tailor is the freaks who left their hats, coats, scarves at the Fillmore. "I send them to Meader's Cleaners first." It's not that he doesn't like his own clothes; he's very tight with his eleven-year-old Mime Troupe corduroy pants and his two sweatshirts. His bounty with friends and performers, with causes and benefits, with his former wife and his son, doesn't extend to spending money on dressing himself. He has soul; he doesn't need to spend money on shirts. He spends money on donuts. He has none of the modern youth-shlock disease which could be called Illusions of Gender. He doesn't need to be surrounded by pretty girls, like James Aubrey or, say, Bernard Cornfeld. He seems to be secure in his masculinity—as secure as a violent and kindly Jewish neurotic Bronze-Star-winning war hero refugee can be imagined to be. He does enjoy wheels, however, his tradition of transportation, from the boyish Vespa to the mighty XKE in which we were now rolling again, top down, feet bare, across the leveled countryside of northern California. We knew we were near home when a rust-colored Continental containing two ladies with identical rust-colored Afro wigs drew alongside and began looking at us, indicating non-Zen delights at the nearest off-ramp.

"Let's come up here again with our women," he said.

Back in San Francisco, we stopped at his office—factory, printing facilities, electronic shop, interlocking sets of rooms and enterprises. Assistants and secretaries trailed after him, asking orders and receiving suggestions: "Throw him out. Say yes, I'll call back. Why not?" They usually trailed off with the question, "Say, Bill, you're not wearing shoes anymore?"

He left for New York the following day to help promote one of his projects. He uses the word f— a lot. He means it. He makes it work for him. He telephoned from New York, between talk shows, to ask what I thought of fighting the "R" rating on a movie. "They say the word f— is an obscenity, but you and I know it's just the shortest distance between two points.

I tried to explain that not everybody knows how essential it is to the life of the streets, in which not everyone is raised. Some have forgotten. The movie-raters are trying to forget.

"Uh-huh, uh-huh," he said, "and by the way"—adding a lot of "R'- and even "X"-rated language—"what I really called to say, Herb, is I had a wonderful time on our pleasure trip and I GOT A F—ING CASE OF POISON OAK, YOU—"

O my brothers, the future is passing swiftly into the past, but Bill Graham has risen through the convulsions of youth-quake into personality, a genius and joy beyond any successful promotion. He is ready for the present again, as he has always been, with a holler, a curse, the compassion of strength, and a bottle of Calamine lotion. Nietzsche said in *The Anti-Christ:* "It is only the powerful who know how to honor, it is their art, their domain for invention."

I had a plaque made, with the following inscription:

ZEN TORTURE SORE FEET PLEASURE HIKE
FIRST PRIZE BILL GRAHAM

and placed it on the belly of a newly-minted Chinese trophy-shop Buddha. I hope he keeps it with his million-selling gold records, his Fillmore posters, his print of Bill Graham playing Bill Graham in *Apocalypse Now*, and his memorabilia of a full life in the magic magnification of media.

I too have poison oak. I itch, burn, scratch, wouldn't have done without this little two-day stroll with Bill Graham-roshi.

Colin Fletcher

The Man Who Walked Through Time

Colin Fletcher is a Welshman, a former World War II British Marine officer, and, since the 1960s, a backpacking authority who lives in California. The Complete Walker has influenced a generation of rec-reational backpackers (though I have never met any high-tech hikers as particular about tea-time and foot care rituals as this guru of the desert).

The Man Who Walked Through Time (1968) is the quintessential Fletcher tale of a solo walk through the Grand Canyon. In bush-whacking one of the world's mightiest chasms, Colin Fletcher was caught in the web of geological time and learned the "simplicity" of nakedness, "a delightful condition."

* * *

When you look down onto the Tonto Platform from the Rim of Grand Canyon you see a flat gray rock terrace that hangs on the very lip of the Inner Gorge. It seems to be quite bare and looks like a very dull place indeed.

When you walk along the Tonto Trail (which runs the whole length of the Tonto Platform and is nowadays, like the Apache Trail, really a wild burro trail) you find that the grayness you saw from above came not from rock but from sparse, dowdy, knee-high bushes. This scraggy fleece part-covers a coarse and often stony soil that varies in color from pale green through gray to almost purple, according to which layers of the many-hued Tonto shale lie close to the surface. And the Platform turns out to be by no means as flat as you had imagined. Even when you swing around a ridge or butte onto the prominent spurs, or headlands, that were all you really saw of the terrace from the Rim, you are always climbing a slope or easing down its far side. You spend less time out on these spurs than you do in sidecan-yons, for the sidecanyons cut back much more deeply than you had imagined. And in these canyons the going is rough.

You are in for another mild surprise too. Although the Platform hangs on the lip of the Gorge, the Tonto Trail tends to hug the inner talus, and you rarely see the Colorado. Occasionally you hear the faint roar of rapids.

If you walk to the edge of the Platform, there is the river, a thousand feet below, at the foot of its plunging black walls. But if you keep to the trail you find yourself walking quite alone, in a world cut off from everything above and below.

Away to the left cuts the black chasm of the Inner Gorge. It is a barrier to more than your body. Because of it, the cliffs and terraces beyond are not a part of your world. You look at them, of course, may even take time to study a particular feature; but mostly (if your mind works the way mine does) everything on the far side of the Gorge moves past as if it existed behind a huge pane of glass.

To your right towers the Redwall. Sometimes you walk close and can pick out a small gray patch where a rock fragment peeled away so recently that iron oxide from the terrace above has not yet had time to seep down and restain the newly exposed surface. Sometimes the trail swings wide, and your eye, encompassing mile after mile of smooth red cliff face, can savor the sweep of each bay and promontory. The Rim, when you can see it, hangs high above and far, far back. The world beyond it lies somewhere out beyond the horizons of your imagination.

When I began to walk through this curiously segregated world I think I was afraid that it would turn out to be as dull as it had looked from the Rim. I need not have worried. . . .

All through the first afternoon I rested beneath the overhang in which I had cached my five gallons of water. Even during the heat of the day it was cool and relaxing there, deep in the shadow of the rock. A bush that by some quirk of chance had germinated far back in a crack in the roof had been forced to grow downward and then outward to meet the light, and a bird's nest neatly woven into its overhanging branches gave the place a comfortable kind of under-the-eaves-of-my-country-cottage feeling. After dark I stood my flashlight on its base and a white alkali-stain on the roof reflected a soft and efficient glow. I slept lightly, the way I tend to if I know that I need an early start next day; and when, soon after four o'clock, I looked out of my picture doorway I saw the morning star slide up over the North Rim. During breakfast, as the night began to slip away, I heard an owl calling me to harness from somewhere in the emerging Redwall; and by the time I had swung halfway around the first spur sunlight came flooding over the buttes like the incoming tide.

All morning I hurried eastward, halting only for brief hourly rests. Spur, sidecanyon, spur, then sidecanyon again. Sometimes the spur-to-spur cycle took an hour, sometimes two; but always there was a steady, rhythmic inevitability about it, comforting and compelling. So compelling that I did not stop for lunch until almost two o'clock. But when I did so at last I knew that I had broken the back of the first long, waterless stretch of the Tonto Platform. And after that the day was different.

But the change stemmed from more than assurance of success. For this was the day I introduced, again more or less accidentally, the week's second catalyst.

Walkers and mountaineers and the like can be divided into two distinct breeds: those who put on the clothes they think are about right, and then stick it out, hour after hour, without apparent discomfort; and those who peel and restore in response to every variation of effort and environment. I belong to the thermally responsive faction: it takes hardly a mile of walking or a side glance of sunshine to strip me down to hat, socks, boots, underpants, and shorts. This was the way I had traveled almost every day since Fossil Bay. But now I had moved not only well into May but also deeper into the Canyon—down to barely three thousand feet above sea level. At noon the day before, in welcome shade, my thermometer had registered 86 degrees. Out in the sun, on bare sand, it had been 126 degrees—and of course I could almost never walk in the shade. But the human body is a remarkably adaptable piece of machinery, and as long as a breeze was blowing I rarely felt too uncomfortable. When the breeze died, though, the heat clamped down.

At lunchtime on the day beyond my five-gallon overhang, the breeze suddenly died. The heat clamped. All at once it occurred to me that in the privacy of the Canyon I could carry my thermostatic clothing system to its logical conclusion. And I promptly stripped to hat, socks, and boots.

Now, nakedness is a delightful condition. And it keeps you very pleasantly cool—especially, I suppose, if you happen to be a man. But as I walked on eastward that afternoon through my private, segregated, Tonto world (exercising due care at first for previously protected sectors of my anatomy) I found I had gained more than coolness. I felt a quite unexpected sense of freedom from restraint. And after a while I found that I had moved on to a new kind of simplicity. A simplicity that had a fitting, Adam-like, in-the-beginning earliness about it.

The new simplicity was there, working, all that afternoon, and all through the days that followed.

Freed from the pressure of haste, the tyranny of film, and now the restraint of clothes, I found myself looking more closely at what went on around me. Not only at a network of white dikes that reached up and out into the black walls of the Inner Gorge, like huge varicose veins serving the molten heart of the earth. Not only at caves hanging high and inaccessible on the Redwall, fascinating as fairy castles can be in childhood. But at the close-ups. At the minutiae. At the network of life that spreads, almost invisible, across the Spartan and apparently inhospitable expanse of the Tonto Platform.

At first I saw only things. Intriguing and often beautiful things, but still just single, unconnected, three-dimensional items.

A prickly pear blazed purple on bare talus. An agave stalk thrust up twenty feet of clustered yellow blooms, and bumblebees droned ponderously around the flowers' entrances, pollen sacs yellow and pendulous. I stopped for lunch, and ants arrived to remove the crumbs: big ants carrying big loads, small ants carrying stupendous loads.

Once, resting in the cool of an overhang, I watched a translucent brown insect scrambling over the stones toward me. It was about half an inch long, six-legged, twin-antennaed, and needle-headed. The upper surface of its body was flat, with cupped edges that made the creature look like a tiny, shallow, pedestrian bowl. I watched for a while as it scrambled nearer. It moved with considerable agility. And some fixed, insatiable purpose seemed to drive it on. Lazily, I wondered why it had such an oddly shaped body. Then my mind meandered off.

A few minutes later I noticed another insect crossing the stones, in the opposite direction. This one, though about the same length, was an ungainly creature, hardly able to haul its heavy, bulbous body along. It moved lethargically, quite without the driving intent of the first. But it too, I noticed, had six legs. And two antennae. And a needle-sharp head. The head looked vaguely familiar, and I bent closer. Then I looked at the body again. It was round and distended, but there was something familiar about that too. And then I saw that the body was distended with a dark-red liquid. And all at once I knew that the liquid was warm as well as red. Was warm mammalian blood. Welsh blood. My blood.

Noon on the trail. I stopped in midstride: three feet from my boots lay a lizard. Cameraless, I crouched slowly down until my eyes were within nine inches of the fat and panting body. The lizard basked on. I took notes. On the roof of the solemn, philosophical, brown-gray head bulged two domes, one above each eye, like a pair of slightly compressed igloos. Around the neck ran a startling collar of blue-gray and white stripes. Back and flanks were speckled; the athletically slim legs, dappled; the long, artistic fingers of the feet, front and rear, a warm golden-brown; and the tail, tapering away almost endlessly, as if reluctant to give way to mere empty space, a uniform and magnificent gold. For a long time the lizard basked on, panting, eyes staring directly ahead in their slightly glazed, reptilinear way. Then, for no apparent reason, it darted off into a patch of scrub.

It was early morning, the day's freshness untarnished. The rattlesnake lay beside the trail, belly up, head pounded almost to pulp, stomach and part of one flank already eaten away by some small-jawed animal. I turned it over. The back was distinctly pink. I stretched the corpse out. It measured a shade over three feet. It was not yet stiff. I examined the scuffle of footprints in the dust and saw that its executioner had been wild burros.

I had been in wild-burro country ever since I crossed the precipitous head of Forster Canyon, back on the far side of Apache Point. The burros came in two brands: buff with black shoulder-and-back stripes, and plain chocolate. All had grizzled muzzles. By effectively maintaining the Tonto Trail through sheer footwork, they seemed to me to have established ownership of the Tonto Platform. Thanks to them there was always—hour after hour, day after day—at least one trail for me to follow.

Often, in fact, the burros had created not one trail but a network. There was usually no doubt about which branch to follow, but sometimes I erred along one created by an obstinate right-wing minority group that liked to wander up the talus toward the Redwall. This let's-go-up-the-hill faction always recognized its mistake in the end and rejoined the main assembly, but to judge by their readiness to deviate again they remained unrepentant. Occasionally a whole web of trails converged at a rolled-bare dust bath. Once, where the soil reflected the junction of contrasting Tonto shales, I was offered and declined two such baths, one purple-red and one green.

There were other reminders of the burros too. Several times a day I would hear, somewhere out in the space and silence, a selection from their wide repertoire of lifelike imitations, ranging from the snort of a dyspeptic colonel to the lowing of a locomotive. And occasionally I would surprise one of them browsing among the green bushes and cottonwood trees that grew on the floors of most sidecanyons, or I would meet one standing with hang-burro mien out in the blazing sun.

Such meetings like my meetings with the rattlesnake and the lizard and the blood-bibbing insect, were at first no more than meetings. No more than the chance intersection of two animals' life-paths.

But after two days of carnival and rhythmic progress along the Platform—spur and sidecanyon, spur and sidecanyon, sunrise and noon and sunset, silence and space and solitude, Gorge and Redwall and distant Rim, sunrise and sunset, spur and sidecanyon—I found myself beginning to see beyond the meetings. I found myself seeing us all not merely as animals that happened to be there on the Platform, but as passing performers in a long, long dance. And I found that I understood this dance not merely with the thin comprehension of intellect, but so radically and so clearly that after a little while its surge and rhythm were as sure as the meetings themselves, if not surer.

I saw the burros now as recent accidental importations by such men as William Bass. I saw them as creatures that had found in the Canyon, and in particular along the Tonto Platform, an empty or sparsely occupied niche in which they could live and thrive and multiply, even in the face of a stupidly conceived Park Policy that at one time sought to eliminate them. I saw them too as the hosts that, above all, made it possible for small insects with shallow blood-bowls on their backs to fill those bowls often enough to keep alive. (It was not often, obviously, that these insects smelled, Fee, Fi, Fo, Fum, the blood of a hot Welshman.)

And I began to see—clearly, in my confused Celtic way—other linkages. I saw the burros as executioners with frenzied hooves that played a minor part in keeping within reasonable bounds the population of pink-backed rattlesnakes. I saw the rattlesnakes as organisms that were in part kept alive by—and also helped keep under control—speckled Western collared lizards that basked in the sun, plump and panting, in order to warm their cold, premammalian blood sufficiently to hunt, or even to digest their food. I saw the lizard as an organism that in part kept itself alive by feeding on small insects that in their turn kept themselves alive by feeding on warm-blooded burros. I saw the lizard too, feeding on other insects that buzzed, busy in bright desert sunlight, around the entrances of yellow flowers clustering on a Maypole-straight agave stalk.

And I saw the agave now as part of the green bedrock of life on earth. As a part of the plant life that captures for this planet the energy of the sun and stores this energy and hands it on to insects that buzz around its yellow flowers sucking nectar, and to other animals that feed on other parts of it, such as certain kinds of lizards, or perhaps a browsing wild burro, or a party of Supai Indians squatting around a mescal pit. A burro or an Indian that in turn gives nourishment to a blood-bowl of an insect that in turn feeds a lizard that in turn feeds a rattlesnake that in turn feeds something else with small jaws. . . .

In other words, as I walked on eastward along the Tonto Platform, almost as naked as the other animals, I began to see everything around me as an intricate, interlocking web of life.

And the web, I saw, covered more than the three dimensions of the Tonto Platform. It also extended back in time.

I saw in the pinkness of the rattlesnake the result of an immensely slow but very sure selection that had taken place during the comparatively recent two or three million years since the Canyon began to approach its present size. A selection favoring individuals that by chance were born pink. For because their color blended with the dominant pink of the Canyon's rock and so protected them from enemies, and so to produce more offspring—which in turn tended more and more often to have pink skins.

Now I saw the lizard not just as an individual organism, but as a life that was helping to carry forward the development of a species that had in its time helped carry forward the development of life from cold-blooded to warm-blooded land animals. I saw it as a twig on a branch of life that may still, for all we mammals know, have a viable future.

I saw that such single-minded creatures as a little walking blood-bowls (which presumably feed on nothing but their favorite food) could hardly have prospered until warm-blooded mammals such as ground squirrels or wild burros or stray Welshman had already gained a footing.

And I saw the flowering agave as a newcomer form of plant life. For brightly-colored flowers would not have evolved successfully if there had been no insects for their bright colors to attract. Individual plants that by chance mutation produced flowers would have gained no advantage for their kind: they would not at that time have attracted insects. Not, at least, insects that could act as unknowing agents for the spread of the plants' reproductive pollen—and thereby increase the number of these plants' progeny so effectively that in the end the newfangled flower bearers would compete out of existence those similar plants that had not happened to produce flowers. Now, there have probably been plants on the land surface of the earth for something like 400 million years—that is, since soon after the laying-down of the mud that is now the shale of the Tonto Platform. But flying insects of the kind likely to cross-pollinate flowers regularly in the course of their own search for nectar did not appear in large numbers until about 180 million years ago—that is, after the creation of the white limestone of the Canyon's present Rim. Soon afterward (10 million years later, say, or 30 million), flowering plants duly began to flourish. They are, as I say, comparative newcomers in the plant world.

But perhaps I am cheating when, in an effort to convey how things looked to me during those hot and rhythmic days along the Tonto Platform, I quote these specific biological details. I rather doubt that during those days I fully understood them all. Yet, oddly enough, it does not matter. For I do not believe that at the time I *thought* very much about this intricate web-in-time: I *felt* it. Felt myself an integral part of everything that went on around me. Felt it with a simple and straightforward certainty I had never known before. Felt myself not only as a part of the web of life as it happened to exist in the present, but as a part of the throbbing, pulsating process that is all we know. A process of which this present web is merely a fingerprint.

As I walked on eastward, spur after spur after sidecanyon, day after day, I think I must have known that the time had not yet come to look too closely at this web. For although the animal meetings were perhaps the highlight events of each day, what occupied my eyes and my mind more steadily—minute after minute, hour after hour, spur after sidecanyon—were still the rocks, that foundation across which the web of life is spread and from which it almost certainly arose.

Edward Abbey

Desert Solitaire

Desert Solitaire (1968) was written as an elegy to the American South-
west the author knew as a U.S. Park Service seasonal ranger. Edward
Abbey described Desert Solitaire *as a tombstone for the desert wilder-*
ness.

"You're holding a tombstone in your hands. A bloody rock. Don't
drop it on your foot—throw it at something big and glassy. What do
you have to lose?"

This is the same Edward Abbey whose novel the Monkey Wrench
Gang *contributed to popular culture the phrase "monkey wrenching"*
(meaning acts of sabotage against despoilers of the environment).

The following excerpt from "Cliffrose And Bayonets" tells of a
patrol Abbey made in Arches National Monument in southeast Utah.

* * *

The sun is rising through a yellow, howling wind. Time for breakfast.
Inside the trailer now, broiling bacon and frying eggs with good appetite, I
hear the sand patter like rain against the metal walls and brush across the
windowpanes. A fine silt accumulates beneath the door and on the window
ledge. The trailer shakes in a sudden gust. All one to me—sandstorm or
sunshine I am content, so long as I have something to eat, good health, the
earth to take my stand on, and light behind the eyes to see by.

At eight o'clock I put on badge and ranger hat and go to work, checking
in at headquarters by radio and taking my post at the entrance station to
greet and orient whatever tourists may appear. None show. After an hour
of waiting I climb in the government pickup and begin a patrol of the park,
taking lunch and coffee with me. So far as I know there's no one camping
in the park at this time, but it won't hurt to make sure.

The wind is coming from the north, much colder than before—we may
have sleet or rain or snow or possibly all three before nightfall. Bad weather
means that the park entrance road will be impassable; it is part of my job
to inform campers and visitors of this danger so that they will have a chance
to get out before it's too late.

Taking the Windows road first, I drive beneath the overhanging Balanced Rock, 3500 tons of seamless Entrada sandstone perched on a ridiculous, inadequate pedestal of the Carmel formation, soft and rotten stone eaten away by the wind, deformed by the weight above. One of these days that rock is going to fall—in ten, fifty, or five hundred years. I drive past more free-standing pinnacles, around the edge of outthrust ledges, in and out of the ravines that corrade the rolling terrain—wind-deposited, cross-bedded sand dunes laid down eons ago in the Mesozoic era and since compressed and petrified by overlying sediments. Everywhere the cliffrose is blooming, the yellow flowers shivering in the wind.

The heart-shaped prints of deer are plain in the dust of the road and I wonder where the deer are now and how they're doing and if they've got enough to eat. Like the porcupine the deer too become victims of human meddling with the natural scheme of things—not enough coyotes around and the mountain lions close to extinction, the deer have multiplied like rabbits and are eating themselves out of house and home, which means that many each year are condemned to a slow death by starvation. The deerslayers come by the thousands every autumn out of Salt Lake and California to harvest, as they like to say, the surplus deer. But they are not adquate for the task.

The road ends at the Double Arch campground. No one here. I check the garbage can for trapped chipmunks, pick up a few bottlecaps, and inspect the "sanitary facilities," where all appears to be in good order: roll of paper, can of lime, black widow spiders dangling in their usual strategic corners. On the inside of the door someone has written a cautionary note:

> Attention: Watch out for rattlesnakes, coral snakes, whip snakes, vine-garoons, centipedes, millipedes, ticks, mites, black widows, cone-nosed kissing bugs, solpugids, tarantulas, horned toads, Gila monsters, red ants, fire ants, Jerusalem crickets, chinch bugs and Giant Hairy Desert Scorpions before being seated.

I walk out the foot trail to Double Arch and the Windows. The wind moans a dreary tune under the overhanging coves, among the holes in the rock, and through the dead pinyon pines. The sky is obscure and yellow but the air in this relatively sheltered place among the rocks is still clear. A few birds dart about: black-throated sparrows, the cliff swallows, squawking magpies in their handsome academic dress of black and white. In the dust and on the sand dunes I can read the passage of other creatures, from the big track of a buck to the tiny prints of birds, mice, lizards, and insects. Hopefully I look for sign of bobcat or coyote but find none.

We need more predators. The sheepmen complain, it is true, that the coyotes eat some of their lambs. This is true but do they eat enough? I mean, enough lambs to keep the coyotes sleek, healthy and well fed. That is my concern. As for the sacrifice of an occasional lamb, that seems to me a small price to pay for the support of the coyote population. The lambs, accustomed by tradition to their role, do not complain; and the sheepmen, who run their hooved locusts on the public lands and are heavily subsidized, most of them as hog-rich as they are pigheaded, can easily afford these trifling losses.

We need more coyotes, more mountain lions, more wolves and foxes and wildcats, more owls, hawks and eagles. The livestock interests and their hired mercenaries from the Department of Agriculture have pursued all of these animals with unremitting ferocity and astonishing cruelty for nearly a century, utilizing in this campaign of extermination everything from the gun and trap to the airplane and the most ingenious devices of chemical and biological warfare. Not content with shooting coyotes from airplanes and hunting lions with dogs, these bounty hunters, self-styled sportsmen, and government agents like to plant poisoned meat all over the landscape, distribute tons of poisoned tallow balls by air, and hide baited cyanide guns in the ground and brush—a threat to humans as well as animals. Still not satisfied, they have developed and begun to use a biochemical compound which makes sterile any animal foolish enough to take the bait.

Absorbed in these thoughts, wind in my eyes, I round a corner of the cliff and there's a doe and her fawn not ten yards away, browsing on the cliffrose. Eating flowers. While she could not have heard or scented me, the doe sees me almost at once. But since I stopped abruptly and froze, she isn't sure that I am dangerous. Puzzled and suspicious, she and the fawn at her side, madonna and child, stare at me for several long seconds. I breathe out, making the slightest of movements, and the doe springs up and away as if bounced from a trampoline, followed by the fawn. Their sharp hooves clatter on the rock.

"Come back here!" I shout. "I want to talk to you."

But they're not talking and in another moment have vanished into the wind. I could follow if I wanted to, track them down across the dunes and through the open parks of juniper and cliffrose. But why should I disturb them further? Even if I found them and somehow succeeded in demonstrating my friendship and good will, why should I lead them to believe that anything manlike can be trusted? That is no office for a friend.

I come to the North Window, a great opening fifty feet high in a wall of rock, through which I see the clouded sky and the hazy mountains and feel the funneled rush of the wind. I climb up to it, walk through—like an ant crawling through the eyesocket of a skull—and down the other side a half-mile to a little spring at the head of a seldom-visited canyon. I am out of the wind for a change, can light up my pipe and look around without getting dust in my eyes; I can hear myself think.

Here I find the track of a coyote superimposed on the path of many deer. So there is at least one remaining in the area, perhaps the same coyote I heard two weeks ago wailing at the evening moon. His trail comes down off the sandstone from the west, passes over the sand under a juniper and up to the seep of dark green water in its circle of reeds. Under the juniper he has left two gray-green droppings knitted together with rabbit hair. With fingertip I write my own signature in the sand to let him know, to tip him off; I take a drink of water and leave.

Down below is Salt Creek Canyon, corraded through an anti-cline to the bed of the Colorado. If I were lucky I might find the trail of bighorn sheep, rumored still to lurk in these rimrock hideaways. In all these years of prowling on foot through the canyons and desert mountains of the south-west I have yet to see, free and alive in the wild, either a lion or a bighorn. In part I can blame only my ignorance and incompetence, for I know they are out there, somewhere; I have seen their scat and their tracks.

As I am returning to the campground and the truck I see a young cottontail jump from the brush, scamper across the trail and freeze under a second bush. The rabbit huddles there, panting, ears back, one bright eye on me.

I am taken by the notion to experiment—on the rabbit. Suppose, I say to myself, you were out here hungry, starving, no weapon but your bare hands. What would you do? What *could* you do?

There are a few stones scattered along the trail. I pick up one that fits well in the hand, that seems to have the optimum feel and heft. I stare at the cottontail hunched in his illusory shelter under the bush. Blackbrush, I observe, the common variety, sprinkled with tightly rolled little green buds, ready to burst into bloom on short notice. Should I give the rabbit a sporting chance, that is, jump it again, try to hit it on the run? Or brain the little bastard where he is?

Notice the terminology. A sportsman is one who gives his quarry a chance to escape with its life. This is known as fair play, or sportsmanship. Animals have no sense of sportsmanship. Some, like the mountain lion, are vicious—if attacked they defend themselves. Others, like the rabbit, run away, which is cowardly.

Well, I'm a scientist not a sportsman and we've got an important experiment under way here, for which the rabbit has been volunteered. I rear back and throw the stone with all I've got straight at his furry head.

To my amazement the stone flies true (as if guided by a Higher Power) and knocks the cottontail head over tincups, clear out from under the budding blackbush. He crumples, there's the usual gushing of blood, etc., a brief spasm, and then no more. The wicked rabbit is dead.

For a moment I am shocked by my deed; I stare at the quiet rabbit, his glazed eyes, his blood drying in the dust. Something vital is lacking. But shock is succeeded by a mild elation. Leaving my victim to the vultures and maggots, who will appreciate him more than I could—the flesh is probably infected with tularemia—I continue my walk with a new, augmented cheerfulness which is hard to understand but unmistakable. What the rabbit has lost in energy and spirit seems added, by processes too subtle to fathom, to my own soul. I try but cannot feel any sense of guilt. I examine my soul: white as snow. Check my hands: not a trace of blood. No longer do I feel so isolated from the sparse and furtive life around me, a stranger from another world. I have entered into this one. We are kindred all of us, killer and victim, predator and prey, me and the sly coyote, the soaring buzzard, the elegant gopher snake, the trembling cottontail, the foul worms that feed on our entrails, all of them, all of us. Long live diversity, long live the earth!

Rejoicing in my innocence and power I stride down the trail beneath the elephantine forms of melting sandstone, past the stark shadows of Double Arch. The experiment was a complete success; it will never be necessary to perform it again.

Patricia Armstrong

In Love with Tundra

Spontaneous enthusiasm and love of Nature can always win me over. But how many people are there nowadays who would admit to feelings of rebirth and freedom at the sight of scraggly, stunted trees?

   Patricia Armstrong's love of tundra has led her around the world in search of plants which thrive in the harshest above-treeline conditions. She has walked many ridgetop miles to commune with tundra flowers; she even shares certain personal qualities with them.

   And me? What flower am I? That's hard for me to say. I might be moss campion, snuggly warm and delicately pretty, until I think of alpine forget-me-nots. My eyes are blue. Then I remember the sky-blue eyes of the Andes gentian in Peru, and I think I'd like to spend forever there at 18,000 feet, watching condors soar over Nevado Cayesh.

This selection originally appeared in Backpacker *magazine.*

* * *

I have always been in love with tundra. It's funny too, because I grew up in the Midwest, farther away from mountains than any other place in the United States. I didn't even see a mountain until I was nearly 25, with a husband and two baby daughters.

We made our first trip to the mountains, accompanied by a babysitter and a rotten old army tent borrowed from friends, at the end of August, 1961. We drove straight through to the Blackfeet Indian Reservation in northwestern Montana. There in the middle of the night we stopped. We were near enough to see the mountains, and we wanted our first view to be at dawn. The five of us contorted around the junk in our beat-up old car and tried to snooze while waiting for the sun. We were awake well before the first fingers of light began to play on the tallest mountains. Ever so gently the peaks began to glow. The rosy luminescence spread slowly from one mountain to another and slid down the ridges to fill the valleys. Every detail stood out against blue shadows. We held our breath.

Too soon, the magic faded and the mountains stood stark and bare, flat and cold, where before they had been so warm and inviting. We crossed into Canada and headed west from Calgary, directly into the Rockies. We set up our first tent camp in Yoho Valley, British Columbia. We had come 2,113 miles in less than three days. We were tired, yet sleep came hard. It was like Christmas Eve. Takakkaw Falls plunged 1200 feet from the base of the Daly Glacier and the Waputik Icefield, the second tallest waterfall in America. The night wind brought the mist up the valley to settle heavily on our tent. Tomorrow we would walk in the mountains, see them up close, feel them.

Dawn finally came at 5:30. It was cold. All our provisions as well as the camp's water supply were frozen. We left the girls in care of the babysitter and began our first day in the mountains.

When I think of how we slept in newspapers and blankets in that heavy army tent and how we carried our jackets in a bucket and took 30 feet of old clothesline with us, I laugh. We have come a long way since then, but some things have never changed. I will always remember our love-at-first-sight encounter with the alpine world. I have never been the same since.

The subalpine forest of the Canadian Rockies is much taller and more lush than the boreal forest of our native Michigan. The Engelmann spruce (*Picea engelmannii*) and subalpine fir (*Abies lasiocarpa*) grow tall in the cool, snowy environment. Dense moss carpets and flowers brightened our path as we headed upward. We climbed 1000 feet in the first mile, switchbacking 27 times.

At 6000 feet the trail leveled off in a beautiful mountain meadow. Flowers danced before our eyes: scarlet Indian paintbrushes (*Castilleja miniata*), pink twinflowers (*Linnaea borealis*), daisies (*Erigeron peregrinus*), white valerians (*Valeriana sitchensis*), grass-of-Parnassus (*Parnassia fimbriata*), harebells (*Campanula rotundifolia*), bluebonnets (*Lupinus sericeus*) and golden groundsel (*Senecio triangularis*). I had never seen so many different colored flowers at one time before. We couldn't even stand without crushing something lovely.

We hiked around Mount Wapta toward Mount Field. The valley fell off on our right. Far below, the greenish-white Emerald Lake looked like a dish of creamed pea soup. Trees with grizzled bare heads and dense green skirts shrank to our size and even smaller. They clustered behind boulders and in the lea of ridges until, finally, there were none. We had reached timberline, our very first timberline. We seemed to stand taller in relation to the world, to see farther and feel closer to the sky. It was a glorifying yet humbling experience.

At timberline the continuous forest ends. Above it trees appear in clumps and are dwarfed and twisted by the wind. These elfin trees are called

Krummholz. They extend upward to the tree limit above which the only trees are prostrate willows and birches. Above these is tundra.

Timberline and tree limit are determined by several factors. The most important is temperature. As one goes upward in elevation, or north or south toward the poles, the temperature drops. When the mean temperature for the hottest month of the year averages 50 degrees Fahrenheit or less, trees begin to disappear. This happens at 72 degrees north latitude and 56 degrees south latitude.

The precise altitude of timberline depends on latitude and precipitation. It is lower close to the poles (2300 feet in Alaska, sea level in Antarctica) and higher near the equator (13,000 feet in Mexico, 12,000 feet in Ecuador). In the Canadian Rockies there is heavy winter snowfall, and timberline is at about 7000 feet. The highest timberlines in the world are in the Himalayas a little north and south of the equator and in the Andes, where the highest mountains occur in the driest altitudes.

Above the last elfin tree, we entered the enchanted land of tundra. From there until permanent snow and ice prevented the growth of most flowering plants, grasses, sedges and flowers enjoyed the unhampered freedom of the heights. Turflike meadows were ablaze with color. Shrubby heaths and tiny tufts among the rocks competed for our attention. It was the pink star-studded pin cushions that grabbed my fancy. I marveled at such courageous beauty flaunting the blast of glacier winds. I flung myself to the ground, eye to eye with moss campion (*Silene acaulis*), my first alpine friend. It is one of the most widespread alpine plants, growing on mountains from Alaska to Mexico and completely around the globe in the arctic. It can be found also in the mountains of New England, and in the Alps, Carpathians, Pyrenees and Apennines of Europe.

Moss campion snuggles its compact cushion among wind-rounded rocks and gravels on the harshest ridges. A long taproot anchors it in granular soil and stores nourishment. It may take 10 years for a cushion to grow big enough to flower, and a 25-year-old plant may be only seven inches in diameter. That day, the plant's flowers smiled among its dense leafy hemisphere only a few inches above the ground, where my cheek felt the warmth of the gravel and the quietness of the wind.

Another plant not far away was the dryad (*Dryas octopetala*). Its tiny fernlike leaves wove dense mats across the scree and its feathery seed heads were spread like a cockatoo's crest. Back-lit by the sun, they made shimmering islands on the broken stones. A few plumes rode the wind and bumped across rocky places. A butterfly buffeted by the same breeze landed on the moss campion. As the insect sucked its life-giving drink from the flower, I looked up to see an eternity of sky, clouds and rugged peaks. My lifelong love affair with mountains had begun.

*   *   *

The altitude, airy views and dazzling clarity of the place struck both of us. Chuck leaped to his feet and jerked me up. We shouted and waved across the valley. Sometimes echoes answered back but mostly there was only the screaming wind. We cavorted on the meadow, dancing hand in hand in wild circles till we fell exhausted to the ground. Then, laughing, we rolled downhill in each other's arms and slid to a stop behind a boulder. We heard the scree go sliding on and on until it vanished and the great silence of the summits shushed us.

Out of the wind, we basked in the warmth of mountain sun. We heard wind-worried sand ping against the rocks and felt the angles and grooves where differential hardness had opposed the eternal etching process. We marveled about the few plants able to smile here despite the hostile winds.

Fellfields, or wind-swept boulder fields, are far better developed in the southern Rockies than in the Canadian Rockies. There, cushions of alpine forget-me-not (*Eritrichium aretioides*), dwarf clover (*Trifolium nanum*), Rocky Mountain nailwort (*Paronychia pulvinata*) and alpine phlox (*Phlox condensata* or *P. pulvinata*) mix their bright colors with moss campion. These hardy plants take their shapes from the rocky places where they live. To appreciate their beauty and smell their lovely fragrances, you must lie down and view them at their level.

We resumed climbing, hand in hand, our bucket swinging in the breeze. Plants became scarcer; here and there in the cold shade of craggy places we found snow. We put our jackets on and continued to climb.

The vascular plant limit and the snow line usually occur at the same altitude. It is wherever the average mean for the warmest month of the year is 32 degrees Fahrenheit. There is no time for blooming and setting seed. The soil is almost always frozen and not a source for plant nourishment. The only plants that can survive are those that don't need warm periods to live. Mosses, lichens and algae are well adapted to this harsh environment.

The zone above the vascular plant limit has been called Aeolian, after the Greek god of wind. Since temperatures there rarely go above freezing for long, plants obtain all their nourishment from wind-blown debris and snow melt. In such dry areas as the low-latitude Himalayas and Andes, the snow line is extremely high, and plants grow at 20,000 feet. In northern North America, the snow line is low, and there are extensive Aeolian zones.

Exploring the Aeolian zone of Mount Wapta and Mount Field required technical rock climbing skills. Before we had gone far, better judgment got the best of us. We didn't know why mountaineers carried rope or how they used it, but we realized our clothesline wasn't good for much. We stood for a long time looking up at the beckoning skyline and out across the dark green abyss. We dared not go on, yet we were reluctant to leave. Sadly, we finally traced our footsteps down the rocky face, across the scree and cushion plants to the tundra meadow of our rapture, and down to our camp in the fir forest. We kept stopping to look back, to remember how it had been. We knew we would have to return.

In the years that followed my husband and I took up climbing. I went back to school to learn about tundra and spent several summers with the University of Colorado in Rocky Mountain National Park, with Michigan State University on the Juneau Icefield in Alaska, and on a 10,000-mile Edlund-Armstrong-Olmsted-Abbott-Corydalis Expedition, of the University of Chicago, to the mountains of the eastern United States. In 1968 I finished my master's research on bryophytes and lichens. Since then the mountains of the Western Hemisphere have become my classroom, and the plants that grow there my instructors and friends.

Nowadays, we carry lightweight mountain tents with snow liners and rain flies. We have good mountain boots, backpacks and down sleeping bags. On the trail I carry a six-by-ten-inch backpacking plant press and some flower books as well as my share of camp gear, climbing and photographic equipment.

Each time I see the forest dwindle into Krummholz—as I pass into the area of "elfinwood"—I feel reborn and free. I still have worldly cares; I must use my judgment to stay alive under conditions often harsh and dangerous. But I am self-sufficient. I have food and shelter on my back and a knowledge of mountains in my head.

I have laughed in the teeth of 100-mile-an-hour winds, slept snuggly in the snow at 30 below, found my way in the darkest night and whitest fog, been soggy wet and mosquito bitten for two weeks straight, and felt the presence of lightning all around and through me. Yet I love it. Like the tundra flowers or the lowly lichens, I have learned to adapt so I can enjoy the worst as well as the best.

My whole family reminds me of certain tundra flowers. My youngest daughter, Becky, is a pink mountain heather, *Phyllodoce empetriformis*. Tough, wiry, stormy mornings and sunny afternoons, a snow-bed plant, sleeps late. Somewhat mischievous, slippery footing on the steeps; yet petite and feminine with dainty chiming bells. Imaginative and talkative.

My older daughter, Jackie, is a dryad, *Dryas octopetala*. A rebel, chumming with her cohorts, taunting the established ways, daring slidey scree. Long shaggy hair back-lit in the sun, radiantly beautiful when happy. Not a part of any community. Aloof, yet clannish with her kind. A hidden potential to heal the world's erosion scars with boundless love.

My best female friend and companion on many tundra treks is an alpine sunflower, *Hymenoxys grandiflora*. A big blonde Swede, she's wholly beautiful. Her sunny countenance and laughing eyes have shared a world of passion and pain with me.

My husband? An elephanthead, *Pedicularis groenlandica*. Unexpected humor, delight of mimicry, cheerful smile despite heavy pack and soaking feet. I take strength and warm comfort from his ever-presence in my mountains.

And me? What flower am I? That's hard for me to say. I might be moss campion, snuggly warm and delicately pretty, until I think of alpine forget-me-nots. My eyes are blue. Then I remember the sky-blue eyes of the Andes gentian in Peru, and I think I'd like to spend forever there at 18,000 feet, watching condors soar over Nevado Cayesh.

When at last I reach the slower, grayer years, I can become an arctic gentian, *Gentiana algida*, pert in blue-black lace and faded scarlet shawl against the eternal snows that must surely come.

Lois Crisler

The Pacific Coast Ranges

The late Lois and Herb Crisler made wildlife films for Walt Disney. Their adventures filming wolves and caribou in Alaska are recounted in Artic Wild *(1956).*

The following account in The Pacific Coast Ranges *(1946) tells of an autumn hike the Crislers made across the core of the Olympic Mountains in Washington state.*

* * *

We left the trail by Oyster Lake, a shallow pool on the top of Appleton Ridge, five miles up from the Olympic Hot Springs. Scarlet huckleberry coated the steep side of the ridge ahead of us. Erratic game trails a few inches wide made imperceptible terraces around it, and along them, heavy with our full packs, we picked our way to a pass above Cat Creek, and contoured in to Cat Creek Basin.

It was a cloudy, dull evening but the basin glowed with color—the rose color of the huckleberry. In low green thickets as we entered, we had jumped groups of elk. Here in the basin itself two bulls were challenging. One big pale cream-colored bull lay couched with majestic command on a shelf by a dark pointed clump of alpine fir, his herd grazing the fuchsia-colored slopes above him. At intervals he answered a vibrating bugle coming from near us, down on the floor of the basin. As we stood silently looking, the challenger, a brown-headed bull, stepped out of a clump of trees. He bugled and moved toward us, his antlers high. He stopped to challenge, first the king up on the hillside, then us, who were standing very still. He pawed, ripped up the ground with his antlers; his sides heaved with the quick fierce bark. Then he slowly advanced. I felt like running, but he got suspicious and turned, moving off slowly and proudly.

We struck Wildcat Ridge the next morning, a jagged cleaver with alpine fir fans flung over it. I stepped on their springy limbs and clung to the boughs, feeling blindly, over sheer space, for a place to get my foot down to the sharp rock. For an hour it was tough going with our heavy packs.

The worst place came near the other end of the cleaver, where Herb grabbed a long fir limb and swung across a steep, bare slope like a pendulum.

He came back for my pack, and I launched out timidly, got astride of my alpenstock half way over, but clawed up onto the rock on the other side, trembling. The cleaver flattened to hold a muddy pool, a game wallow, by the bear and deer tracks, and on the grass near, under the low firs, I sprawled flat on my back to regain my nervous equilibrium.

From there around the bare southern flank of Mount Carrie, a seldom-climbed wildnerness peak, seven thousand feet high, we contoured along game trails. Four thousand feet below us the Hoh River made a silvery scratch through its gray gravel bars. The dark-timbered ridges south of it rose into the white crests of Mount Olympus and Mount Tom, another peak rarely climbed. We had been following an elk "travel trail," which gave us in places very good footing, but it drifted down onto a ridge while we kept our elevation, running into one place so sheer, above a thousand-foot drop, that I lost my nerve for the second time and stuck to the mountainside like a postage stamp, till Herb, ahead and almost at a standstill himself, conceded, "Turn around. We'll try it lower."

Game trails are plainest where the choice of travel routes is the scarcest. If they run out or seem to spread over the country in "feeding trails," the chances are that the going is fair anywhere along this strip. But you must be on the alert and try to pick up the travel trail when leaving this area to cross a rough strip. If you start across without a game trail, you are liable to get into very rough going or even get stuck.

When we broke around a "corner" of the mountainside into Eleven Bull Basin, the shallowest and briefest of shelves, we halted silently to watch a bear browsing just ahead of us, before we even noticed two more a little higher. We camped at Eleven Bull that night in the low black firs at the edge of the drop-off. I had laid my bag in a game trail, which made a slight cradle for me, and in the morning I heard a rustling beyond the foot of my bag. The head of a doe, her tall ears up, was looking at me over the bushes. It was probably that she had never seen a human being before. She vanished as I sat up, then came slipping back to peep and stare.

In sunshine we climbed out of the basin to head a rock gorge and hit a travel trail. Around the middle of a cliff that to me had looked impassable, it opened foot by foot as we advanced, getting us safely across. We were traveling above timber, and now from back of us and far below, a fog front moved in from the Pacific. We paused occasionally to watch it moving up the Hoh Valley toward us. Overhead the sun hazed and we were in a cool world between two cloud layers. Across the valley Mount Olympus and Mount Tom looked wild, white, and desolate above the bluish, timbered mountainsides. The wind from ahead of us and the undulating fog river moving up from behind were battling below us now. Suddenly the vapors sifted up through the treetops toward us, and in five minutes, chill and light-moving, had softly closed us in.

"Can you find the way?" I asked with anxiety. Herb traveled steadily ahead. In an hour the wind had won and the fog was drawing back toward the ocean. We passed bear and bucks, scores of elk, and a flock of pine grosbeaks.

About noon Herb stopped and looked a moment, then quietly drew back with a smile, turning to me. "There's your first view of Cream Lake," he said.

Beside a clump of alpine scrub I stood and looked silently down at the basin below and ahead of us. Seated at the base of a circle of mountains, with Mount Ferry white beyond, and Mount Olympus off to the right, a great mountain basin opened out—the largest, the wildest I had seen in the Olympics. Far below us spread the "seat," a pale green valley marked with blue water channels. At its extreme edge, beside the drop-off, lay a spot of color, the creamy, glacial blue-green of Cream Lake itself. We jolted down the steep mountainside, foot below foot, till at last the descending skirts of the slope swept out in green, to the level shore of the lake. There we camped.

Flat on the ground in our bags that night, we looked up at the black spires of the firs against the stars. Every few minutes sounded the clear keen bugle of an elk, sometimes near, sometimes far.

We ascended the basin in the sunny morning, picking huckleberries as we went, my freshly washed spare shirt drying like a flag from my alpenstock. The third lake we came to lay cradled in clean white living rock. I stripped and went in. As I dried on a blue bandanna, big raindrops hit my bare back softly, falling from a momentary haze overhead.

To our right opened out a wide pass looking toward the shining Hoh Glacier on Mount Olympus. We bore to the left of the pass, contouring around the south side of Mount Ferry into a saddle, then heading southward over rock and snow toward Mount Olympus along the crest of the Bailey Range. The wild region at the head of the Goldie spread far below the crags to our left, and jagged peaks and snow fields to our right.

There is one place where this spine of the Olympics widens a little, and the firs, centuries old, a few feet high, spread their dense skirts over its windward edge—a place where we could lay our eiderdown bags that night, pull the drawstrings snug around our necks, and fall asleep, to waken now and then under dense stars, in the profound stillness on this spit of land in the sky, with the void on each side and white mountains dim beyond.

We were near our goal now. The next day, over snow and dark jagged rock, we climbed up and down into swales along the very crest of the Bailey Range again, then up a rather wide snow field, to break over into the head of the Queets Basin. The basin did not open out suddenly, but in a succession of steep descents and little basins.

Camp that night was deeply satisfying. The toil and uncertainties of the trip were over; only the delight remained. There is an inimitable delight about making camp in the wilderness. The problems presented all must and can be solved immediately—the wood show, the water show, the "bedroom." There is none of the circuitousness with which food and shelter are obtained in civilization.

We camped on a wide grassy spur under crags crowned by sharp-spired clumps of alpine fir, overlooking the Queets Basin, across which rose Mount Barnes and Mount Queets. Toward dawn I wakened sleepily. It was very still. Fog was studying what it could do: folding in, dim white, then falling away to let in a window of dark crag and swallow it again; or half disclosing a black, pointed fir, then veiling it. It was like watching preliminary studies for the creation of a world.

As we climbed away toward the Dodwell-Rixon Pass, the mists were dissolving against the blue sky and off the shining glacier; the huckleberry brush shone crimson and translucent against the long sun just topping the ridge ahead. It was the Olympic symbiosis at its best. We dropped down the Elwha snow finger and out to our homeward trail. For six days we had not followed nor crossed a man-made trail nor seen a human being. Ah, wilderness!

Belmore Browne

The Conquest of Mount McKinley

Few people realize that dog sledding can involve much more walking than it does riding. Often the musher walks or trots beside the sled for many grueling miles in the harshest of winter conditions.

This practice was part of Belmore Browne's fun in the winter of 1912 as he and his partner, Professor Parker, attempted to move their supplies far enough into the interior to make a summit assault on Mount McKinley, as described in Browne's book, The Conquest of Mt. McKinley *(1913).*

* * *

Now the value of dogs in the north fluctuates with the seasons. When the trails begin to harden and winter throws its mantle of snow across the land there is corresponding boom in the dog market, while in the springtime when the dogs' usefulness vanishes with the melting snows they can be purchased for a song. In order to profit by the spring "slump" we commissioned Arthur Aten to buy dogs for us, and when the summer of 1911 arrived we possessed a strong and well-trained team.

But plans are made but to be broken. With the coming of spring came a call of "Gold!" from the north. With feverish haste we packed and stood ready. Then followed travel-worn letters that told us that "strikes" were being made along the glaciers, of Prince William's Sound. Mount McKinley was for the time, forgotten, and we spent our summer among the ice-fed fiords.

With the coming of winter our thoughts drifted back to the big mountain and when the first snow flurry came down from the Kenai Mountains we were ready to advance. Aten and La Voy were the only men of the old party to join Professor Parker and the writer. Our journey was to be entirely different in character from the work we accomplished in 1910, for speed in dog travel depends on a small party, and we no longer needed the large number of men necessary for relay packing. It was with the keenest regret however that we started on the long trail without our old companions.

As we were to enter the Alaskan Range just east of Mount McKinley our route would lead us up the familiar waterways of the Susitna and Chulitna rivers. But as Cook Inlet was choked with ice during the winter time, we were forced to leave the steamer at Seward.

Seward lies at the head of Resurrection Bay on the south side of the Kenai Peninsula. It is from this port that the incompleted railroad, so often mentioned in the newspapers, starts on its long journey to the interior. Striking directly through the heart of the Kenai Peninsula the railroad winds and tunnels for eighty miles through magnificent mountain scenery to tide-water on Turnagain Arm at the head of Cook Inlet. At this point construction has ceased, but a winter trail leads from the end of the line to Susitna Station via Knik Arm. Beyond Susitna Station a winter trail now leads over the Alaskan Range at the head of the Kichatna to the Kuskoquim and the gold fields of the Iditerod. This three-foot strip of foot-hardened snow is the only link now joining the village that will some day be a city with the wildnerness that in days to come will be an inland empire. The road is not operated in the winter time but the grade is too valuable to stand idle, and after the ties and tracks are covered with snow the scream and rumble of the loco-motive gives way to the jingle of dog bells.

At intervals of about ten miles, "road-houses" stand offering food and rest to man and dog. They are one of the most important of Alaskan insti-tutions, and on all the winter trails that criss-cross the great land, one will find these resting-places which make rapid travel possible.

Now only one man can drive a dog team. When "the going is bad" an extra man can *help*. But the Seward trail was supposed to be a good trail.

For that reason Professor Parker and I turned over our outfit to Aten and La Voy in October. They were to relay our supplies to Susitna Station and then up the Susitna as far as they could, returning to Susitna Station to meet us in February. At Seward La Voy met a "sour-dough" fresh from the Iditerod. He had come over the long trail bound for "the outside" and sold his dogs, sled, and fur sleeping-robe for a ridiculously low price. This addition gave us fourteen dogs for the heavy hauling, and each one had more than earned his cost before our freight rested at Susitna. A telephone line that connected the road-houses was a great help to us. Our companions 'phoned the news of their progress to Brown & Hawkins—the leading merchants of Seward—who kindly forwarded the messages by mail. In this way we were able to keep track of our companions until the day arrived when we too were to start on the long trail.

It was during the last days of January that our steamer drifted in between the fog-draped cliffs of Resurrection Bay. Only ten years before I had been in the same harbour; but now a bustling Alaskan town was scattered over what had then been a green spruce-covered point, and along the water front I could see the trestles of the new railroad whose right of way we were going to follow with our dog teams. The mountains alone were unchanged and looked down through the fog rifts as they did in the old days. To me this is one of the most striking facts in our great country—the rapidity of growth. I have heard an Englishman earnestly comparing (unfavourably) the transportation facilities of a Western city with those of London when I could remember the days when the stumps of forest trees were still obstructing the main avenue of that city! When I first saw Resurrection Bay it was little more than a wilderness fiord. When our little steamer, that, in any other land, would long since have been condemned, came to rest, a canoe came gliding from the shore. The man who paddled it was calling aloud for a minister. The minister was wanted by one Bill or Tom and "he wants to get married *bad*" the canoe-man added, "for he has two kids already!" Such was Seward in the old days, but even then it was historical ground. The Russians had settled there when Alaska belonged to the White Bear, and the first wooden man-o'-war ever launched on the Pacific coast was built by them in this sheltered harbour.

On our sail along the Alaskan coast we had been overcome with forebodings of trouble through the mildness of the winter. No winter like it could be remembered, even by "the oldest inhabitant." Our wildest fears were realised as we walked to our hotel along the Seward streets for the thin glare of ice that covered the ground was melting perceptibly.

Our first task was to find a traveller with a dog-team who was going to Susitna Station, for besides our personal duffle of fifty pounds to the man the invariable forgotten or left-over things had swelled our belongings to a weight of three hundred pounds. Fortune led us to the United States mail-carrier, Vause by name, who was starting over the trail in a few days.

He turned over his second team to us, partly loaded with second-class mail matter—which under his contract he is not forced to deliver. This raised our load to five hundred pounds while he carried an equal bulk of letters on the lead-sled. For a number of days we kicked our heels about the streets of Seward, waiting for the weather to turn cold. In the meanwhile the town was stirred by the arrival of the Iditerod gold shipment.

The gold was packed in small wooden chests—one hundred pounds to the chest—which were handled with grunts and groans by the bank clerks who took them from the dog sleds. The populace stood packed about, but fully one half of their interest was centred on the two magnificent, perfectly matched dog teams that had pulled the treasure from the banks of the Kuskoquim, four hundred miles to the north.

The dogs were owned and driven by "Bob" Griffith, better known as "Dog" Griffith among the trail men. He knew dogs better than a Kentucky horsemen knows horses, and had participated himself in the greatest sporting event of this world—"The Nome Sweepstake"—when men race an unlimited number of wolf-dogs over four hundred miles of frozen Alaskan trail.

We met him later as he wanted tallow to feed to his dogs and I had an over supply to trade. From his lips and those of Mitchell, the driver of

Griffith's second team, we heard picturesque but awful things concerning the condition of the Susitna trail. On the theory that the longer we waited the worse things would be, we set the following day for our time of departure.

An earthquake—the precursor possibly of the Katmai eruption that buried Kadiak Island in ashes—rattled the frame houses as we prepared our outfit for the trail.

We said good-by to Seward and its hospitable citizens on the first of February. We crossed a piece of rough trail through the waste of burnt and slashed timber common to Alaskan towns before reaching the shelter of the woods.

In the shelter of the timber we found snow enough to grease our sled runners and before long we were trotting along the line of the railroad.

Vause led with a five-hundred-pound load of mail lashed on a Nome sled, drawn by five dogs. Professor Parker travelled with the lead-sled, while I followed them at the gee-pole of the second Nome sled loaded also with 400 (four hundred) pounds, and drawn by four dogs.

Unless one has been in the north it is hard to realise the importance of the "broken trail." In the winter time the whole country is covered with several feet of soft, powdery snow. This snow is seldom crusted until the spring thaw sets in, and in consequence it is difficult to travel through; even a man on snowshoes may find it arduous work. But after a man has walked over it his snowshoes leave a broad path that freezes hard, and on this narrow strip of frozen crust dogs can pull a loaded sled. As the trail is used it grows broader, firmer, and smoother, until in time it becomes in reality a "winter trail."

After a snow-storm, or a heavy drifting wind, the trail must be rebroken, and at times when it becomes completely effaced you feel your way with a sharpened pole lest you lose the trail and the benefit of its firm foundation.

Now dog-driving, when you have a heavy load and the going is bad, is about as strenuous a job as a man can tackle. Even one week of idleness will allow hardened muscles to become soft, and after many months of city life, no matter how conscientiously one has *exercised* according to civilised standards, the body is in no condition to stand the demands of the trail.

On our first day's run we put twenty-one miles of soft snow behind us. The trail was in execrable condition. The warm weather had rotted the snow, and the sleds in consequence were continually breaking through and turning over into the soft snow beside the trail. Now when a sled turns over or "killapies" its outside runner has a fiendish way of catching under the hard lip of the trail; put five hundred pounds on top of the sled and it is a man-sized job to lift it back onto the trail again. When you have trotted twenty-one long, soft snow miles punctuated frequently with these sled episodes your very bones cry out against your past months of idleness.

Another source of bruises and bad language that we encountered were the numerous trestles. There was a drop of about three feet from the surface of the trail to the ties.

The snow had fallen through between the timbers which were capped with cones of hard ice. We would nurse our dogs as gently as possible to the edge of the trestle and then give them the word to "Mush!" Vause's dogs being under his constant supervision and at the head of our line took the bridges quietly, a thing which few dog teams will do. As I was a stranger to the dogs I drove and as they were behind they took the bridges with a rush. The "gee-pole" or steering-pole is lashed to the right-hand runner of the sled in such a position that the end comes level with your right hand when you stand six feet in front of the sled. When the sled slid from the level of the trail the gee-pole first swept out into space and then plunged down to the level of the ties. As it is absolutely necessary to hold on to the gee-pole to guide the sled, we had to take the drop-off on the run, leap out into space, land, somehow, on the ice-capped ties, and *keep running* while the ice scraped the skin from the knuckles of our right hands. It was dashing, bone-breaking work, and would have made good moving picture "stuff," but when you are wedged between ice-capped ties with the steel runners of a four-hundred-pound sled grinding your back, it's hard to appreciate the picturesque side of things!

About twelve miles from Seward stands the first road-house, and here we got a bite to eat and rested the dogs. Some miles beyond we came to our first trouble; the bridge over Snow River had been washed out by a freshet and the rails and ties hung in midair, held only by the spikes and fish-plates. One look at this aerial route was enough, and we descended to the naked gravel bars of the river bed and by doubling our two dog teams relayed the sleds over a jury-bridge of logs.

When we reached the railroad again it had been transformed by the late freshet into a ridge of ice. On the top of this "ice tight-rope" we juggled with sleds and dogs. Once, my foot slipped and I landed with my sled and dogs in a tangled heap at the base of the ridge. Night overtook us beyond Snow River, and it was inky black when we saw the lights of our night's shelter.

Vause was trail-hardened, having carried mail since the first snow, and to him our day had been only a moderately strenuous one. But to me— fresh from the flesh-pots—it savoured of "hard labour."

With all this work however there goes the invariable recompense; back of all these aches, and strains, and cuts, and bruises lies the knowledge that you are being made over; it is only nature's way of doing the job. It is always hard when you first "hit the trail," but as you think of the days to come, when, with a body as hard as those of the dogs you drive, you can trot unwearied the long day through, the game seems well worth the candle.

Robert Marshall

Alaska Wilderness

Robert Marshall (1901–1939) was a U.S. Forest Service planner and visionary whose work led to the establishment of the National Wilderness Preservation System. One of America's most famous official wildernesses, the Bob Marshall Wilderness in Montana, is a tribute to his wildlands preservation leadership.

Wilderness is a peculiarly twentieth-century concept. Our present urban delight in the "untrammeled" character of the backcountry continues to grow in proportion to its scarcity.

Bob Marshall experienced true wilderness at a time (the 1930s) just before every place on the map became "managed" by administrators. The arduous-but-joyous hikes he made throughout Alaska have become the stuff of legend among the outdoor fraternity. They were also what killed him. He died very young of a heart attack, probably caused by overexertion. His brother George Marshall's introduction to the posthumously-published Alaska Wilderness *explained that Bob's*

> *"joy at discovering the Arctic wilderness among the dramatically magnificent mountains, canyons, and rivers of the Koyukuk drainage of the Brooks Range north of the Arctic Circle in Alaska was matched by his pleasure in coming to know intimately the sourdoughs and Eskimos who comprised the remarkable civilization which existed on its borders. Bob found in both the wilderness and in this frontier community some of the essentials of freedom of the human spirit for which he fought and which seemed so lacking in the twentieth-century world of the nineteen-thirties."*

Bob Marshall was the best type of wilderness devotee; he loved the backwoods people as well as their land. He revelled in the pleasures of the city as well as those of roadless areas. He was complete.

Near the end of his short life he wrote to his former Alaskan partner, Ernie Johnson, "I can't think of anything more glorious than to be on the trail with you again and exploring some more of what still remains to me the most beautiful country I have ever seen. . . . There is still much exciting country to explore there and it would be too bad not to take advantage of it."

[The following adventure took place in August 1930.]

*   *   *

On the morning of our eighth day below the Arctic Divide, it was still raining, our tent was beginning to leak, and the prospects of clearing seemed so remote that we decided to pull out. We shouldered what we fortunately thought were 60-pound packs apiece—later they turned out to weigh 70— and started down the long seventeen-mile grind to the mouth of Ernie Creek. Before starting we ditched a week's food supply, including 8 pounds of sugar which nearly broke my heart, and took with us only 12 pounds of this most concentrated food. The packs felt so heavy at first, especially to Al who had less experience in back packing than I, that when after two hundred yards I let out a loud cheer at the completion of one one-thousandth part of our journey home, Al answered with a disgusted grunt. We stopped about three times per mile, sitting down always on a sloping bank or rock so that we could rest the packs without removing them. Shoulders straining, backs straining, heads straining against the headstraps, we scarcely appreciated the grandeur of the Valley of Precipices. On the whole the going was fairly good; but the last five miles, through clumps of sedges, made a substantial installment on the required payment for our one week in heaven.

We pitched our tent near Ernie Johnson's cabin at the Ernie Creek forks and used his stove for cooking. The cabin at this season was too damp and dirty for sleeping. As it alternately rained and snowed the next day we stayed close to camp, but I spent much of the time making growth measurements and stand tables in the timber adjacent to the cabin.

The following day we were off before seven for a two-day exploration of the upper North Fork—Al's exploration to be largely by pan and shovel, mine by map and camera. We took no sleeping bags or tent, planning to "siwash" out for the night—to camp Indian fashion without equipment. Thus we had very light loads, just my photographic and Al's prospecting equipment, a little food, a pot and frying pan, and the gun.

We covered the eleven miles above our starting point in about four hours, and reached a large stream coming in from the east which I later named Amawk Creek, meaning wolf creek. The scenery was superb—on the left a high gray stone ridge cut by six deep gulches; on the right the multipinnacled summits of three mountain masses rising 5,000-6,000 feet above the valley floor and divided by two great gorges. In the center, the upper North Fork, as it twisted back and forth across the valley, was in continual foam. We picked a campsite about half a mile above Amawk Creek, and, after an abbreviated lunch, continued on our way, Al to pan and I to explore.

Near our campsite, the upper North Fork turned toward the north. Straight gray stone walls rose steeply on either side of the valley through which the river had cut. After five miles, I reached a second sizable stream coming in from the east, which a little later I named Alinement Creek. From this point the upper North Fork continued in a northerly direction for several miles to the Arctic Divide. I gave this northern extension of the upper North Fork the name Nakshakluk Creek, meaning creek of the blocked pass, because a mile upstream it issued from a deep canyon which blocked the way.

Near the mouth of the junction of Nakshakluk and Alinement creeks, where I was standing, Charlie Irish of Noland and Ernie had been hunting before. Apparently no human being had been up Alinement Creek, however, which flowed in from the east; so I determined to explore it.

A mile and a half brought me to a small permanent icefield. I slipped across, then passed a little knoll, and suddenly found myself five hundred feet from a band of seventeen sheep. They ran up the mountainside while I snapped three pictures. As I continued up the valley I observed that the north divide consisted of the unusual group of almost equally high peaks in perfect alinement which I had marveled at from Limestack. They were a little more than a mile apart, and there were seven of them in the ten miles between Nakshakluk Creek and the final fork of Alinement Creek. Below each rocky, snow-capped summit, a deep gulch with a heavy flow of water descended. These numerous breaks in the topography added excitement to the exploration of this unknown river, for it was always a mystery as to just what would be in the deep draw ahead.

Although, on the whole, the valley of Alinement Creek was much less precipitous than the Valley of Precipices or the Grizzly or Kenunga Creek valleys, the country was enough on end to suit the most ambitious climber. Best of all, it was fresh—gloriously fresh. At every step there was the exhilarating feeling of breaking new ground. There were no musty signs of human occupation. This, beyond a doubt, was an unbeaten path.

Then for a short distance I wished it were a lot more beaten. The river kept boiling down the narrow valley, now sharp up against one steep side, now flush against the other. Occasionally I had to leave the bed and climb over high cliffs. But usually I could pick my way around at the base. At one such place, where a schist ledge came down straight to the edge of the river, the rock near the base had fragmented and I could use its right-angled cleavage for a precarious footing.

There was a stretch of about forty yards which totally absorbed my attention as to how to place my feet. When I looked up, my heart stood still, as the books say. About 150 feet ahead were three grizzlies. This may seem like a long distance to a catcher trying to throw a man out stealing second, but not to a man faced by three bears, eleven miles from the closest gun, hundred and six from the first potential stretcher bearer, and three hundred from the nearest hospital. As in Goldilocks, the first bear was small, probably a two-year-old, the second was of medium size, the third appeared like two elephants plus a rhinoceros. They reared up, one after the other, from little to gigantic, just like so many chorus girls going through some sprout in sequence. They stood for a moment and then got down on their four legs and disappeared into the willows.

I continued upstream. As the water from each deep gulch was subtracted from the volume of the main creek it became noticeably smaller. When I finally came to the last forks, only a little brook was left. Here, virtually at the head of the upper North Fork, I reluctantly turned around.

I made the fifteen miles back to Al and our siwash camp at a four-mile-an-hour clip. The feeling of striding through untrammeled terrain was only a little less keen than going out. It had cleared, and the spectacle at the Nakshakluk Creek forks was one of wild grandeur. Downstream, framed by the cliffs where the river cut through Graystone Ridge rose a jagged rock wall more than 4,000 feet high and three miles long. Directly across Nakshakluk Creek rose the paired pinnacle of Twoprong Mountain, each prong jutting straight up into the sky. Upstream was the dark canyon from which Nakshakluk emerged, and across the canyon appeared massive Inclined Mountain, with its dark, tilted strata. The Alinement peaks, one after the other, seemed alive as the late afternoon sun played queer pranks around their snowy tips, while real life was added to the scene by five sheep feeding on one of the low, grassy hills near the forks.

When I reached our camp I found that Al had made the best possible preparations for a cold night without blankets. He had cut willow and spruce boughs to lie upon, inclined slightly toward the fire, and had collected a great quantity of dry wood. In addition, a delicious macaroni and vegetable dinner awaited me. The night passed as nights without blankets usually do when there is no cut bank to reflect the fire's heat. We were alternately roasting and chilling, with little sleep, but beyond that, not too uncomfortable. At two o'clock in the morning a fairly strong wind came up followed by snow. By half past five we started, but visibility was so limited that we realized further exploration for the day was useless and returned through a heavy snowstorm to our camp near Ernie's cabin. We just stopped once to examine the deep gorge separating Doonerak from Wien Mountain. A big creek came out of it, seemingly leaping from the clouds in two sheer falls of 500 and 200 feet. The upper fall was the largest and most impressive single plunge I have seen in northern Alaska.

Had the weather been even tolerable the next day, we would have climbed Hanging Glacier Mountain. But it was storming all around us, showed no indications of clearing, and it seemed to be time to get out. We shouldered our packs, now reduced to 65 pounds each, and started on the long trailless trek to Wiseman, ninety-one miles away.

Our seven-day journey back to civilization can be summarized in three words—damn hard work. These could not, however, be repeated ninety-one times, once for each mile, because there was a vast difference among the miles. Some, along gravel bars, we hardly noticed. Others were such, that it seemed ridiculous anyone of his own free will should put himself to such grinding effort. Opposite one gulch it took us fifty-five minutes to make half a mile. We were forced to proceed along a very steep side hill, where even without pack a person would have had a hard time worming his way through the tangled alder thickets. With brute strength we simply tore our way through the brush. There was also a very difficult stretch where the river takes a great loop to the west. We had to climb uphill for four miles through sedge tussocks and over half-frozen moss into which we would sink to our ankles at every step. It was snowing steadily that day, which made our rests chilly and uncomfortable and our footing very slippery. As I looked dimly through the storm up the North Fork, frozen along the banks and completely surrounded by the snow-covered landscape, I was ready to believe that this really was the Arctic. The worst going was at Jack Delay Pass. Here the sedge tussocks were so high and grew so close together to make walking between them impossible. But it was also impossible to walk on top of them for any distance, because they would roll over, plunging us off into muck. This would happen about once in every twenty steps and as we took about two thousand steps to the mile I think it conservative to say that at least a hundred times in each of three endless miles we would find ourselves sitting on the ground, a 65-pound pack anchoring us firmly in the mud, with an overhanging cliff of sedge formation nearly waist-high towering above us. We would grit our teeth, gather energy, and pull ourselves up the necessary three feet—only to do it all over again within the next twenty paces.

Nevertheless, there was genuine exhilaration in triumphing over the toughest conceivable travel. Tired we would be, but never worn out; difficult as the going was, we always had plenty of reserve. It was the kind of stimulation I had received earlier in my life from such varied activities as climbing the five slashed summits of the Adirondack's Dix Range in one day with my brother George and our friendly Adirondack mountain guide Herb Clark; racing through twenty-nine stormy Idaho days out of thirty in November, 1927, to finish a program of experimental work, coming home from the woods each night soaked through and then doing office work until long after midnight; staying up forty hours without sleep on a water-relations study at Johns Hopkins; or suddenly, after hard concentrated study, getting a glimmer of the significance of the quantum theory. I could give many other examples but the principle is always the same. It is the great stimulus for mental and physical adventure alike—simply the joy of triumphing over something which is difficult to accomplish.

There were two pleasant half-day interludes on our homeward journey. In the first we climbed the Redstar Mountain, fifteen miles south of the junction of the North Fork and Ernie Creek. This mountain had excited our interest on every one of the three previous occasions when we passed it, because it was capped by a red, star-shaped blotch, probably 2,000 feet across. We had been too rushed or too wet to stop before, but this time, despite snow flurries all around, we determined to investigate the source of this brilliant coloration. The ascent proved very easy, about 2,500 feet in elevation and four miles in distance with only the last 400 feet steep. We found that the entire top of the mountain as well as the tops of the higher peaks immediately north, were an igneous upthrust, the only one we had seen in this vicinity. The red, a vermilion, was only superficial, the interior of the rock under its coating being a steel gray. Much of the vermilion substance, all pulverized, was scattered in the rock crevices and over a large area. What it was mystified us as much as ever. Al picked up some of it for analysis at the Alaska School of Mines in Fairbanks.

The second interlude came when I shot a moose on the afternoon after we left the camp near Ernie's cabin. The first shot, at about 700 feet, tore off a hind leg, and the rest was simple. Like the Indians, we made camp where the moose died, dressed him, and cached most of the meat—I planned to return with a dog team, when the first snow came. We cooked a feast which included the tongue and two huge T-bone steaks. The moose was a young bull which Al estimated to weight about 450 pounds dressed. Shooting the moose gave me a dual pleasure. First, I never tasted more delicious meat than that we enjoyed at every meal for two days. Second, when in the future certain of my friends would chide me for being a reluctant nimrod and when it would be too complicated to explain that a living wild animal is more beautiful to me than a dead one, I would be able to elevate my nose a trifle and remark: "Oh, deer (or elk, or goats as the case may be) seem too tame after moose."

The last night out the thermometer dropped to 15. The following day it remained cool all morning and we did not perspire while staggering up the steep mountainside to Pasco Pass. Once through it, our last real difficulty was over, and the remaining eleven miles to Wiseman were downhill. We reached the house of the Pingels on Nolan Creek in time for a noon dinner, after a most hearty reception. We spent most of the afternoon around Nolan, telling our tales, hearing the latest news and enjoying the company of other human beings, after four weeks of wilderness. After 101 trailless miles of back packing, from Grizzly Creek to Nolan, the seven miles of road to Wiseman seemed easy, even though excessively muddy. I sat down flat once. When we hit the last mile from the foot of the big hill into Wiseman we were going strong and struck a four-mile-an-hour pace into town. Everybody dropped around to the roadhouse that evening and it was very pleasant to talk with our friends. Very pleasant too it was to find seventeen letters awaiting me.

Thus ended a glorious trip. I had not felt the slightest eagerness to get back to civilization. There had been much hard work, but never any real discomfort and we had traveled efficiently. It had been just an active unexciting trip physically, but the most thrilling in aesthetic pleasure.

Our record of exploration included the ascent of six until then unclimbed mountains, three of them on the Arctic Divide; the visiting of three major unexplored valleys and six minor valleys, gulches, and chasms; and the mapping of forty-two miles of until then untraversed valleys.

Our scientific record included the study for growth of six stands of timber, the laying out of four sample plots to determine the size of trees and number per acre; the launching of an experiment testing tree establishment beyond timber line; the collecting of rock samples which we brought back for identification; and the opening of animal stomachs to determine feeding habits.

We had prospected six creeks and had found gold in none of them; and we had seen a black bear, two moose, seven grizzly bears, and three score sheep.

Our personal statistics included the carrying of packs and leading of horses for two hundred sixteen miles, side-tripping with light packs for a hundred and seventy miles; the killing and partly eating of three sheep, one moose, and one grizzly bear; the catching and enjoying of one hundred and twelve grayling; and the gathering of delicious blueberries and cranberries.

I should like to conclude the account of this trip with a few words about my partner. Although we had no important interests in common aside from this particular journey, Al was considerate, affable, and eager to help me in accomplishing my purposes. He was the most resourceful person imaginable. He could do everything from patching up the split hoof of a horse to repairing my camera. He was better than I in every one of the many activities of our trip except for walking, back packing, mapping, and photographing. He did twice as much work around camp as I did, yet never even hinted that he was doing more than his share of the work; nor was he disgruntled that my objectives were entirely realized while his ended in total failure.

Additional Reading

Abbey, Edward. *Desert Solitaire: A Season in the Wilderness*. New York: McGraw-Hill, 1968.

Adamson, George. *My Pride and Joy*. New York: Simon and Schuster, 1987.

Allen, Benedict. *Who Goes Out in the Midday Sun?: An Englishman's Trek Through the Amazon Jungle*. New York: Viking, 1985, 1986.

Armstrong, Neil, Michael Collins and Edwin E. Aldrin, Jr. *First on the Moon: A Voyage with Neil Armstrong, Michael Collins and Edwin E. Aldrin, Jr*. Boston: Little, Brown and Company, 1970.

Armstrong, Patricia. "I'm In Love with Tundra." *Backpacker* 15 (June 1976, Volume 4, Number 3).

Bailey, Anthony. "Reporter at Large." *New Yorker* (June 2, 1980).

Belloc, Hilaire, ed. *The Footpath Way: An Anthology for Walkers*. London: Sidgwick & Jackson, Ltd., 1911.

Belloc, Hilaire. *The Path to Rome*. New York: Longmans, Green, 1902.

Beston, Henry. *Northern Farm: A Chronicle of Maine*. New York: Rinehart, 1948.

Blanchard, Smoke. *Walking Up and Down in the World: Memories of a Mountain Rambler*. San Francisco: Sierra Club Books, 1985.

Bonython, C. Warren. *Walking the Flinders Ranges*. Adelaide, Australia: Rigby, 1971.

Bonython, C. Warren. *Walking the Simpson Desert*. Adelaide, Australia: Rigby, 1980.

Booth, Alan. *The Roads to Sata: A 2,000 Mile Walk Through Japan*. New York: Viking, 1985.

Brooks, Paul. *Roadless Area*. New York: Knopf, 1964.

Brown, Hamish M. *Hamish's Groats End Walk*. London: Victor Gollancz Ltd., 1981.

Browne, Belmore. *The Conquest of Mount McKinley: The Story of Three Expeditions Through the Alaskan Wilderness to Mount McKinley, North America's Highest and Most Inaccessible Mountain*. New York: G. P. Putnam's Sons, 1913. Boston: Houghton Mifflin Co., 1956.

Browne, Waldo Ralph. *Joys of the Road: A Little Anthology in Praise of Walking*. Chicago: Browne's Bookstore, 1911. Freeport, New York: Books for Libraries Press, 1970.

Cahill, Tim. *Jaguars Ripped My Flesh: Adventure is a Risky Business*. New York: Bantam, 1987.

Chatwin, Bruce. *In Patagonia*. New York: Summit Books, 1977.

Cherry-Garrard, Apsley. *The Worst Journey in the World: Antarctic 1910–1913*. London: Chatto & Windus, 1965.

Chesterton, G. K., in *The Oxford Book of Literary Anecdotes*, James Sutherland, ed. New York: Oxford University Press, 1975.

Chiles, Lawton. "Lawton Chiles Walks-and-Talks Through Florida." Mimeographed diary, 1970.

Chitty, Susan and Thomas Hinde. "Making Each Day Extraordinary." *Quest/77* (September/October 1977).

Churchill, Winston. *My African Journey*. London: The Holland Press, 1962.

Clark, Ronald W. *Freud: The Man and the Cause*. New York: Random House, 1980.

Clyde, Norman. *Norman Clyde of the Sierra Nevada: Rambles Through the Range of Light*. San Francisco: Scrimshaw Press, 1971.

Crawford, Mary. "Trekking With Harry." *Mountain Gazette* VII (November 1977, Number 2).

Crisler, Lois. *Arctic Wild*. New York: The Curtis Publishing Co., 1956.

Crisler, Lois. "The Wilderness Mountains." In *The Pacific Coast Ranges*, Roderick Peattie, ed. New York: Vanguard, 1946.

Critchfield, Richard. *Shahhat: An Egyptian*. Syracuse, New York: Syracuse University Press, 1978.

de Saint-Exupéry, Antoine. *Wind, Sand and Stars*. New York: Harbrace Paperbound Library, 1939, 1940, 1967.

Edelman, Bernard, ed. *Dear America: Letters Home From Vietnam*. New York: W. W. Norton & Co., 1985.

Eiseley, Loren. *The Star Thrower*. New York: Harcourt Brace Jovanovich, 1978.

Evans, Griffith. "A Seven Block Walk of Architectural Whims." *The Globe and Mail* (Toronto) (July 1, 1974).

Fermor, Patrick Leigh. *A Time of Gifts: On Foot to Constantinople: From the Hook of Holland to the Middle Danube*. New York, Harper & Row, 1977.

Fermor, Patrick Leigh. *Between the Woods and the Water: On Foot to Constantinople from the Hook of Holland: The Middle Danube to the Iron Gates*. New York: Viking, 1986.

Fisher, Ronald M. *The Appalachian Trail*. Washington, D.C.: National Geographic Society, 1972.

Fleming, Peter. *Brazilian Adventure*. New York: Charles Scribner's Sons, 1933. New York: Houghton Mifflin Co., 1983.

Fletcher, Colin. *The Man Who Walked Through Time*. New York: Knopf, 1971.

Fletcher, Colin. *The Thousand Mile Summer*. New York: Vintage Books, 1964, 1987.

Fletcher, Colin. *The Winds of Mara*. New York: Knopf, 1973.

Fossey, Dian. *Gorillas in the Mist*. Boston: Houghton Mifflin Co., 1983.

Frankl, Viktor E. *Man's Search for Meaning: An Introduction to Logotherapy*. New York: Washington Square Press, 1964.

Frome, Michael. *Strangers in High Places: The Story of the Great Smoky Mountains*. New York: Doubleday, 1966.

Gareth, Caitlin. "Walking My Dog in Montrose." *The Magazine of the Houston Post* (October 28, 1984).

Gavron, Daniel. *Walking Through Israel*. Boston: Houghton Mifflin Co., 1980.

Gibbons, Euell, "Stalking the Nearby Places." *Organic Gardening and Farming* XX (November 1973, Number 11).

Gide, Andre. *Travels in the Congo*. New York: Knopf, 1929.

Gilbert, Douglas and Clyde S. Kilby. *C.S. Lewis: Images of His World*. Grand Rapids, Michigan: Eerdmans, 1973.

Glazebrook, Philip. *Journey to Kars: A Modern Traveller in the Ottoman Lands.* New York: Atheneum, 1984.

Glover, James M. *A Wilderness Original: The Life of Bob Marshall.* Seattle: Mountaineers, 1986.

Gold, Herbert. *A Walk on the West Side: California on the Brink.* New York: Arbor House, 1981.

Gutkind, Lee. *The People of Penn's Woods West.* Pittsburgh: University of Pittsburgh Press, 1984.

Hall, Wilson. "Alabama's Secret Wilderness." *Backpacker* 30 (December 1978/January 1979, Volume 6, Number 6).

Halle, Louis J. *Spring in Washington.* New York: Harper & Brothers, 1957.

Halliburton, Richard. *The Royal Road to Romance.* Indianapolis: The Bobbs-Merrill Co., 1925.

Harman, Michael G. *The Arizona Limited or Across the Continent Afoot.* Richmond, Virginia: Southern Publishing Co., 1909.

Harvey, Andrew. *A Journey in Ladakh.* Boston: Houghton Mifflin Co., 1983.

Hay, John. *The Great Beach.* New York: Ballantine, 1963.

Hemingway, Ernest. *A Moveable Feast.* New York: Charles Scribner's Sons, 1964.

Higham, Roger. *Island Road to Africa.* London: J. M. Dent & Sons Ltd., 1968.

Hillaby, John. *A Walk Through Europe.* New York: Houghton Mifflin Co., 1972.

Hillaby, John. *Journey Home.* New York: Holt, Rinehart and Winston, 1984.

Hillaby, John. *Journey to the Jade Sea.* London: Constable and Company, Ltd., 1964.

Hoagland, Edward. *African Calliope: A Journey to the Sudan.* New York: Random House, 1979.

Hoagland, Edward. *Walking the Dead Diamond River.* New York: Random House, 1973.

Hodson, Peregrin. *Under a Sickle Moon: A Journey Through Afghanistan.* Boston: Atlantic Monthly Press, The Atlantic Traveller, 1987.

Holzach, Michael. *Deutschland Umsonst: Zu fuss und ohne geld durch ein wohlstandsland.* Hamburg: Hoffman Und Campe Verlag, 1982.

Idriess, Ion L. *My Mate Dick.* Sydney: Angus & Robertson Ltd., 1962.

Jenkins, Peter. *A Walk Across America.* New York: Morrow, 1979.

Jenkins, Peter. *The Walk West.* New York: Morrow, 1981.

Kazin, Alfred. *A Walker in the City.* New York: Grove Press, 1951.

Kerasote, Ted. *Navigations.* Harrisburg, Pennsylvania: Stackpole Books, 1986.

Kerouac, Jack. *The Dharma Bums.* New York: Buccaneer Press, 1958.

King, Harry, ed. *South Pole Odyssey: Selections from the Antarctic Diaries of Edward Wilson.* Dorset, UK: Blandford Press, 1982.

Konopa, Charles. "The Reason Why." Unpublished.

Kubly, Herbert. *Native's Return: An American of Swiss Descent Unmasks an Enigmatic Land and People.* New York: Stein and Day, 1981.

Kyme, Hector E. *A Million and More Strides.* London: Robert Hale, 1975.

La Bastille, Anne. *Woodswoman.* New York: E. P. Dutton, 1976.

Lawrence, D. H. *Mornings in Mexico.* London: M. Secker, 1927. Layton, Utah: Peregrine Smith Books, 1987.

Levin, Bernard. *Hannibal's Footsteps.* New York: Crown Publisher, Inc., 1985.

Lindsay, Vachel. *Adventures, Rhymes and Designs.* New York: Eakins Press, 1968.

Lindsay, Vachel. *Adventures While Preaching the Gospel of Beauty.* New York: M. Kennerly, 1904.

Lovell, Mary S. *Straight On Till Morning: The Biography of Beryl Markham.* New York: St. Martin's Press, 1987.

Lunt, Dudley Cammett. *The Woods and the Sea: Wilderness and Seacoast Adventures in the State of Maine.* New York: Knopf, 1965.

MacDonald, Hugh, ed. *On Foot: An Anthology Selected by Hugh MacDonald.* New York: Oxford, 1942.

Mailer, Norman. *The Armies of the Night: History as a Novel/The Novel as History.* New York: New American Library, 1968.

Malone, Joe. "Roaming the Streets of Henry Miller, Then and Now." The Brooklyn College Alumni Literary Review (Fall–Winter 1981–82, Volume 2).

Manning, Harvey. *Walking the Beach to Bellingham.* Seattle: Madrona, 1986.

Markham, Beryl. *West With the Night.* New York: Houghton Mifflin Co., 1942. Berkeley, California: North Point Press, 1983.

Marshall, Robert. *Alaska Wilderness: Exploring the Central Brooks Range.* Berkeley, California: University of California Press, 1956, 1970.

Matthews, James. *Voices: A Life of Frank O'Connor.* New York: Atheneum, 1983.

Matthiessen, Peter. *The Cloud Forest: A Chronicle of the South American Wilderness.* New York: Viking, 1961.

Matthiessen, Peter. *The Snow Leopard.* New York: Viking, 1978.

Mehta, Ved. *Mahatma Gandhi and His Apostles.* New York: Viking, 1977.

Meinertzhagen, Richard. *Kenya Diary (1902–1906).* London: Eland Books, 1957, 1983.

Merrill, John. *Walking My Way.* London: Chatto & Windus, 1984.

Moffat, Gwen. *Space Below My Feet.* New York: Houghton Mifflin Co., 1961.

Moorehead, Alan. *A Late Education: Episodes in a Life.* New York: Harper & Row, 1970.

Moorhouse, Geoffrey. *To the Frontier.* New York: Holt, Rinehart and Winston, 1984, 1985.

Morris, James. *Coronation Everest.* London: Faber and Faber, 1958.

Morton, H. V. *A Traveller in Italy.* New York: Dodd, Mead & Co., 1964, 1982.

Murie, Olaus. *Journeys to the Far North.* Palo Alto, California: American West Publishing Co., 1973.

Murphy, Dervla. *Eight Feet in the Andes.* London: J. Murray, 1983. Woodstock, New York: The Overlook Press, 1986.

Murray, Geoffrey. *The Gentle Art of Walking.* London: Blackie & Son, Ltd., 1939.

Nabokov, Vladimir. *Speak, Memory: An Autobiography Revisited.* Rev. ed. New York: Putnam, 1966.

Naipaul, Shiva. *North of South: An African Journey.* New York: Simon and Schuster, 1979.

Newby, Eric. *A Short Walk in the Hindu Kush.* New York: Doubleday, 1958. New York: Penguin Books, 1981.

Newby, Eric. *On the Shores of the Mediterranean.* Boston: Little, Brown, 1984.

Nicolson, Adam. "The Alps, On Foot." *The New York Times Magazine* (March 16, 1986).

Nicolson, Adam. *The National Trust Book of Long Walks in England, Scotland and Wales.* New York: Harmony Books, 1981.

Nicolson, Adam. *The National Trust Book of Long Walks in France.* London: Weidenfeld & Nicolson, n.d.

Oakes, George W. *Turn Right at the Fountain: Walking Tours of London, Oxford, Cambridge. . .* 4th ed. New York: Holt, Rinehart and Winston, 1981.

Oakes, George W. *Turn Right at the Pub.* 3rd ed. London: Congdon & Weed, 1985.

O'Connor, Peter. *Walking Good: Travels to Music in Romania and Hungary.* London: Weidenfeld and Nicolson, 1971.

O'Sullivan, Kitty. *The Plodding Shoe.* Auckland, New Zealand: n.p., 1953.

Origo, Iris. *War in Val D'Orcia: An Italian War Diary 1943–1944.* Boston: Godine, 1947, 1984.

Palmer, Howard. *Mountaineering and Exploration in the Selkirks: A Record of Pioneer Work Among the Canadian Alps, 1908–1912.* New York: G. P. Putnam's Sons, 1914.

Rawicz, Slavomir. *The Long Walk: A Gamble for Life.* New York: Harper & Row, 1956.

Ridgway, John. *Road to Osambre: A Daring Adventure in the High Country of Peru.* New York: Viking, 1986.

Schneebaum, Tobias. *Keep the River On Your Right.* New York: Grove Press, 1969.

Shipton, Eric. *That Untravelled World: An Autobiography.* London: Hodder and Stoughton, 1969, 1970.

Shoumatoff, Alex. *In Southern Light: Trekking Through Zaire and the Amazon.* New York: Simon and Schuster, 1986.

Smedley, Agnes. *The Great Road: The Life and Times of Chuh Teh.* New York: Monthly Review Press, 1956, 1972.

Smith, Roger, ed. *The Winding Trail.* London: Diadem Books, 1981.

Snyder, Gary. *Jack's Book: An Oral History of Jack Kerouac.* Barry Gifford and Lawrence Lee, eds. New York: St. Martin's Press, 1978.

Solzhenitsyn, Aleksandr I. *The Gulag Archipelago.* New York: Harper & Row, 1973.

Somerville-Large, Peter. *From Bantry Bay to Leitrim.* London: Arrow Books, 1974.

Somerville-Large, Peter. *To the Navel of the World.* London: Hamish Hamilton, n.d.

Spangler, Sharon. *On Foot in the Grand Canyon: Hiking the Trails of the South Rim.* Boulder, Colorado: Pruett Publishing Co., 1986.

Statler, Oliver. *Japanese Pilgrimage.* New York: William Morrow and Company, Inc., 1983.

Stuhlmann, Gunther, ed. *The Diary of Anaïs Nin, 1931–1934.* New York: The Swallow Press and Harcourt, Brace & World, Inc., 1966.

Sussman, Aaron and Ruth Goode. *The Magic of Walking.* New York: Simon and Schuster, 1967, 1980.

Sutton, Ann and Myron. *Yellowstone: A Century of the Wilderness Idea.* New York: Macmillan, 1972.

Tourte, Jo. *A Pied Autour du Monde: Trois Ans de Camping.* Paris: J. Susse, 1947.

Trent, George D., ed. *The Gentle Art of Walking: A Compilation from the New York Times.* New York: Arno Press/Random House, 1970.

Trevelyan, George Macauley. *Walking*. Hartford, Connecticut: E. V. Mitchell, 1928.

Vyvyan, Lady Clara Coltman (Rogers). *Down the Rhone on Foot*. London: Owen, 1955.

Waite, John. *Mean Feat: A 3,000-Mile Walk Through Portugal, Spain, France, Switzerland and Italy*. Sparkford, Yeovil, Somerset, England: The Oxford Illustrated Press, 1985.

Waugh, Evelyn. *Ninety-two Days: The Account of a Tropical Journey Through British Guiana and Part of Brazil*. New York: Farrar & Rinehart, Inc., 1934.

White, E. B. *Essays of E. B. White*. New York: Harper & Row, 1977.

Wickes, George, ed. *Lawrence Durrell and Henry Miller: A Private Correspondence*. New York: E. P. Dutton & Co., 1964.

Zochert, Donald, ed. *Walking in America*. New York: Knopf, 1974.